The Ancient Egyptian Book of the Moon: Coffin Texts Spells 154–160

The Ancient Egyptian Book of the Moon: Coffin Texts Spells 154–160

Gyula Priskin

Archaeopress Egyptology 22

ARCHAEOPRESS PUBLISHING LTD
Summertown Pavilion
18-24 Middle Way
Summertown
Oxford OX2 7LG

www.archaeopress.com

ISBN 978-1-78969-198-6
ISBN 978-1-78969-199-3 (e-Pdf)

Cover image: Old Moon in the New Moon's Arms, photo © Yuri Beletsky

This book is available direct from Archaeopress or from our website www.archaeopress.com

Contents

Preface 1

1. Introduction 3

2. The spells 22
   - 2.1. Spell 154: the origins of the month 22
   - 2.2. Spell 155: lunar invisibility 40
   - 2.3. Spell 156: the waxing moon 72
   - 2.4. Spell 157: the full moon 90
   - 2.5. Spell 158: the waning moon 122
   - 2.6. Spell 159: the moon at the eastern horizon 141
   - 2.7. Spell 160: a solar eclipse 158

3. General Commentary 177
   - 3.1. The major themes of the spells 177
   - 3.2. Textual layers in the Book of the Moon 188
   - 3.3. The text variants from Deir el-Bersha and Asyut 194
   - 3.4. The survival of the spells in the Book of Going Forth by Day 203

4. Conclusion 230

Bibliography 235

Index 250

Preface

The text of this book is essentially identical to my PhD thesis, the first draft of which I submitted to Eötvös Loránd University, Budapest, in 2017. My work there was warmly encouraged by my supervisor, Gábor Schreiber, and I wish to express my deepest gratitude to him for his cooperation. I would also like to take this opportunity to thank him for letting me participate in his archaeological mission in western Thebes, thus from time to time giving me – the 'archetypal desk scientist' – a taste of real Egyptological research in the field. I am also very much indebted to my reviewers, Katalin Kóthay from the Museum of Fine Arts, Budapest, and Zoltán Imre Fábián from Károli Gáspár University, Budapest, for their astute remarks and suggestions concerning the different manuscripts of my dissertation during the doctoral process at Eötvös Loránd University. They, no doubt, greatly contributed to presenting my work in a more intelligible and scholarly way. Naturally, any mistakes, errors, or unsubstantiated claims left in the book are entirely my fault. I also say a warm thank you to Tamás Bács, head of the Egyptological programme of the Doctoral School of History at Eötvös Loránd University, and the other members of the panel hearing the final defence of my thesis, for their help and assistance in bringing my doctoral studies to a conclusion. Finally, I am extremely grateful to the many colleagues and friends with whom I have discussed the ideas, or some of the ideas, that are put forward in the present book.

1. Introduction

This book is about seven Coffin Texts spells (154–160) that were written in ancient Egypt at the beginning of the 2nd millennium BCE.[1] My initial interest in them arose when, as part of my master's course at Eötvös Loránd University, I decided to focus my scholarly attention on the role of the moon in ancient Egyptian thinking. An early result of my research was the translation and interpretation of Coffin Texts spell 155.[2] Since this text bears a title which expressly mentions a lunar phenomenon, the invisibility of the moon (*psḏn.tjw*), it naturally fitted into my agenda. With time, however, I came to realise that this text did not stand alone but was part of a series of spells that all dealt with the moon. So I extended the scope of my enquiries to this group of spells, which I started to call the ancient Egyptian Book of the Moon. While I was working on the material, I published two short summaries of my preliminary findings,[3] predicting the appearance of a detailed analysis of the texts with extensive commentary. The present volume fulfils this pledge, giving a new translation of the spells that brings out their lunar character more pronouncedly than any of the existing renderings.[4] This is of course not to disparage the achievements of previous translators; the lunar allusions of the texts are often quite obvious from their works, too.

Certainly, spells 154–160 of the Coffin Texts have long been known to form one composition because in their titles all of them, mostly in connection with different localities, promise the knowledge of the *bas*,[5] that is the powers or essential qualities ('souls') that make a thing distinctively what it is.[6] These spells are also frequently cited in discussions about the lunar concepts of the ancient Egyptians,[7] yet so far these two quite noticeable aspects of the spells have not been intertwined more tightly. My major claim here is, however, that the purpose of these spells is to describe the moon. A careful reading of the texts will reveal that – underlying the thematic unity postulated in the first place by the references to the *bas* – the real editorial principle of this group of spells is a chronologically ordered account of the phenomena that happen during a lunar month. After the introduction (spell 154) which explains the origins of the month, the separate texts represent the successive stages of the monthly cycle: the period of invisibility (spell 155), waxing (spell 156), events around the full moon (spell 157), waning (spell 158), the arrival of the last crescent at the eastern horizon (spell 159), and again the conjunction of the sun and the moon when a solar eclipse can occur (spell 160).

---

1 *CT* II, 266a–388c.
2 Priskin 2013.
3 Priskin 2015b: 182–185; Priskin 2016a.
4 Sethe 1922; Speleers 1946: 86–92; Faulkner 1973: 132–139; Barguet 1986, 571–578; Carrier 2004, 370–397.
5 Sethe 1922: 1–4; Lapp 1990: 229; Bickel 1994: 266–267; Quirke 2003: 173; Hays 2008: 190; Robinson 2008: 128.
6 Allen 2001a: 161.
7 Parker 1950: 12; Derchain 1962a: 24; Leitz 1994: 269–271; Servajean 2003: 446; Lieven 2007: 199; Eaton 2011: 236–240; Arquier 2013: 122–126.

Despite giving a systematic description of the lunar events as they unfold along the month, and thus being the oldest written composition about the earth's satellite anywhere in the world, the Book of the Moon was in all probability not spurred by what we would now call scientific interest. It must be noted, nevertheless, that it belongs to the rare class of ancient Egyptian literary works that treat all aspects of a particular topic in depth.[8] What prompted the writing of the Book of the Moon is obvious from the circumstances where we encounter it. It is part of a large collection of spells, the Coffin Texts, that represent the second great wave of literary production in terms of Egyptian funerary literature.[9] Whereas the oldest corpus of religious spells, the Pyramid Texts, were initially – as their name suggests – carved on the walls of Old Kingdom pyramids,[10] the Coffin Texts augmented and superseded their antecedents at the end of the Old Kingdom, and especially during the Middle Kingdom. They were – and here the appellation is also quite revealing – primarily written in ink on the different surfaces of coffins that were made for the members of the elite at various places throughout Egypt, most notably among them Asyut, Beni Hasan, Deir el-Bersha, el-Lisht, and Meir.[11]

Whether there was a clear divide between the Pyramid and Coffin Texts, as earlier research opined,[12] or they represented an essential continuity, as is now often emphasised,[13] the two corpora were surely created to enhance the chances of the deceased for resurrection by enabling them to overcome the difficulties that unfolded in connection with the transition from one life to the next one. This is the context in which the Book of the Moon was born. Numerous concepts existed side by side about rebirth, in accordance with the ancient Egyptian mindset that saw no irreconcilable differences between notions that would for us often seem mutually exclusive. Even if we only consider the astral aspects of resurrection, the analysis of funerary texts and monuments shows us that three intertwined strands of tradition were perpetuated. Although the emphasis put on them may change with time, it is clear that all three of them permeate Egyptian thought throughout the different stages of mortuary literature. One is connected with the stars,[14] and claims that eternal life is possible as a star in the sky, especially in the company of the 'imperishable ones' (*jḫm.w-sk*, literally 'those who do not know destruction'), that is the circumpolar stars that are always seen in the night sky and never set below the horizon.[15] According to another set of beliefs resurrection could be effected by repeating the life-cycle of the sun.[16] Each night the sun enters the netherworld and thus dies, but at dawn it triumphantly

[8] Baines 2007, 41.
[9] Hornung 1999: 7–12; Willems 2014: 124–135.
[10] Hornung 1999: 1–6.
[11] Hornung 1999: 7.
[12] Breasted 1912; David 2002: 154.
[13] Mathieu 2008; Willems 2008 and 2014; Smith 2009b; Hays 2011; Morales 2013.
[14] Wallin 2002: 90–100.
[15] This is the common understanding of the term. Rolf Krauss believes that the imperishable ones included all the stars north of the ecliptic, see Krauss 2001: 86–130.
[16] Wallin 2002: 101–127

re-emerges from the eastern horizon to illuminate the world of the living; it is, in essence, reborn every day. Finally, rebirth is to be achieved by acquiring the ability of the moon to renew its cycle, by copying its successful transition from waning and total invisibility (death) to waxing and flourishing.[17]

The moon in funerary literature

At this point, to put the Book of the Moon into perspective, we may take a brief overview of how the moon appears throughout time in Egyptian funerary literature. A short summary of this kind may help to highlight the delicate changes by which the role of the moon shifted and its importance grew. We have to bear in mind, however, that the passages in the large corpora of funerary literature having something to say about the moon can be classified into two groups, one comprising the texts whose lunar content is obvious, while the other encompassing those descriptions that modern researchers suspect to have lunar connotations (i.e. their lunar content is a matter of interpretation, and thus it sometimes can be contested). Obviously, into the first group belong such texts that expressly mention the moon or lunar feast days, while the second group can deal with a wide range of subjects.

Although the earliest collection of mortuary spells, the Pyramid Texts, are usually associated with the ideas of stellar and solar rebirth,[18] it does not mean that references to the moon are entirely absent. It is true, however, that these mostly do not go beyond simply mentioning lunar feasts or just naming the moon in a context that otherwise is not predominantly lunar. The Egyptian name for the moon was *jꜥḥ*, and we encounter this designation three times within the Pyramid Texts. The king is said to be born in his months as the moon,[19] or the moon is his brother as he is ferrying over to the imperishable stars,[20] while at the third place the moon is identified as the king's father.[21] In every case the moon is associated with the Morning Star, or more literally, the Morning God (*nṯr-dwꜣ.j*), a celestial entity whose exact identity is debated, but nevertheless belongs to the eastern side of the sky,[22] so the moon in these passages seems to be strongly linked to the idea of astral rebirth in the east.

Another group of spells with a clear-cut lunar content are the texts that mention different feast days of the lunar month. It must be pointed out, however, that only sixteen spells in the Pyramid Texts include references to such feasts, making up about two percent of the total number of utterances,[23] so lunar feasts by no means play a crucial role in early mortuary literature. The five monthly feast days mentioned in the Pyramid Texts – blacked-out moon, first-crescent day, the sixth day, the seventh day,

[17] Wallin 2002: 56–89.
[18] Allen 2002: 62.
[19] *Pyr.* §732.
[20] *Pyr.* §1001.
[21] *Pyr.* §1104.
[22] Krauss 1997: 217–226; Goebs 2008: 21.
[23] Eaton 2011: 231–232.

and the fifteenth day (half-month) – occur mostly in connection with offerings made to the deceased and purification rituals.[24] Two interesting spells link the beginning and the middle of the lunar cycle (the first-crescent day and the day of the full moon, the fifteenth day) with the idea of baldness and its remedy in the form of hair-spittle.[25] These descriptions no doubt testify to an ancient concept that understood the monthly waxing of the moon as a head gradually becoming bald after being fully covered by hair during invisibility, when the moon is totally dark.[26]

Lunar gods also make their appearance in the Pyramid Texts, though, again, they are only scarcely referred to. Khonsu is mentioned only once, in the framework of the so-called 'cannibal hymn'.[27] Recently it has been claimed that this text, rather than being connected with a gruesome offering ritual, is the description of the cosmic phenomenon by which the rising sun cancels out the lights of the nocturnal celestial bodies.[28] In this context Khonsu is described as a blood-thirsty divine being that slays the enemies of the deified king (i.e. the sun), so we must suppose that he in fact here is identified with the sickle of the moon, and perhaps more particularly, with the sickle of the waning moon in its final phases, when the thin crescent of the moon, rising shortly before sunrise from the eastern horizon, indeed presages the appearance of the solar disc in the morning.

Thoth, the lunar god par excellence of the ancient Egyptians,[29] gets more numerous mentions in the Pyramid Texts. In connection with lunar phenomena, Thoth can either be the moon itself, or he can act as a protector or assistant of the moon.[30] Since, however, he can fulfil various roles in different mythological cycles, he does not always appear in the spells in connection with his lunar connotations, or at least these connotations are not straightforward. Nevertheless, there are some particular passages in which he seems to feature almost certainly because of his close associations with the moon. A very good example for this is utterance 210 that speaks about two companions 'who cross the sky, [and] who are Re and Thoth',[31] and in which the speaker identifies himself with the statements: 'I go round the sky like Re, I traverse the sky like Thoth'.[32] From the parallels with the sun god Re it seems highly likely that in these passages Thoth represents the moon.

Thoth is sometimes involved in helping the deceased to get from one side of the sky to the other, as for example in utterance 270, in which the celestial ferryman is linked with two divine entities: Thoth and 'He-who-looks-backwards' (*Ḥr=f-ḥꜣ=f*, *Mꜣ=f-ḥꜣ=f*),

[24] Eaton 2011: 232.
[25] Utterances 324 and 684, see *Pyr.* §§320–321, §§2055–2056.
[26] Derchain 1962a: 20; Eaton 2011: 236.
[27] *Pyr.* §402.
[28] Goebs 2003.
[29] Derchain 1962a: 36.
[30] Boylan 1922: 62.
[31] *Pyr.* §128; Faulkner 1969: 39.
[32] *Pyr.* §130; Faulkner 1969: 39.

who is in all probability the designation of the waning moon.[33] This latter being also has a counterpart named 'He-who-looks-forward' (*Ḥꜣ=f-m-ḥꜣ=f, Ḥr=f-m-ḫn.t=f*), and together these two figures seem to refer to the opposite facets of the moon during waxing and waning. [34] Thus it may be said that in the Pyramid Texts the moon most characteristically appears as a celestial ferryman that facilitates the deceased's voyage in and between the different regions of the netherworld. It is usually assumed that this ferryman transports the deceased across the Winding Waterway, the band of the sky where the sun, moon, and the planets move,[35] from the south to the north, that is to the region of the circumpolar stars, a prime area for netherworldly existence.[36] Having said that, it is equally possible that the moon as a celestial ferryman likewise also assists the dead soul to depart from the west and reach the eastern part of the sky (the place of sunrise, and thus that of rebirth), as during its monthly cycle the moon gets from the west (first crescent after sunset) to the east (last crescent before sunrise).[37]

Another spell of the Pyramid Texts (utterance 359) that talks about the lunar ferryman also contains references to the eye of Horus, which was of course – as can be deduced primarily from later sources – a very important symbol of the moon.[38] There are numerous references to the eye of Horus in the Pyramid Texts, but as it was the general designation for offerings and also had solar connotations,[39] it is again not always clear whether a particular reference to it should be interpreted in lunar terms or not. Since the general tone of utterance 359 – with its allusions to the fight between Horus and Seth, their injuries, Thoth, and the ferryman called He-who-looks-backwards – seems to be lunar, it is quite probable that this spell is one of several passages in the Pyramid Texts in which the eye of Horus is the equivalent of the moon.

In the Coffin Texts references to the moon are not only more numerous, but they also become longer and more sophisticated. This is precisely one of the reasons why we can identify one distinct set of these texts – the subject matter of the present volume, spells 154 to 160 – as a composition that gives an extended account of the lunar cycle. There are, however, further spells that – based either on their title or content – concern themselves with the major theme of lunar phenomena. In this category fall, among others: spell 6, which in all probability talks about the appearance of the first crescent – the 'feather' in the sky – on the western horizon following the blacked-out moon,[40] spell 207 in which two goddesses are invoked with the hope of being reborn as the

33 Krauss 1997: 75.
34 Krauss 1997: 67–85; Allen 2002: 63.
35 Krauss 1997: 49–63.
36 Krauss 1997: 17–48; Allen 2002: 63.
37 For the motif of the eastward crossing of the Winding Waterway, see Krauss 1997: 34–37.
38 Derchain 1962a: 20–24.
39 Westendorf 1980.
40 Goedicke 1989; Willems 2005.

moon,[41] spell 246 in which the speaker assumes the identity of the invisible moon,[42] and spells 824 and 1096 that associate the moon with Thoth and the eye of Horus.[43] Indeed, it is in the Coffin Texts that the eye of Horus first appears as the undisputed symbol of the moon, as for example spell 1096 specifies: "This is Thoth who is in the sky; the Eye of Horus is on his hands in the Mansion of the Moon'.[44]

Lunar feast days continue to be mentioned, and the Coffin Texts include references to seven of them: blacked-out moon, first-crescent day, the fourth day, the sixth day, the seventh day, the eighth day, and half-month day.[45] Some of the spells that talk about these feasts are leftovers from the Pyramid Texts, but new spells are also created, so that the number and proportion of the spells mentioning lunar feasts slightly increase (sixteen in the Pyramid Texts as opposed to forty in the Coffin Texts).[46] In addition to offerings and purification, which were the primary contexts of these spells in the earlier corpus, a new role emerges for the lunar feast days in the instructions that give information on the performance of the texts: spell 695 is prescribed to be recited on certain days of the lunar month.[47] Lunar days are also associated with themes that are connected with protection, transformations, and the adverse conditions of the netherworld: not eating excrement and not walking upside down.[48] These conditions, though they were also described in other contexts in the Pyramid Texts, had not been elaborated in connection with the lunar feast days earlier.[49]

Just as in the Pyramid Texts, the moon is expressly mentioned in several spells of the Coffin Texts. In two very similar spells (93 and 152) the speaker addresses an entity that is called the 'Sole One' (*Wꜥ*), and is identified as someone who shines or rises in the moon.[50] Since the purpose of these spells, as their titles suggest, is to go forth by the day and live after death, they seem to testify to a belief that resurrection in the next life was comparable with the behaviour of the moon, though the dead are not yet directly identified with the moon itself. Spell 176 also refers to some divinities who are in the great moon, and probably alludes to the situation when the moon is in conjunction with the sun, because the stated purpose of the spell is to go forth to the place in the sky where Re is.[51] A very similar statement is made in spell 853.[52] In an obscure passage the mansion of the moon is identified as the place where Thoth makes judgement.[53] Spell 467 describes the topography of the Field of Rest (or, alternatively,

[41] Willems 1996: 253–255.
[42] See my interpretation of this spell below.
[43] Faulkner 1978: 14, 152.
[44] Faulkner 1978: 152.
[45] Eaton 2011: 233.
[46] Eaton 2011: 231, 233.
[47] *CT* VI, 329q–r; Eaton 2011: 233.
[48] Eaton 2011: 233.
[49] Eaton 2011: 233.
[50] *CT* II, 64b, 260c–d.
[51] *CT* III, 62g.
[52] *CT* VII, 56l–57e.
[53] *CT* III, 339e.

Field of Offerings), an area in the netherworld where the deceased spend their days, and the moon here appears in connection with verdant vegetation.[54] In a series of spells that deal with fishing nets, the moon is referred to in connection with lunar festivals,[55] and again with its mansion.[56] These spells, it must be emphasised, introduce a new theme because the fishing net and lunar motifs did not feature together in the Pyramid Texts. The moon is also mentioned twice in spell 824 that was supposed to make the effective spirit of the deceased powerful.[57]

As for the lunar gods, Khonsu appears in about fifteen spells.[58] A recurring motif in spells 187 and 195 is that the deceased meets him on his way back from Punt, the mythical land that in funerary literature represents east, that is, the place of sunrise.[59] Interestingly enough, both in spells 195, and 573, the Coffin Texts variant of the cannibal hymn, Khonsu features in a passage which also makes a reference to the time of lunar invisibility (*psḏn.tjw*). This may offer further support for the identification of Khonsu with the sickle of the waning moon in the east, at least in the particular contexts of the Pyramid and Coffin Texts. Spell 311 is concerned with becoming Khonsu himself,[60] showing the increased importance of the god. The violent nature of Khonsu is still alluded to, since in spell 994 he is said to live on heads (*ꜥnḫ=j m tp.w jnk Ḫnsw*).[61]

Thoth is mentioned much more frequently than Khonsu in the Coffin Texts, and this is no doubt partly due to the relatively large portion of spells that were recorded in his chief cult centre, Hermopolis (or its necropolis at the time, Deir el-Bersha).[62] Again, Thoth may be included in a text because of his many roles in different mythological cycles. However, it is in the Coffin Texts that his identity with the moon is first expressly stated, because one variant of spell 1096, which was already mentioned above, identifies the god holding the eye of Horus in the mansion of the moon as Moon-Thoth (*Jꜥḥ-Ḏḥw.tj*).[63] It may be added that the role of Thoth in saving the lunar eye (the sound eye, *wḏꜣt*) is also emphasised in a preceding spell (1094).[64]

At the beginning of the New Kingdom, a new collection of spells, known as the Book of Going Forth by Day (Book of the Dead), supersedes the older corpus of the Coffin Texts.[65] In it the lunar themes that already appeared in the Pyramid and Coffin Texts continue to be perpetuated. The relative proportion of texts mentioning lunar day

[54] *CT* V, 371b–g.
[55] *CT* VI, 25c, 45c.
[56] *CT* VI, 27n.
[57] *CT* VII, 24g–25s.
[58] Molen 2000: 395.
[59] Meeks 2000: 57–58.
[60] *CT* IV, 67r.
[61] *CT* VII, 208b–c.
[62] Gestermann 2004.
[63] *CT* VII, 380a–b (B1L).
[64] *CT* VII, 372d–379b.
[65] Hornung 1999: 13–22.

feasts increases, as seventeen of the 192 chapters include such references.[66] On the one hand they often emphasise the deceased's knowledge about these feasts, while on the other the rubrics of some spells stipulate that the rituals described should be performed on specific days of the lunar month.[67] Spells addressing the moon as the Sole One made their way into the Book of Going Forth by Day (chapters 2 and 65), just as the moon keeps being mentioned in its role as the celestial ferryman, and in connection with fishing (chapters 99 and 153). Chapter 99 also includes references to the eye of Horus falling on the eastern side of the sky, thus it is a direct descendant of utterance 359 of the Pyramid Texts. While Khonsu only appears twice in the Book of Going Forth by Day (spells 83 and 153), Thoth is frequently mentioned. It is quite clear that for example in spell 80 he features in his lunar capacity, because the deceased claims that he has equipped the god in the mansion of the moon.[68] Spell 80 also talks about the filling of the eye in relation to the sixth or fifteenth day of the month,[69] so it is clearly one of the truly lunar spells of the Book of Going Forth by Day.

There are further important new developments. It is in the Book of Going Forth by Day that the deceased first undoubtedly assumes the identity of the moon when he claims that he will never perish because he is the moon among the gods (chapter 8, see the papyrus of Ani).[70] Osiris is now unequivocally associated with the moon, since for example in one variant of spell 183, dated to the 21st/22nd dynasty, he is named as the 'Lord of the Blacked-out Moon' (*nb psḏn.tjw*).[71] The identity of the moon with Osiris is also apparent from one variant of chapter 162 (Ptolemaic Period), a hymn to the god in which he is likened to the rising moon.[72] It is also very important that in the vignettes attached to the spells of the Book of Going Forth by Day the pictorial representations of the moon start to occur. The vignette to chapter 186 for example shows the lunar crescent over the western mountains from which a cow goddess and a hippopotamus goddess emerge.[73] In another vignette known as chapter 143 and belonging to spells 141 and 142, the blacked-out moon is shown to travel aboard the barque of Re,[74] as is suggested by the instructions for spell 141 which prescribe it to be recited on the day of lunar invisibility.[75]

In the New Kingdom, primarily in the royal mortuary sphere, new compositions began to be inscribed on the walls of the tombs and on funerary equipment. These compositions, though their main theme was the nocturnal journey of the sun,[76]

[66] Eaton 2011: 234.
[67] Eaton 2011: 234.
[68] Allen 1974: 70.
[69] Lepsius 1842, pl. 30; Allen 1974: 70.
[70] Faulkner 1994: pl. 18.
[71] Budge 1912: pl. lxxii; Allen 1974: 202.
[72] Allen 1974: 158.
[73] Allen 1974: 210 n. 327.
[74] Lepsius 1842: pl. lix. The larger disc in the barque is the sun, the smaller one is the moon, see Priskin (forthcoming).
[75] Lepsius 1842: pl. lviii; Allen 1974: 117.
[76] Hornung 1999: 26–111.

also featured pictorial representations of the moon. In the Book of What is in the Netherworld (Amduat), the moon appears in the second hour of the night, sailing in its own barque in the wake of the barque of the sun god.[77] In the tomb of Ramesses VI the lunar disc is also depicted in one of the corridors as part of an enigmatic composition.[78] The lunar disc also appears in private tombs, for example on the vaulted ceiling in the tomb of Sennedjem (TT 1), set against the background of the starry sky.[79] It is then not surprising that in the tombs of Maya (Saqqara) and Khaemhat (TT 57) a hymn to the moon rising on the eastern horizon was also inscribed on the walls.[80] Another composition that devoted a chapter to the moon was the Fundamentals of the Course of the Stars (Book of Nut) that made its debut on the walls of the Osirieon in Abydos (under Seti I), and was also preserved and annotated in hieratic/demotic papyri later in Graeco-Roman times.[81]

In the tomb of Senenmut (reign of Hatshepsut), on some water clocks, and then in some Ramesside memorial temples and royal tombs a pictorial representation of the sky, known as the astronomical diagram, came into use.[82] It was a pictorial composition, rather than a textual one, so its lunar contents were represented by a procession of divinities who corresponded to the days of the lunar month and converged from the two sides on the drawings of the northern constellations in the middle. Similar processions, the constellations being replaced by a symbol of the moon, were frequently depicted later in the temples of the Graeco-Roman Period.[83] Some astronomical diagrams are also thought to have incorporated the representations of the lunar months as well.[84] The use of the astronomical diagram in the funerary sphere, just as is the case with many of the compositions originally appearing around the middle and second half of the 2nd millennium BCE, continued after the demise of the New Kingdom.[85]

While the Book of Going Forth by Day continued to be used into Ptolemaic times, from the Late Period onwards yet another set of new compositions started to augment or replace it. Some of these picked upon a theme that had already been alluded to in the earlier mortuary spells and elaborated it further, so that in the end whole new compositions were created.[86] The moon frequently occurred in these new compositions, too. For example, in one of the commonly used later texts, which was centred around the topic of breathing, The Letter for Breathing Which Isis Made for Her Brother Osiris, we read that Isis compiled the lines of this work, *inter alia*, to make

[77] Hornung 1999: 43 fig. 15.
[78] Darnell 2004: 224–230.
[79] Porter and Moss 1960: 4; Hodel-Hoenes 2000: 259 fig. 186.
[80] Bosse-Griffiths 2001: 137–138.
[81] Lieven 2007: 94–106.
[82] Neugebauer and Parker 1969: 8–38; Symons 2014: 99.
[83] For these processions, see Priskin 2016c: 112–113.
[84] Symons 2014: 99.
[85] Neugebauer and Parker 1969: 38–84.
[86] Smith 2009a: 17–18.

the *ba* of Osiris appear in the sky as the disc of the moon.[87] A special composition that grew out of the Book of Going Forth by Day was the hypocephalus, which was essentially a disc made of cartonnage, bronze or other material, and put under the head of the deceased, displaying excerpts from chapter 162 and relevant drawings (vignettes) ordered in a number of registers.[88] One of these showed the encounter between the barques of the sun and the moon, most probably on the day when the latter became invisible due to its closeness to the rising sun.[89]

A crucial stage in the funerary procedure, mummification, has also received a lot of attention and a manual entitled The Embalming Ritual, preserved on three papyri from the 1st century ce,[90] was composed. It contained two types of texts: instructions for the different, ritually charged embalming techniques and recitations to be spoken along these actions. According to one of these, the deceased's *ba* will rejuvenate like the moon.[91] As part of mummification, a cloth is also to be placed in the right hand of the deceased with the images of Re (the sun) and Min (the moon) depicted on it.[92] Since Min is often associated with the invisible moon,[93] this cloth in the grasp of the right hand most probably evokes the conjunction of the sun and the moon in the east, although later on reference is also made to the rising of the full moon on the fifteenth day of the month,[94] and the text also specifies Min's role as the instigator of the appearance of the moon in the west (i.e. the first crescent of waxing).[95]

Other texts that were now used in the mortuary sphere had been originally conceived for temple use, especially in connection with the cult of Osiris.[96] These compositions reinforce that by this time (Late Period/Ptolemaic Period) the identification of Osiris with the moon was firmly established. In a text entitled The Rite of Introducing the Multitude on the Last Day of Tekh,[97] Osiris is called the lunar pillar, that is the moon, who as a phoenix goes forth to the sky and becomes the left eye to spread light over the earth with his rising.[98] According to another papyrus, belonging to the genre known as the glorifications of the god, Osiris emerges as the moon, and also as the bull of the sky on the day of the sound eye, that is the day of the full moon.[99] The motif of Osiris, or his *ba*, appearing as the sound eye or the left eye of Atum (the full moon) is repeated in other similar compositions.[100] The texts also intimate that Osiris

[87] Smith 2009a: 469.
[88] Varga 1998: 29–31.
[89] Priskin 2015a.
[90] Smith 2009a: 215.
[91] Smith 2009a: 230.
[92] Smith 2009a: 240.
[93] Cauville 2011: 42–43.
[94] Smith 2009a: 241.
[95] Smith 2009a: 243.
[96] Smith 2009a: 18–19.
[97] Tekh (*tḫ*) was an alternative name of the first month of the Egyptian calendar, see Smith 2009a: 152.
[98] Smith 2009a: 157.
[99] Goyon 1965: 100, 140.
[100] Smith 2009a: 76, 112, 131–132, 140, 144–145, 189.

is rejuvenated at the beginning of the month, perhaps more specifically on the second day of the lunar month, when the first lunar crescent appears.[101]

The moon outside the funerary sphere

Besides the vast corpus of funerary literature, there are of course other sources that tell us a lot about the significance of the moon in ancient Egypt. These start to surface right from the beginnings of ancient Egyptian history. While there are not many direct references to the moon in the written records of the Old Kingdom, one cultural achievement of this period strongly suggests that the Egyptians were already keenly observing lunar phenomena from the earliest times. It is the civil calendar, and although it totally disregarded the actual lunar cycles, that is it was in no way synchronised with or adjusted to observational months, its overall structure – the fact that one civil year comprised twelve thirty-day months – certainly indicates that the people who devised it had been fully aware of the moon's cyclical behaviour over the yearly period. So prior to the inauguration of the civil calendar – which surely took place by the middle of the 3rd millennium BCE, as, after some sporadic instances under the 3rd dynasty,[102] civil dates began to be recorded in large numbers during the 4th dynasty[103] – the Egyptians must have accumulated quite an extensive body of knowledge on the moon. In modern Egyptological literature this obvious conclusion has led to wide speculations about the possible existence and precise workings of an Egyptian lunar calendar in the Old Kingdom or perhaps even earlier.[104] The discussion of this debate falls outside the scope of this introduction, but it should be noted that the civil calendar does stand witness to an early familiarity with the lunar world on the part of the Egyptians.

Intertwined with the introduction and use of the calendar is the celebration of festivals. Sources from the New Kingdom indicate that the Egyptians distinguished between two types of festivals: the 'feasts of heaven' (*ḥ3b.w n.w p.t*) that were set according to lunar phenomena and recurred every month, and the 'seasonal feasts' (*tp trw*) that were tied to the civil calendar and occurred only once a year.[105] Monthly feasts, as we could see, were regularly referred to in the spells of funerary compositions. From the earliest times they also appear in feast lists that were at the beginning, in the Old Kingdom, recorded on the walls of tombs, but later on also in temples and other contexts.[106] Some seasonal feasts were also influenced by the moon; a good example from the New Kingdom is the annual Beautiful Feast of the Valley that commenced on the day of the blacked-out moon (*psḏn.tjw*) in the second month of

[101] Smith 2009a: 136, 140, 168, 171, 190.
[102] Depuydt 2001: 89.
[103] Verner 2006.
[104] Depuydt 1997: 16–17.
[105] Spalinger 1996: 1–2.
[106] Spalinger 1996.

the Shemu season.[107] The observance of festivals was therefore also largely a matter of the observation of the moon, and since feasts seem never to have been neglected throughout Egyptian history, knowledge about lunar phenomena must have been cultivated and appreciated continuously.

While literacy in the Old Kingdom was quite limited, and only the Middle Kingdom saw its more widespread development with the arrival of truly literary genres,[108] it must be said that apart from funerary literature our sources on the moon from this era are rather meagre. In one of the characteristic compositions of the period, preserved on papyri and foretelling *a posteriori* how the founding father of the 12th dynasty, Amenemhat I, would come into power, entitled The Prophecies of Neferti, the moon appears in the propagandistic description of chaos preceding the new golden age of the said dynasty. During these wretched times, the text goes, the sun is much like the moon, a pale replica of itself that fails to dazzle the living and is beset with some irregularities.[109] The lack of lunar attestations may possibly be due to the fact that the temples erected in Middle Kingdom times, which would have presumably yielded some lunar texts and scenes, largely perished because they were built mostly of mudbrick, and because in many cases later edifices replaced them.[110]

However, it must also be noted that a series of lunar dates have come down to us from the Middle Kingdom in the so-called Illahun papyri that preserved much information concerning temple service in this town at the entrance to the Fayum region.[111] This indicates that cult activities, just like important feasts, continued to be regulated by the phases of the moon. A rather small object also strongly suggests that a cult of the moon was flourishing. It is a container in the shape of a half-cylinder, partitioned into five compartments; at both ends a circle or disc is inscribed onto the surface, and it encloses the figure of a pig surrounded by fifteen dots.[112] Both the pig and the number fifteen have strong lunar connotations (the full moon putatively arrives on the fifteenth day of the month),[113] so this rather peculiar bowl was in all probability used for some cult activities connected with the moon.

With the advent of the New Kingdom the sources on the moon seem to explode. This in part results from the better preservation of monuments and records, but other factors must also have been at play. For one thing, most of the pharaohs at the end of the 17th and the beginning of the 18th dynasties, and also often their immediate kin, bore names that alluded to the moon or the lunar god Thoth – Jahmes, Jahhotep,

[107] The Epigraphic Survey 1934: pl. 142.
[108] Lichtheim 1975: 3–12.
[109] Lichtheim 1975: 142–143.
[110] Shafer 1997: 4.
[111] Luft 1992.
[112] Friedman 1998: 137, 218.; Lieven 2007: 178 n. 987.
[113] For the association of the pig with the moon, see below and my discussions in Priskin 2015b: 170–171; Priskin 2016b: 86–88.

Thutmose being the most salient examples.[114] This possibly shows that the lunar cult was in the ascendancy at the time. A heightened interest in the moon around this period is probably also indicated by the introduction of a new sign in the writing of *psḏn.tjw*, the day of lunar invisibility, most likely depicting how the lunar disc is absorbed by the sun during conjunction.[115] Before long a depiction of the lunar disc in the company of Anubis also appears in the memorial temple of Hatshepsut at Deir el-Bahari.[116]

Besides their allegiance to the lunar gods Jah and Thoth, the founding dynasties of the New Kingdom, originating and being seated in Thebes, were also under the protection of the main local god, Amun, who with time – and assimilating the nature of the sun god, Re – became the official state god of the period.[117] The triad of Amun, besides his consort, Mut, included the child Khonsu, who was also one of the pre-eminent lunar gods.[118] Thus a lunar dimension became an inseparable element of the Theban cultural and theological landscape and it manifested itself in various ways. Khonsu had a temple built within the main enclosure of Amun at Karnak (construction started under Ramesses III), though some parts of it were only decorated in later times.[119] Since theological doctrines in Thebes were inextricably connected with the idea of kingship, through Khonsu lunar rituals were also incorporated into the ceremonies that symbolically represented and advertised the power of the pharaoh.[120]

In the second half of the 18th dynasty the deification of Amenhotep III meant not only his identification with the solar god, but also with the moon, as his inscriptions in the temple of Soleb in Nubia attest to it.[121] Later, after the interlude of Akhenaten, the jewellery of Tutankhamun, recovered from his famous and almost intact tomb in the Valley of the Kings, includes some pieces that feature lunar motifs, for example the elaborate pectoral showing a beautifully represented scarab as it lifts a barque with the left eye and lunar disc on board, the latter encompassing the figures of Thoth, the pharaoh himself, and Re-Harakhty.[122] It was also in the reign of Tutankhamun that his general and later successor Horemheb had a statue made with inscriptions including a hymn to Moon-Thoth.[123] In his famous decree, aimed at restoring law and order after the Amarna upheaval, Horemheb declares that he will be reborn like the moon.[124]

In the memorial temple of Ramesses II on the Theban west bank, also known as the Ramesseum, the New Kingdom astronomical diagram decorated the ceiling of one of

[114] Bryan 2000: 209.
[115] Depuydt 1998.
[116] Ritner 1985.
[117] Tobin 2001: 82–83.
[118] Tobin 2001: 84.
[119] Baines and Malek 2002: 92.
[120] Goyon 1983.
[121] O'Connor 2001: 147–148.
[122] James 2000: 230–231.
[123] Lichtheim 1976: 100–103.
[124] Galán 2000: 259 n. 30.

the vestibules in front of the sanctuary.[125] It is there that this composition was first depicted outside a tomb, and as far as the moon is concerned, it should be noted for two things. First, in the procession of lunar divinities the pharaoh himself is included, suggesting that in one form or another Ramesses II participated in the lunar cult, and he deemed it important to have himself represented in such a context. This ambition is also underlined by the text running at the edge of the whole celestial diagram, as it expresses the wish that Re should create for the king his forms as the moon.[126] Second, unlike any other astronomical diagrams, the one in the Ramesseum shows the ancient Egyptian constellation of the boat together with the drawings of discs, and some of these – judged from a comparison with later images of some decans that featured in the zodiacs of the Graeco-Roman era – represent the full moon and the blacked-out moon at the vernal and autumnal equinoxes, respectively.[127]

From the Third Intermediate Period perhaps the most interesting source on the moon that should be mentioned is the historical document known as the Chronicle of Prince Osorkon.[128] It reports that in a certain year a rebellion or some sort of unrest broke out in the country, although the sky did not swallow the moon.[129] As pointed out by many commentators, this statement most probably refers to the fact that although a lunar eclipse – which was surely seen as an ominous event – did not take place, the peace and quiet of Egypt was disturbed.[130] The sentence about the moon thus implies that its behaviour in general, and irregular behaviour in particular – i.e. a lunar eclipse – had a direct effect on the well-being of the land of Egypt. A golden bracelet owned by one of the sons of the 22nd dynasty pharaoh, Sheshonk I, also testifies to the currency of lunar ideas at the time.[131] Its external decoration shows the squatting figure of the divine child as he is emerging from a lotus bud, which is the visual representation of the child's birth. On his head he wears the lunar disc and crescent, so the whole scene possibly attests to the role of the moon in divine birth. Since the bracelet was worn publicly, it surely carried a message that was easily recognisable for those seeing it.

In the Late Period bronze figurines showing the god Osiris with the lunar disc and crescent on the head appeared.[132] According to the captions that were written on these objects, they show the composite deity Osiris-Moon, and they were no doubt deposited in temples as votive offerings, seeking the benevolence of the god. The production and use of these statuettes certainly indicates that by this time Osiris was not only closely associated with the moon, but was straightforwardly identified with it. Although the Osiris-Moon figurines were primarily intended for cult activities that

[125] The Epigraphic Survey 1963: pl. 478.
[126] Priskin 2016b: 99.
[127] Priskin 2016b.
[128] Caminos 1958.
[129] Caminos 1958: 88–89.
[130] Caminos 1958: 88, with references; Thijs 2010: 181.
[131] Russmann 2001: 218–219.
[132] Griffiths 1976.

took place in temples, since Osiris was the lord of the netherworld par excellence, they also testify to the increasing selenisation of afterlife beliefs.[133] On the other hand, from the royal sphere we may mention that in the 26th dynasty Egypt once more had a pharaoh with the name Jahmes (Amasis),[134] though the choice of this king for such a throne name was probably dictated by a deference to the great founding ruler of the 18th dynasty, rather than by his great enthusiasm for and strong involvement in the lunar cult.

Most of our Egyptian records with substantial lunar content date from the Graeco-Roman Period. Possibly the earliest of these is the texts and scenes on the propylon at Karnak that was built under Ptolemy III Euergetes to the south of the temple of Khonsu.[135] A well-known passage here likens the different phases of the lunar cycle to the life stages – infancy, childhood, and old age – of a human being.[136] As mentioned earlier, the Khonsu temple was erected in the New Kingdom, surely in the place of an earlier building that already stood there in the Middle Kingdom, but some parts of the decoration were reworked in Ptolemaic times. Unfortunately, the major temple precinct of Thoth at Hermopolis has all but disappeared by the time serious and modern studies could have been effected on it, though some parts of it were still standing just around the middle of the 19th century CE.[137] As for Jah, it seems that this divinity, if he was in fact ever more than just the deified form of the moon,[138] did not have a local cult, so no temple enclosure was devoted to him anywhere in Egypt.

Apart from the temples of the lunar gods, the moon also became an important element for other temples that were built in Ptolemaic and Roman times, and in this respect two developments are worth noting. On the one hand, as the figure of Osiris had taken on ever more lunar attributes, the information on the moon – both written and pictorial – formed an essential part of the Osirian chapels that were customarily placed on the roofs of the major temples at this time.[139] The best example for this is of course found at Dendera, where these sanctuaries and their decoration are well-preserved.[140] Numerous lunar motifs occur there, including the ones in the famous round zodiac on the ceiling of the second room in the east.[141] On the other hand, since temples were generally envisaged as the architectural representations of the cosmos, including the sky, the ceilings or upper registers of walls in the pronaos now displayed appropriate astronomical scenes.[142] These were much more intricate than the blue ceilings of the New Kingdom temples dotted with stars, and thus included the

[133] Koemoth 1996: 203–204.
[134] Josephson 2001.
[135] Clère 1961.
[136] Clère 1961: pl. 60; Derchain 1962a: 43.
[137] Baines and Malek 2002: 126–127.
[138] Derchain 1962a: 51.
[139] Zivie-Coche 2008: 10.
[140] Cauville 1997.
[141] Cauville 1997: pl. 60.
[142] Finnestad 1997: 194.

complex representations of the lunar cycle, for example in Edfu, Dendera, and Esna.[143] In the pronaos of the Edfu temple the pictures of the lunar scenes on the eastern and western walls are also accompanied by lengthy horizontal lines that expound the movement of the moon in relation with the sun.[144] This text was possibly copied from a composition that was kept in the temple library, and contained the core knowledge on the subject that a priest was expected to be familiar with.[145]

From the Late Period onwards Egypt's contacts with the Aegean proliferated, and as a result Greek authors started to write accounts of the land in the Nile valley, viewed by them as a cradle of civilisation and wisdom. The moon is mentioned several times in these descriptions, which augment our knowledge about the Egyptians' view of lunar phenomena. Three of these descriptions may be cited here to hint at the kind of information they contain. Herodotus visited Egypt during the first Persian occupation (5th century BCE), and he paints a vivid picture about the great lunar feast of the month of Pachons (the month named after the lunar god Khonsu) by reporting on the consumption of pork at this particular event.[146] Plutarch, working at the turn of the 1st and 2nd centuries CE, wrote a lengthy treatise on the cult of Isis and Osiris, and in it he repeatedly stressed the close connections between the moon and the god who ruled the netherworld.[147] Finally, the Christian apologetic writer, Clement of Alexandria (2nd century CE), informs us about the procession of priests at an Osirian festival, possibly as he witnessed it on the streets of his own town, and he relates that one of the officiants – the hour watcher – carried four papyrus rolls, two of which dealt with the movements and encounters of the sun and the moon.[148]

The overview of Egyptian lunar knowledge on the previous pages, which is of course far from exhaustive, clearly indicates that the Book of the Moon had a wide background on which it could rely for its descriptions, themes, and motifs. We sometimes tend to overlook the importance the moon played in the ancient Egyptians' world view. This is partly due to the common perception that Egyptian thought was preoccupied with the sun god Re, and the cult built around him. The moon thus could only have had a limited role. Perhaps nothing epitomises this bias more than the simple fact that the pharaoh had a 'son of Re' name, and not a 'son of Jah' or 'son of Thoth' name. While of course it is true that the solar cult reigned supreme all throughout Egyptian history, the lunar attestations collected above also prove that as a strong undercurrent the moon had a significant presence in a number of Egyptian records, and it was acknowledged that the moon had a profound influence on the world in general, and on the lives of the Egyptians in particular. The Book of the Moon provides one of the earliest insights into this sometimes neglected area of Egyptian thought.

[143] Priskin 2016c: 113–143.
[144] Chassinat 1928: 207–208, 211–212.
[145] Depuydt 1998: 79.
[146] Herodotus, *The Histories* II.47, see Godley 1920: 335.
[147] Plutarch, *De Iside et Osiride*, see Griffiths 1970.
[148] Clement of Alexandria, *Stromateia* 6.4.35, see Stählin 1906: 449.

The Book of the Moon

The synoptic edition of the hieroglyphic texts constituting the Book of the Moon – i.e. Coffin Texts spells 154–160 – can be found in Adriaan de Buck's seminal work recording the Coffin Texts known in his time.[149] Ten coffins have preserved the complete composition, one of which has come down to us from Asyut, while the rest originate from Deir el-Bersha. Fragmentary copies that lack some parts or entire spells exist on yet another coffin from Deir el-Bersha and six coffins from Asyut, plus there is a short fragment of spell 154 from Meir. The distribution of the texts strongly suggests that the Book of the Moon was created in Deir el-Bersha (on this subject, see also chapter 3.2. on the textual layers of the composition). Therefore I have chosen one of the texts from this location as the basis for my new annotated translation. The choice I have made is also dictated by my previous work on the subject. As I have already mentioned, first I focused on Coffin Texts spell 155, and I had the impression that this particular chapter of the Book of the Moon had been best preserved on the coffin of Sen (B4LB according to the siglum in *CT* II).[150] He bore the titles 'chief physician' (*wr swnw*) and 'steward' (*jm.j-r pr*) and – as his coffin was found in the burial complex of the nomarch Djehutihotep – he was undoubtedly one of the distinguished members of the local elite at Hermopolis that flourished during the time of Senwosret II and Senwosret III.[151] Since, however, the Book of the Moon is a complex composition, its individual spells deriving from different sources (see the relevant chapter below), what is true for one spell may not hold fast for the entire composition. Indeed, we shall see that Sen's text is at some points inferior to other versions and has to be augmented. Despite this, and since the mistakes in it are not really numerous, I still deem the text on Sen's coffin the best starting point for the overall presentation of the composition. To make things clear, at the appropriate places I shall indicate the necessary emendations.

As for the new translation that I here offer for Coffin Texts spells 154–160, two further things should be noted. First, the translation of these spells, just like perhaps the translation of almost any passage in the Coffin Texts, is inevitably fraught with many difficulties. In my opinion, apart from the fact that the spells 'resemble disconnected scraps of conversation for which the context has been lost',[152] the most serious obstacles to full comprehension stem from four major factors. These are (1) the use of a specialised vocabulary, (2) textual corruption, (3) the deliberate opacity with which the ancient authors recorded their thoughts, and, somewhat corollary to all the previous points, (4) our insufficient understanding of the cultural background of the texts. In fact, the spells of the Book of the Moon have been pinpointed as perhaps the ones presenting the most difficulties in terms of understanding and interpretation within

[149] *CT* II, 266a–388c.
[150] Priskin 2013: 28.
[151] Willems 1988: 76–77.
[152] Mueller 1972: 99.

the entire collection of the Coffin Texts.[153] So, while I believe that my translations of the spells make a great contribution to understanding these texts better, by no means do I claim that every detail of them has become thoroughly intelligible for me.

On the other hand, one circumstance really offers help to understand a treatise about the moon written at the beginning of the 2nd millennium BCE. While our modern world is miles apart from that of the ancient Egyptians, and our concepts of what we see around us are shaped by the fact that we live in a secular, urbanised social environment, in contrast to the rural and religious intellectual landscape of ancient Egyptian society, at the root of things we experience the same reality. When we look up the sky and see for example the crescent of the waxing moon, we think of it as the earth's satellite, a smaller sphere of solid material orbiting our planet, whose surface is lit up by the sun to various degrees according to the moon's position along its orbit. When the ancient Egyptians looked up, they saw the feather of the west or, probably when the crescent was seen in the day sky, the wing of Thoth, or the opening of an eye. Yet on their face value the developments that unfold on the 'giant screen' of the sky are essentially the same: after one or two days when only stars can be observed in the night sky, a thin white crescent appears in the west just after sunset; then – as the month progresses – it grows bigger and is spotted increasingly to the east at nightfall. Following the day of the full moon, when the complete lunar disc emerges from the eastern horizon and crosses the sky in its entirety, the white disc begins to dwindle, rising closer and closer to dawn on successive days. This cycle, no matter how it is explained away by different cultures, repeats itself continuously, and it is this relentless visual display that we have in common with the ancient Egyptians which helps us to understand how they made sense of it.

Secondly, none of the standard collections of Coffin Texts translations – all based on de Buck's hieroglyphic edition (*CT*) – uses a Deir el-Bersha coffin as their source text for spells 154–160. Louis Speleers gives a synoptic translation without specifying a particular coffin,[154] Raymond O. Faulkner presents the text variant on Nakht's inner coffin coming from Asyut (S2P in de Buck's designation),[155] Paul Barguet does the same,[156] and Claude Carrier still adheres to the same coffin as his starting point.[157] One is left to wonder whether the preference for the S2P coffin is simply the outcome of its first position in de Buck's publication (i.e. the text of S2P runs along the left-hand margin), and had he chosen a different arrangement, we now would be reading translations of a quite different kind. Whatever prompted the popularity of Nakht's text, it means that a new rendering of spells 154–160 based on Sen's copy will unavoidably be different from the translations most researchers are currently

[153] DuQuesne 1998: 619.
[154] Speleers 1946: 87-88.
[155] Faulkner 1973: 133-134.
[156] Barguet 1986: 572-573.
[157] Carrier 2004: 376-379.

familiar with, irrespective of my agenda to highlight the inherent lunar character of these texts. This fact in itself adds to the justification of my enterprise here.

In connection with this last statement, the remark is perhaps worth making here that in ancient Egypt the concept of the authorship of a written composition – and consequently, the concept of the originality of a given composition – was quite different from modern European categories.[158] This means that the Egyptians did not view their literary works as the single, unalterable products of individuals, but rather as the pieces of a common cultural memory that could be shared and worked on by those who perpetuated the texts.[159] While I firmly believe that the Book of the Moon was originally compiled in Hermopolis, this does not imply that the composition recorded there – any of the ten copies – should be viewed as an *Urtext* in the modern sense, that is, a literary work that later copyists necessarily vied to emulate or faithfully reproduce. In fact, as I just made the hint above, the Asyut version of the Book of the Moon displays some marked differences in comparison with the texts coming from Deir el-Bersha. It is somewhat corollary to this ancient Egyptian approach to literature, and the varied contents of the composition, that the Coffin Texts sequence 154–160 could legitimately be analysed in other contexts as well, such as for example the distribution of the offerings, mummification, or the nature of temple cults and festivals. However, my aim here is not to offer an all-encompassing description of the spells under scrutiny, which would anyway inevitably result in a cumbersomely large volume, but to underline the primary lunar character of these texts.

The structure of the present book follows a simple pattern. After the introduction, I will look at the individual spells, one after the other, and offer a detailed commentary on them. Each chapter in this section is introduced by the hieroglyphic transcription of the spell, as is given in de Buck's edition of the Coffin Texts. It is followed by the transliteration, translation, and the comments about the different lines. The next section offers a more general commentary on the composition and comprises four chapters. The first one reiterates the main lunar themes of the Book of the Moon for making its structure and logic clearer. The next chapter analyses the contents of the spells in relation to each other in order to distinguish the different textual layers that exist within the composition.[160] The following chapter examines the copies of the Book of the Moon that have come down to us from Deir el-Bersha and Asyut, and establishes the chronology of their creation. The final section in the general commentary looks at the survival of the Book of the Moon by examining how the spells made their way into the corpus that superseded the Coffin Texts, i.e. the Book of Going Forth by Day. At the end of the book, a short conclusion closes the discussion, summarising the major findings and once more highlighting the uniqueness of the composition.

[158] Derchain 1996; Parkinson 2002: 24–25.
[159] Luiselli 2003: 343.
[160] See also Priskin 2017a.

2. The spells

2.1. Spell 154: the origins of the month

The hieroglyphic text

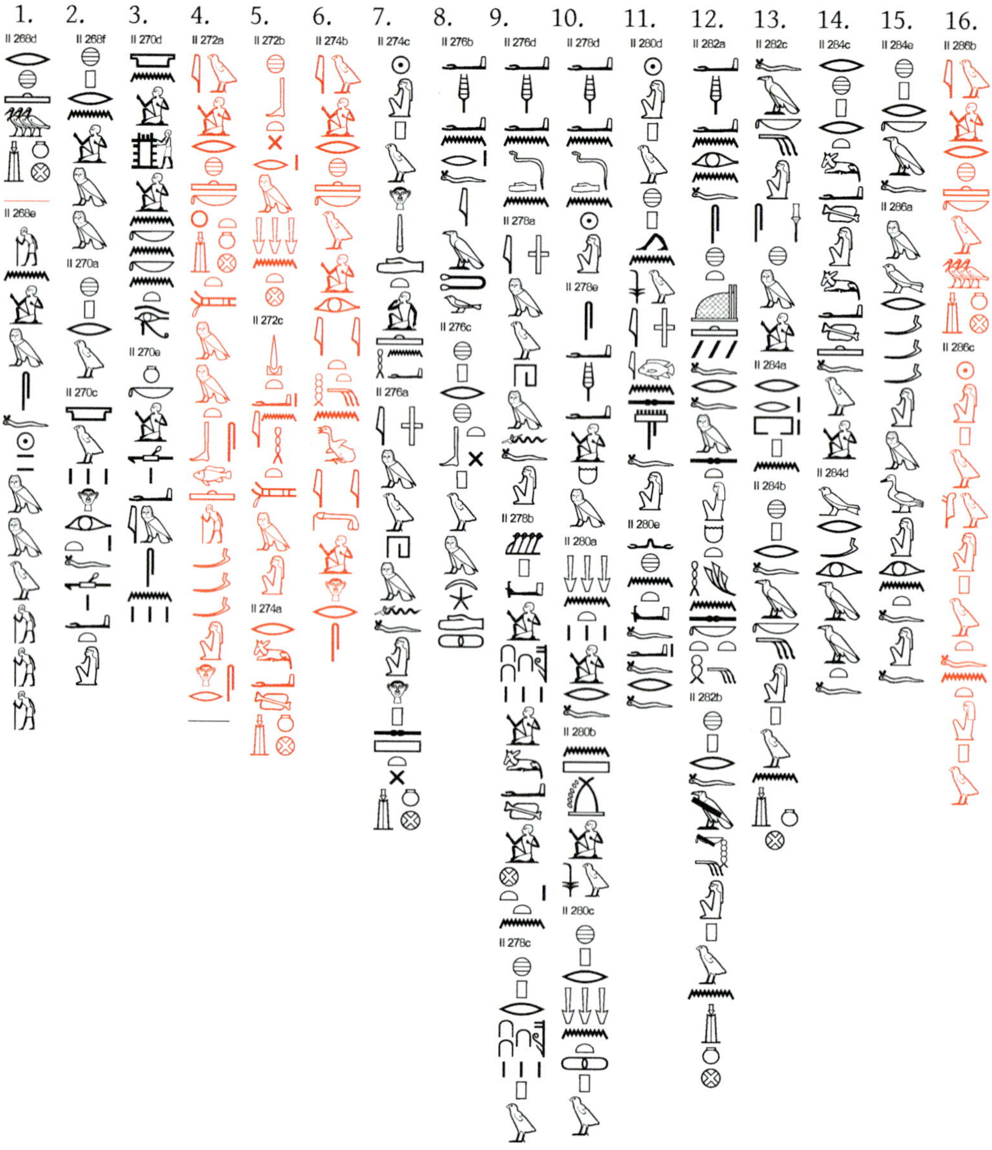

Transliteration and translation

1. *rḫ bꜣ.w Jwn.w wr.n⸗j m sf.wj m-m.w wr.w*
2. *ḫpr.n⸗j m-m ḫpr.w wn.w-ḥr jr.t⸗f wꜥ.t*
3. *wn n⸗j qd⸗j nknk.t jnk wꜥ jm⸗sn*
4. *jw⸗j rḫ.kw jr.t Jwn.t(j) tmm.t bsj wr-mꜣ.w ḥr⸗s*
5. *ḫb.t r m sn.wt ḏꜣ.t ꜥjn ḥtm r jwꜥ Jwn.w*
6. *jw⸗j rḫ.kw jry.t ḥnk.t n ṯꜣ.y ḥr⸗s*
7. *Rꜥ pw ḥr mdw.t ḥnꜥ Jm.j-whm⸗f ḥr psš.t Jwn.w*
8. *ꜥḥꜥ.n r⸗f jꜣṯ ḫpr ḫb.t pw m ꜣbd*
9. *ꜥḥꜥ.n ḏd.n Jm.j-whm⸗f šsp⸗j mꜥbꜣ⸗j jwꜥ⸗j n.t tn ḫpr mꜥbꜣ pw*
10. *ꜥḥꜥ.n ḏd.n Rꜥ sꜥḥꜥ⸗j ḥm sn.wt⸗j r⸗f nš⸗j sw ḫpr sn.wt pw*
11. *Rꜥ pw ḫpj.n(⸗f) sw Jm.j-jns⸗f n ḫn.t⸗f ꜥ⸗f*
12. *ꜥḥꜥ.n jrj.n⸗f sḫt⸗f r⸗f m s.t ḥm.t ḥnsk.t ḫpr⸗f pw n Jwn.w*
13. *fꜣk sḫm r r-pr pn ḫpr fꜣk pw n Jwn.w*
14. *ḫpr.t jwꜥ jwꜥ⸗f wj wr mꜣꜣ jt⸗f*
15. *ḫpr.kꜣ⸗f m wr-mꜣw m sꜣ jrj n jt⸗f*
16. *jw⸗j rḫ.kw bꜣ.w Jwn.w Rꜥ pw Šw pw Tfn.t pw*

1. Knowing the *bas* of Heliopolis. I became great yesterday among the great ones.
2. I have come into being among the beings who watch his sole eye.
3. Open to me so that I could build up the injured eye – I am one of them.
4. I know the eye of Heliopolis into which not even the greatest of seers has been initiated,
5. The diminishing of the part in the *senut*, and how the destroyer extends the arm against the heir of Heliopolis.
6. I know how a braided lock of hair of a man is made upon it.
7. It was the case that Re had a discussion with He-who-is-in-his-fire over the division of Heliopolis.
8. Then his part was injured and that is how the diminishing of the month came into being.
9. Then He-who-is-in-his-fire said: 'I will take my harpoon and I will inherit this town'. And that is how the harpoon came into being.
10. Then Re said: 'I will erect my flagpoles against him and I will repel him'. And that is how the *senut*-festival came into being.
11. It was the case that Re encountered He-who-is-in-his-red-cloth before he could turn his hand against him.
12. Then he made a trap for him in the form of a woman with braided hair, and that is how he came into being in Heliopolis.
13. The bald man holds power in this temple, and that is how the bald man came into being in Heliopolis,
14. Before the heir to the heritage came into being, that is me, the great one who sees his father;

15. He will come into being as the greatest of seers, as the son who acts for his father.
16. I know the *bas* of Heliopolis. It is Re, it is Shu, it is Tefnut.

Commentary

Line 1

rḫ bꜣ.w Jwn.w wr.n=j m sf.wj m-m.w wr.w

Knowing the *bas* of Heliopolis. I became great yesterday among the great ones.

Although – in contrast to practically all the other coffins – it is not highlighted by red ink, the title on Sen's coffin is short and unambiguous: 'Knowing the *bas* of Heliopolis'. Longer titles exist on the Asyut coffins and two coffins from Deir el-Bersha (B2Bo and B1L). They are more or less similar; here I am going to cite the variant that is found on the coffin of Djehutinakht (B2Bo):

rḫ rḫ.t.n Ḏḥwtj m sṯꜣ wꜣḥ tp tꜣ ꜣḫ m ẖr.jt-nṯr ʿq ḥr nb.w Jwn.w pr.t r p.t wbꜣ dwꜣ.t jn bꜣ ʿnḫ mwt jw=j rḫ.kw bꜣ.w Jwn.w

Knowing what Thoth knows about making whole, enduring on earth and being effective in the necropolis, entering into the lords of Heliopolis, coming forth to the sky and opening up the netherworld by the living and dead *ba*. I know the *bas* of Heliopolis.

It must be noted that the beginning of this longer title is slightly corrupt, and the word *sṯꜣ* is a meaningless hapax legomenon.[161] The parallel versions show that instead of *rḫ rḫ.t.n Ḏḥwtj m sṯꜣ* we should read *rḫ rḫ.t.n Ḏḥwtj m swḏꜣ*,[162] with the sense that I indicated in my translation. The whole phrase on these coffins adds the word *nḥḥ* at the end, so possibly it stands for 'knowing what Thoth knows about making whole eternally' or 'knowing what Thoth knows about making eternity whole'. A very similar collocation of words is included in Coffin Texts spell 442, with the difference that the

[161] Not included in Molen 2000.
[162] *CT* II, 266b, coffins S9Ca and S9Cb.

other Egyptian word denoting eternity, *ḏ.t*,[163] features there; for the entire phrase the translation 'making eternity hale' has been suggested.[164]

Since on the Asyut coffins the word appears as , previous translators render the expression *swḏꜣ.w* as 'protective spells', 'protective formulas',[165] but I believe that in the light of the later contents of the spell, which include references to the injured eye and the loss from the month's length, the words 'making whole' reflect the original connotations of *swḏꜣ* more appropriately. For this we should also consider that in the text of the spell no protective formulas are mentioned or written down, so my proposal at the same time perhaps suits the general context better. The word *swḏꜣ* is of course related to *wḏꜣ.t* 'the sound eye' or 'the whole eye' (*wedjat*-eye), and therefore it is not impossible that here it was also chosen to somehow evoke the idea of the moon and the lunar cycle.

Thoth's connection with making the eye whole or complete is well-known,[166] so his appearance in the longer title of the spell is certainly not unjustified. However, the spell is about the *ba*s of Heliopolis, which city was of course the intellectual capital of ancient Egypt, and as such, the primary cult centre of the solar god, Re.[167] Thoth is not known otherwise to have particularly strong ties with Heliopolis, but the reference to him can equally be explained by his general association with knowledge and wisdom.[168] He was also the pre-eminent lunar god,[169] and – notwithstanding the fact that Heliopolis was the seat of solar theology – we should not forget that the city was also involved in the cult of the moon. This is indicated for example by a passage in chapter 153 of the Book of Going Forth by Day which mentions court cases that are heard on the day of the full moon in the temple of the moon in Heliopolis.[170] This text goes back to Coffin Texts spells 474–475, though there the temple of the moon is not mentioned together with Heliopolis.[171] Since Heliopolis lies under the modern settlement of Cairo, the existence of this temple cannot be archaeologically verified, just as in fact this ancient city is very poorly excavated, and we do not even know too much about the exact layout of the sun temple there.[172]

Another hint at the moon's significance in Heliopolis is that chapter 125 of the Book of Going Forth by Day links the completion of the *wedjat*-eye in Heliopolis with the last day of the second month of the Peret season.[173] This statement alludes to the

163 *CT* V, 301c (S14C^{b}).
164 Faulkner 1977: 79.
165 Faulkner 1973: 132; Barguet 1986: 571; Carrier 2004: 371.
166 Boylan 1922: 72–73.
167 Quirke 2001: 73.
168 Boylan 1922: 92–97.
169 Boylan 1922: 62–75; Stadler 2012: 1.
170 Allen 1974: 152; Lapp 1997: pl. 57.
171 *CT* VI, 18n.
172 Quirke 2001: 73, 96–99.
173 Lapp 1997: pl. 65.

appearance of the full moon on the day that incidentally splits the core year of 360 days into two equal halves; as such, this date probably had some symbolic significance. The connection between the moon and Heliopolis is also already apparent from utterance 720 of the Pyramid Texts in which the celebrations of the full-moon and the sixth-day festival (*sn.wt*) are associated with a person who is described as the 'foremost of Heliopolis' (*ḫnt.j-Jwn.w*).[174]

As for the *bas* of Heliopolis, it should also be noted here that in later sources their primary role was to greet and glorify the rising sun.[175] In the lunar cycle the rising sun has an important part to play at the time of conjunction, that is when at the end of the waning period the moon gets so close to the sun from the viewpoint of an earthbound observer that no light is reflected from its surface, and thus it becomes invisible. Spell 154, as we shall see, contains more references to this particular moment, so the appearance of the *bas* of Heliopolis falls in line with the wider context of the allusions to the blacked-out moon.

The sign that starts the next sentence, 𓀗, showing an old man leaning on a stick, can be read variously as *jꜣw, smsw,* or *wr*.[176] I opted for the reading *wr*, because on some other coffins the corresponding verb is spelled out in this way.[177] This interpretation is perhaps further strengthened by another Asyut variant, where we find a synonym of *wr*, *ꜥꜣ* 'to be large' as the verb introducing the sentence.[178] The claim that the reciter of the spell became great among the great ones must refer to the theme of initiation that is also present in the following lines of the spell, where he identifies himself as a being within a group of beings that observe the sole eye, and also as someone who knows more than the high priest of Heliopolis, the 'greatest of seers' (*wr-mꜣ.w*). Thus the verb also resonates with the *wr* in this title that is mentioned shortly afterwards. While purification rites and requirements in connection with the priestly office in ancient Egypt are relatively well-documented,[179] we seem to know quite little about other aspects of initiation that determined how individual persons could become officiants of particular cults.[180] Our text seems to suggest that for the position that is somehow connected with the observation of the sole eye and the reconstruction of the injured eye, it was important to become a member of a group of people who possessed a great amount of wisdom and knowledge.

The claim that the speaker of the text became great yesterday may be another subtle allusion to the onset of lunar invisibility. Its defining point is the transition from the night to morning when the very thin last crescent of the waning moon is no longer

[174] *Pyr.* 2237d; Faulkner 1969: 310.
[175] Guglielmi and Buroh 1997: 114.
[176] Gardiner 1957a: 444.
[177] *CT* II, 268e, coffins S9Ca, S9Cb, B9C, B2P; *CT* II, 269e, coffins B1L, B17C, B1C.
[178] *CT* II, 268e, coffins S2P, S2P, S1Tü, S2C.
[179] Sauneron 1960: 36–37; Quack 2013: 118–128.
[180] Baines 1990: 1–2; Jasnow and Zauzich 2005: 54–55.

seen emerging only to a small height over the eastern horizon just before sunrise. Since the Egyptian day lasted from sunrise to sunrise (or dawn to dawn, as the use of the term *psḏn.tjw* suggests),[181] the observation whether the last crescent occurred immediately before it or not could have still partly belonged to the end of the previous day. So when the speaker emphasises that he became great yesterday – that is, he acquired his great knowledge yesterday – he may be intimating precisely this moment of the lunar cycle when the lack of the last crescent was acknowledged before the sun rose to signal the beginning of a new day.

Lines 2-3

ḫpr.n=j m-m ḫpr.w wn.w-ḥr jr.t=f wꜥ.t
wn n=j qd=j nknk.t jnk wꜥ jm=sn

I have come into being among the beings who watch his sole eye.
Open to me so that I could build up the injured eye – I am one of them.

Spell 154 as a whole functions as the introduction to the Book of the Moon, and gives a mythological explanation for the fact that observable months are not of uniform length. The period that it takes for the moon to get to the same position in its orbit in relation to the earth is not constant. For someone standing on the earth, therefore, it seems that sometimes the same lunar phase (for example the full moon) recurs after 29 days, whereas at other times it does so after 30 days. In the parlance of modern astronomy we express this irregularity by saying that the synodic month – from one phase to the next identical one – has an average length that equals 29.53059 days. In ancient Egypt the beginning of lunar invisibility (conjunction, blacked-out moon) marked the arrival of a new month.[182] This was the time when the change from one month to the next one was tracked.

Consequently, as I already indicated above, spell 154 is closely associated with the time of lunar invisibility (also known as the astronomical new moon), and this event is also alluded to in the second line, because the expression 'sole eye' most probably refers to this celestial phenomenon. At the time of conjunction the moon is situated between the sun and the earth (in front of the sun from the perspective of observers on the earth), and thus it becomes invisible. If we put this situation into an ancient Egyptian mythological framework, this is the moment when from the two eyes of Horus, the sun and the moon, only the first can be seen in the sky. The sole eye is then nothing other than the sun hiding the moon. This interpretation may get some support from a scribal error in the other copy of the spell on Sen's coffin (B4L[a]) where the copyist of the text first started to record the relevant expression as 'the (sole) eye of Horus', and

[181] Parker 1950: 10; Hornung, Krauss, and Warburton 2006: 49–51.
[182] Parker 1950: 9–23; Krauss 2006: 387–388.

then, realising his mistake, he crossed out the hieroglyph standing for the name of the god by a red stroke, and wrote the usual third person pronoun (*=f*) into the text.[183]

Quite a detailed description of the union of the sun and the moon – as the two celestial eyes – at the time of their conjunction is found on the eastern wall of the pronaos of the Edfu temple (1st century BCE). The closing part of the long horizontal inscription next to the lunar scene of the topmost register on the eastern side declares: 'Re merges with the moon, their lights unite as one, the rays of the right eye shine for the left eye. The two eyes are joined as one, and the two luminaries are in the heaven above Edfu according to their celestial regulations' (*jꜥb=f Rꜥ m-ḥr jwn-ḥꜥꜥ snsn jꜣḫ.w=sn m-sp bꜣq jꜣḫ.w n jmn.t r jꜣb.t ḫnm jr.tj m-sp ḥꜣy.tj m ḥr.t ḫnt Ḥw.t-Ḥr.w-nḫt mj n.t-ꜥ=sn m nw.t*).[184] Though this is of course a much later source, the idea is clearly the same: at conjunction only one celestial eye, the sun, can be observed in the sky.

The reciter of spell 154, however, does not only pay a lot of attention to the moon in conjunction with the sun, but aims at building up the injured eye. This ambition surely refers to the reappearing lunar crescent at the beginning of waxing, and possibly to the whole period of waxing. Once more, the same motif is present at Edfu, but this time on the western wall, next to the lunar scene showing the capture of the *wedjat*-eye by a net, and thus referring to the appearance of the first crescent over the western horizon just after sunset. A caption to the scene reads: 'building up the *wedjat*-eye, rejuvenating the glorious eye, netting its pupil and putting it in its place' (*sps wḏꜣt srnp ꜣḫ.t jḥ ḏf=s dj m s.t=f*).[185] Though this text speaks about the building up of the *wedjat*-eye, and not the injured eye, with the verb *sps* instead of its synonym *qd* found in the Coffin Texts, the parallels between the two assertions are still very obvious.

In sum, at the beginning of spell 154 the speaker defines himself as one of those people who closely follow the changes of the moon, especially at the times when it is absent from the sky for a short period, and when the injured eye is being reconstructed during the waxing phases.

Lines 4–6

jw=j rḫ.kw jr.t Jwn.w tmm.t bsj wr-mꜣ.w ḥr=s
ḫb.t r m sn.wt dꜣ.t ꜥjn ḥtm r jwꜥ Jwn.w
jw=j rḫ.kw jry.t ḥnk.t n ṯꜣ.y ḥr=s

I know the eye of Heliopolis into which not even the greatest of seers has been initiated, The diminishing of the part in the *senut*, and how the destroyer extends the arm against the heir of Heliopolis.

[183] *CT* II, 270c.
[184] Chassinat 1928: 211–212.
[185] Chassinat 1928: 210.

I know how a braided lock of hair of a man is made upon it.

I translate the group of signs  as the eye of Heliopolis, but this writing leaves room for an alternative interpretation, as is also suggested by the parallel text variants. On most of the Asyut coffins a seated god complements the group, whereas on the coffin of Nakht (S2P) even the plural strokes appear, and these details provide a good ground for interpreting the expression in question as the ennead of Heliopolis (*psḏ.t Jwn.w*), which is indeed the understanding of previous translators.[186] However, the simple circle denotes the eye at other places in the Deir el-Bersha text variants,[187] and although the stroke signalling a logogram here is missing from the group constituted by the circle and the loaf of bread, it is still eminently possible that here the eye is meant, all the more so because in the examples cited the stroke is also lacking. Even one of the scribes copying the text in Asyut took the group to mark the eye (see S9C[a]), and he wrote the traditional hieroglyph of this body part in the appropriate place. Since in the previous line the sole eye referred to the two celestial eyes being in conjunction, the expression 'the eye of Heliopolis' is certainly also a designation of the same phenomenon, that is the invisible moon in the vicinity of the sun.

According to the text, the greatest of seers has not been initiated into the knowledge about the eye of Heliopolis. This title, *wr-mꜣ.w* 'greatest of seers', probably implies that its holder was very much skilled in the observation of the sky and astronomical phenomena,[188] though neither can it be ruled out that it should be translated as 'the one who sees the great one'.[189] The lunar (and solar) context of spell 154 vouches for its ultimate connection with celestial observations, and thus makes it more likely that the signs stand for the eye of Heliopolis. There is some contradiction between the two parts of the statement that not even the greatest of seers knows the eye of Heliopolis. This may be perhaps resolved if we consider that in actual fact two very similar titles containing the *wr-mꜣ.w* element existed: the ('simple') 'greatest of seers',[190] and the 'greatest of seers of Heliopolis' (*wr-mꜣ.w Jwn.w*).[191] We may suppose that this latter was ranked even higher than the earlier one, so someone with this title had a more profound knowledge of things than an ordinary *wr-mꜣ.w*. Therefore the boasting of the speaker of *CT* 154 may allude to the distinction between the two types of greatest of seers. Since the greatest of seers of Heliopolis was undoubtedly the highest official of the sun cult, the claim also – and again – implies that it incorporated the knowledge of lunar phenomena, too

One of the key expressions in the whole spell is *senut* (*sn.wt*). In Sen's text the word has a town determinative, and this must be due to the fact that there existed an eponymous

[186] Faulkner 1973: 132; Barguet 1986: 571; Carrier 2004: 370.
[187] *CT* II, 296a, 334c, 343a.
[188] Clagett 1995: 490.
[189] Kahl 2007: 49.
[190] Jones 2000: 386 no. 1428.
[191] Jones 2000: 386 no. 1429.

shrine,[192] which was basically the sacred enclosure – or one of the sacred enclosures – of Re in Heliopolis.[193] From the wider context, and several other text variants,[194] it is also obvious that the expression should be interpreted in another semantic field as well, because the morpheme *sn.wt* could also signify the sixth day of the lunar month.[195] Certain sources suggest that some sort of a link or connection may have existed between the shrine in Heliopolis and the sixth day of the month. For example, in spell 314 of the Coffin Texts the deceased expresses a wish with the following words: 'may I be with Horus on the day when the festival is celebrated and when the offerings are repeated, on the sixth and seventh days of the lunar month in Heliopolis' (*wn=j ḥnꜥ Ḥr.w hrw jr.t ḥꜣb wḥm ꜥꜣb.t sn.wt dnj.t m Jwn.w*).[196] Possibly the offerings were presented in the shrine of the city. The expression *senut* was also frequently associated with a particular district of Heliopolis, Kheraha; I will discuss the nature of this connection below, in the comments on lines 9–10.

The mention of the *senut* puts the speaker's claim about being great among the great ones (line 1) into a new light, because it is already well-documented in the Old Kingdom that there existed the title *wr sn.wt* 'the great one of the *sn.wt*-shrine'.[197] It is worth noting that one of the leading figures of the 6th dynasty, Nyankhnesut bore several titles – apart from the one just indicated – that closely relate to astronomical observation on the one hand, and to the themes of spell 154 on the other: *wr-mꜣ.w Jwn.w* 'the greatest of seers in Heliopolis',[198] *ḥr.j-sštꜣ n p.t* 'privy to the secrets of the sky',[199] and *ḥm-nṯr bꜣ.w Jwn.w* 'the prophet of the *bas* of Heliopolis.[200]

The text is concerned with the diminution in the part of the *senut*, and what lies behind this statement can only be understood if we take into consideration the further associations of *senut*, especially in connection with its role to designate the sixth day of the lunar month. This was not just a simple day in the calendar, but in the Heliopolitan doctrine it embodied the fullness of the moon.[201] Quite obviously, the Heliopolitan priests were aware that in reality the moon became full on the fifteenth day of the month (or, in a few number of cases, on a day that fell close to the fifteenth day), but the *senut* could symbolically express the full moon because according to a relevant mythological notion the eye representing the moon consisted of six parts.[202]

Since the six constituent elements corresponded to six different fractions (the dimidiated series 1/2, 1/4, 1/8, 1/16, 1/32, 1/64), the sum of which totalled a little less

[192] *Wb.* IV, 152.16.
[193] Kees 1922: 125; Wilkinson 2000: 162
[194] cf. for example B2Bo, B4Bo, B9C, B2P.
[195] *Wb.* IV, 153.4–6.
[196] *CT* IV, 95g–h.
[197] Leahy and Mathieson 2001: 37.
[198] cf. Jones 2000: 386 no. 1429.
[199] cf. Jones 2000: 621 no. 2276.
[200] Leahy and Mathieson 2001: 37–41.
[201] Smith 2002: 122.
[202] Junker 1911: 101.

than unity (63/64), the six parts of the eye did not only represent the idea of wholeness, but in a way also its imperfection.[203] This arithmetic exercise may have had something to do with astronomical observations as well, and may have alluded to the average length of the synodic month and the possible differences between the durations of the individual months.[204] Although some researchers doubt the early development and use of the Horus-eye fractions,[205] the analysis of spell 155 will demonstrate that they had a part to play in lunar reasonings at least already in the Middle Kingdom, and the appearance of *senut* in spell 154, with its associations of the full moon and full (30-day) month, can only be truly appreciated if we suppose that the Horus-eye fractions were known at the time.

The statement that 'the destroyer extends the arm against the heir of Heliopolis', which is to be taken as a hostile gesture,[206] only becomes clear when we consider the next line of the spell, informing us that the reduction in the month resulted from a row between Re and a serpent called He-who-is-in-his-fire. Thus the two participants of the argument are the heir of Heliopolis, that is Re, and the destroyer who has a serpent determinative in the other text variants, and consequently must be identical with the creature later referred to as He-who-is-in-his-fire.

Next we learn that at some point a braided lock of hair is made upon the eye of Heliopolis, and the speaker's claim about this detail must be connected with the idea that the full moon was a bald head, whereas when the earth's satellite was waxing and waning it was covered by hair to various degrees.[207] Indeed, the remark about the lock of hair in line 6 can be contrasted with the appearance of a bald man in line 13. Spell 154 of the Coffin Texts is therefore one of the few sources in which this concept about the moon repeatedly turning bald is attested.

The earliest evidence in this regard comes from utterance 684 of the Pyramid Texts, which states: 'The king will sit beside you, Osiris, the king will spit on your scalp, he will not let it be ill, the king will not let it be bald, according to the king's daily speech at the half-monthly festivals and at the monthly festivals' (*ḥms N r rmn=k Wsjr psg N sm3=k Wsjr n rdj=f mr=f n rdj N nqm=f r r n N rꜤ nb r tp.jw smd.wt tp.jw 3bd.w*).[208] The time expressions in this passage pointing to the beginning and middle of the lunar month suggest that here Osiris' head is indeed a symbol of the moon.[209] Another vestige of the concept may be the divinity called He-whose-hair-is-parted (*Wp-šn.wj*) in utterance 493 of the Pyramid Texts,[210] and although it has been proposed that this being is Horus

[203] Robins and Shute 1987: 14–15.
[204] Priskin 2002.
[205] Ritter 2002.
[206] cf. Faulkner 1973: 133.
[207] Derchain 1962a: 20; Eaton 2011: 236.
[208] *Pyr.* §2055a–c.
[209] The saying is repeated in *Pyr.* §2056a–c, where Horus replaces Osiris.
[210] *Pyr.* §1061a.

in his solar capacity,[211] since this particular text shows great affinities with Coffin Texts spell 246, another lunar text (see below), it is more likely that He-whose-hair-is-parted is essentially a lunar entity.

Some Late Period and Ptolemaic documents call the sixteenth day of the lunar month *ḥbs-tp* 'covering the head',[212] and this designation also provides evidence for the identification of the moon with a human head. During most lunations waning starts on the sixteenth day, so this is the time when the gibbous moon replaces the full lunar disc. The covering of the head therefore must have referred to the development by which the first thin dark strip marred the full lunar disc, which was mythically conceived as the first speck of hair on the bald scalp of the full moon.[213] It is worth noting that the sources citing the covering of the head as the name of the sixteenth day of the month link this event with Heliopolis. In the papyri recounting the wrongdoings of Seth (pBM 10252 and pLouvre 3129), in connection with the aversion of a lunar eclipse we learn that the celebration of *ḥbs-tp* takes place in Heliopolis.[214] Another papyrus, dated to the 7th century BCE and collecting various mythological episodes of certain cult places in the Delta (pBrooklyn 47.218.84), also puts the covering of the head in Heliopolis, specifying that it lasted as long as the first crescent reappeared on the third day of the month.[215]

Lines 7–8

Rꜥ pw ḥr mdw.t ḥnꜥ Jm.j-whm=f ḥr psš.t Jwn.w
ꜥḥꜥ.n r=f jꜣṯ ḫpr ḫb.t pw m ꜣbd

It was the case that Re had a discussion with He-who-is-in-his-fire over the division of Heliopolis.
Then his part was injured and that is how the diminishing of the month came into being.

Here the text talks about the diminishing of the month (*ḫb.t pw m ꜣbd*), and not that of the *senut*, so the connection of the narrative with the length of the month is more straightforward. The reduction in the month's length is the outcome of a debate between Re and the serpent called He-who-is-in-his-fire. This name evokes the moon being in conjunction with the sun – i.e. being between the earth and the sun – because when the last crescent disappears at the end of the month, the moon gets so close to the sun from the perspective of an earthbound observer that no light is reflected from it towards the earth, and it cannot be observed immediately before sunrise on the

[211] Allen 2005: 432.
[212] Parker 1953.
[213] Eaton 2011: 236.
[214] Altmann 2010: 93.
[215] Meeks 2006: 14.

eastern horizon. In other words, the moon enters the fire of the sun and dwells in its immediate vicinity, but is invisible.

The sun's association with fire is self-evident,[216] and various passages within the Coffin Texts also underline this identification.[217] One obvious example is spell 1033 which states that the fire that is bright or burning towards the deceased is around Re (*sḏ.t tw wbḫ.t r=tn ḥ3.t Rʿ*).[218] Indeed, the idea that the invisible moon commingles with the fire of the sun is also apparent from Coffin Texts spell 246, in which the deceased speaks as if he himself were coming into contact with it:

r n ʿq m sḏ.t pr.t m sḏ.t r-ḥ3 p.t jnk Sfg-jr.w pw ḥr.j-jb j3ḫ.w ʿq=j m sḏ.t prj.n=j m sḏ.t n dm (w)j j3ḫ.w n ns wj Gmm.w-wr jnk ds mds jm.j ʿ Ḏḥw.tj n dbn=j n dbn=j ʿ=k Ḥr.w ʿ=k Wr wḏ3.t 3ḫ.t nb ḏf3.w

Spell for entering into fire and coming out of fire in the back of the sky. I am He-with-hidden-form amidst sunshine, I enter into fire and come out of fire, the sunshine has not pierced me, He-who-is-always-found-great has not burnt me. I am the flint-knife and the flint-sickle that are in the hand of Thoth. I have not gone around, I have not gone around your arm, Horus, your arm, the Great One, and the Sound Eye is radiant and has provisions.[219]

This spell, which is also full of subtle lunar imagery that I discuss elsewhere,[220] was possibly prompted by the deceased's wish to acquire the ability of the moon to survive in the vicinity of the sun, in accordance with their ambition to join Re for a successful afterlife. Each month, after the moon entered the fire of the sun, it demonstrated its endurance, because the first waxing crescent inescapably appeared one or two days

[216] Wilkinson 1992: 161.
[217] Hornung 1999: 11.
[218] *CT* VII, 263a; Faulkner 1973: 129–130.
[219] *CT* III, 337a–338b.
[220] Priskin 2018. In my paper I argue that He-with-hidden-form is the designation of the invisible moon, He-who-is-always-found-great refers to the sun (the unchanging solar disc), while the flint-knife and flint-sickle in Thoth's hand allude to the last and first crescents of the moon during waning and waxing, respectively.

later, thus serving as a 'role model' for the dead. With its description, spell 246 serves to underline the point that according to Egyptian beliefs at the time of conjunction the moon passed through the fiery environment of the sun, so the name He-who-is-in-his-fire was also an appropriate designation of the blacked-out moon in spell 154.

Because He-who-is-in-his-fire acts as the adversary of Re, he is conceptualised as a snake and has the corresponding determinative. In the two early Ptolemaic papyri mentioned above (pBM 10252 and pLouvre 3129), He-who-is-in-his-fire leads twenty enemies of the sun god poised at the gate of the horizon,[221] and this information supports the astral and solar connotations of the being. His identification with the invisible moon is further backed up by his reappearance in spell 160, once more as the enemy of the sun god, because there he is responsible for stopping the solar barque on its daily journey (see the relevant chapter below). As such, he is the instigator of a solar eclipse, and this event – by the laws of nature – can only happen at the time of lunisolar conjunction when the moon gets directly between the earth and the sun. This again shows that He-who-is-in-his-fire is an alias for the blacked-out moon.

From the text it is not entirely clear whose part is injured; it may be the sun god or the moon behind the name He-who-is-in-his-fire. If the suffering party is the sun, then the statement is perhaps based on the recognition that the light of the moon eventually originates from the sun, i.e. the moon only reflects the light that falls upon it from the direction of the sun. If the moon is at the receiving end of the debate, the reduction may refer to a hollow month which only lasts for 29 days (i.e. one day short of the full 30-day month). Howsoever it is the case, the strife between Re and He-who-is-in-his-fire may be a distant predecessor of the story told by Plutarch by which Thoth had won in a game of dice from the moon a certain amount of light of each day to create the epagomenal days and to make the birth of the gods possible.[222] Besides the association with the *senut* and, indirectly, with the fractions of the eye of Horus, it is this resemblance to this much later motif that suggests the translation of the word 𓂋𓏤 as 'part'. Previous translators generally believed that it referred to Re's mouth.[223]

Lines 9–10

ꜥḥꜥ.n ḏd.n Jm.j-wḥm=f šsp=j mꜥbꜣ=j jwꜥ=j n.t tn ḫpr mꜥbꜣ pw
ꜥḥꜥ.n ḏd.n Rꜥ sꜥḥꜥ=j ḥm sn.wt=j r=f nš=j sw ḫpr sn.wt pw

Then He-who-is-in-his-fire said: 'I will take my harpoon and I will inherit this town'. And that is how the harpoon came into being.
Then Re said: 'I will erect my flagpoles against him and I will repel him'. And that is how the *senut*-festival came into being.

[221] Schott 1929: 63.
[222] Griffiths 1970: 135.
[223] Faulkner 1973: 132; Barguet 1986: 571; Carrier 2004: 370; Eaton 2011: 236–237.

The theme of the debate spoiling the relationship of Re with He-who-is-in-his-fire is further embellished here with a dialogue between them that contains more clues to the lunar interpretation of the text. The weapon that He-who-is-in-his-fire – the moon in conjunction – wants to use to press his case is quite telling in this respect, since the harpoon called *mʿbꜣ* and written as  is homophonous with the word for the number 30, and as we can see, its hieroglyphic writing includes the number itself (the sign for ten repeated thrice). He-who-is-in-his-fire threatens to inherit Heliopolis with the help of his harpoon and would like to overthrow Re, who himself was named the heir of Heliopolis in a few lines earlier. The text implies that the existence of the harpoon is the result of the mythical incident recounted in spell 154, and this is the first time when the aetiological motif – an explanation of how things came into existence – appears in the Book of the Moon. We will see that this motif regularly recurs in some of the chapters of the composition.

Re answers the threat of He-who-is-in-his-fire with a statement that is also based on a pun, because in his reply the word for flagpoles, 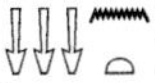 *sn.wt*,[224] resonates with the homophonous  *sn.wt*, which of course denotes the festival of *senut* on the sixth day of the lunar month. The two adversaries in their speeches therefore seem to allude to both the full month of 30 days (*mʿbꜣ*), and the hollow month of 29 days (through *sn.wt*). It must be noted that the *senut* was already closely associated with the idea of struggle in utterance 493 of the Pyramid Texts where the king asserts: 'I am great because of my *bas*, and the *senut* belongs to me in Kheraha (*wrr⸗j ḥr bꜣ.w⸗j nnk sn.wt m ẖr.j-ʿḥꜣ*).[225] Kheraha was part of Heliopolis and its name means 'the place of fighting', 'battlefield', literally '(the place) which is under the fighting',[226] so it naturally evokes the act of fighting in connection with the *senut*. Later sources, for example the papyrus about the myths in the Delta (pBrooklyn 47.218.84), relate that Kheraha was the site where Re, or Atum, fought his enemies in an epic battle,[227] though these stories do not necessarily have any astral connotations. The strife between the sun god and his adversaries may have encompassed more than one semantic layers. Utterance 483 of the Pyramid Texts and spell 154 of the Coffin Texts certainly add astronomical dimensions to the fight.

Lines 11–12

Rʿ pw ḥpj.n(⸗f) sw Jm.j-jns⸗f n ḫn.t⸗f ʿ⸗f
ʿḥʿ.n jrj.n⸗f sḫt⸗f r⸗f m s.t ḥm.t ḥnsk.t ḫpr⸗f pw n Jwn.w

It was the case that Re encountered He-who-is-in-his-red-cloth before he could turn his hand against him.

[224] *Wb.* IV, 152.8.
[225] *Pyr.* §1062b–c.
[226] Gardiner 1947: 134–136.
[227] Meeks 2006: 16.

Then he made a trap for him in the form of a woman with braided hair, and that is how he came into being in Heliopolis.

The name He-who-is-in-his-red-cloth, on the analogy of He-who-is-in-his-fire, also refers to the moon in conjunction with the sun, but this time at the opposite end of the sky over the western horizon. Because of atmospheric refraction the setting sun – just as the rising sun, for that matter – tends to attain a red hue, so now the invisible moon dwelling in its vicinity can rightly be called He-who-is-in-his-red-cloth. It is clear from the location of such mythical places as the Island of Fire and the Lake of Fire in the east, that the primary fiery nature of the sun was linked to its morning form as it rose from the eastern horizon.[228] That is perhaps why the invisible moon changes its name as it gets to the western side of the sky. The being called He-who-is-in-his-red-cloth also appears in utterance 254 of the Pyramid Texts: 'You see Re in his fetters, you praise Re in his bindings, under the protection of the great one, He-who-is-in-his-red-cloth' (*mꜣꜣ=k Rʿ m jnṯ.wt=f dwꜣ=k Rʿ m pr.wt=f m sꜣ wr Jmj-jns.w=f*).[229] Unfortunately the context here is rather obscure, but this passage nevertheless also underlines the close ties between Re and the divine being called He-who-is-in-his-red-cloth. Furthermore, in spell 619 of the Coffin Texts He-who-is-in-his-red-cloth appears in a passage that talks about the arrival of the deceased to the west, and this also suggests that the name should be associated with the western direction.[230]

Behind the two names of the invisible moon in spell 154 must lie the cognizance that at the time of conjunction the moon moves simultaneously with the sun through the day sky, so that at dusk – likewise to the sun – it is also near the western horizon. The same idea is also expressed much later, on the eastern wall of the pronaos of the Edfu temple. Here the description of the first day of the lunar month, *psḏn.tjw*,[231] starts with an account of sunrise emphasising the role of Isis and Nephthys in lifting up the solar disc.[232] Then we read: 'It (= the solar disc) completes its course with its radiance and its rays hide the light of the moon. Horus unites with his counterpart, and his mother, Nut, conceals him in her armpits for Min, which is his place on the day of the invisible moon' (*mḥ.n=f šn=f m psḏ.w=f sdg.n psḏ.w=f mꜣw.t n jʿḥ snsn Ḥr.w m sn.nw=f sdg sw mw.t=f m ḥṯṯ.t=s n Mnw s.t=f psḏn.tjw*).[233] Starting from the east the invisible moon, hidden in the light of the sun, reaches west, as is indicated by the reference to the armpits of Nut. Since the arching figure of Nut, embodying the sky, gives birth to the sun in the east, her arms are obviously in the west.

According to the text, He-who-is-in-his-red-cloth had no chance to attack Re, who then set a trap for him, and that is how he came into being. The personal pronoun here

[228] Grieshammer 1977.
[229] *Pyr.* §285c–d.
[230] *CT* VI, 232e–233c.
[231] The term *psḏn.tjw* is discussed in Borghouts 1971: 84–87.
[232] Chassinat 1928: 211. For an annotated translation of this part of the text, see Priskin 2017b.
[233] Chassinat 1928: 211.

most probably refers to Re, but it cannot be ruled out either that its antecedent is the other protagonist, He-who-is-in-his-red-cloth. The trap is embodied in the person of a woman with braided hair, and utterance 254 of the Pyramid Texts may again provide a clue to understanding this detail. A few lines before the appearance of He-who-is-in-his-red-cloth, we can read: 'Look, here she comes to meet you, the Beautiful West comes to meet you, with her beautiful locks of hair' (*mk sj jwj=s m ḫsf=k Jmn.t nfr.t m ḫsf=k m nꜣb.wt nfr.t*).[234] The woman with braided hair thus could be identical with the goddess called Beautiful West, who is the personification of the western direction.[235] This may once more reinforce the proposition that He-who-is-in-his-red-cloth designates the moon moving in unison with the setting sun in the west. Since the new crescent of the waxing moon appears in the west after sunset, the west as a trap perhaps expresses the idea that if the sun reaches the western horizon without any disturbance, either on the first or second day of lunar invisibility, there is bound to be no solar eclipse in that month (i.e. the invisible moon has been unable to launch an attack against it).

These lines thus perhaps give a symbolic account of the situation when during conjunction no solar eclipse occurs. Along its orbit the moon gets between the sun and the earth during each lunation, and thus becomes invisible for a while, but a solar eclipse only takes place when the earth, moon, and sun are perfectly aligned. In astronomical terms, the plane of the moon's orbit around the earth is slightly tilted from the plane on which the earth orbits the sun, so the two planes do not meet at every conjunction. At the same time, the two planes are always close enough to make the moon invisible. In the majority of the months no eclipse occurs. The text, with its reference to the avoidance of a hostile attack, perhaps alludes to this common situation.

Lines 13–15

fꜣk sḫm r r-pr pn ḫpr fꜣk pw n Jwn.w
ḫpr.t jwꜥ jwꜥ=f wj wr mꜣꜣ jt=f
ḫpr.kꜣ=f m wr-mꜣw m sꜣ jrj n jt=f

The bald man holds power in this temple, and that is how the bald man came into being in Heliopolis,
Before the heir to the heritage came into being, that is me, the great one who sees his father;
He will come into being as the greatest of seers, as the son who acts for his father.

These lines perhaps have two layers of meaning. The bald (or shorn)[236] man on the one hand may refer to a particular priest or priestly position, who fulfils his duties

[234] *Pyr.* §282b–c.
[235] Leitz 2002a: 365–366.
[236] The term implies that the person is bald because he deliberately got rid of his hair.

in a temple precinct in Heliopolis. From the logic of the text, this temple is either identical with the *senut* shrine, or includes this shrine, and the priest serving in it has a great knowledge about the movements of the sun and the moon. The speaker thus defines himself as the heir of this person, the next greatest of seers, who can likewise become very familiar with celestial phenomena. Spell 660 of the Coffin Texts attests to the fact that there indeed existed a priestly position in Heliopolis which was held by people with shorn heads, and which was somehow connected with the observation of the moon, since the deceased declares: 'N (consumes) breakfast and supper at the seventh-day festival because he has heard the shout from the mouths of the bald men of Heliopolis (*jꜥ.w ms.wt n N pn n dnj.t n-n.tjt sḏm.n=f jhm m r n fꜣk.w n.w Jwn.w*).[237] Indirectly the connection between the shorn priest and the *senut* is reaffirmed, since the seventh-day festival (*dnj.t*) immediately followed on the *senut* (the sixth day), and these two lunar days were frequently mentioned together in a number of sources (see above).[238]

On the other hand, because of the association of the moon with the hairy or hairless head, the bald man can also evoke the full moon, and can be juxtaposed with the mention of the man with a braided lock of hair alluding to the other lunar phases. As I argued, with the reference to yesterday, the lines at the beginning of the spell imply that the greatest of seers gains his legitimacy at the opposite end of the month, when he precisely observes the disappearance of the last crescent at the onset of lunar invisibility. Therefore the expressions connected with hair contrast the two defining moments of the lunar cycle, the full moon and the blacked-out moon. This seems logical, but the precise connotations of these ideas are really difficult to fathom.

Even more obscure are the claims of the speaker about the temporal dimension of the course of events and his identification with the great one who sees his father. However, as the sixth day of the month was mentioned earlier in the text, we must bear in mind that in later sources the protective deity of the eighth day of the month was called He-who-sees-his-father (*mꜣꜣ-it=f*).[239] Quite possibly then the bald man and the person who sees his father are subtle allusions to the middle of the waxing period, when metaphorically the moon starts to shed its hair in earnest, anticipating the arrival of the full moon. So in this way spell 154 does not only refer to the time of conjunction, but surely to the first few days of a lunation. Two days are specifically mentioned through the expressions of the *senut* (*sn.wt*, the sixth day) and He-who-sees-his-father (*mꜣꜣ-it=f*, the eighth day).

Line 16

jw=j rḫ.kw bꜣ.w Jwn.w Rꜥ pw Šw pw Tfn.t pw

[237] *CT* VI, 283j–k.
[238] Eaton 2011: 244.
[239] Leitz 2002c: 199.

I know the *bas* of Heliopolis. It is Re, it is Shu, it is Tefnut.

The closing line identifies the *bas* hinted at in the title of the spell with Re and the first generation of the Heliopolitan ennead, Shu and Tefnut. Their position in this divine group may itself explain why they feature among the *bas* of Heliopolis. In later texts Shu and Tefnut can represent the two eyes of Horus, that is the sun and the moon.[240] Nevertheless, besides the obvious connection with Heliopolitan theology, perhaps a pun also lies behind the group of gods named in the last line of the text. Re, as the solar deity par excellence, naturally embodies the sun, while Shu may allude to the invisible moon. The phoneme *šw* can also mean 'to lack', 'to be empty'.[241] This verb is used in utterance 412 of the Pyramid Texts, which contains a lot of lunar references and most probably evokes the time of the blacked-out moon. The king is first equated with the stars that surround Re, and then the relevant passage reads: 'You will be born in your months like the moon, Re will lean on you in the horizon, the imperishable stars will follow you. Provide for yourself until Re comes; you will be purified and you will come forth for Re, the sky will not be devoid of you forever' (*msj=k jr ꜣbd.w=k mj jꜥḥ twꜣ Rꜥ ḥr=k m ꜣḫ.t N š(m)s ṯw jḫm.w-sk j.ꜥbꜣ ṯw jr jw Rꜥ N wꜥb=k prj=k n Rꜥ n šw p.t jm=k N ḏ.t*).[242] The promise that the sky will not lack (*n šw*) the presence of the king in his capacity as the moon clearly shows that the verb *šw* could be used to refer to the absence of the moon from the sky. Whether a pun with the name Shu was meant in spell 154 cannot be told with any certainty.

On the Asyut coffins further statements augment the closing of the spell, but these do not go beyond generalities and only reiterate the themes of the longer title:

wꜣḥ tp-tꜣ ꜣḫ m ẖr.t-nṯr ꜥq ḥr nb.w Jwn.w pr.t r p.t wbꜣ dwꜣ.t

Enduring on the earth, being effective in the necropolis, entering into the lords of Heliopolis, going forth to the sky, and opening up the netherworld.

[240] Derchain 1962a: 52.
[241] *Wb.* IV, 426.7–15.
[242] *Pyr.* §§732b–733d.

2.2. Spell 155: lunar invisibility

The hieroglyphic text

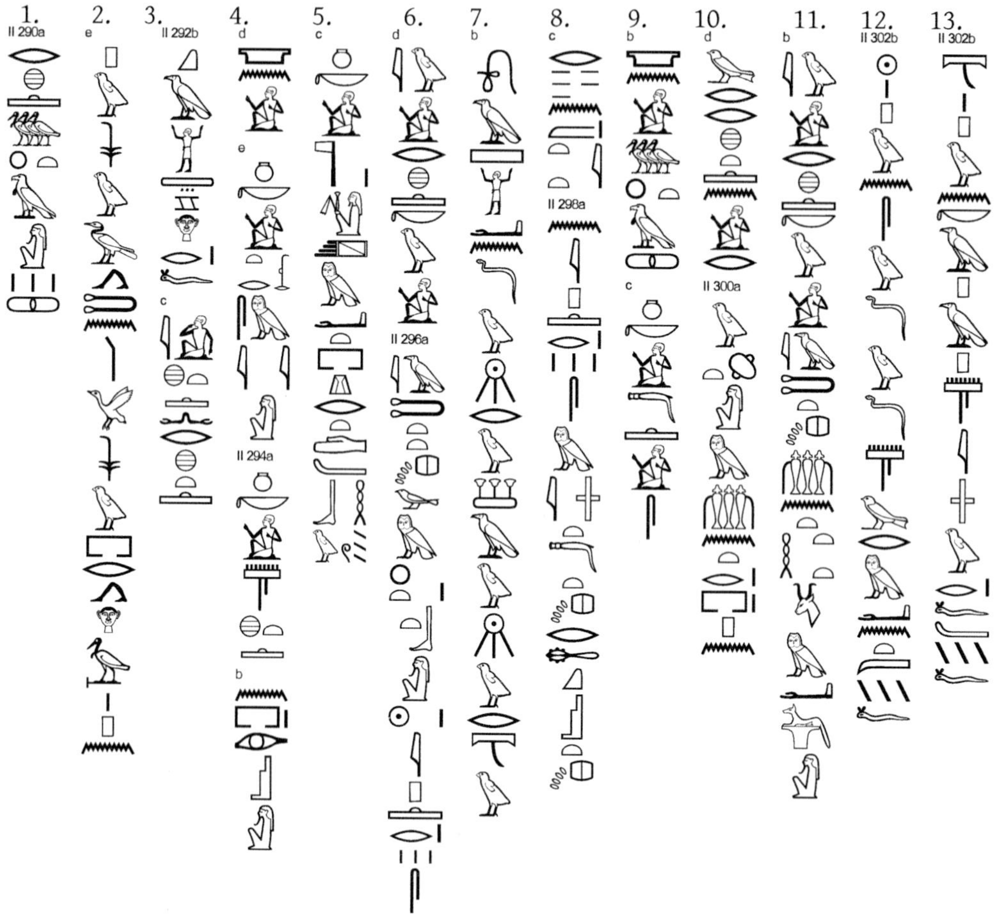

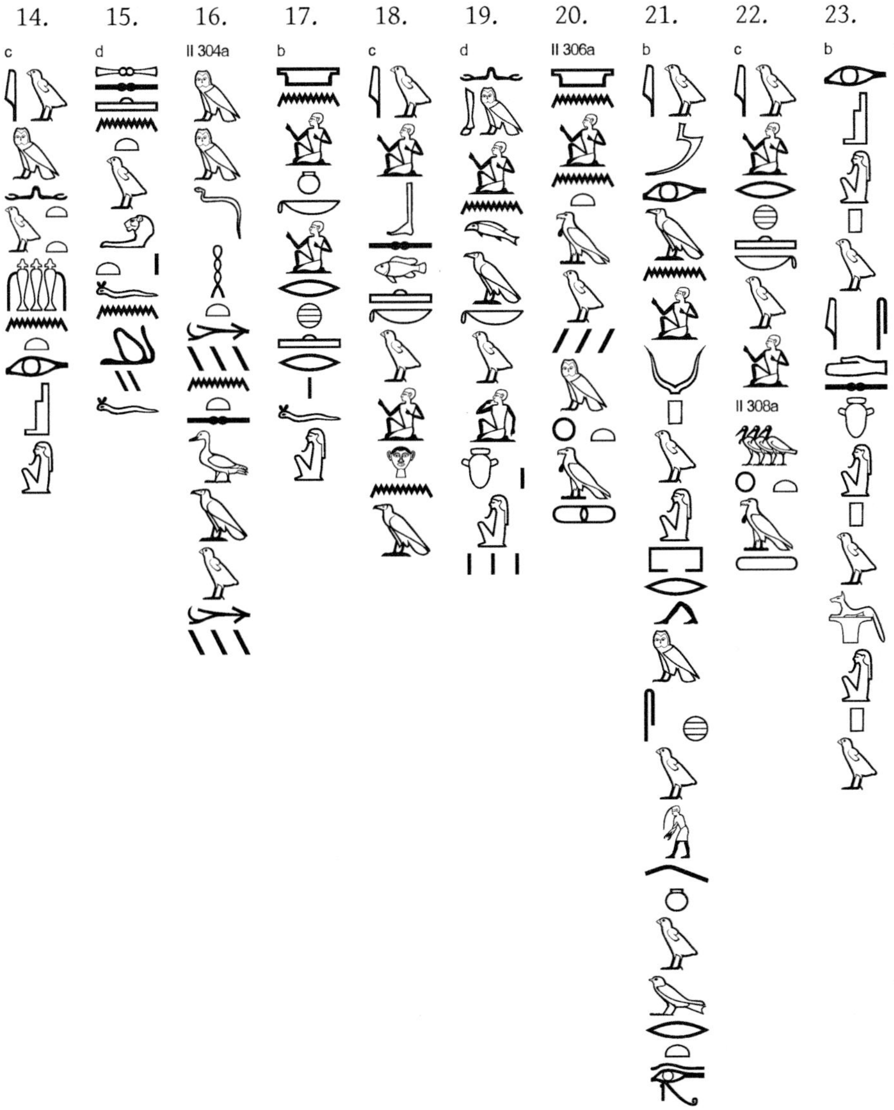
14. c
15. d
16. II 304a
17. b
18. c
19. d
20. II 306a
21. b
22. c
II 308a
23. b

Transliteration and translation

1. *rḫ bꜣ.w psḏn.tjw*
2. *pw sw ꜥq(.w) ṯnw sw pr(.w) ḥr bꜣ pn*
3. *qꜣ tꜣ ḥr r⸗f j.ḫt n rḫ.t*
4. *wn n⸗j jnk tr(.w) sm.y jnk ḥbs(.w) ḫ.t n pr Wsjr*
5. *jnk nṯr jr.j sjꜣ m ꜥ.t ẖr dbḥ.w*
6. *jw⸗j rḫ.kw jꜣṯ.t m jr.t Tby jp r.w⸗s*
7. *wꜣš ꜥnḏw r wšꜣ.w wḫ.w*
8. *r 5-nw n gs twt n jp r.w⸗s m jmj.t mḥ.t r ẖqs.t*
9. *wn n⸗j bꜣ.w psḏn.tjw jnk mḥ⸗j s(j)*
10. *wr rḫ.t.n⸗j r wtj m ḫnt r-pr pn*
11. *jw⸗j rḫ.kw jꜣṯ.t ḫnt ḥt.t m ꜥJnpw*
12. *hrw pw n swḏwḏ wr-m-ꜥn.wt⸗f*
13. *grḥ pw n kꜣpꜣp jmj.w r⸗f*
14. *jw m jwtt ḫnt Wsjr*
15. *ṯs.n.tw ḥꜣ.t⸗f n pḥ.wj⸗f*
16. *m mḏḥ.t n.t sꜣw*
17. *wn n⸗j jnk rḫ(.w) r⸗f*
18. *jw⸗j bsj.kw ḥr nꜣ*
19. *n wḥm⸗j n ẖꜣk.w-jb*
20. *wn n⸗j ntjw m psḏn.tjw*
21. *jw mꜣꜣ.n⸗j wp.w pr(.w) m sḫ.w n.w Wr.t*
22. *jw⸗j rḫ.kw bꜣ.w psḏn.tjw*
23. *Wsjr pw Jsds pw Jnpw pw*

1. Knowing the *bas* of the moon's invisibility.
2. Who is he who enters, where is he from who comes forth upon this *ba*,
3. the earth being high on account of his spell? That is an unknown thing.
4. Open to me because I am one who respects the observed one, because I am one who makes the covering in the house of Osiris,
5. and because I am the god in charge of the full moon period in the room where the vessel containing the fractional components of the eye is stored.
6. I know what is missing from the eye of Tebi when its parts are counted,
7. and when dawn is stronger than the glow of the darkened night.
8. The fifth part of an entire half for counting its parts between what is in the filling eye and the ailing eye.
9. Open to me, the bas of the moon's invisibility, for I am one who completes the eye,
10. for what I know is more than the embalmer of the temple knows.
11. I know what is missing from the eye canal in the hand of Anubis
12. on this day of covering his great fingernails,
13. on this night of hiding his teeth.

14. It is a void out of Osiris,
15. when one has joined his front with his back
16. as the hewn out part of the beam.
17. Open to me because I am one who knows his spell.
18. I have been initiated into these matters,
19. and I will not reveal it to ill-intentioned people.
20. Open to me, those in the moon's invisibility.
21. I have seen the gelder come out of the slaughterhouse of the Great Eye.
22. I know the *bas* of the moon's invisibility.
23. It is Osiris, it is Isdes, it is Anubis.

Commentary

Line 1

rḫ bꜣ.w psḏn.tjw

Knowing the *bas* of the moon's invisibility.

The first line is the title of the spell, though on Sen's coffin it is not highlighted with red ink. On five out of the ten coffins coming from Deir el-Bersha the title stands this short, while a significantly longer version is found on the inner coffin of Djehutinakht (B2Bo):

rḫ bꜣ.w psḏn.tjw ʿq r pr Wsjr n h̭d.w wnn m šms.w n Wsjr sḫm m mw tm šm sẖd tm wnm ḥs tm mt ky sp m ẖr.t-nṯr jn bꜣ ʿnḫ.y mt.y

Knowing the *bas* of the moon's invisibility, entering the house of Osiris in Djedu, being among the followers of Osiris, having control over water, not walking upside down, not eating excrement, not dying a second time in the necropolis by the living and the dead *ba*.

The additional elements in this long title are, however, commonplace phrases that keep being repeated in the Coffin Texts in order to express the most obvious wishes of the deceased. In the underworld the Egyptians customarily wanted to be close to Osiris, tried to evade final annihilation (the second death) and hoped that they could avoid such abominations as going about upside down or consuming bodily refuse – these abhorrent activities of course highlighted the otherworldly conditions of the realm of the dead.[243] The only part of the extended title that does not recur elsewhere is the phrase 'entering the house of Osiris in Djedu', and it is included in the title on another Deir el-Bersha coffin (B1Y), and then regularly features on the coffins from Asyut. One may therefore wonder whether this circumstance implies that the Egyptians editing spell 155 felt that this clause was different from the others in the long title and it gave some meaningful extra information concerning the theme of knowing the *bas* of the moon's invisibility, or again, it just expressed in yet another way the basic desire of being close to Osiris by claiming to have access to his property. Patrik Wallin consents to this latter view and sees here the expression of the wish to join in the ritualised pilgrimage to Osiris' main centre in the north.[244]

There is of course quite an easy explanation why some copyists may have felt that a direct reference to Osiris was appropriate at the beginning of spell 155. The closing of the spell is in fact a straightforward response to the very first phrase of the title, as it names in no uncertain terms the *bas* of the moon's invisibility: they are Osiris, Isdes and Anubis. Whether this statement is an early attestation of the process by which Osiris became thoroughly identified with the moon is a moot point, and I will discuss it in my comments to line 24 below. Nevertheless, the extended title relates Osiris to Djedu (Busiris), his chief Lower Egyptian cult centre in the middle of the Delta. If it could be proved that the lunar cult played a significant role in the ritual activities there, then this fact would explain the mention of this town in the title of a spell that claims to be concerned with the *bas* of the moon's invisibility. However, there is not much evidence hinting at such a connection in the Coffin Texts. One exception may be spell 339 that lists the localities where Thoth (here clearly in his judicial function) is supposed to vindicate Osiris against his enemies before the councils of magistrates, and it claims that in Djedu it should happen on 'the day when the *wedjat*-eye is given to its owner' (*hrw pw n rd.t wḏꜣ.t n nb=f*).[245] While the *wedjat*-eye was most frequently conceived as a symbol of the restored left eye of Horus, that is, the full moon,[246] in the absence of a wider lunar context it may not necessarily be equated with the moon here, so this piece of evidence remains inconclusive. But, as we shall see it later, it is precisely *CT* 155 that hints at the connection of the lunar cult with the house of Osiris in Djedu (see comments to lines 4 and 5 below).

To translate the term *psḏn.tjw*, Leo Depuydt proposes the technically more appropriate expression 'last crescent invisibility',[247] for the event that inaugurated the new lunar month in ancient Egypt was the morning when the last crescent of the waning moon could no longer be seen above the eastern horizon. From the Egyptian sources it also

[243] Assmann 2005: 128.
[244] Wallin 2002: 72.
[245] *CT* IV, 338c.
[246] Smith 2002: 124.
[247] Depuydt 1998: 73.

transpires, however, that *psḏn.tjw* did not only refer to a momentary event, that is, the disappearance of the last crescent, but also to the whole period when the moon was invisible (see discussion below). Therefore here I render *psḏn.tjw* 'the moon's invisibility', because on the one hand I would find the use of 'last crescent invisibility' a bit cumbersome, and on the other I think my rendering elicits the sense of duration to a greater extent than Depuydt's choice of words. I must also note that I use the term 'the moon's invisibility' interchangeably with the modern expression 'new moon' (the traditional translation of *psḏn.tjw*), as in its wider sense (astronomical new moon) it also conveys the idea of the non-presence of the lunar disc.

Lines 2–3

pw sw ꜥq(.w) ṯnw sw pr(.w) ḥr bꜣ pn
qꜣ tꜣ ḥr r⸗f j.ḫ.t n rḫ.t

Who is he who enters, where is he from who comes forth upon this *ba*,
the earth being high on account of his spell? That is an unknown thing.

That *pw* here on its own at the beginning of the sentence is equivalent to *ptr* 'who? what?' (etymologically *pw* plus the enclitic particle *tr*) has long been established.[248] The expression 'this *ba*' surely refers to the deceased, but in the following line Sen's inscription differs from all other versions in a minute, yet perhaps quite significant detail. On most coffins in *CT* II, 292b we have 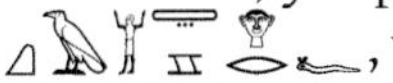, while singularly on B2Bo (Djehutinakht's inner coffin) 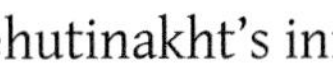, and this can of course be interpreted as *qꜣ tꜣ ḥr r⸗f* 'the earth is being high on him'.[249] Sethe then goes on to conjecture that the whole statement alludes to the mound that is elevated over the tomb.[250] However, Sen quite clearly has a stroke next to the sign of the mouth, so the hieroglyphs should definitely be read *qꜣ tꜣ ḥr r⸗f* 'the earth being high on account of his spell' (though admittedly it is also quite plausible that the stroke after the mouth sign is merely a scribal error). Obviously, there is a marked difference between the two renderings, as the reference to a spell gives quite a different sense to the passage. My interpretation, however, on the one hand finds its echo in line 17, where the speaker boasts about knowing his spell, and on the other can be set against another passage in the Coffin Texts that may shed some light on the link between the earth's highness and a written or orally recited utterance.

In spell 314 the deceased assumes a series of priestly positions which supposedly help him to draw near Osiris, and here he makes the claim: 'I am the *wab*-priest in Djedu on the day when what is high is made high, I am the god's servant in Abydos on the day when the earth is exalted' (*jnk wꜥb n Ḏd.w sw sqꜣ qꜣꜣ.t jnk ḥm-nṯr n ꜣbḏ.w hrw ḥꜥw.t tꜣ*).[251]

[248] Sethe 1922: 28; Faulkner 1982: 27.
[249] Faulkner 1973: 133; Carrier 2004: 376.
[250] Sethe 1922: 29.
[251] *CT* IV, 95i–l.

Now, this passage made its way into the Book of Going Forth by Day, and there in spell 1 it ends with exactly the same expression as in *CT* 155: 'I am the *wab*-priest in Djedu, made wise in Abydos, (on the day) when what is in the high one is made high, I am the god's servant in Abydos on the day when the earth is high' (*jnk wꜥb m Ḏd.w sbq m ꜣbḏ.w sqꜣ jm.j-qꜣꜣ.t jnk ḥm-nṯr m ꜣbḏ.w hrw n qꜣ.w tꜣ*).[252] In these excerpts the references to height and, more specifically, to the height of the earth quite plausibly pertain to the mound over the tomb of Osiris, and I think the same applies to *CT* 155.

Eventually of course, as in theory anyone's tomb in ancient Egypt may be conceived as the replica of Osiris' tomb, the heap of earth hinted at in line 3 of *CT* 155 could also relate to the speaker's own burial place. But this is not the issue here. What matters is that surely there was an Osirian ritual connected with building a mound over the divine tomb. Consequently, I think that what the assertion 'the earth is high on account of his spell' really wants to emphasise is the speaker's ability to take part in ritual activities and his aptitude for producing the right speech acts during these rituals. These then lead to the desired effect, that is the mounting of earth over the tomb. The *BD* descendant of Coffin Texts spell 314, though of course dates from a much later time (Ptolemaic era), highlights the connection between the act of making the earth high and intellectual capacities by referring to the experience of becoming knowledgeable (*sbq m ꜣbḏ.w*). Understanding the clause 'the earth being high on account of his spell' as advertising the intelligence of the speaker is quite in keeping with the rest of spell 155.

Lines 4–5

wn n=j jnk tr(.w) sm.y jnk ḥbs(.w) ḫ.t n pr Wsjr
jnk nṯr jr.j sjꜣ m ꜥ.t ẖr dbḥ.w

Open to me because I am one who respects the observed one, because I am one who makes the covering in the house of Osiris,
and because I am the god in charge of the full moon period in the room where the vessel containing the fractional components of the eye is stored.

Faulkner believes that *tr* here is the enclitic particle,[253] but that is certainly an erroneous view, and I agree with Sethe that it is the participle of the verb *tr* 'to respect, to esteem'.[254] In a similar fashion, I take *sm.y* to be the passive participle of *sm* 'to pay attention to someone, to respect',[255] thus meaning 'the observed one' – for this see also the separate entry in the *Wörterbuch*, with essentially the same meaning.[256]

[252] Lepsius 1842: pl. 1.
[253] Faulkner 1973: 134.
[254] *Wb.* V, 318.1–8; Sethe 1922: 29.
[255] *Wb.* IV, 120.7.
[256] *Wb.* IV, 120.9.

My rendering is therefore quite similar to that of Barguet's,[257] but I think it is really difficult to give a good translation here, because two words in line 4 – *sm.y* and *ḥbs* – make subtle allusions to the names of specific days of the lunar month, and thus different stages of the lunar cycle. The names of the 30 days of the lunar month are revealed at a much later time in Graeco-Roman temple inscriptions.[258] In these lists the fourth day is called *pr.t-sm* 'the going forth of the *sem*-priest'. According to a papyrus with mythological content written in the 7th century BCE, already cited in the previous chapter, this event signals the moment when Horus has recovered the faculties of his eye after the period of distress caused by Seth: 'Horus opened his eyes, and he could see with them. ... His strength grew, so he went forth at dawn – one calls it the going forth of the *sem*-priest on the fourth day following every instance of the moon's invisibility' (*wn Ḥr.w jr.tj⸗fj m33⸗f jm⸗sj ... ꜥ3 pḥ.tj⸗fj prj.ḫr⸗f m ḥḏ-t3 pr.t-sm ḫr.tw r⸗f ḥr hrw 4 n psḏn.tjw nb*).[259] One may not be far off from the truth to interpret this poetic description as referring to the appearance of the new crescent – in the evening of the third day of the lunar month at the latest – and to a corresponding ceremony heralding the waxing phase of the moon at the end of that evening (dawn of the fourth day). Therefore the expression *sm.y* also evokes that stage of the lunar cycle when the crescent of the moon is seen waxing.

This interpretation is reinforced by the second part of line 4 which seems to be connected with the other side of the lunar cycle, waning. For *ḥbs ḫ.t* three possibilities may be considered. First, suspecting a more abstract sense behind *ḥbs* 'to clothe things, to cover things (with cloth)' the phrase may mean 'to keep things secret', and that is the understanding of practically all previous translators.[260] For this compare *Wb.* III, 65.10, and *CT* III, 311c, where *ḥ3p* 'to hide, to keep secret' and *ḥbs* are used interchangeably on different coffins. Secondly, it can of course have the literal meaning, 'to cover', just as I translated it here. However, I believe that covering here is not just a general term, but – and that is the third possibility – it has some quite sophisticated lunar connotations, which can again be understood in connection with the lunar day names.

The verb *ḥbs*, as expounded earlier, occurs in one name variant for the sixteenth day of the lunar month, *ḥbs tp* 'covering the head', though of course, the attestations of this designation also date from the Graeco-Roman Period.[261] Already Ludwig Borchardt conjectured that covering here describes the appearance of the first narrow strip of darkness on the lunar disc after full moon.[262] More interestingly, the term *ḥbs* is found closely associated with *psḏn.tjw* in the mythological papyrus already mentioned, where we read: 'As for the covering of [...] in Heliopolis until the third day after the moon's

[257] Barguet 1986: 572.
[258] Parker 1950: 11–12; for a recent edition of one list from Dendera, see Cauville 2008: 32–34.
[259] Meeks 2006: 14 (pBrooklyn 47.218.84, IV, 5–6).
[260] Sethe 1922: 27; Faulkner 1973: 133; Barguet 1986: 572; Carrier 2004: 377.
[261] Parker 1953: 50.
[262] Borchardt 1935: 23 and 40.

invisibility – Seth seizes the eye of Horus' (*jr ḥbs [...] m Jwn.w ḥr hrw 3 n psḏn.tjw Stẖ jṯj.n⸗f jr.t-Ḥr.w*).[263] Unfortunately, the object of the verb is lost in this manuscript, but a marginal note to the text does refer to *ḥbs tp*. Then the association of the expression with both the sixteenth and third day of the lunar month can only be explained if we assume that it designated the entire period when the moon first gradually became covered (waning) and then remained totally covered (invisible) during conjunction.[264] Similarly, in line 4 of *CT* 155 the phrase *ḥbs ẖ.t* may after all refer to a specific activity in the cult of the moon – a re-enactment of the process by which increasingly larger portions of the lunar disc turned dark along the second half of the month – and not just generally to keeping secrets or clothing ritual objects. If it really does, then it also must be surmised that the house of Osiris was a place where some events concerning the lunar cult were unfolded. It must be added that in the expression *ḥbs ẖ.t* the second element, *ẖ.t*, may also have some lunar connotations, as some Graeco-Roman texts used this word to denote the constituent parts of the lunar eye,[265] for which the most commonly employed expression was of course *dbḥ.w*. So it is surely not by coincidence that this latter word makes an appearance in the next line (see below).

That the statements about the respect for the observed one and the act of clothing or covering should be understood in a lunar context is strongly suggested by line 5 which in my opinion contains further unmistakable references to lunar phenomena in general, and to the names of lunar days in particular. The key word here is *sjꜣ*, written  on Sen's coffin. Since this word is missing from the Asyut texts, i.e. there it has been corrupted into a form that has little resemblance to its original, most of the existing translations fail to grasp its significance. Only Servajean takes it into consideration,[266] and he renders it as *sjꜣ.t* 'cloth'.[267] Dirk van der Plas and Joris F. Borghouts are apparently of the same opinion, as in their word index to the Coffin Texts they list the reference to *CT* II, 294c under the same word.[268] However, it is very unlikely that the sign  should be read *sjꜣ.t*, though Servajean's justifiable conjecture that this particular type of cloth was later associated with the waxing moon should be kept in mind.[269] The word *sjꜣ.t* is always written with the clothes determinative  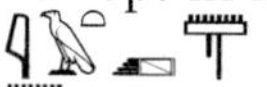 in the Coffin Texts, and only once is it not spelled out phonetically  .[270] On its own once stands for the verb 'to know, to perceive',[271] and once in a very fragmentary text perhaps for *Sjꜣ*, the divine personification of the concept

[263] Meeks 2006: 14 (pBrooklyn 47.218.84, IV, 2–3).
[264] Meeks 2006: 79.
[265] Aufrère 1991: 199.
[266] Servajean 2003: 446.
[267] cf. *Wb.* IV, 29.3–7.
[268] Plas and Borghouts 1998: 244.
[269] Servajean 2003: 453–456.
[270] *CT* V, 373a.
[271] *CT* II, 116s.

'knowledge, perception',[272] though there too an ensuing stroke very probably belongs to it.[273] Neither word would be satisfactory here.

However, a clue to understand the sign is provided by the closing lines of spell 156 of the Coffin Texts, the next chapter of the Book of the Moon, where appears with the determinative . It must be noted immediately that in the Coffin Texts this sign is often not the animal hide but the variant of the hieroglyph representing the night , i.e. the misreading of the pertinent hieratic sign.[274] That this is surely the case here is shown by the fact that on two Deir el-Bersha coffins (B2P and B17C) the word is indeed written with  (another variant of ), while in most other inscriptions the mediating form  is used (the same as is found in *CT* II, 302b on Sen's coffin).[275] I must emphasise that I take the combination 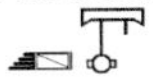 as one word with the latter sign as determinative, and think that the rendering of the clause in *CT* II, 324c as *sštꜣ sjꜣ grḥ pw* 'it is the secret of the knowledge of the night' with a double direct genitive is unnecessarily protracted.[276] The word replacing *sjꜣ* in the Asyut versions of *CT* 155,  *ꜣꜥw* 'leather document case', having  as a determinative, also suggests it indirectly that in *CT* II, 294c once had the same determinative, too. Therefore the unity of the sign *sjꜣ* with the night hieroglyph as a determinative in *CT* II, 324c can hardly be doubted – all the more so, because the word *sjꜣ* can perfectly be made sense of in a lunar setting.

In the Graeco-Roman lists of lunar days the fourteenth and the seventeenth days of the month are equally called *sjꜣ.w*, spelled either  or .[277] I believe therefore that in spells 155 and 156 of the Coffin Texts the same expression occurs, and I translate it 'full moon period' in accordance with the astute observation of Richard A. Parker that the fourteenth and the seventeenth days of the lunar month bear the same name because, due to the complexities of lunar observation, the full moon appears within this time window.[278] In other words, if the first day of the lunar month is established by, say, the invisibility of the last crescent in the morning (at dawn), it is not a foregone conclusion that full moon will occur on day fifteen – it may be observed on either the fourteenth, fifteenth, sixteenth, or seventeenth day, but never before day fourteen or after day seventeen. Parker's original conjecture is also backed up indirectly by Plutarch who says that 'the Egyptians relate that the death of Osiris occurred on the seventeenth (of the month), when the full moon is most obviously waning'.[279]

It must be added that – at least for the Graeco-Roman lunar day lists – technically speaking a more appropriate translation of *sjꜣ* would be 'the window of time in

[272] *CT* IV, 286d.
[273] *contra* Molen 2000: 449.
[274] Faulkner 1981: 173.
[275] See Faulkner 1981: 173.
[276] For this rendering, see Carrier 2004: 383.
[277] *Wb.* IV, 31.12; Cauville 2008: 33.
[278] Parker 1950: 13.
[279] Plutarch *De Iside et Osiride* 42, see Griffiths 1970: 185.

which full moon may be observable'. It is not altogether impossible, however, that the fourteenth and seventeenth days of the lunar month gained their names from an antecedent expression meaning just 'full moon', and I think *sjꜣ* is used in that sense here. I see of course no contradiction between the mention of the full moon and the primary focus of the spell, the moon's invisibility, as these two events are inherently interrelated. From the later sources we also have the impression that the Egyptians generally had a predilection for the waxing phase of the moon and its apotheosis, the full moon, as for example the scenes showing the fourteen stairs leading up to the full lunar disc indicate.[280] The reasons for this are not difficult to see: it is this part of the lunar cycle that exhibits the powers of regeneration most forcefully. On the other hand, it is equally clear that the whole lunar cycle, including the waning period, is often represented in the Graeco-Roman temples.[281]

Another key word that needs some explanation here is *dbḥ.w*. One of the lexical items it can be associated with is the verb *dbḥ* 'to ask for, to require, to need something', and its derivative *dbḥ.w* 'cult objects, paraphernalia'.[282] Thus in *CT* 155 it may be understood in a general sense, describing the totality – or any – of the things that are needed during the performance of a ritual. Since in the Asyut texts the word is followed by a clothes determinative, the interpretation of most previous translators has been to render it as 'ritual robe'.[283] However, the word's orthography on Sen's coffin, 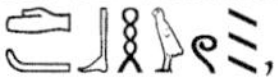, is quite different and I think that van der Plas and Borghouts are justified in connecting it with the expression that occurs in *CT* V, 190g and VII, 17q.[284] They translate it as 'halyard', that is a rope for raising and taking down the sail of a ship. Rami van der Molen is more cautious in his hieroglyphic dictionary of the Coffin Texts and does not venture to offer a translation.[285] Neither does he cite *CT* II, 294c as a source for the word, but that may be due to an oversight of the Deir el-Bersha text variants. While van der Molen's reluctance to translate the word indicates that the two remaining attestations are equally opaque, they may nevertheless shed some additional light on the meaning of *dbḥ.w*.

That both in *CT* V, 190g and VII, 17q *dbḥ.w* refers to some nautical equipment is quite apparent, as spell 404 lists the parts of the boat that ferries the deceased over to the island of the Field of Reeds, and the particular section in spell 818 is also about this journey on water in the underworld. In both spells *dbḥ.w* collocates with *sgrg.w*,[286] but the meaning of this word is equally elusive ('yards? of ship'),[287] so this connection does not add significantly to our understanding of *dbḥ.w*. Interestingly enough, in spell 404 – which catalogues the secret names of the underworld ferry – we read that 'the

[280] Herbin 1982: 239–243.
[281] Priskin 2016c.
[282] *Wb.* V, 439.6–440.1 and V, 440.3–14.
[283] cf. especially Faulkner 1973: 134 n. 4.
[284] Plas and Borghouts 1998: 319.
[285] Molen 2000: 790.
[286] cf. *CT* V, 190c and VII, 17q itself.
[287] Molen 2000: 568.

name of its (i.e. the boat's) *dbḥ.w*: they are the staffs of Ra which are in Hermopolis' (*rn n dbḥ.w=s mꜣw.wt pw n.t Rꜥ jm.jt Wnw*),[288] so here for some reason *dbḥ.w* is associated with the lunar cult centre, Hermopolis. Though van der Plas and Borghouts make a separate entry for it,[289] I think the same word occurs in *CT* V, 169e, with a slightly different spelling : 'the Great One's stern-post and tiller when he is with the *dbḥ.w*' (*jm.j-tp wr ḫr.j-ꜥ wr jw=f ḥnꜥ dbḥ.w*; S1C). From the use of the preposition *ḥnꜥ*, Faulkner believes that people are meant here (and he of course makes a derivation from 'ask for').[290] But whatever the precise meaning of *dbḥ.w* when used in a nautical setting, this word clearly does not fit the context of *CT* 155, so I think there, despite the orthographic similarities, a different expression is used.

Some spellings of the word on the Deir el-Bersha coffins (B1L and B4Bo) – ,  – are, if anything, more suggestive of a connection with another lexical entry, that of *dbḥ* 'a measure, measuring vessel'.[291] Indeed, I think this is the word used here, but in a more restricted sense that is usually thought to be first attested from the Graeco-Roman Period. When talking about the eye of Horus or the *wedjat*-eye late texts often make references to the *dbḥ.w*, that is the constituent parts of the eye that are needed to make it whole (for an example see the excerpt from Esna below). As the foregoing definition implies, this expression is commonly seen as a specialised use of the general word *dbḥ.w* 'requirements'.[292] However, such late writings as , 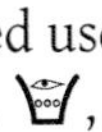,  etc.[293] suggest that the components of the eye were also conceived as being contained in a vessel.

It would of course be all too easy to dismiss the significance of this pictorial representation and say that it arose from a late pun between the words *dbḥ.w* 'requirements' and *dbḥ* 'measuring vessel' were it not for the evidence supplied by the Rhind Mathematical Papyrus. According to its colophon, this papyrus is a copy of an older document that was recorded under Amenemhat III,[294] and it is generally accepted that the contents of the papyrus reflect Middle Kingdom knowledge.[295] Problem 80 has a direct bearing on *CT* 155, as it specifies the *dbḥ* in terms of two measures for grain, the *hekat* and the *hin*. The term in the introduction to the problem is usually understood as referring to a measuring vessel,[296] but as the problem itself is no more than the listing of six fractional values, it may equally be rendered 'series of fractions'. Thus the beginning of problem 80 should be read: 'As for the set of fractions

[288] *CT* V, 190g–h (B5C).
[289] Plas and Borghouts 1998: 319.
[290] Faulkner 1977: 44 n. 11.
[291] *Wb.* V, 441.10–13; Pommerening 2005: 62–65.
[292] *Wb.* V, 440.12.
[293] Daumas 1988: 775–777.
[294] Peet 1923: 3.
[295] Robins and Shute 1987: 58.
[296] Peet 1923: 122–123; Pommerening 2005: 64.

one measures with for the governors of the storehouse.' (*jr dbḥ ḫ3y.w jm=f n jr.jw-ʿ.t n šnʿ*).[297]

The fractional values then recorded in the rest of the problem correspond to the dimidiated series (1/2, 1/4, 1/8, 1/16, 1/32, 1/64) known as the Horus-eye fractions in Egyptology. Thus Peet transcribes the subdivisions of the *hekat* with the hieroglyphs for the relevant parts of the eye. It must be noted, however, that the identity of the hieratic signs with these hieroglyphs has been questioned lately.[298] Going here into the details of this debate would cause us to stray too far from the subject in question, but I must point out that in my opinion *CT* 155 provides indirect evidence in favour of maintaining the Horus-eye notation, for the consistent presence of the grain determinative in the expressions *j3ṯ.t, mḥ.t* and *ḫqs.t* that occur in further lines of the text (*CT* II, 296a, 298a, and 300b) in relation to the eye of Tebi clearly creates a link between a celestial eye and the *dbḥ*. We have seen that in a roughly contemporaneous document, the Rhind Mathematical Papyrus, this term can be understood either as a measuring vessel the contents of which are to be divided by the dimidiated fractions, or as these fractions themselves. That the word in *CT* 155 should have the same sense is strongly suggested by the reference to counting the parts of the eye in line 6.

Considering all this, it is not impossible that the *dbḥ.w* was an actual cult object in Hermopolis, originally 'a vessel containing the fractional elements of the eye'. After all, *CT* 155 unambiguously describes it as something that can be stored in a room (for this see also the comments to line 23 below). The fractional elements may have been represented by different amounts of grain equal to a half, a quarter etc. of the vessel. The completion of the eye – representing the time elapsing during the month (note the night determinative in *dbḥ.w* on B4Bo!) – was ritually enacted by filling the vessel with these amounts. The question persists whether this cultic device was created by conforming to an already existing capacity measuring system, or conversely, whether it had served as a model for grain measuring using dimidiated fractional amounts. Later on *dbḥ.w* became to mean the 'fractional elements of the eye as conceived to be contained in a vessel', and hence more generally 'components of the eye'. While this scenario seems quite likely to me, I must add that the precise etymological or semantic relationship between the similarly written 'vessel', 'requirements', 'components of the eye', and even perhaps 'piece of nautical equipment', still remains open for conjecture. On the last point it should be noted that the spelling of *dbḥ.w* in *CT* 155 as if it was a rope for shipping may have been deliberately used as a device to distract from, or to mask, the real sense of the word.

So, despite the difficulties posed by some obscure expressions, the gist of lines 4 and 5 has now become clear. The lunar setting is obvious and the speaker emphasises his constant allegiance to the moon. In so doing, he equates himself with a god who, given

[297] See Peet 1923: pl. W.
[298] Ritter 2002.

the nature of the clues, can be no one else but Thoth. A later hint dropped in line 9 will make it absolutely certain that the speaker assumes the identity of this divinity. He is proud to assert his ability to keep track of all the phases of the lunar cycle, and especially that of waxing, which he invokes through refined allusions. Line 5 ends with an emphasis on the responsibilities concerning the components of the lunar eye, because now the speaker goes on to hint at the more precise nature of his outstanding knowledge about them.

Lines 6–8

jw=j rḫ.kw jȝṯ.t m jr.t Tby jp r.w=s
wȝš ʿnḏw r wšȝ.w wḫ.w
r 5-nw n gs twt n jp r.w=s m jmj.t mḥ.t r ẖqs.t

I know what is missing from the eye of Tebi when its parts are counted,
and when dawn is stronger than the glow of the darkened night.
The fifth part of an entire half for counting its parts between what is in the filling eye and the ailing eye.

I have already highlighted the peculiar spelling of *jȝṯ.t* with the grain determinative, and the significance of this detail. This word is usually written with the determinative of mutilation, compare 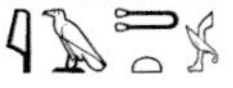 in the Asyut texts, but three other Deir el-Bersha coffins (B2P, B1L, and B1C) follow suit and repeat Sen's orthography. The grain determinative is surely a deliberate feature of the spelling of the word, and not something that resulted from the confusion of hieratic signs, because – as also pointed out earlier – it likewise appears in the semantically kindred words *mḥ.t* and *ẖqs.t*.

The eye of Tebi has in the past usually been associated with the sun,[299] but the overall context here makes it unambiguously clear that it designates the lunar eye, and more specifically the injured eye that must be restored.[300] The next phrase saying its parts are being counted also indicates that here the lunar eye is meant. The texts of the Graeco-Roman Period that touch upon the theme of counting the parts of the eye in the vast majority of the cases associate this activity with the moon.[301] Thus for example a passage in Esna describes Thoth in his well-known lunar avatar of a bull: 'It is the fiery bull that counts the components of the eye with his correctness. It is the mighty bull that shines with precision on the fifteenth day of the month' (*kȝ psj pw jp dbḥ wḏȝ.t m ʿqȝ=f kȝ nḫt pw psḏ.tj r mtr m smd.t*).[302] Alexandra von Lieven thinks that these lines bring up the image of the full moon,[303] but a text in Dendera proves that the picture is a bit more complex than that. There, in a hymn to Osiris written in one

[299] Sethe 1922: 30; *Wb.* V, 261.9; Piankoff 1954: 38; Hornung 1963: 45.
[300] Meeks 1998: 1188.
[301] For the rare instances where the act of completion concerns the solar eye, see Aufrère 1991: 201 n. 1.
[302] Lieven 2000: 84.
[303] Lieven 2000: 86.

of his chapels on the roof of the temple, we read: 'you are the fiery bull that hides at the time of the moon's invisibility and emerges at the beginning of the month' (*ntk kꜣ psj kꜣp m psḏn.tjw bsj m bjꜣ tp ꜣbd*).[304] It follows from this that the fiery bull is rather the waxing phase of the moon, not just full moon,[305] so the counting of components is not a momentary occasion but may encompass a period of time. In this period, as *CT* 155 suggests, even the time of the moon's invisibility can be included in some way.

I propose to make an emendation to the end of line 7, where I believe instead of  we should have , and thus a direct genitival construction reading *wšꜣ.w wḫ.w* 'the glow of the darkened night'. Again, this corruption of the text may have come about by the misreading of the hieratic signs for and .[306] I take *wḫ.w* to be a passive participle of the verb *wḫ* 'to be dark at night',[307] and thus a nuance of meaning is added to the basic word 'night',[308] although it is also possible that the ending only reflects the quasi-plural ending of the preceding word. In the latter case *wḫ.w* is used adjectivally, but the meaning of the phrase remains essentially unchanged. As for *wšꜣ.w*, it is usually written with the night determinative,[309] but its replacement here with  is perhaps meant to put an emphasis on the dim light of the night, the source of which is of course the stars and the moon itself.

The whole line then I think describes the events on the morning sky as they develop around the end of the lunar month. For in the second half of the month the ever diminishing lunar crescent is seen rising on the eastern horizon closer and closer to the time of dawn, until one morning it completely disappears from the celestial dome. That is the moment when dawn defeats the dwindling light of the lunar crescent. Astronomically speaking this is of course the period of conjunction, when the moon is between the sun and the earth, and it thus becomes invisible. While the interpretation of line 7 as pointing to the morning of last crescent invisibility is in full accord with the title of *CT* 155, all possible arguments need to be gathered in favour of it, because we have seen that just a couple of lines before reference was made to the full moon. However, the well-discernible parallel between lines 7 and 12–13 (see comments to lines 14–16) does establish it beyond doubt that the event described here is the moon's invisibility.

It is then, at new moon, that the parts of the lunar eye are reckoned and the absence of the missing element is acknowledged. I think that – instead of alluding to the two-dimensional spectacle by which the shiny surface of the moon gradually becomes invisible (this topic will be dealt with in the following section of the spell) – the next line describes the calculation of the eye in its temporal aspect. To disclose this layer

[304] Cauville 1997: 283.
[305] See also Chassinat 1966: 281 n. 2.
[306] See Möller 1909: 8 no. 91, and 55 no. 574.
[307] *Wb* I, 352.3.
[308] *Wb.* I, 352.8.
[309] cf. *Wb.* I, 370.2–4.

of meaning, however, a couple of textual peculiarities must first be clarified. To begin with, the very first group of signs  poses a problem as on its own it obviously lends itself to at least three interpretations. First it may be seen as the combination of a cardinal number with the word 'part, item', thus standing for 'five parts' (though this use, because of the possible confusion with fractions, was rare; for an example see the writing *t-jm.j-tꜣ r 4* 'four pieces of *t-jm.j-tꜣ* bread' in the Old Kingdom mastaba of Neferhotep).[310] Alternatively  may be understood as the representation of a fraction reading 'one-fifth', as writing numerals under the mouth sign was the ordinary way to record fractions in hieroglyphic. In all probability, the numeral in a fraction had a sense of ordinality by default, because for example  was comprehended as 'the fifth part (which concludes a row of equal parts)'.[311] As a consequence of this inherent ambiguity, there is the third possibility, that  may also have an ordinal sense, such as in a list, corresponding to the expression 'the fifth part or item'.

As the first option is quite unlikely, it seems expedient only to consider the interpretations according to which the group  is either a fraction or a phrase containing an ordinal number. If it is understood as 'one-fifth', first it must be stressed that some dates recorded in the Graeco-Roman temples provide unequivocal proof for the use of fractions with a temporal sense. Thus in a date the hieroglyphs 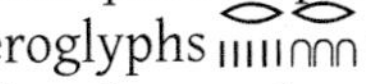 stand for day 7 of the month, because these fractions must be referred to the number 30, so that $(1/5+1/30)\times30=7$.[312] Therefore I think the same procedure applies to line 8 of *CT* 155, but – contrary to the Graeco-Roman texts, where the reference number is always assumed but never given explicitly – here the reference number is also recorded by the expression *gs twt* 'entire half'. This I of course take to mean the half of an entire month (a 30-day month, see below), that is fifteen days. In support of the view that 'half' can surely mean the half of the month, I can cite here the divine epithet 'Pleasing is his look as that of the moon at the half of the month' (*nḏm-ptr⸗f-mj-jꜥḥ-gs-ꜣbd*).[313] So the text speaks about the *r-5-nw n gs twt* '1/5 of 15 days'. That a phrase in which a fraction is linked to an integer by the preposition *n* should be understood this way is proved by an innovative writing of the 70-day period of embalming on some ostraca from Deir el-Medina: '1/20 of 1400 (days) with (lit. on the hands of) Anubis' (*r-20 n 1400 ḥr ꜥ.wj Jnpw*).[314]

It does not take a mathematician to work out that the period thus signalled is three days. This is a meaningful figure in terms of the moon's invisibility, as it denotes the maximum length of time elapsing from last crescent invisibility to first crescent visibility. Just as full moon may occur over a range of time encompassing the fourteenth and seventeenth days of the lunar month, in a complementary fashion, the lunar disc may be hidden for almost three days and in the minority of cases may become visible

[310] Hassan 1948: pl. lii.
[311] Gardiner 1957: 196.
[312] Chassinat 1932: 5; for a list of dates similarly written, see Priskin 2002: 78.
[313] Leitz 2002b: 167.
[314] Fischer-Elfert 1983: 44.

only on the evening of the third day of the month.[315] So line 8 reveals that the speaker is aware of this somewhat unruly behaviour of the moon but nevertheless is skilled enough in the observation of crescents to follow the lunar changes accurately. For another ancient Egyptian account of the three days of lunar invisibility at conjunction, see the excerpts from pBrooklyn 47.218.84 above.

In the light of the fact that here the speaker is alluding to the period of time when the moon is invisible, the precise meanings of the terms *mḥ.t and ẖqs.t* can be clarified. In modern renderings these are usually taken to mean 'the full eye' and 'the injured eye', respectively,[316] but these expressions convey the idea of a state, rather than that of a process. On top of that, in the imagination of a modern reader 'the full eye' inevitably evokes the expression 'full moon'. However, since line 8 defines the invisibility of the moon as something that separates *mḥ.t* from *ẖqs.t*, the earlier definitely does not mean full moon and can only be conceived as the entire period when the lunar disc fills up, from first crescent to full circle of brightness, i.e. the waxing moon. This is of course pretty evident from Graeco-Roman sources as well, because they indicate that the filling of the eye happened towards the middle of the month.[317] In contrast, *ẖqs.t* corresponds to the time when the lunar disc is, so to speak, being constantly injured, that is the waning phase – in line 8 its use is appropriate because it also includes the last crescent, the phase immediately preceding the moon's invisibility. Grammatically speaking, *mḥ.t* and *ẖqs.t* in this sense are more likely to be feminine active imperfective participles, and to bring out this aspect of theirs I translate them as 'filling eye' and 'ailing eye'. While from the perspective of the new moon, chronologically the waning phase precedes the waxing one, in *CT* 155 'the filling eye' comes first, possibly for reasons of decorum again. It must also be noted that, because of their grain determinative, in Sen's inscription *mḥ.t* and *ẖqs.t* are strictly speaking not 'eyes', but I keep referring to them as such because they are surely connected with the celestial eye of the moon.

It is also possible that the allusion to the injury of the lunar eye in line 8 is much more complex, but here we are entering the ground of speculation far more than in any other part of my study. Some parallel texts in *CT* II, 296c (see B1L, S2P, and S3P), by affixing the ordinal ending *-nw* to the numeral five (), suggest that the expression may as well be read 'the fifth part, fifth item'.[318] In this way a list is evoked which, in my opinion, can be nothing other than the series of fractions alluded to by *dbḥ.w* a few lines earlier. Then the group  on Sen's coffin would still stand for a fraction, but in a form of deliberate cryptic writing it is not 1/5, but the fifth fractional component of the eye, that is, 1/32. This must without doubt be the fifth part of the eye, because the

[315] Parker 1950: 13.
[316] *Wb.* II, 119.4 and III, 401.1.
[317] Smith 2002: 121; Koemoth 1996: 203.
[318] See the modern translations of Sethe 1922: 27; Faulkner 1973: 133.

mathematical papyri testify to the principle that the Egyptians always arranged series of fractions in a descending order.[319]

Now, calculating with 1/32 instead of 1/5 we get 0.46875 days (1/32×15=1/3 1/8 1/96), and this figure may also be seen as having some relevance for the new moon. To understand this I must refer back to an earlier article of mine in which, prompted by the cryptographic writings of dates in Graeco-Roman inscriptions, I worked out that the superimposition of the series of Horus-eye fractions on the period of 30 days resulted in a figure – 29.53125 ((1/2+1/4+1/8+1/16+1/32+1/64)×30=29 1/2 1/32) – that is in fact a very good approximation of the length of the mean synodic month (29.53059 days).[320] It falls short of 30 days by 1/64, that is 1/64×30=0.46875 days, and this of course – because of a simple mathematical identity – equals 1/32×15 days, the computation suggested by one reading of line 8.

In this way *CT* 155 may hint at the knowledge of a concept comparable to the modern term 'mean synodic month', describing the average amount of time that separates two identical phases of the moon in reality. As I pointed out elsewhere, the Egyptians could easily have arrived at such a notion at any time in their history by noticing that twenty-five of their civil years comprised exactly 309 lunar months.[321] The first unequivocal proof for the recognition of this relation, a scheme listing the beginnings of lunar months, either twenty-nine or thirty days long, in terms of the civil calendar over a 25-year period, pCarlsberg 9,[322] dates from the 2nd century CE but the discovery may have been effected much earlier.

The irregularity of lunations, as just indicated in the previous paragraph, shows up in the structure of lunar calendars as the alternation of 30-day 'full' months and 29-day 'hollow' months, so in this framework *mḥ.t* and *ẖqs.t* would stand for these periods, respectively. Since in writing the feminine active perfective participles looked the same as their imperfective counterparts, now the static, finished nature of the expressions would be acted upon. The term 'full month' would have been particularly apt in ancient Egypt, as it in fact filled out the 30-day month that was idealised in the civil calendar. Some support for this interpretation may be offered by the use of the phrase *gs twt* 'entire half', which presupposes that there was also a half that was not whole, corresponding to the hollow month of twenty-nine days. All in all, if it is accepted that  stands for 1/32, then the description of conjunction is more abstract and it alludes to the realisation that the lunations are always 'injured' insofar as they never comply with exactly thirty days in reality.

While from the two interpretations presented above, the one pointing to three days is certainly more mundane and harmonises well with the rest of the spell, I would not

[319] Peet 1922: 16.
[320] Priskin 2002: 78.
[321] Priskin 2002: 78–79.
[322] Neugebauer and Parker 1969: 220–225 and pl. 65.

categorically rule out the second one, even if it could be met with serious objections. For one thing it is purely hypothetical that *mḥ.t* and *ẖqs.t* denoted the full and hollow lunar months. On the other hand, the Horus-eye fractions did exist in ancient Egypt, they were indeed closely associated with the moon, so they may have been put to use in a numbers game about conjunction. Therefore I intend to preserve the possible ambiguity of the original text by the rendering 'the fifth part', because with some contrivance it may be fitted into both reasonings. Whichever way we look at the issue, one thing is for certain: these lines of spell 155, though cloaked in cryptic vocabulary and writings, do propagate the astronomical skills of the speaker. They can in fact be juxtaposed with the autobiographical inscriptions of a Deir el-Bersha official from the beginning of the Middle Kingdom, Djehutinakht (not identical with the owner of B2Bo). In his tomb he asserts: 'I know the hours of the night in all its seasons' (*jw=j rḫ.kw wnw.wt n.t grḥ m jtr.w=f nb*).[323] The precise understanding of the rest of the inscription is again hampered by the use of obscure terminology. The publisher of the text, Harco Willems thinks that it concerns the determination of the decans on the first days of the three Egyptian seasons.[324] The exact details in this case may also remain undiscovered, but Djehutinakht's tomb inscription stands witness to the willingness of the local elite at Deir el-Bersha to publicise their specialised skills in astronomy. It is this intellectual climate in which lines 6–8 of *CT* 155 were also born.

Lines 9–10

wn n=j bꜣ.w psḏn.tjw jnk mḥ=j s(j)
wr rḫ.t.n=j r wtj m ẖnt r-pr pn

Open to me, the *bas* of the moon's invisibility, for I am the one who completes the eye, for what I know is more than the embalmer of the temple knows.

The appearance of the construction *jnk sḏm=f* in line 9 is just another grammatical feature that shows the closely related nature of *CT* 155 with the autobiographies of Middle Kingdom officials, as this kind of nominal sentence is most characteristic of such texts.[325] The imperative at the beginning of the line, just as in lines 4, 17, and 20, indicates that a new section of the spell is started. The exaggeration that the speaker's knowledge exceeds that of the embalming priest's and the appearance of Anubis in line 13 suggest that the setting in which the statements of the following section of the text should be interpreted is the embalming of the corpse and the rituals associated with it. Unfortunately, from the time when the Coffin Texts were written no documents detailing the ritual procedures of embalming have come down to us. A potential hint in the Coffin Texts of the ties between mummification and lunar phases will be mentioned in the next section, but if we want to seek out further possible clues

[323] Willems 2006: 437.
[324] Willems 2006: 440–442.
[325] Allen 2001b: 273.

as to the role of the moon in the embalming rituals, we must rely on much later papyri that are more voluble in describing mummification. The chief sources are pBoulaq III and pLouvre 5125, both dating from the 1st centuries CE.[326]

The two types of texts recorded on these papyri, technical instructions for different, ritually charged embalming procedures and recitations to be spoken along these actions, cannot be said to be particularly revealing about an emphatic role of the moon during mummification. This is of course not to deny that some lunar references are made. For example on a piece of cloth destined for the right hand it should be inscribed that this hand has seized the moon (*ꜣmm.n=k jꜥḥ*).[327] The involvement of the moon in this rite can be much loftier than it seems at first sight, as the cloth in question is the one called *sjꜣ.t*, and it resonates well with 'full moon'.[328] In one of the recitations the deceased's identity with the moon is also established: 'Your *ba* will look upon your corpse forever since you keep on renewing like the moon' (*mꜣꜣ bꜣ=k ḥr ẖꜣ.t=k ḏ.t jw=k wḥm rnpj mj jꜥḥ*).[329] This idea is of course well-known from late sources, and its first clear indications show up in New Kingdom material. The iconographic evidence will be discussed below, but the concept is also expressed verbally in the Book of Going Forth by Day, where for example in a spell about Hermopolis (*BD* 8) the dead person claims: 'I am the moon among the gods, I will never perish' (*jnk jꜥḥ jm.jw nṯr.w nn tm=j*).[330] Though the moon was a potent symbol of regeneration already in the Pyramid Texts and the Coffin Texts, the direct identification of the deceased with the moon seems to have come about during the New Kingdom (see Introduction).

So, apart from equating the dead with the moon and some sporadic references, the late mummification manuals do not establish a strong connection with lunar phenomena. By this I mean there are no indications that for example certain rites or procedures were performed in observation of particular phases of the moon. Either the relevant body of knowledge was lost or such information has never existed. Why then would the speaker of *CT* 155 compare himself to the embalmer priest? As it will turn out, the answer to this question has more to do with the eye, and the epithet of Thoth that he has earned as the healer of the eye of Horus, for now from the statement 'I am the one who completes the eye' it becomes absolutely unambiguous that the speaker assumes the identity – and responsibilities – of Thoth. In spell 17 of the Book of Going Forth by Day it is stated about the deceased that 'he filled the *wedjat*-eye after its illness on the day when the two companions fought ... and it is Thoth himself who did this with his fingers' (*jw mḥ.n=j N wḏꜣ.t m-ḫt hꜣb=s hrw pwj n ꜥḥꜣ rḥ.wj ... jn gr.t Ḏḥw.tj jrj nn m ḏbꜥ.w=f ḏs=f*).[331] Accordingly, in Ptolemaic temple inscriptions Thoth has the epithet 'the

[326] See Sauneron 1952.
[327] Sauneron 1952: 30.
[328] Servajean 2003: 446–457; though he fails to make the connection with the lunar day names.
[329] Sauneron 1952: 11.
[330] Budge 1913: pl. 18.
[331] Budge 1913: pl. 8; for the Coffin Texts antecedent (spell 335), see *CT* IV, 237a–239a (T3Be).

one who fills the eye with its components' (*mḥ.w wḏꜣ.t m dbḥ.w=s*).[332] However, as the manipulator of the eye, Thoth was also a doctor and a medical papyrus dated to the 18th dynasty calls him 'the physician of the eye of Horus' (*swn.w pwj n jr.t Ḥr.w*).[333] This role of Thoth makes a comparison with the embalming priest more than appropriate.

Lines 11–13

jw=j rḫ.kw jꜣṯ.t ḫnt ḥt.t m ʿJnpw
hrw pw n swḏwḏ wr-m-ʿn.wt=f
grḥ pw n kꜣpꜣp jmj.w r=f

I know what is missing from the eye canal in the hand of Anubis
on this day of covering his great fingernails,
on this night of hiding his teeth.

Anubis is here of course mentioned in his pre-eminent role as the god supervising the embalming process, but the reference at the same time may be more concrete and point to the priest who – wearing a jackal mask – impersonated him during the embalming rituals.[334] That these rituals in the time of the Middle Kingdom were somehow tied to lunar phenomena is well illustrated by a passage in Coffin Texts spell 45 which informs us that 'Anubis turns your (i.e. the deceased's) stench pleasant before your seat in the embalming booth, he gives you incense at all seasons, from which nothing is deducted on the day of the new moon' (*snḏm Jnpw stj=k ḫnt s.t=k m sḥ-nṯr rdj=f n=k snṯr r tr nb n ḫbj jm n psdn.tjw*).[335] Obviously here it is implicated that the day of the moon's invisibility had a distinguished place in the time-frame determining the anointing of the dead body. The connection of Anubis the embalmer with the moon becomes more pronounced in some later scenes in the temple of Hatshepsut at Deir el-Bahari, the mammisi of Nectanebo I, and the Graeco-Roman birth houses. These depictions show Anubis bending over the lunar disc essentially in the same posture as he is usually represented attending the corpse of Osiris on his mummification bier.[336] Thus it seems that the mummified body in its entirety could be seen as the representation of the lunar disc, the point of course being to imbue the physical remains of a person with the inherent qualities of rebirth associated with the moon. This identification serves as a background for the detailed references of *CT* 155 to the acts of mummification.

The word 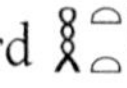 *ḥt.t* makes it clear that the speaker is still rephrasing his knowledge of the missing parts of the celestial eye of the moon. While both Faulkner and van der Molen believe that elsewhere in the Coffin Texts (cf. *CT* VII, 83d and 453c) *ḥt.t* is

[332] Chassinat 1935: 26.
[333] Reisner 1905: 6 (pHearst XIV, 6).
[334] DuQuesne 2001: 14–16; Seeber 1980: 1197.
[335] *CT* I, 195g–196c.
[336] Ritner 1985: 152.

a variant of *ḥty.t* 'throat',[337] I think that in *CT* 155 it is a different word, or perhaps the same word used in a different sense, that can be related to an expression occurring in spell 301 of the Pyramid Texts where it undoubtedly has ophthalmological – and eventually lunar – connotations: 'Behold, the king has brought to you (i.e. Horus) your great left eye ... Accept it from the hand of the king whole, its fluid whole, its blood whole, its canals whole' (*mk jnj.n n⸗k N jr.t⸗k wr.t jꜣb.t ... šsp n⸗k sj m ꜥ N wḏꜣ.t mw⸗s jm⸗s wḏꜣ.t ṯr.w jm⸗s wḏꜣ.t ḥt.w jm⸗s wḏꜣ.t*).[338] Acting on an earlier remark of Sethe, Faulkner surmises that here *ḥt.w*, written as , is also connected with 'throat' and describes some ducts or vessels ('throats') of the eye.[339] I concur with his view, adding that perhaps the most obvious candidate would be the tube in the eye that connects the optical nerve disc with the lens (hyaloid canal).

When seen in cross section,[340] this canal bisects the eyeball into two halves, and the analysis of the rest of the sentence will unravel why the speaker intends to draw attention to the concept of duality and the existence of complementing semicircles in connection with the eye, that is the lunar disc. Of course the hyaloid canal is a minute detail in the structure of the eye, and would only be readily recognisable to a keen observer of this organ.[341] This fact puts further stress on the speaker's statement that he – in the disguise of Thoth – knew more than the embalming priest. If there were people in ancient Egypt who had immensely deep knowledge about human anatomy, they must have been those attending to the mummification of the deceased, as in fact their daily chores would have been comparable to the work of a modern forensic pathologist. The speaker's familiarity with the 'throat of the eye' (the eye canal, or canal of the eye) means that he must have seen an eye cut open, so he does have such experience in the treatment of dead bodies that can emulate or even outdo the expertise of professional embalmers. An officiant of Thoth, as the example of Sen shows, could bear the title 'Chief Physician' *wr swn.w*, and Anubis in his role as embalmer was also called *pꜣ wr swn.w* in later demotic texts,[342] so this again shows that the comparison made in *CT* 155 is not at all inappropriate.

Still alluding to the role of Thoth as an eye specialist, three coffins (B2Bo, B4Bo and B9C) replace *jꜣṯ.t ḫnt ḥt.t* with *ḥḏ(.t) ḫnt qn.t* in *CT* II, 300b, which should be translated 'the missing part of the eye fat'. In the medical papyri of the 20th dynasty *qn.t* describes the fat of the eye as the symptom of an eye disease, possibly pinguecula,[343] so this variation also underlines the connection of this part of the spell

337 Faulkner 1978: 44 and 164; Molen 2000: 361.
338 *Pyr.* §451.
339 Faulkner 1969: 91 n. 11.
340 cf. Gray 1918: 1006 fig. 869.
341 The hyaloid canal is in fact barely visible to the naked eye, so of course it cannot be ruled out that the text speaks of another feature of the visual organ. Furthermore, the hyaloid canal was discovered relatively late in Western science, but despite this the Egyptians could have been well aware of this feature of the eyeball, since its obscurity in Europe was – at least, partly – due to the canonical ban of the church on the study of human anatomy.
342 Ritner 2008: 56.
343 *Wb.* V, 41.3; Nunn 2002: 202.

with the description of the eye. Perhaps even a pun is intended between *ḥdj* 'missing, lacking' and 'white'.[344] The word *ḥḏ.tj* for the white of the eye is attested from the New Kingdom onwards,[345] and as the fat of the eye is basically a condition that leads to the swelling of the white or yellowish part of the eye, it is not difficult to provide an explanation for such a wordplay.

Lines 12 and 13, forming a split column in the hieroglyphic original, present great difficulties of interpretation. Followed by the clothes determinative, both *swḏwḏ* and *kꜣpꜣp* on their face value refer to putting or laying a piece of textile over something, thus covering or even bandaging something. The expression *kꜣpꜣp* may be linked with *kꜣp* 'to cover, roof over' or perhaps more closely to  *kꜣp.t* 'patch of linen to cover the opening of a pot', and it is a noteworthy detail that an etymologically related word  is used in the medical papyri to denote the drooping of the eyelid.[346] It is, however, even more likely that *kꜣpꜣp* was a sort of 'abracadabra' word,[347] specially coined for the purposes of *CT* 155 because of its resemblance to the general word *kꜣp* 'to hide, to take cover', which as we have seen could be used, at least in Graeco-Roman times, in a lunar context to describe the disappearance of the moon at conjunction.[348] The singular nature of *kꜣpꜣp* is accentuated by the lack of attestations for the word *swḏwḏ* – it remains an enigma, even in its Asyut variant, spelled with *d*'s (*swdwd*).[349] It also needs to be pointed out that *kꜣp* is the name of the ninth day of the lunar month,[350] but I must admit that it completely eludes me whether this fact has any relevance here, and if so, what it would be.

Neither is it entirely clear what are being covered. Since on Sen's coffin at the end of this section the phonetic elements and the determinative of the word 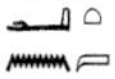 *ʿn.t* 'claw, fingernail' are distinctly visible, I take the whole group of hieroglyphs following *swḏwḏ* to be part of a composite construction starting with the adjective *wr* 'great' as for example in the epithet *wr-m-jꜣw.t≠f* 'great in his office'.[351] Thus by analogy here we have 'great in his fingernails', which for reasons of style I rephrased as 'his great fingernails' in my translation. After *kꜣpꜣp* we have  *jmj.w-r* 'what are in the mouth' and because of the determinative without doubt the teeth are meant here (I take the appearance of the viper after the mouth sign a scribal error, though for   the alternative reading *jmj.w-r≠f jbḥ.w≠f* 'what are in his mouth, his teeth' may also be considered). In support of these interpretations I must mention that teeth and fingernails are mentioned twice side by side in the Pyramid Texts,[352] though the contexts there do not seem to be related to our passage.

[344] *Wb.* III, 212.16 and *Wb.* III, 206.16 'von Fett'!
[345] *Wb.* III, 211.9.
[346] *Wb.* V, 104.11–13.
[347] cf. the modern translation of Carrier 2004: 379.
[348] Cauville 1997: 283; see also above.
[349] Molen 2000: 468.
[350] Parker 1950: 11.
[351] cf. Jones 2000: 380–381 no. 1411.
[352] *Pyr.* §791c and 1358d.

The expressions 'covering his fingernails' and 'hiding his teeth' may have referred to actual moments in the embalming process, but it is more likely that in spell 155 these activities are mentioned in order to bring out the pictorial contrast between two hieroglyphs used in the recording of these phrases, the signs 𓂩 and 𓌉. These representations can very easily be seen to form a contrastive pair, as the first sign has a downward pointing end, in opposition to the upwardly curved tip of the latter sign. The duality - and yet at the same time, the essential identity - of the two clauses in which they appear is made prominent in the original by the split column. Obviously, the moon does have a very characteristic dual nature of opposing qualities, that of course being the periods of waxing and waning. Therefore, despite all the obscurities of the wording of this passage (but remember that *kꜣp* later does refer to new moon), these hieroglyphic characters - and the sentences containing them - in all probability make a figurative allusion to the disappearance of the lunar disc at new moon.

To understand this, we only have to recall precisely how this event unfolds. Immediately before conjunction, the thin crescent of the waning moon - with a curvature bulging to the left - is seen on the eastern horizon in the morning hours, just before dawn breaks. After the period of invisibility lasting one to two and a half days, the new moon - here in the literal sense denoting the first showing of the thin crescent of the waxing moon, now curving in the rightward direction - appears in the evening sky above the western horizon. Now, if we equate 'fingernails' (the sign 𓂩) with the last phase of the waning crescent, and conversely, 'teeth' (the sign 𓌉) with the first phase of the waxing crescent, even the times assigned to the acts of 'covering' and 'hiding' them match the temporal aspect of the moon's invisibility, as the disappearance of the last crescent is a morning event (*hrw*), while the invisibility of the would-be first crescent is associated with the evening (*grḥ*), as it will in fact reveal itself after sunset. Thus lines 12 and 13 describe in figurative language the transitory nature of the moon's invisibility from the two viewpoints of the old moon and new moon, represented by the liminal qualities of the last crescent and first crescent, respectively. In short, these two clauses refer to the time when no part of the lunar disc is seen (conjunction).

Lines 14–16

jw m jw.tjt ḫnt Wsjr
ṯs.n.tw ḥꜣ.t=f n pḥ.wj=f
m mḏḥ.t n.t sꜣw

It is a void out of Osiris,
when one has joined his front with his back
as the hewn out part of the beam.

Here we also encounter some difficult vocabulary, especially in line 16. The meaning of *jw.tjt* 'void' (literally 'that which does not exist'), still describing the injury to the eye, that is the disappearance of the lunar disc, is corroborated by an assertion made in spell 80 of the Book of Going Forth by Day: 'I have saved the eye of Horus from its nothingness as the fifteenth day of the month has come' (*šdj.n=j jr.t ḥr.w m jw.tj=s jj.n smd.t*).[353] The joining of Osiris' front with his back may again refer to an actual stage in the mummification process, as the verb *ṯs* 'to tie, to join' is well-known from funerary texts to refer to the assemblage of body parts.[354] However, underneath the simple practical meaning of the words it is not difficult to see once again the poetic description of the transition from the waning phase of the moon to the waxing one. Then the body of Osiris here is clearly identical with the moon, and thus these lines express verbally the same idea that is later represented iconographically with the depictions of Anubis bending over the lunar disc-cum-Osiris. In fact, the later temple scenes could be seen to form a vignette to the text of *CT* 155. Consequently, the circle that Anubis tends in these illustrations is not just the lunar disc in general, or the full moon brought as a gift to the newborn child, but the representation of the invisible new moon.[355] To resolve the dichotomy of this statement, just compare a schematic figure showing the lunar phases in any modern astronomical textbook.

For the full appreciation of the poetic metaphor involving Osiris' body it would be advantageous to grasp the exact meaning of the next phrase in line 16, but at the moment the lack of evidence supporting a good definition for the word *mḏḥ.t* prevents us from doing so. It is surely a derivative of *mḏḥ* 'to hew wood', and though it may be taken to mean woodwork or wood that has been processed by hewing,[356] for reasons that will become clear shortly I think here it designates the part of a wooden beam or board that has been hewn out. The word *s3w* no doubt refers to a larger piece of wood, a beam,[357] and the whole expression 'the hewn out part of the beam' is quite reminiscent of the Osiris beds that in some burials accompanied the dead from the New Kingdom onwards. One type of these beds was prepared by hacking out a shape of Osiris from a piece of wood, itself forming an Osirian silhouette, thus creating a hollow space in the material.[358] This hollow space is more pronounced in the related group of objects known as Osiris bricks, though in these the figure of the god was sunk into pottery, not wood.[359] The god was brought to life symbolically by filling this depression with mud and seeds of barley that eventually sprouted. I therefore think line 16 may be interpreted as drawing a parallel between the impressions in Osiris beds and the moon. Just as Osiris is clearly there yet invisible in the hollow part of the beds, so the moon is hidden yet still continuing its existence during conjunction.

A very late source may also offer some guidance for the understanding of this passage. The 2nd century CE Greek author Plutarch relates that for the burials of Osiris the

[353] Lepsius 1842: pl. 30.
[354] *Wb.* V, 397.15.
[355] *contra* Ritner 1985: 151.
[356] *Wb.* II, 190.6 and 192.6–7.
[357] *Wb.* III, 419.14.
[358] See Tutankhamon's specimen; Carter 1933: 81 and pl. lxii.
[359] Tooley 1996.

Egyptians cut wood in order to fashion a crescent-shaped coffin 'because the moon, whenever it approaches the sun, becomes crescent-shaped and suffers eclipse'.[360] The link between the hewing of wood and the moon's invisibility cannot be more direct, and the burials of Osiris Plutarch mentions were surely connected with the interment of Osiris effigies made of – similarly to the contents of the earlier Osiris beds – a paste of mud and sprouting barley during the Khoiak festivals. A possible point of connection between these properly mummified figures and the description of Osiris in *CT* 155 is that the effigies were in fact made in two halves and they acquired their final shape when these separate parts were joined.[361]

In another passage Plutarch suggests that the light of the moon was seen in Egypt as beneficial for the sprouting of plants,[362] and the same idea is also propounded in some Egyptian records.[363] This again prompts the inference that the joining of Osiris' front with his back has multiple connotations. On one level it is a metaphorical expression of the transition from old moon to new crescent because of the references to front and back, while on another it captures the moment of inertness in the making of a corn Osiris: his shape has been formed in the wood (understanding the whole phrase *ṯs.n.tw ḥꜣ.t⸗f n pḥ.wj⸗f* to express the establishment of the intactness of the body), yet it is only an empty receptacle now, a silhouette as devoid of life as a seed without the vivifying light of the moon. When this light manifests itself, i.e. the waxing of the moon begins, so do the seeds spring to life and animate the figure of Osiris. The time of inertness is therefore synonymous with the moon's invisibility. The different layers of meaning are thus in unison and complement each other quite nicely.

At this point it is worth stopping for a moment to look back at lines 4–16 again. It must be noticed that a clear parallelism exists between the two sections of the text, lines 4–8 and lines 9–16. The first unit, making allusions to the counting of the components of the eye of Tebi, and the second one, cloaked in the language of mummification, both describe the events unfolding around the time of the new moon. While lines 4–8 refer to the temporal aspect of this natural phenomenon, lines 9–16 portray how one visually observes the arrival of the new moon. Within the two main sections, even the semantically analogous clauses can be distinguished:

1. Pride in knowledge

Open to me because I am one who respects the observed one, because I am one who makes the covering in the house of Osiris,	Open to me, the *bas* of the moon's invisibility, for I am the one who completes the eye,

[360] Plutarch *De Iside et Osiride* 42, see Griffiths 1970: 185.
[361] Cauville 1997: 28.
[362] Plutarch *De Iside et Osiride* 41, see Griffiths 1970: 183.
[363] Smith 2002: 126.

2. Reference to priestly duties

and because I am the god in charge of the full moon period in the room where the vessel containing the fractional components of the eye is stored.	for what I know is more than the embalmer of the temple knows.

3. Hinting at knowledge of the missing part of the eye

I know what is missing from the eye of Tebi when its parts are counted,	I know what is missing from the eye canal in the hand of Anubis

4. Specifying the time of mutilation

and when dawn is stronger than the glow of the darkened night.	on this day of covering his great fingernails, on this night of hiding his teeth.

5. Specifying the exact nature of the mutilation

The fifth part of an entire half	It is a void out of Osiris,

6. Hinting at the bilateral nature of mutilation

for counting its parts between what is in the filling eye and the ailing eye.	when one has joined his front with his back as the hewn out part of the beam.

Lines 17–19

wn n=j jnk rḫ(.w) r=f
jw=j bsj.kw ḥr n3
n wḥm=j n ḫ3k.w-jb

Open to me because I am one who knows his spell.
I have been initiated into these matters,
and I will not reveal it to ill-intentioned people.

This part of the text does not pose difficulties of translation, except for perhaps *n3* in line 18 and *ḫ3k.w-jb* in line 19. As for the latter, its usual translation is 'rebel' or 'enemy',[364] but these words would not make much sense here, so I translated as 'ill-intentioned

[364] *Wb.* III, 363.14–16; Wilson 1997: 761–762.

people', as this expression, while having roughly the same meaning, better suits the present context. In line 18 *nꜣ* is clearly the neutral plural demonstrative pronoun,[365] but because in the Asyut texts it is followed by the sign , previous scholars suspected that it might refer to some embalming materials or unguents.[366] However, all the other Deir el-Bersha coffins write , indicating clearly that the word originally pointed to some intangible concepts, knowledge, and the replacement of  with  is only a corruption. In this instance it was possibly not brought about by the misreading of hieratic signs; more likely the hieroglyph  has seeped into the text through some copyists who only grasped the medical undertones of the spell.

On the other hand, this oversight and all the other cases of textual corruption that characterise the Asyut texts illustrate well the point that the speaker makes in this passage, since the misconstrued expressions crept into spell 155 precisely because the copyists working with the text had only a limited understanding of what the contents of the spell were really about. There are of course differing views on the role and extent of initiation in ancient Egypt,[367] but I think the textual vagaries of *CT* 155 give a good example of how the restriction of knowledge actually worked. For it may reasonably be assumed that the cult of the moon was not widespread in the Middle Kingdom, and those echelons of the elite that happened to live outside the Hermopolis area were unfamiliar with the details of ritual activities or the special vocabulary involved in the cult.

For these people the comprehension of spell 155 would have been an especially arduous task, because this text – quite in harmony with the claims made in the lines under discussion – intentionally veiled its message under a cloak of subtle allusions and a series of inside metaphors. If a modern researcher can begin to penetrate the text deep enough to uncover its multiple levels of meaning, it is only because the academic discipline of Egyptology has collected – from quite disparate sources that range over three millennia – much more information than was available to a person of average education at a particular point of time in ancient Egypt. Thus I believe that the speaker does not make an empty claim here: he indeed kept the secrets of his trade, as his words were only truly understandable to the high-ranking officials of the lunar cult. Most of those actually copying the lines, though they must have recognised the prestige of the text, were left in the dark as to the true significance of its contents.

Lines 20–21

wn n=j ntjw m psḏn.tjw
jw mꜣꜣ.n=j wp.w pr(.w) m sẖ.w n.w Wr.t

[365] *Wb.* II, 199.2.
[366] Faulkner 1973: 133; Barguet 1985: 572; Carrier 2006: 379.
[367] Baines 1990: 1–2; Jasnow and Zauzich 2005: 54–55.

Open to me, those in the moon's invisibility.
I have seen the gelder come out of the slaughterhouse of the Great Eye.

The two main sections of spell 155, lines 4–8 and 9–16, describe the state of affairs at new moon. The next three lines about the initiation of the speaker are inserted into the text to separate those descriptions from what he is saying now, because here something markedly different is hinted at. In short, line 21 – appearing quite appropriately at the end of a text whose main concern is the invisibility of the moon – expresses the joy over getting the first glimpse of the new crescent and celebrates the arrival of the first sign that makes the renewal of the moon assured. On the funerary level it is the realisation of rebirth and the expression of the happiness the deceased feels about their own regeneration.

The *sḫ.w n.w Wr.t* 'the slaughterhouse of the Great Eye' is yet another picturesque metaphor for the new moon, now building on the idea that the moon was also seen as a bull (see the excerpts from Esna and Dendera above). This concept is best expounded in a Ptolemaic inscription about Khonsu, the Theban moon god, on the propylon of his temple at Karnak.[368] It states that the sun and the moon are two bulls that traverse the sky and when they are born in the east they meet each other as the two great luminaries of the sky (*snsn kꜣ.wj*). This encounter of the two bulls no doubt describes the events at full moon, because then both the sun and the moon travel the entire span of the celestial dome from east to west, by day and night respectively. Further in the lines we read that 'the forms of the moon are, when it is young, a fiery bull, and when it is old, a steer, because he has darkened' (*jꜥḥ m jr.w⸗f ḏr sẖrd⸗f kꜣ psj m kḥkḥ⸗f sꜥb pw ḥr jrj.n⸗f snk*).[369] So when the moon grows old, that is when it wanes, the lunar animal is called *sꜥb* 'a steer, a castrated bull',[370] and this designation immediately elucidates the whole message of line 21.

The expression *wp.w* 'the one who cuts up corpses, flesh-cutter'[371] must surely have a more restricted meaning here, and it refers to a person who castrates bulls, a gelder. When he leaves the slaughterhouse, it means that he can no longer carry out his duties, that is the castration of the bull – the waning phase of the moon, including the time of its total invisibility during conjunction – is over. In other words, claiming to have seen the emergence of the gelder from the slaughterhouse is a cleverly formulated assertion intimating that the most eagerly awaited event around the time of the new moon is about to happen or has already taken place. This spectacle is of course the sighting of the newly illuminated crescent. When it appears just after sunset above the western horizon, it is a sure sign of the fact that darkness has been overcome, the lunar bull will rejuvenate itself and a new cycle of regeneration will be started.

[368] Derchain 1962a: 43.
[369] Sethe and Firchow 1957: 74.
[370] *Wb.* IV, 44.1.
[371] *Wb.* I, 302.5.

Lines 22–23

jw=j rḫ.kw bꜣ.w psḏn.tjw
Wsjr pw Jsds pw Jnpw pw

I know the *bas* of the moon's invisibility.
It is Osiris, it is Isdes, it is Anubis.

The last lines of the spell name the gods who act as the *bas* of the moon's invisibility. As for Osiris, the first records that explicitly identify him with the moon date from the New Kingdom.[372] There has been at least one attempt to seek out the possible allusions to such an identification in the Pyramid Texts,[373] and Derchain contemplated the possibility that some passages in the Coffin Texts (*CT* IV, 372a–b, 373a–b) may point in this direction.[374] However, these reasonings do not constitute conclusive evidence for the existence of direct links between the moon and Osiris at an early stage, and are rightly met with reservations.[375] It is in this light that we have to judge the references to Osiris in spell 155. Although in the closing line he is listed as one of the *bas* of the new moon, this does not necessarily mean a great deal – after all, Anubis also features in the list and he has never been especially closely associated with the moon. More conducive are lines 14–16 where Osiris does appear as a substitute image for the new moon, and it also must be remembered that the act of covering – referred to in line 4 with a sure intent on lunar connotations – is also done in the house of Osiris.

Therefore it seems to me quite plausible that the involvement of Osiris in the lunar cult had already been effected to some degree when *CT* 155 was written. It may not have gone as far as the thorough identification of Osiris with the moon, but the fundamentally common essence of these two entities must have been acknowledged. As later sources unanimously agree, we have to suspect that the basis for such an association was the similar regenerative capabilities of both Osiris and the moon. In all likelihood spell 155 documents the early development of this concept when it was certainly not widespread. The general tone of the spell – the deliberate use of cryptic language that is hard to follow – can even be understood to intimate that the recognition of the close ties between Osiris and the moon was limited at this time to an exclusive group of officials, set apart from the rest of the learned elite either on account of their exalted positions in the cult, or their particular locality, or perhaps both. Certainly, the Hermopolitan origin of *CT* 155 suggests that the main instigators of the Osiris-moon ideology resided in the fifteenth Upper Egyptian nome.

[372] Ritner 1985: 152; Griffiths 1980: 240.
[373] Kees 1956: 145.
[374] Derchain 1962a: 45.
[375] Griffiths 1980: 239–240.

Isdes is one of the divine forms in which Thoth can appear, but most of the texts that contain information about him date from the Graeco-Roman Period.[376] Apart from spell 155, he appears only twice in the Coffin Texts, in *CT* 27 where he is addressed by a hymn of the deceased, and also in *CT* 349 in a corrupted passage.[377] I think that this rarity is precisely the reason why he is included among the *ba*s of the moon's invisibility. Quite possibly, only a very few readers of spell 155 could work out at the beginning of the 2nd millennium BCE that he was identical with Thoth, so the mention of his name was yet another device to mask the real message of the text. Neither in *CT* 27 nor in the later sources does Isdes seem to be particularly connected with the lunar capacity of Thoth.[378] If the role of Isdes in *CT* 155 is only to act as a pointer to Thoth, then of course this latter deity must also be counted among the *ba*s of the moon's invisibility. Given the overwhelming evidence showing Thoth as a lunar god,[379] this perhaps does not require further explanation; I can only recapitulate here that one of the most graphic descriptions of Thoth as the moon is found in the Book of the Moon, in the rubric of Coffin Texts spell 156.

The role of Isdes in relation to the moon, however, may be much more significant if his close connection with a seemingly other god, Isden is accepted. These two divinities were surely identical in Graeco-Roman times,[380] and it is quite likely that the name Isden is only a variant of Isdes that arose from mistaking the *ds*-jar in the hieroglyphic spelling of the latter for a *nw*-jar.[381] In certain texts at Dendera accompanying ritual scenes it is said of the pharaoh: 'As Isden, he is in the Mansion of the Bird Net filling in the *wedjat*-eye with its fractional components' (*sw m Jsdn ḫnt Ḥw.t-jbṯ.t mḥ(.w) wḏ3.t m dbḥ.w⸗s*).[382] So in this late inscription Isden/Isdes appears precisely in the role of completing the lunar eye with its elements, which explains quite nicely why he is included among the *ba*s of the moon's invisibility at the end of a Coffin Texts spell which itself makes reference to the fractional components of the lunar eye and to the act of counting them (lines 5-6). Since the sanctuary in Hermopolis identified as the Mansion of the Bird Net in the Dendera text was also called the 'Mansion of the Moon' or 'Mansion of the Month' (*Ḥw.t-3bd*),[383] one may even wonder if the room housing the components of the eye (line 5) was indeed found in that building.

Anubis has never been seen as a deity having particularly close ties with the moon.[384] The contents of *CT* 155, the later temple scenes showing him bending over the lunar disc, and also the much later papyri detailing the mummification rituals all indicate that he earned his place among the *ba*s of the moon's invisibility through

[376] Boylan 1922: 201.
[377] *CT* IV, 384c. See Faulkner 1973: 283 n. 9.
[378] Leitz 2002a: 560-561; Stadler 2009: 278.
[379] Boylan 1922: 62-75.
[380] Leitz 2002a: 558-561.
[381] Stadler 2009: 278.
[382] Chassinat 1935: 139.
[383] Gauthier 1927: 48-49.
[384] See Altenmüller 1975a.

his embalming role. As Osiris, and all the people who upon their death assumed his identity, came to be imbued with the regenerative powers of the moon, Anubis the embalmer was not only tending a divine or human corpse, but also a celestial body. His expertise about the former was extended to the latter, and his actions could have been seen as especially congruent with the new moon, as the state of death corresponded to that particular lunar phase for obvious reasons. So this is perhaps why the author of the text made him accompany Osiris and Isdes.

2.3. Spell 156: the waxing moon

The hieroglyphic text

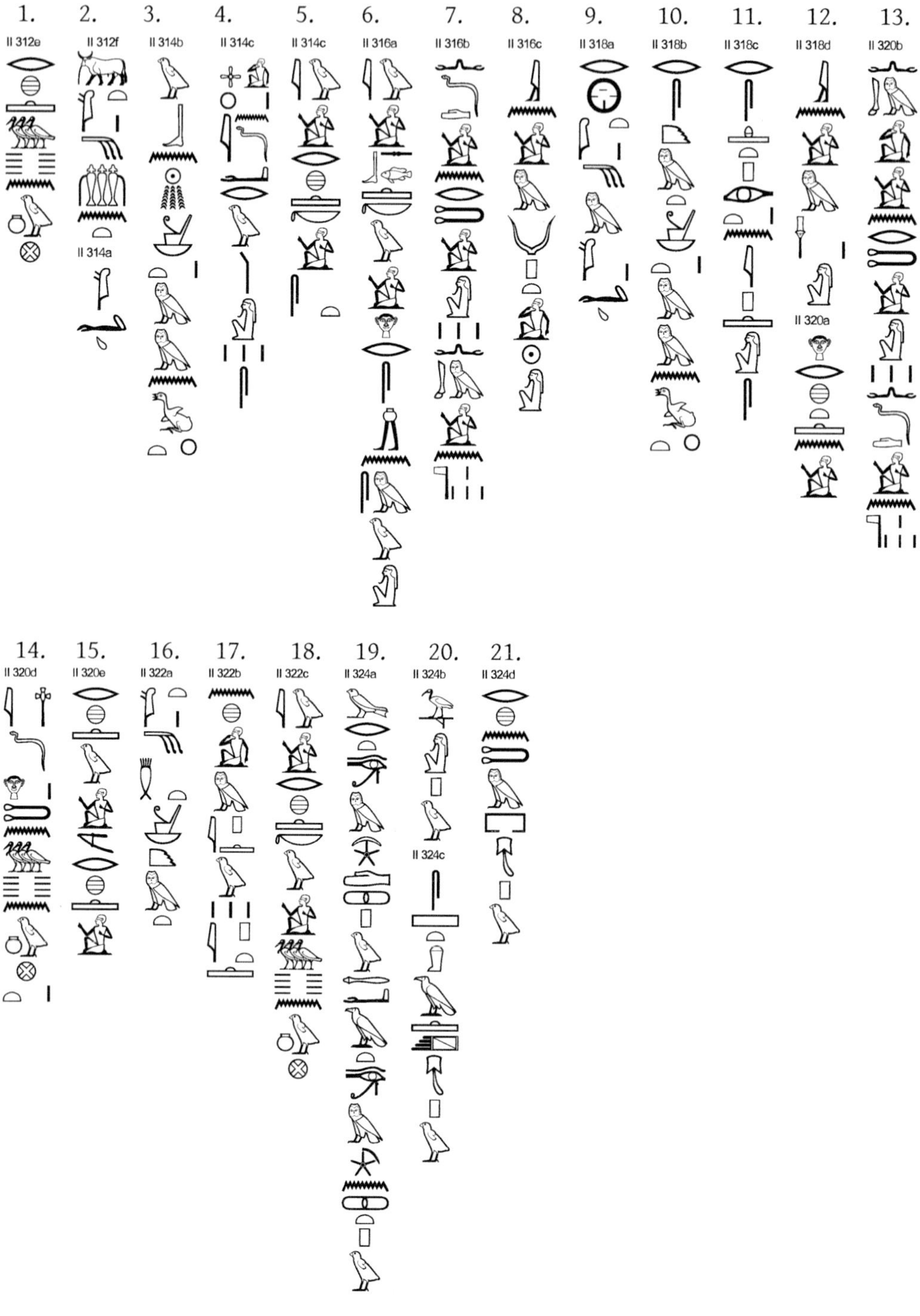

Transliteration and translation

1. *rḫ bꜣ.w Ḫmnw*
2. *wn šw.t ḫnt qꜥḥ*
3. *wbn dšr.t m mnṯꜣ.t*
4. *wnm jr.t jn ḏꜥr.w⸗s*
5. *jw⸗j rḫ.kw st*
6. *jw⸗j bs.kw ḥr⸗s jn sm.w*
7. *n ḏd⸗j n rmṯ n wḥm⸗j n nṯr.w*
8. *jj.n⸗j m wp.t Rꜥ*
9. *r smn.t šw.t m qꜥḥ*
10. *r skm.t dšr.t m mnṯꜣ.t*
11. *r sḥtp jr.t n jp(.w)⸗s*
12. *jj.n⸗j m sḫm ḥr rḫ.n⸗j*
13. *n wḥm⸗j n rmṯ n ḏd⸗j n nṯr.w*
14. *jnḏ ḥr⸗ṯn bꜣ.w Ḫmnw*
15. *rḫ.<k>w mj rḫ*
16. *šw.t rd.t(j) dšr.t km.t(j)*
17. *nḫ m jp.w jp.t*
18. *jw⸗j rḫ.kw bꜣ.w Ḫmnw*
19. *šr.t m ꜣbd pw ꜥꜣ.t m smd.t pw*
20. *Ḏḥw.tj pw sštꜣ sjꜣ pw*
21. *rḫ.n⸗ṯ m pr-grḥ pw*

1. Knowing the *bas* of Hermopolis.
2. The feather is thrust into the shoulder,
3. and the Red Crown rises in the *mentjat*-bowl,
4. the eye is consumed by those who inspect it.
5. I know this,
6. because the *sem*-priest initiated me into this.
7. I have not told it to other people, nor have I repeated it to the gods.
8. I have come on an errand for Re
9. to establish the feather in the shoulder,
10. to make the Red Crown whole in the *mentjat*-bowl,
11. and to pacify the eye for the one who takes count of it.
12. I have come as a divine power for what I know.
13. I have not repeated it to other people, nor have I told it to the gods.
14. Hail to you, *bas* of Hermopolis!
15. My knowledge is like that of a wise man.
16. The feather has grown and the Red Crown is whole,
17. so now there is rejoicing over what has had to be counted has been counted!
18. I know the *bas* of Hermopolis.

19. It is the small eye on the second day of the lunar month, it is the great eye on the fifteenth day of the lunar month.
20. It is Thoth, it is the secret of the full moon,
21. and it is what you have learnt in the house of the night.

Commentary

Line 1

rḫ bꜣ.w Ḫmnw

Knowing the *bas* of Hermopolis.

As is the case with spells 154 and 155, the title of the spell is not highlighted in red on Sen's coffin. The text of spell 156 on the Deir el-Bersha coffins starts off with this line, except for two coffins. One of these is the coffin of Djehutinakht (B2Bo) which features the following introductory formula:

ꜥq ḥr jmj.w Ḫmnw ḥs.t mr tp tꜣ šꜣ s r ꜥq.w ꜥꜣ m ẖr.t-nṯr j[n] bꜣ ꜥnḫ(.w) mwt(.w)

Entering among those who are in Hermopolis, being praised and loved on earth, having great provisions in the necropolis by the living and the dead *ba*.

The other exception is Gua's coffin (B1L); here also a longer introduction precedes the standard text of the spell:

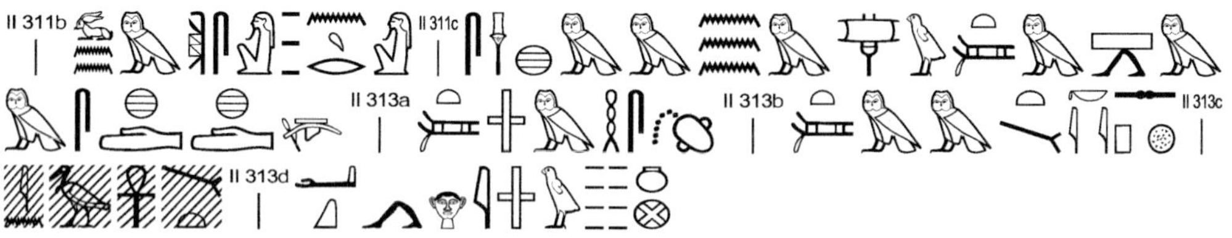

wnn m šms.w n Wsjr sḫm m mw m ṯꜣw tm šm m sḫdḫd tm wnm ḥs tmmwt ky sp [jn bꜣ ꜥnḫ mwt] ꜥq ḥr jmj.w Ḫmnw

Being among the followers of Osiris, having power in water through breathing, not walking upside down, not eating excrement, not dying another death by the living and dead *ba*, entering among those who are in Hermopolis.

It is clear, however, that these longer introductions express wishes that conform to the general aspirations of the deceased in the netherworld which are often repeated in other spells of the Coffin Texts, too.[385] They do not convey information that would be specific to the moon, or in a wider sense, to the lunar world, except perhaps the reference to the idea that the deceased wants to be associated with Hermopolis, the main cult centre of the principal Egyptian lunar god, Thoth. It is quite possible that this general, easily recognisable and understandable character is the reason why the introductory formula on Gua's coffin is repeated in the Asyut text variants.

The *bas* of Hermopolis play an important role in hailing the invisible moon and the appearance of the first crescent in the lunar scene on the eastern wall of the pronaos of the Edfu temple.[386] They are depicted there as ibis-headed human beings, that is, with the iconography of Thoth, in front of the lunar barque that carries the symbols of the full, waning, and blacked-out moon.[387] The words they utter allude not only to the invisible moon, but also to the ensuing event: 'The *bas* of Hermopolis who witness the revelation of the *wedjat*-eye on new-crescent day, following the god when he is the child of the day of invisibility while his mother hides him in her armpit (from the time when) Nut gives birth to the eastern feather (= the waning crescent) until the living see the feather of the west' (*bꜣ.w Ḫmn.w ntj dgꜣ wn-ḥr wḏꜣ.t m ꜣbd šms nṯr m ḫj n psḏn.tjw sdḫ sj mw.t=f m ḥṯṯ.t=s msj (sj) Nw.t m šw jꜣb.tj r dgꜣ (sj) ꜥnḫ.w m šw jmn.tj*).[388] Since, as we shall see below, spell 156 is the oldest document that establishes a connection between the *bas* of Hermopolis and the new crescent, it is difficult to tell whether this concept originates from it, or it just reflects common knowledge that was preserved in both *CT* 156 and the much later Edfu inscription.

Line 2

ṯwn šw.t ḫnt qꜥḥ

The feather is thrust into the shoulder,

The feather here – as is obvious from other Coffin Texts spells, notably 6 and 9[389] – is used beyond any doubt figuratively, and refers to the new crescent appearing over the western horizon just after sunset.[390] It is precisely this association that lies behind the inclusion of the feather in the various signs that denote the direction of west.[391] In ancient Egypt, as is clear from the analysis of the previous spell of the Book of the Moon, the lunar month started with the disappearance of the waning crescent (last crescent invisibility, to be observed on the eastern horizon). In the majority of the

385 Assmann 2005: 158.
386 Chassinat 1929: pl lxix.
387 Priskin 2016c: 120–128.
388 Chassinat 1928: 213.
389 *CT* I, 16c–19a, 29a–31a.
390 Kees 1925: 8; Goedicke 1989: 61; Willems 2005.
391 Willems 2005; Meeks 2006: 32, 292.

cases the first crescent of the new lunation was seen on the evening of the second day of the lunar month (*ꜣbd*), and this is the event that will be evoked in line 19 of the present spell by the description of the small eye, i.e. the smallness of the moon. In some lunations (about 30% of the months) the first crescent only appeared on the evening of the third day.[392] The previous spell about the invisibility of the moon (*psḏn.tjw*) closes with the claim that the reciter has seen the gelder come out of the slaughterhouse, in accordance with the belief that the waning moon is incorporated by an ox (a castrated bull).[393] The whole statement then symbolically intimates that the strife of the moon is about to end, and the appearance of the new crescent can be expected. So in this case very tangibly spell 156 follows on spell 155 in a logical, chronological order. The second spell of the Book of the Moon is about the very beginning of the month, the period of lunar invisibility, whereas the third one, spell 156, kicks off with the event that takes place either on the second or third day of the month, the appearance of the first crescent. In turn, as we shall see, it will encompass the waxing moon until the time when the full moon sets in.

According to the text, the feather – the first crescent of the waxing moon – is thrust (*ṯwn*) into the shoulder (*qꜥḥ*). These two words also have strong lunar connotations. The verb *ṯwn* describes the action by which a bull butts something or someone with its horns,[394] but it must also be mentioned that in the Graeco-Roman lists of the lunar days it is equated with the twenty-seventh day.[395] Certainly, at this time the waning crescent is similarly quite thin, though its arc faces the opposite direction from the curve of the waxing crescent. The use of the verb 'to thrust, butt, gore' seems to suggest that the Egyptians associated the thin lunar crescent – regardless whether it appeared during the waxing or the waning phases – with the horns of a bull. This association is perhaps closely linked to the personification of the waxing moon with a fiery bull (*kꜣ psj*), and of the waning moon with a castrated bull (*sꜥb*). As regards the hieroglyphic text, the reading of the sign showing the bleeding bull is beyond any doubt, because in the Asyut text variants it is phonetically spelled out as *ṯwn*. Rather interestingly, on the coffin of the Deir el-Bersha official, Neferi, this word is replaced by a completely different expression: *sṯꜣ* 'to drag, to pull along'.[396] It is not impossible that for the choice of this word the scribe was influenced by some other related lunar myths in which it is stated that Seth's finger is removed (*sṯꜣ*) from the eye of Horus.[397] This motif is also about putting an end to the injury of the eye of Horus (the waning and invisible moon), so it could naturally be integrated into the message of spell 156.

The shoulder must, in the context of the spell, refer to the relevant body part of the arching sky goddess, Nut, which is in fact situated in the west according to her

392 Parker 1950: 13.
393 Derchain 1962a: 43
394 *Wb.* V, 359.11
395 Wilson 1997: 267.
396 *CT* II, 313f (B17C).
397 *Wb.* IV, 352.12; Derchain 1962a: 24.

schematic representations. In some descriptions of the moon dated to the Ptolemaic era it is emphasised that the invisible moon – at the end of its own period lasting for one or two days – reaches the 'western' body parts of Nut, although in these late inscriptions the destination of the moon is Nut's armpits, and not her shoulders (see the quotation from Edfu above).[398] To designate this place the word *ḥṯṯ.t* is used. Its translation in the late texts as 'armpit' seems secure, because Nut is said to hide the moon here, but it must be noted that the same word can in a more general sense mean the shoulder or the shoulder area of the body.[399] In any case, shoulder and armpit are the 'two sides of the same coin', that is they denote the same general area of the upper torso, so the later descriptions of the moon offer support for the interpretation that spell 156 makes a reference to the shoulder of Nut. It must be mentioned, though, that the Asyut versions speak of the shoulder of Osiris. This augmentation of the text could still relate to the west, stemming from the common association of Osiris with this direction, evidenced by his widespread epithets such as 'Lord of the West' or 'Foremost of the Westerners'.[400] In light of this, I do not think we should seek a connection of the shoulder with a constellation representing Osiris in the sky (presumably 'Orion'), as has been tentatively suggested.[401]

Another avenue for the association of the shoulder with the moon is opened up by an inscription on the enclosure wall of the Edfu temple about the body parts of the hippopotamus representing the archenemy of the local god, Horus, that is Seth. It reads: 'his shoulder is to be under the protection of Thoth on this day of the blacked-out moon' (*s3 Ḏḥwtj rd.t n=f qʿḥ=f hrw pfj n psḏn.tjw*).[402] The connection between the shoulder of the hippopotamus and the moon might be indicated by the detail that according to other passages this body part should be stored in Hermopolis or in the sanctuary of Thoth.[403] These motifs about the shoulder must be related to the stories about the fighting between Horus and Seth, in which both of them turn into a hippopotamus to outmanoeuvre each other.[404] The lunar aspects of their strife – Seth injures the eye of Horus representing the moon – are of course well-known.[405] It is, however, very unlikely that we should seek a direct link between the shoulder of the hippopotamus described at Edfu and Coffin Texts spell 156, because here the shoulder belongs to either Nut or, according to the Asyut version, to Osiris. A reference to a shoulder in a lunar context, in any case, may have been prompted by a wordplay between the corresponding Egyptian expressions (*jʿḥ* - *qʿḥ*).

---

398 For another example, see Chassinat 1928: 211.
399 *Wb.* III, 204.15–17.
400 Leitz 2002c: 583; Leitz 2002e: 783–786.
401 Nyord 2003: 83 n. 64.
402 Chassinat 1931: 147.
403 Chassinat 1931: 85, 89.
404 Lichtheim 1976, 218–219.
405 See below the comments on spell 157.

Line 3

wbn dšr.t m mnṯ3.t

and then the Red Crown rises in the *mentjat*-bowl,

Whereas the identification of the feather with the first crescent is fairly secure, the reference of the Red Crown in the next line is not so straightforward, not least because the other thing named, the *mentjat*-bowl, is equally obscure. The connotations of the verb *wbn*, 'to rise (in the east)',[406] suggest that the Red Crown is identical with the full moon rising on the eastern horizon. Due to the atmospheric scattering of light the full moon near the horizon – just as the sun near the horizon – may appear to have a red hue.[407] The Red Crown thus may specifically refer to this phenomenon. From a number of sources it is quite clear that in ancient Egypt the royal crowns were used as metaphors for the moon, and more particularly, for the full moon. Chapter 80 of the Book of Going Forth by Day most probably identifies the counterpart of the Red Crown, the White Crown, with the full moon when it says: 'I have saved the eye of Horus from its nothingness as the fifteenth day has come ... I have equipped Thoth in the house of the moon and taken possession of the White Crown' (*šdj.n=j jr.t-Ḥr.w m jw.tj=s jj.n smd.t ... ʿpr.n=j Ḏḥwtj m ḥw.t-jʿḥ jtj.n=j wrr.t*).[408] Since in late texts the equipping of the moon is repeatedly associated with the full moon, it can hardly be doubted that the White Crown is the symbol of the full lunar disc. This identification is first described in utterance 468 of the Pyramid Texts, in a passage that also mentions the Red Crown. After citing the two key moments of the waxing moon, the day of the first crescent (the second day of the lunar month) and the middle of the month (the fifteenth day of the full moon),[409] the text reads: 'O King, the dread of you is the intact eye of Horus, (namely) the White Crown ... O King, I provide you with the eye of Horus, the Red Crown, rich in power and many-natured' (*h3 N pn šʿ.t=k pw jr.t-Ḥr.w wḏ3.t ḥd.t tw ... h3 N ḥtm ṯw m jr.t-Ḥr.w dšr.t wr.t b3.w ʿš3.t wn.w*).[410] Here the eye of Horus, that is the moon, is associated with both the White Crown and the Red Crown. The White Crown is linked to the intact eye and thus once more denotes the full moon. The signification of the Red Crown is perhaps identical, and its epithets – 'rich in power' (literally, 'having great *bas*') and 'many-natured' ('having plentiful existences') – surely point to the moon.

It must be admitted, though, that the precise understanding of the text is hampered by the fact that the phrase *ʿš3.t wn.w* is a hapax and does not recur elsewhere.[411] The word is surely connected to the verb 'to be' and thus the whole expression may

[406] *Wb.* I, 292.9–293.11.
[407] Goebs 2008: 158–159.
[408] Lepsius 1842: pl. xxx, 80.4–6.
[409] *Pyr.* 897c.
[410] *Pyr.* 900a–901b. Translation from Faulkner 1969: 157.
[411] *Wb.* I, 307.13.

try to convey the idea that the moon – the Red Crown – throughout its 'life-cycle', i.e. its phases, manifests itself in many forms. This may be in unison with Willem's understanding that the rising of the Red Crown implies a reference to the first half of the lunar cycle (waxing), through which the elevation of the moon increases day by day (it appears towards dusk at a higher position until the first quarter).[412]

The Red Crown appears in an undisputable lunar context in the tomb of Petubastis at Qāret el-Muzawwaqa in the Dakhla oasis (1st century CE). What is more, in the lower register on the western half of the south wall in the pillared tomb chamber this crown seems to stand for the full moon in a rather peculiar, but still decipherable scene.[413] We see Khonsu spearing his enemy,[414] followed by two figures: a Janus-like, two-faced child holding symmetrically depicted snakes in his hands, and a rearing cobra (uraeus) wearing the Red Crown. Above both figures there is a *wedjat*-eye: the eyebrow of the one above the child is painted greenish, just as the child itself, while the same part of the second eye is reddish, matching the colour of the uraeus. The whole scene must be related to the great lunar feast in the month of Pachons,[415] and the two *wedjat*-eyes, with their accompanying characters below, refer to the blacked-out moon and the full moon.

Certain details suggest that the two-faced child corresponds to the invisible moon. The half body of a falcon is appended to the torso of Khonsu which is also of the same greenish colour as the child and the eyebrow of the first *wedjat*-eye. This form of depiction is also characteristic of ithyphallic figures with an upraised left hand that resemble the traditional iconography of Min.[416] Min was often associated with the blacked-out moon in Graeco-Roman texts,[417] so the avian features of Khonsu and the child with the same colour alludes to this phase of the lunar cycle. The beginning of the month was also described by identifying the moon with a child,[418] so this again suggests that the two-faced infant represents lunar invisibility. His two faces indicate that the invisible moon, as the marker of the onset of the new lunar month in Egypt, was also the borderline between the two opposing phases of the lunar cycle, waxing and waning. Consequently, the rearing uraeus, with the Red Crown on its head and its differently coloured *wedjat*-eye, refers to the full moon. Therefore this scene in the late tomb of Petubastis confirms the association of the Red Crown with the full moon.

Given the scarcity of source material, it is really difficult to establish on what grounds the *mentjat*-bowl is associated with the moon, and more precisely, with the full moon. This vessel is frequently depicted in the object frieze of Middle Kingdom coffins where it is shown as a shallow bowl with a flaring rim and possibly a spout.[419] The vessel

---

412 Willems 2005: 211.
413 Osing et al. 1982: pls. 20–21, 31.
414 Unfortunately, the depiction of the enemy is lost.
415 cf. Chassinat 1930: 354–355; Grimm 1994: 105, 197.
416 Kemp 1991: 85.
417 Cauville 2011: 42–43.
418 Clère 1961: pl. 60; Derchain 1962a: 43.
419 Willems 1996: 213–215.

is put on a rather slender cylindrical pot-stand and evidence seems to suggest that the term can either mean the bowl or the stand, or perhaps the whole ensemble in its entirety.[420] This has prompted Willems to render the term as 'support' in his translation of the relevant part of *CT* 156.[421] Roughly contemporaneously with the Coffin Texts, a message addressed to a deceased relative – a 'letter to the dead' – was written on a *mentjat*-bowl which in this case meant the pot-stand.[422] The name of the bowl also appears in offering lists and the information provided by these indicates that the *mentjat* was primarily used for storing water.[423] In the offering lists the *mentjat*-bowl often features next to another, red-coloured container of liquid called *dšr.t*. The designation of this vessel is homophonous with the name of the Red Crown. While the similar role the two bowls played may have had something to do with the presence of the *mentjat* in spell 156, I must admit that I cannot figure out a clear explanation why the *mentjat* is referred to in the description of the rising full moon in our text. It is a noteworthy detail, however, that on the Deir el-Bersha coffins the determinative of the *mentjat*-bowl is a circle, except for Gua's coffin (B1L) where – possibly on the influence of the parallel expression of the shoulder – a lump of meat fulfils the same grammatical function.[424] This may be taken to suggest that the *mentjat* did not originally refer to a bowl or pot-stand, but rather to a body part of Nut which – in contrast to her shoulders in the west – is situated in the east and makes the rising of the full moon possible.

When we look at lines 2 and 3 together, the most likely conclusion is that – despite the obscurity of some of the words used – their descriptions demarcate the starting and end points of the waxing phases: the first crescent above the western horizon and the full lunar disc over the eastern horizon. This interpretation will find strong support towards the end of the spell where the same two antithetic events of the first half of the lunar cycle are named in more certain terms as the small eye on the second day and the great eye on the fifteenth day of the lunar month (see commentary on line 19 below).

Line 4

wnm jr.t jn ḏꜥr.w=s

the eye is consumed by those who inspect it.

To grasp the meaning of *ḏꜥr.w*, spell 249 of the Coffin Texts may be used as a starting point, because we can read there: 'I am Thoth who seizes the great ladies, I have come to examine the eye of Horus. I have brought it and counted it, and I have found it complete, counted, and sound' (*jnk Ḏḥwtj ḥmꜥ wr.wt jj.n=j ḏꜥr jr.t Ḥr.w jnj.n=j st*

[420] Willems 1996: 215.
[421] Willems 2005: 211.
[422] Gardiner 1930: 19–20.
[423] *Wb.* II, 92.7
[424] *CT* II, 315b.

jp.n=j st gm.n=j st km.t jp.t wḏꜣ.t).[425] From this excerpt it is clear that Thoth is the one who carries out the action that is described by the verb *ḏꜥr*, while the rest of the passage stresses the complete and sound condition of the eye of Horus. Although the basic meaning of *ḏꜥr* is 'to seek out', 'to look for', from the context of spell 249 it may equally follow that here the word has its more specialised meaning, used in medical texts, where it denotes the action 'to examine' ('to seek out illness').[426] Thoth was, through his association with the healing of the eye of Horus, deemed as an eye specialist,[427] and the examination of the eye here should be interpreted in that context. In medical texts the verb *ḏꜥr* often collocates with the word 'finger' as its subject, so it means 'to seek out or feel illness with the finger',[428] and we should not forget that in spell 335 of the Coffin Texts,[429] and in its descendant, spell 17 of the Book of Going Forth by Day the healing of the eye of Horus is associated with Thoth's fingers: '*N* filled the *wedjat*-eye after it was injured on the day when the two combatants fought ... and it was Thoth himself who did it with his fingers' (*jw mḥ.n N pn wḏꜣ.t m-ḫt hbj=s hrw pwj n ꜥḥꜥ rḥ.wj ... jr-gr Ḏḥwtj jrj nn m ḏbꜥ.w=f ḏs=f*).[430] Although in *CT* 156 *ḏꜥr.w* is definitely in the plural, it is not impossible that we have a false plural here, and the plural strokes at the end resulted from the ending *.w* of the original participle. If this is the case, then the phrase in line 4 should be translated as 'the eye is consumed by its examiner', and from the context of spell 249 of the Coffin Texts it follows that this person is Thoth. If, however, the plural form of *ḏꜥr.w* is deliberate, then the examiners perhaps refer to a group of medics, the members of which are Thoth and other divinities known for their healing abilities, including perhaps some hypostases of Thoth himself (such as for example Isdes, mentioned at the end of the previous spell in the Book of the Moon).

As we could see, the motif of healing the eye of Horus already appears in spell 155, when its reciter claims that he knows more about the anatomy of the eye than the embalmer priest, who must otherwise be also very skilled in handling the different organs of the human body. This medical context makes sense to the act of eating or consuming the celestial eye by its examiner. In ancient Egyptian medical practice the act of consuming, swallowing, or touching by the mouth (licking) was often a very important magical means of the healing process.[431] Thoth thus eats the ailing eye to make it hale and sound again, which in lunar terms means that the waning and invisible periods of the moon are over, and it starts waxing again.

[425] *CT* III, 343a–g.
[426] *Wb.* V, 540.13–14.
[427] Boylan 1922: 72.
[428] Breasted 1930: 92; cf. *Wb.* V, 540.15.
[429] *CT* IV, 232a–239a.
[430] Lepsius 1842: pl. viii.
[431] Wilson 1997: 235; Ritner 2008: 102–110.

Lines 5–7

jw=j rẖ.kw st
jw=j bs.kw ẖr=s jn sm.w
n ḏd=j n rmṯ n wḥm=j n nṯr.w

I know this,
because the *sem*-priest initiated me into this.
I have not told it to other people, nor have I repeated it to the gods.

Sources already from the Old Kingdom indicate that the title *sm* (*sem*-priest) was held by the deceased's son, and the bearer of this position had a very important role in the ceremony of opening the mouth and in other ritual activities connected with the funeral.[432] At the same time the *sem*-priest – if it is in fact the same title – was very much involved in the observation of the moon. This is quite clear from the papyrus collecting the myths of the Delta region (pBrooklyn 47.218.84) that was mentioned previously.[433] In connection with the name of the fourth day of the lunar month, *pr.t-sm* 'the going forth of the *sem*-priest', we learn that this event took place when Horus regained the faculty of his eyes after being impaired in his vision due to the injuries that Seth had inflicted upon them: 'Horus opened his eyes, and he could see with them. ... His strength grew, so he went forth at dawn – one calls it the going forth of the *sem*-priest on the fourth day following every instance of the moon's invisibility' (*wn Ḥr.w jr.tj=fj mꜣꜣ=f jm=sj ... ꜥꜣ pḥ.tj=fj prj.ẖr=f m ḥḏ-tꜣ pr.t-sm ẖr.tw r=f ḥr hrw 4 n psḏn.tjw nb*).[434] As I already pointed out, what may lie behind the going forth of the *sem*-priest was the fact that in a few number of cases the first crescent of the waxing moon only appeared on the evening of the third day of the lunar month. Thus presumably rituals or ceremonies customarily hailed the waxing moon on the morning of the fourth day, and the officiant responsible for these rites must have been the *sem*-priest. It must be added that the same duties of the *sem*-priest in the observation of the first crescent are also mentioned in the Fundamentals of the Course of the Stars.[435]

Therefore this role of the *sem*-priest is the reason why he is mentioned in our text; consequently, what he initiated the speaker into is the knowledge about the observation of the moon, and especially the sighting of the first crescent of the waxing moon. The reference to this initiation here, however, may be entirely symbolic, and just wants to allude to the – presumably commonly known – connection between the *sem*-priest and the beginning of a lunation. On the other hand, the exclusive nature of lunar knowledge is also emphasised in *CT* 155, and the penultimate line of spell 156, talking about the 'secret of the full moon' (*sštꜣ sjꜣ*), will also underline this theme. Surely, the observation of the moon was a prerogative of a narrow group of skilled people holding the appropriate priestly titles.

[432] Schmitz 1984: 833–834; Wilson 1997: 837.
[433] Meeks 2006.
[434] Meeks 2006: 14 (pBrooklyn 47.218.84, IV, 5–6).
[435] Lieven 2007: 97–101, 177–184, 455–463.

Line 8

jj.n=j m wp.t Rʿ

I have come on an errand for Re

This line identifies the speaker as the messenger or envoy of Re, and in the present context he must be Thoth, so – just as in the previous spell – the speaker assumes the identity of the pre-eminent lunar god here. Since on the cosmic level Re is the sun and Thoth is the moon, the idea that the latter is the nocturnal substitute of the earlier already surfaces in the Pyramid Texts: 'Oh, these two companions who cross the sky ... *N* circles the sky like Re, *N* traverses the sky like Thoth' (*rḥ.wj jpw ḏꜣ.j p.t Rʿ pj ḥnʿ Ḏḥwtj... dbn N p.t mj Rʿ ẖns N p.t mj Ḏḥwtj*).[436] One of the epithets of Thoth – although only documented from the Graeco-Roman era – is *wpw.tj* 'messenger',[437] so this may give further support for the identification. From a wider perspective, it was clear for the Egyptians that the moon received its light from the sun and that their movements were interlinked.[438] This is transparent from such Egyptian sources as the inscriptions on the propylon to the temple of Khonsu at Karnak,[439] the lunar texts in the pronaos of the Edfu temple,[440] and also from various representations that show the symbols of the sun and the moon together.[441] Clement of Alexandria also relates that at least two books carried by the astronomer-priests during ritual processions dealt with the subject of the relationship between the orbits of the sun and the moon.[442] That the speaker sees himself as fulfilling the task of Re in *CT* 156 may just acknowledge the inherent relationship that exist between the two brightest celestial bodies.

Lines 9–10

r smn.t šw.t m qʿḥ
r skm.t dšr.t m mnṯꜣ.t
r sḥtp jr.t n jp(.w)=s

to establish the feather in the shoulder,
to make the Red Crown whole in the *mentjat*-bowl,
and to pacify the eye for the one who takes count of it.

These lines describe the nature and objective of the errand that the speaker carries out for Re, and they effectively correspond to the actions that were mentioned in lines 2 and 3. On the lunar level they denote the first crescent (the feather in the

[436] *Pyr.* §§128–130.
[437] Boylan 1922: 183.
[438] Derchain 1962a: 28.
[439] Clère 1961.
[440] Chassinat 1928: 207–208, 211–212..
[441] See my analysis of the scenes in Priskin 2016c.
[442] Clement of Alexandria, *Stromateia* 6.4.35, see Stählin 1906: 449.

shoulder), and waxing resulting in the appearance of the full moon (making the Red Crown whole and pacifying the eye). While the last two statements do not cause any real difficulties in terms of translation (apart from the obscure nature of the *mentjat*-bowl), the first one – though its general message is quite clear – presents a series of problems. This results from the fact that the verb after the preposition *r* is written with a peculiar hieroglyphic sign (⊖) that is not easy to understand and lends itself to various interpretations. In fact, this sign is not part of the ordinary repertoire of hieroglyphic writing and actually belongs to the realm of cryptography, so much so that it seems from the collation of the different text variants that even most of the ancient copyists were at a loss in understanding its true meaning.

The verb in question is spelled out phonetically only on the coffin of Neferi (B17C) as *smn.t*, which is the infinitive of the causative verb *smn* 'to make something endure', 'to establish'.[443] According to Gertrud Thausing this reading stems from the decipherment of the enigmatic sign on the coffin of Gua (B1L), which she believes represents the hieroglyph 𓋴 (folded piece of cloth) inscribed into the town sign (⊗), and thus it should be read *s* + *m* (in) + *n.t* (town), that is together *smn.t*.[444] However, it is clear that the phonetically written *smn.t* with the usual orthography of the sign 𓏠 is only one possible interpretation of the cryptographic group on Gua's coffin, and various text variants on some coffins from Deir el-Bersha (B2Bo, B9C) and on all the coffins from Asyut testify that the Egyptians regarded the circle surrounding the *s* not as the town hieroglyph, but rather as the sign standing for the eye. So, on the coffins from Deir el-Bersha we find 𓋴𓅓o𓏏𓏤, as the eye was represented so often with just the circle, whereas in Asyut they resolved the riddle with the more common spelling 𓋴𓅓𓁹𓏏𓏤.

Thausing explains this by citing the Graeco-Roman word *mn.t* or *mnd.t* which was used to denote the eyes or the pupil of the eye.[445] With this the reading *smn.t* can be justified along the same principles (*s* + *m* + *mn.t* resolves into *smn.t*). In my opinion, this is the correct understanding of the cryptography in *CT* II, 318a, all the more so because the sign of the eye itself could carry the phonetic value *mn* in some Graeco-Roman texts,[446] and Thausing original reasoning with the town hieroglyph is superfluous, as it in fact cannot be backed up by contemporaneous or later evidence. The numerous texts variants displaying the eye in one form or another prove that the Egyptians took the circle in this part of the text as the sign standing for the eye. The suggestion of Kurt Sethe that the obscure hieroglyph should be read *srd.t* 'to make grow',[447] and it results from the confusion between the hieratic signs for the owl and the rhizome of the lotus plant, should also be rejected.[448]

[443] *Wb.* IV, 131–134.7.
[444] Thausing 1941: 52.
[445] Thausing 1941: 52; Wilson 1997: 440.
[446] Daumas 1988: 148.
[447] Sethe 1922: 42.
[448] Willems 2005: 211 n. 27.

While the solution put forward above for the cryptic sign in spell 156 is certainly alluring and fits the context well, some lingering problems may also be pointed out. First, as in line 2 Neferi's coffin features the verb *sṯꜣ* instead of *ṯwn*, unanimously attested in all the other variants, his text seems to have some idiosyncrasies, and thus his choice for the word *smn.t* in *CT* II, 318a may equally be just one of the possible solutions to the enigmatic hieroglyph in question. Second, in Sen's and Sepi's versions the sign definitely does not contain an inscribed *s*. On Sepi's coffin (B2P) it is perhaps closest to the later hieroglyph showing a (tear)drop or the pupil within the iris (ϴ),[449] and thus may stand for *ḏfḏ* or *ḏfḏf*, but no verb can be matched with these phonetic sequences that would suit the context of spell 156.

In Sen's text the sign is different and seems to include several small dots. Still, it is highly likely that it is a depiction of the eye, or a particular part of the eye, for example the pupil. Again, from Graeco-Roman times we have evidence that the pupil was also called *km* 'the black part of the eye',[450] which word is homophonous with the verb *km* 'to complete'.[451] Then it is not impossible that this wordplay is the ultimate reason for the enigmatic sign in *CT* II, 318a. Some versions of chapter 114 of the Book of Going Forth by Day (which text is of course the direct descendant of Coffin Texts spell 156) indicate that the verb could indeed refer to the lunar feather, because for example in the papyrus of Nebseni we can read: 'I know that the feather has grown and has been completed as it was counted' (*jw⸗j rḫ.kw šw.t rwḏ.tj km.tj jp sj*).[452] If we accept this reading, then there would be a parallel between lines 9 and 10, because they would contain the base verb *km* and its causative offspring *skm*, both meaning 'to complete', 'to make whole'.

Line 10 voices yet another objective of the speaker, and that is to pacify the eye. Besides its literary meaning, the verb used here, *sḥtp*, may have some other distinct connotations as far as the lunar cycle is concerned. Since it is the causative form of *ḥtp*, which verb is used to describe the setting of the celestial bodies on the western horizon,[453] the action of making the eye set in the west may be evoked. Indeed, it is in the first half of the lunar cycle, during waxing, that the moon sets on the western horizon; in contrast, after the day of the full moon it just travels a certain distance towards the west before the sun rises and starts to cancel out its light. Also, as in medical texts *sḥtp* can have the meaning 'to reduce pain',[454] the myth about the moon as the left eye of Horus may be alluded to, because in this framework waning and invisibility are associated with the ailing, injured eye, and it is during waxing that this injury is healed, leading to the appearance of the sound eye (*wḏꜣ.t*) at full moon.[455]

[449] cf. the entries in *Wb.* V, 572.9–573.17.
[450] *Wb.* V, 124.13.
[451] *Wb.* V, 128.3–130.2.
[452] Lapp 2004: pl. 19 114.6–7.
[453] *Wb.* III, 191.11–14.
[454] *Wb.* IV, 222.19.
[455] Wallin 2002: 80–85.

The pacification of the eye is done for someone who takes count of it. This person is undoubtedly Thoth. Once more we have to turn to Graeco-Roman sources for the best evidence to support this claim. In a scene showing the offering of cloth (*mnḫ.t*) to a number of divinities in Khonsu's chapel in the temple of Edfu,[456] Thoth is identified as 'He who counts for himself his left eye' (*Jp-n⸗f-jꜣb.t⸗f*).[457] As mentioned above, an earlier allusion to the role of Thoth as the divinity responsible for counting the eye may be found in spell 335 of the Coffin Texts and spell 17 of the Book of Going Forth by Day, where he is said to have restored it with the assistance of his fingers. The act of counting is of course also emphatically mentioned in the previous spell of the Book of the Moon, in which, as argued, the speaker assumes the identity of Thoth. In the temple of Esna, Thoth is said to count the constituent parts of the *wedjat*-eye in his form as the fiery bull,[458] so there he seems to be especially connected with the waxing phases. This once more underlines that in spell 156 the person counting the eye must be identical with Thoth.

Lines 12–13

jj.n⸗j m sḫm ḥr rḫ.n⸗j
n wḥm⸗j n rmṯ n ḏd⸗j n nṯr.w

I have come as a divine power for what I know.
I have not repeated it to other people, nor have I told it to the gods.

Just as in the previous spell, the speaker of *CT* 156 identifies himself with Thoth. This is clearly indicated by the statement that he has come as a divine power (*sḫm*), because this word is often used as an epithet of Thoth.[459] Already in the Pyramid Texts this nature of the god is apparent in connection with his role as the manipulator of the eye of Horus: '*N* is a divine power who claims his seat, that is Thoth whom Atum calls to the sky so that *N* take the eye of Horus to him' (*N pw sḫm dbḥ s.t⸗f Ḏḥwtj njs.w Tm jr p.t šdj N jr.t-Ḥr.w n⸗f*).[460] That the eye of Horus here should be understood as a symbol of the moon is implied on the one hand by the reference to the sky, and also by the description of the eye earlier in the texts as 'mighty and filled' (*jr.t-Ḥr.w wsr.t mḥ.t*).[461] Later sources also reflect the identification of Thoth as *sḫm*, and his epithets include. 'the *sḫm* of the gods', the divine *sḫm*', the great *sḫm*', and the venerable *sḫm*'.[462] The word *sḫm* is written with the eponymous sceptre (), and Thoth – besides being described in writing as a divine power – in visual representations appears as the sceptre itself, with facial features added to the depiction of the object. Such an image is found in the

[456] Rochemonteix 1892: pl. xxviib.
[457] Rochemonteix 1892: 274; Leitz 2002a: 215.
[458] Lieven 200: 84.
[459] Stadler 2012: 3.
[460] *Pyr.* §§2247d–2248a (utterance 724).
[461] *Pyr.* §2246e.
[462] Boylan 1922: 196.

temple of Seti I in Abydos (New Kingdom).[463] As for line 13, it repeats the statements of line 7, only in a reverse order, possibly to avoid monotonous repetition (line 7: *n ḏd=j ... n wḥm=j*, line 13: *n wḥm=j ... n ḏd=j*)

Lines 14–15

jnḏ ḥr=ṯn bꜣ.w Ḫmnw
rḫ.<k>w mj rḫ

Hail to you, *bas* of Hermopolis!
My knowledge is like that of a wise man.

The signs  at the end of the geographical name Hermopolis are obviously scribal errors that must have got into the text through an interference with the word  'town'. Line 15 differs greatly from the Asyut variants showing  . The standard interpretation of this line is the following: 'Hail to you, *bas* of Hermopolis, who know what Re desires' (*jnḏ ḥr=ṯn bꜣ.w Ḫmnw rḫ=w mr Rꜥ*).[464] The clearly legible text on Sen's coffin, however, is undoubtedly different, yet it hardly makes any sense. After the verb *rḫ* we have what seems to be the first person singular dependent pronoun, and this grammatical construction could be interpreted in two ways. On the one hand, the pronoun can be the object of the verb, which in this case is understood as an imperative, so the whole expression should read 'Know me!'.[465] This meaning does not really fit the context, so the other vague interpretation may be that *rḫ wj* is a participial or adjectival construction in which the dependent pronoun *wj* functions as the subject.[466] This would be an extremely rare grammatical construction which would not lead to any intelligible solutions as regards the meaning of line 15. Therefore it is a distinct possibility that the text is to some extent corrupt here. In my interpretation the initial word *rḫ* is followed by the first person singular ending of the stative, only the hieroglyph of the basket was for some reason omitted – a mistake that is shared by all the text variants.

The hoe, normally carrying the phonetic value *mr*, here in line 15, just as at numerous other places in the Coffin Texts, stands for the preposition *mj* 'like, according to'.[467] In two variants from Deir el-Bersha (B1C, B17C), the word is recorded with the usual sign. The hieroglyphs after the preposition can be seen as a *sḏm=f* form with the verb *rḫ* followed by the first person singular suffix pronoun, but it is more likely that here we have the noun *rḫ* meaning 'the knowing one, wise man',[468] where the human figure at the end acts as the determinative. This expression is of course a set phrase coming

[463] Stadler 2012: 7 fig. 10.
[464] cf. Faulkner 1973: 134; Barguet 1986: 573; Carrier 2006: 380–382.
[465] Nyord 2003: 82 n. 57.
[466] For the rare instances of first person singular adjectival sentences in which the dependent pronoun wj is the subject, see Gardiner 1957a: 109.
[467] cf. Molen 2000: 159.
[468] *Wb.* II, 445.17–18.

from the active participle of the verb *rḫ*. Thus the literal translation of the line would perhaps read 'I know like a wise man', but to reflect the connotations of the probable stative verb form in the original, expressing a state, rather than an action, I feel that the wording 'my knowledge is like that of a wise man' is more appropriate.

Lines 16–17

šw.t rd.t(j) dšr.t km.t(j)
nḫ m jp.w jp.t

The feather has grown and the Red Crown is whole,
so now there is rejoicing over what has had to be counted has been counted!

The stative forms of the verbs *rd* 'grow' and *km* 'complete' in line 16 express that the waxing period of the lunar cycle has been completed and now the full moon has arrived. This is, according to the text, also the time to take count of what has had to be counted, which must likewise be a reference to the middle of the month, or to the first half of the month from the retrospection of the full moon. No doubt, the appearance of the full lunar disc had a distinguished place in the course of days, as is attested in the lists of lunar feasts of all periods,[469] and in the descriptions of the lunar cycle, for example by its designation as the 'encounter of the two bulls' (*snsn kꜣ.wj*, i.e. the encounter of the two mighty lights in the sky).[470] The auspicious nature of the event is underlined by the use of the verb *nḫ* at the beginning of line 17, which is obviously the shorter form of the duplicate *nḫnḫ* 'to rejoice', 'to jubilate', which form is used in the Pyramid Texts.[471] This equivalence is supported by the replacement of the word with the semantically kindred *ršw* in the majority of the text variants. Another detail worth noting is the determinative after the word *jp.t* 'counting', which sign is often interchangeable with  denoting festivals (see for example the hieroglyphic text of line 19). This is perhaps due to the understanding of the act of counting as a festive occasion.[472] Line 17 as a whole is most probably an adverbial sentence with the infinitive of *nḫ* as the subject, so its literal meaning should be given as something like this: 'there is rejoicing in the calculations of counting'; for stylistic reasons I rephrased this statement into the form that I included in my translation.

Lines 18–21

jw=j rḫ.kw bꜣ.w Ḫmnw
šr.t m ꜣbd pw ꜥꜣ.t m smd.t pw
Ḏḥw.tj pw sštꜣ sjꜣ pw
rḫ.n=ṯ m pr-grḥ pw

[469] Eaton 2011: 231–235.
[470] Derchain 1962a: 30–31; Wilson 1997: 870–871.
[471] *Wb.* II, 312.11.
[472] For this, see Barguet 1986: 573.

I know the *bas* of Hermopolis.
It is the small eye on the second day of the lunar month, it is the great eye on the fifteenth day of the lunar month.
It is Thoth, it is the secret of the full moon,
and it is what you have learnt in the house of the night.

As has been correctly interpreted by previous researchers, the references to the small eye at the beginning of the month and the great eye in the middle of it describe the first crescent of the waxing moon and the full moon, respectively.[473] In connection with this statement, we must notice the presence of a widely used ancient Egyptian literary device, the thought couplet, in the rubric of *CT* 156. The two clauses containing the verb *rḫ* 'know' frame the nucleus of the assertion which clearly consists of two parallelisms. Thus both 'it is the small eye on the second day of the lunar month' and 'it is Thoth' refer to the beginning of the month – the connection in the first clause is obvious, while in the second one the name of the god invokes the feast of Thoth that was held on the first day of the lunar month (*psḏn.tjw*).[474] Similarly, 'it is the great eye on the fifteenth day of the lunar month' and 'it is the secret of the full moon' both describe the middle of the lunar month, and here the allusions are more palpable.

In my commentary on *CT* 155 I have already established that the expression *sjꜣ* can be associated with the period of the full moon. To my knowledge, another key expression, *pr-grḥ* 'the house of the night' is unattested elsewhere. While in the writing of *sjꜣ* the night sign is a determinative, here it must function as an ideogram. Thus the designation *pr-grḥ* may point to a temple precinct of Thoth, or to a part of his sacred enclosure, where the knowledge about the observation of the moon, and possibly of other celestial bodies, was recorded and archived. It may have been the place itself where the astronomer-priests (*wnw.tj*) worked at night and observed the night sky.

The *bas* of Hermopolis, as they are defined at the end of *CT* 156, display a marked difference as compared to the rest of the chapters in the Book of the Moon. In all the other spells the *bas* are divinities, whereas here in spell 156 the *bas* of Hermopolis are concepts. In the case of the second *ba* it can perhaps be argued that it has something to do with the god Sia, which was the understanding of some of the copyists of the descendant of spell 156, chapter 116 of the Book of Going Forth by Day,[475] but the third *ba* is undoubtedly described by a somewhat convoluted phrase.

---

473 Parker 1950: 12; Wallin 2002: 63.
474 cf. Cauville 2008: 32.
475 Lepsius 1842: pl. xliv.

2.4. Spell 157: the full moon

The hieroglyphic text

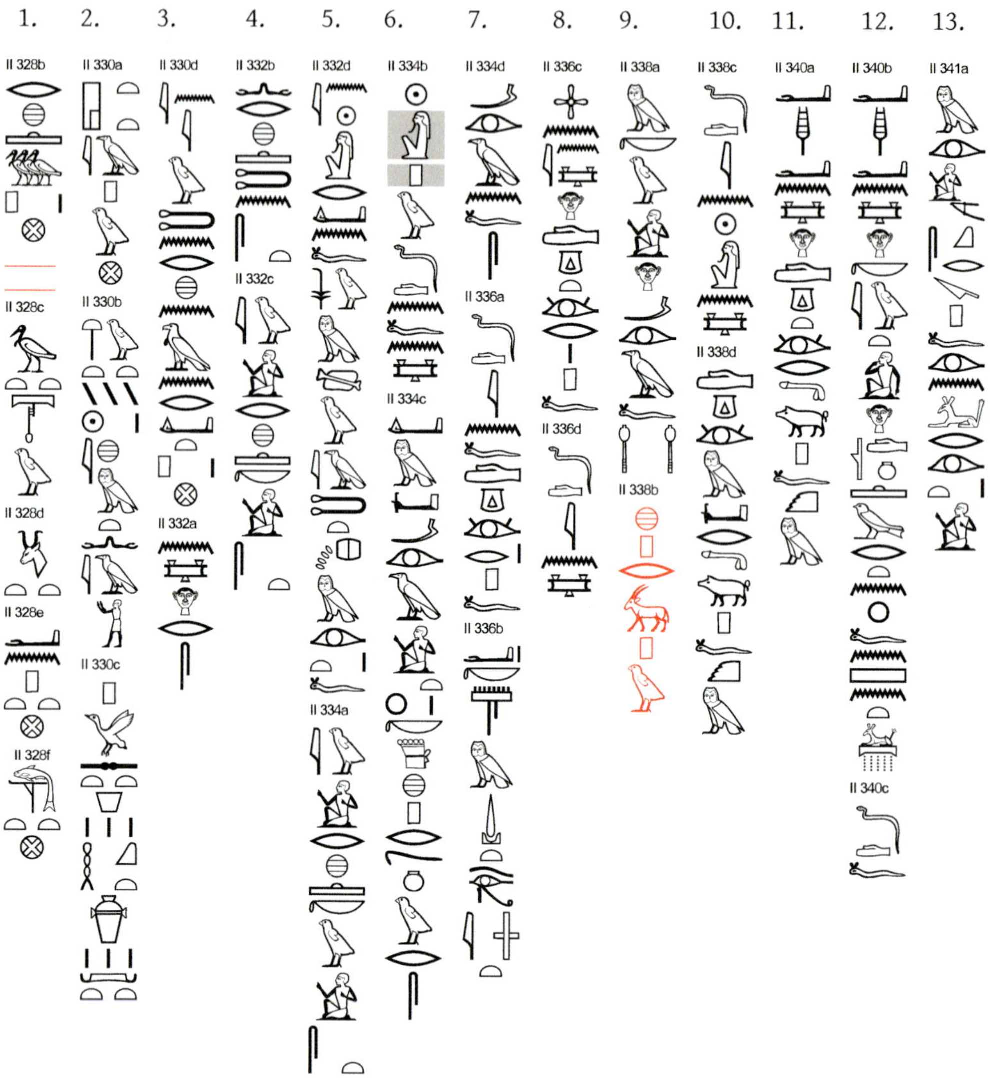

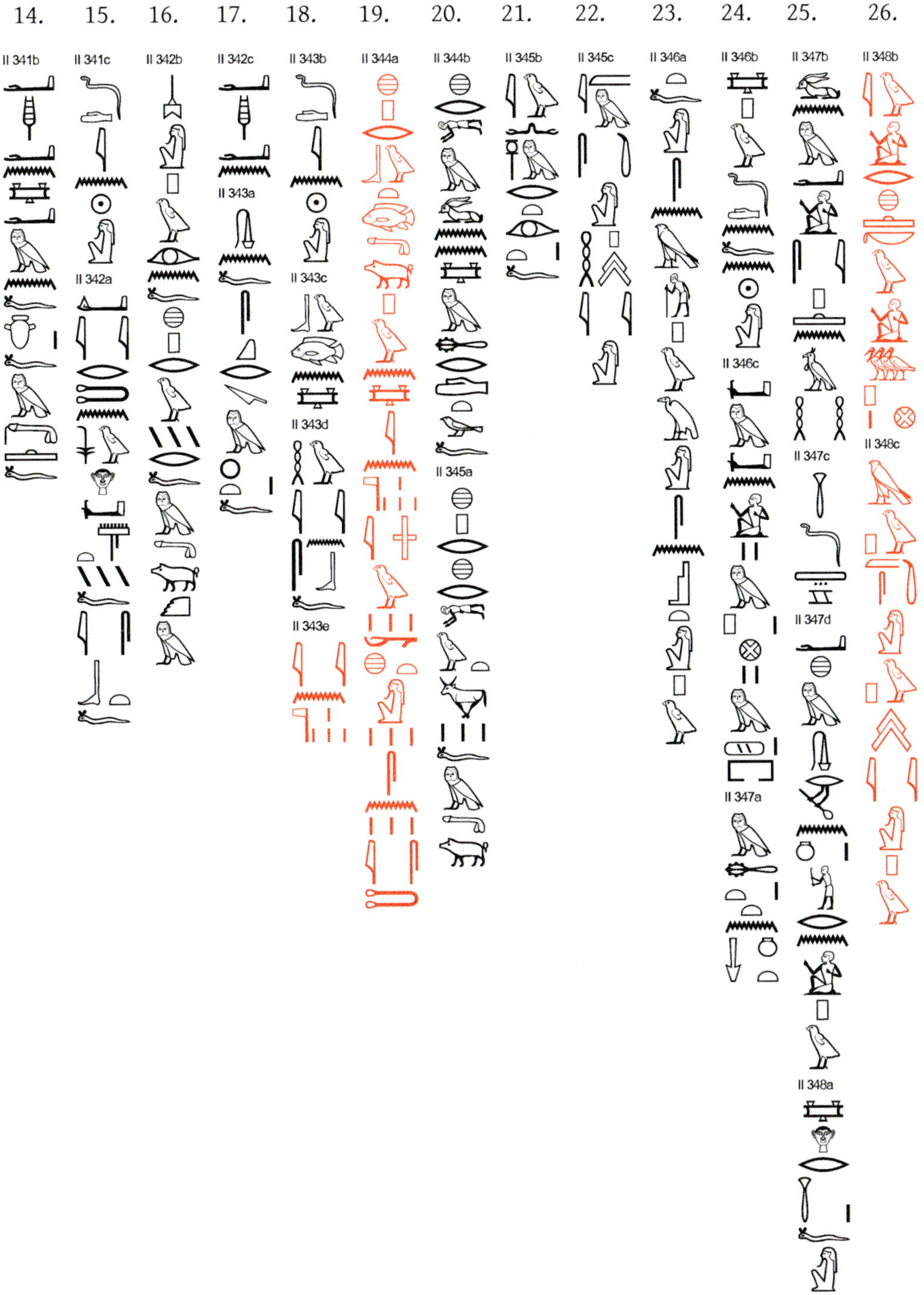
14. II 341b
15. II 341c II 342a
16. II 342b
17. II 342c II 343a
18. II 343b II 343c II 343d II 343e
19. II 344a
20. II 344b II 345a
21. II 345b
22. II 345c
23. II 346a
24. II 346b II 346c II 347a
25. II 347b II 347c II 347d II 348a
26. II 348b II 348c

Transliteration and translation

1. *rḫ bꜣ.w Pj bꜣ.tjt grḥ.w šsꜣ.tjt ꜥnp.tjt Ḥꜣ.t-mḥ.ytjt*
2. *ḥw.tjt-jꜣpw šw.tjt jḫm(.w) jꜣw Rꜥ pꜣsw.tjt ḥnq.t St.t*
3. *jn jw=ṯn rḫ.tjwnj rd.t Pj n Ḥrw ḥr=s*
4. *n rḫ=ṯn st jw=j rḫ.kw st*
5. *jn Rꜥ rdj n=f sw m jsw jꜣṯ.t m jr.t=f jw=j rḫ.kw st*
6. *Rꜥ pw ḏd.n=f n Ḥrw jmj mꜣꜣ=j jr.t=k ḏr ḫpr nw r=s*
7. *mꜣꜣ.n=f s(t) ḏd.jn=f dg r pf ꜥ=k ḥbs(.w) m wḏꜣ.t jmj.t*
8. *wn jn Ḥrw ḥr dg.t r pf ḏd.jn Ḥrw*
9. *mk wj ḥr mꜣꜣ=f ḥḏ.wj ḫpr mꜣ-ḥḏ pw*
10. *ḏd.jn Rꜥ n Ḥrw dg m-dj r(rj) pf km*
11. *ꜥḥꜥ.n Ḥrw ḥr dg.t r(rj) pf km*
12. *ꜥḥꜥ.n Ḥrw ḥr kjw.t ḥr qd wr[.t] n jr.t=f nšn.t ḏd=f*
13. *m(k) jr.t=j mj sqr pf jrj.n Stẖ r jr.t=j*
14. *ꜥḥꜥ.n Ḥrw ꜥm.n=f jb=f m-bꜣḥ=f*
15. *ḏd.jn Rꜥ dj r=ṯn sw ḥr ḥnk.wt=f j.s(n)b.t=f*
16. *Stẖ pw jrj.n=f ḫpr.w r=f m rrj km*
17. *ꜥḥꜥ.n stj.n=f sqr m jr.t=f*
18. *ḏd.jn Rꜥ bwj <rrj> n Ḥrw ḥwj snb=f jj.n nṯr.w*
19. *ḫpr bw.t rrj pw n Ḥrw jn nṯr.w jmj.w-ḫt=sn jsṯ*
20. *ḫr m wnn Ḥrw m ẖrd.t=f ḫpr ḫr.wt=f m rrj*
21. *jw.t mr.t jr.t=f*
22. *Jms.tj Ḥp.j <Dwꜣ-mw.t=f Qbḥ-sn.w=f>*
23. *jt=sn Ḥr.w-sms.w pw mw.t=sn ꜣs.t pw*
24. *Ḥr.w pw ḏd.n=f n Rꜥ jmj n=j 2 m Pj 2 m Nḫn m ẖ.t tn sn.wt*
25. *wn m-ꜥ=j sjp nḥḥ wꜣḏ tꜣ ꜥḫm ẖnn.w rn=j pw Ḥr.w-ḥr-wꜣḏ=f*
26. *jw=j rḫ.kw bꜣ.w Pj Ḥr.w pw Jms.tj pw Ḥpj pw*

1. Knowing the *bas* of Pe. Oh, the ones belonging to the *ba* of the night, the ones belonging to the night sky, Mendesians, inhabitants of the fish nome,
2. the ones of the *jꜣpw*-estate, the ones in the shade who do not know the praise of Re, the ones who belong to the makers of Nubian beer!
3. Do you know why Pe was given to Horus?
4. You do not know it, but I know it.
5. It was given to him by Re in compensation for the injury to his eye, I know it.
6. It was the case that Re said to Horus: 'Let me see your eye because this happened to it'.
7. As he looked at it, he said: 'Take a look at this part as your hand covers the sound eye there'.
8. And Horus looked at that part and said:
9. 'Behold, I see it as altogether white'. And this is how the oryx came into being.
10. Then Re said to Horus: 'Now look at this black pig'.

11. Horus looked at the black pig.
12. Then he shouted because of the grave condition of his raging eye, saying:
13. 'Behold, my eye is like the injury that Seth has inflicted on my eye'.
14. Then Horus collapsed before Re.
15. Then Re said: 'Put him in his bed until he gets well'.
16. It was Seth who took the form of a black big,
17. and caused an injury to his eye.
18. And then Re said: 'The pig is an abomination for Horus'. 'If only he recovered' said the gods.
19. This is how the pig became abominable for Horus by the gods in his retinue.
20. Because when he was a child, his sacrificial animal was the pig,
21. That is before the injury to his eye.
22. Imseti, Hapi, <Duamutef, Qebehsenuf>!
23. Their father is the elder Horus, their mother is Isis.
24. It was the case that Horus said to Re: 'Give me two in Pe and two in Nekhen from the group of these brothers.
25. Let me be the counter of eternity, the one who makes the earth verdant, the queller of disturbance in my name Horus-on-his-papyrus-column'.
26. I know the *bas* of Pe. It is Horus, it is Imseti, it is Hapi.

Commentary

Line 1

rḫ bȝ.w Pj

Knowing the *bas* of Pe.

As in all the first five spells of the Book of the Moon, the title promises to provide information about the *bas* of a locality (with the exception of spell 155 which, as we have seen, is concerned with the *bas* of the invisible moon). In Egyptian sources the *bas* of Pe usually appear together with the *bas* of Nekhen (Hierakonpolis), and this is also true for the Book of the Moon, because the *bas* of Nekhen will be the subject of the next spell (*CT* 158). The *bas* of the northern Egyptian town of Pe,[476] and of the southern Egyptian town of Nekhen, are sometimes seen as the representatives of the dual nature of Egyptian kingship.[477] In connection with this concept, probably the most common view is that the *bas* of Pe and Nekhen stand for the smaller territorial units of the Nile valley before the unification of Egypt, or perhaps more precisely for the royal ancestors who reigned in these regions.[478] This association may explain why they often feature in royal contexts. Depictions of the *bas* of Pe and Nekhen show

[476] Pe is a district of Buto, which was itself a very important settlement in the north of the country, see Altenmüller 1975b: 887–889.
[477] Vernus and Yoyotte 2003: 37.
[478] Žabkar 1968: 15–22.

them with the ceremonial *hn.w* gesture, which possibly originates from a ritual dance of some sort.[479]

These attestations, however, do not offer much help to understand why the *bas* of Pe and Nekhen play an important role in the lunar spells of the Coffin Texts. It is only in the Graeco-Roman Period when the *bas* of these ancient localities appear in a unanimously lunar context. On the ceiling of the pronaos of the Dendera temple, in the strip depicting the lunar cycle (first strip on the western half of the ceiling), they surround the barque that carries Osiris in the company of Isis and Nephthys.[480] According to its captions, the scene represents the moment when Osiris enters the moon on the fifteenth day of the month, that is when the full moon sets in.[481] This corresponds well with the Book of the Moon, because here also the *bas* of Pe are referred to in a text that, as we shall see in this analysis, relate the mythological stories connected with the time of the full moon.

The title of the spell is quite terse on Sen's coffin, and the coffins from Deir el-Bersha follow suit, with the exceptions of B1Y and B1L that display a longer, quite fragmentary title. With the help of the Asyut text variants, they can be easily reconstructed:

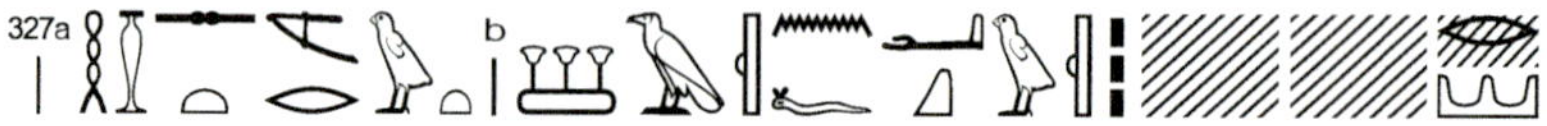

ḥs.t mr.wt šꜣ n=f ꜥq.w [m ẖr.t-nṯr]

Being praised and loved, and receiving offerings in the necropolis.

These are again general wishes that are quite often voiced in the Coffin Texts, so they cannot be directly linked to the particular contents of spell 157 with its allusions to the full moon. The longer titles on the Asyut coffins also belong to this same genre (as an example I give the version on S2P):

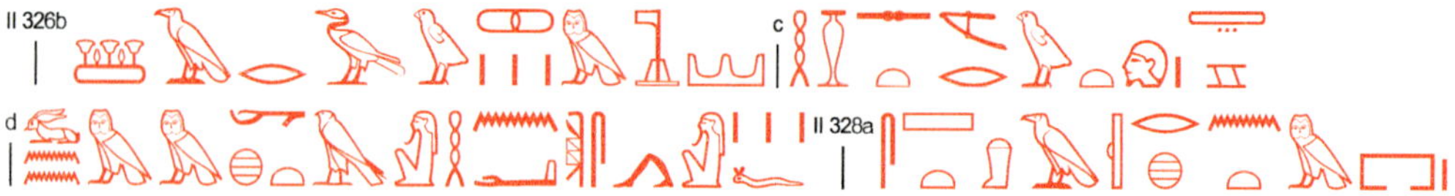

šꜣ r ꜥq.w m ẖr.t-nṯr ḥs.t mr.wt tp tꜣ wnn m m-ḫ.t Ḥr.w ḥnꜥ šms.w=f sštꜣ rḫ.n=ṯ m pr

[479] Junker 1940: 26.
[480] Cauville 2012: pl vi.
[481] Cauville 2012: 48–49.

Receiving offerings in the necropolis, being praised and loved on earth, being in the retinue of Horus together with his followers, the secret that you have learnt in the house.

The only remarkable detail here is the last statement, 'the secret that you have learnt in the house', which corresponds with the definitions of the last *ba* of the previous spell, 'the secret that you have learnt in the house of the night', though here the specification of the house as being connected with the night is missing.

Lines 1–2

b3.tjt grḥ.w šs3.tjt ꜥnp.tjt Ḥ3.t-mḥ.ytjt
ḥw.tjt-j3pw šw.tjt jḫm(.w) j3w Rꜥ p3sw.tjt ḥnq.t St.

Oh, the ones belonging to the *ba* of the night, the ones belonging to the night sky, Mendesians, inhabitants of the fish nome,
the ones of the *j3pw*-estate, the ones in the shade who do not know the praise of Re, the ones who belong to the makers of Nubian beer!

The text starts with an invocation to a rather large group of disparate beings. Grammatically these beings are defined by the plural feminine forms of *nisbe* adjectives. With the exception of *b3.t*, all the other nouns are also feminine in their singular common form, so it is not impossible that the word *b3.t* is used in the text because of the proximity of these other grammatically feminine nouns. The feminine derivative of *b3* with the *.t* ending, which seems to be included in *CT* 157, only appears much later again, in Graeco-Roman sources, as a designation for Hathor.[482] Thus I believe that the first group of divinities in line one should be understood as the *bas* of the night, who may have been seen as feminine, but not necessarily. Also, the expression 'night' has a plural *w* at the end, so a more literal translation '*bas* of nights' may be considered, but the ending here may again be just a sign of scribal sloppiness.

It seems to be a fair supposition that the list of beings invoked at the beginning of spell 157 has not been compiled haphazardly, and the members included in it are associated with or linked to lunar themes. However, the nature of this connection is for the most part obscure. While those belonging to the *bas* of the night or to the night sky can easily be seen as having something common with the moon, with the rest of the beings we can only make more or less well-informed guesses as to why they feature in a text about the mythological associations of the full moon.

It is worth noting that in *CT* II, 328d we find the hieroglyph  on the Deir el-Bersha coffins, whereas in all the Asyut text variants the sign  is recorded at the same place. This interchange is also present in spell 155: while in *CT* II, 300b the texts from

[482] *Wb.* I, 412.11; Wilson 1997: 305–306.

Deir el-Bersha write ,  or , the Asyut coffins replace it with . It is not impossible then that these two hieroglyphs,  and , are confused because their hieratic forms were somehow similar, though the documented hieratic writings do not show outstanding similarities.[483]

The reading of the nucleus of the second element in the list as *šsꜣ.t* seems secure, because this word on the one hand fits the context, and on the other is known to have appeared in texts that had lunar connotations. For example a passage from utterance 320 of the Pyramid Texts reads: ‘*N* has cleared the night, *N* has conducted the stars of the hours, the divine powers appeared in glory and dignified *N* in his form as Babi, *N* is the son of the unknown one, who delivered *N* to He-with-yellow-face, the lord of the night skies. Be great, you, lords, hide yourselves, you, common people, from *N*, because *N* is Babi himself, the lord of the night skies, the bull of the baboons, who lives on the ones that do not know him’ (*ḏsr.n N grḥ sb.n N wn.wt ḫꜥ sḫm.w sꜥḥ=sn N m Bꜣby N pj sꜣ pw n jḫm.t msj.n=s N n qnj-ḥr nb šsꜣ.wt wr ṯn nb.w jmn ṯn rḫ.t tp-ꜥ N N pj Bꜣby nb šsꜣ.t kꜣ jꜥn.w ꜥnḫ m ḫm=f*).[484] Philippe Derchain believes that in this text Babi, who is normally known as a demonic baboon representing sexual potency and vigour, refers to the moon, and his identity with this celestial body is reflected by his epithet ‘lord of the night skies’.[485] The name ‘He-with-yellow-face’ may also point to the moon,[486] as in fact the moon was associated with the face when it acted as the celestial ferryman with the names ‘He-whose-face-is-backwards’ or ‘He-who-sees-backwards’.[487] The word *šsꜣ.t*, as the determinative of its common spelling indicates,[488] is undeniably connected with the night, but its exact meaning is hard to grasp. The expressions ‘nightfall’, ‘starry sky’, ‘night sky’ are its usual translations, and according to the *Wörterbuch* ‘nightfall’ is the most common understanding of the word; the analysis of Erik Hornung shows, however, that it alludes to the dome of the night sky.[489] This meaning fits the context of *CT* 157 nicely, so I use it in my translation, though perhaps ‘nightfall’ would equally be appropriate, because the full moon indeed appears on the eastern horizon at around the time when the sun sets in the west.

The following two groups invoked are obviously related, because Mendes (*ꜥnp.t*) was the seat of the sixteenth nome in Lower Egypt (the fish nome, *Ḥꜣ.t-mḥyt*). The connection of the region with fish stems from the cult of a divine being there also called Hatmehit (*Ḥꜣ.t-mḥ.yt*, ‘foremost of the fishes’),[490] who is the consort of the chief god of the area, the ram of Mendes (Banebdjedet, *Bꜣ-nb-Ḏd.t*, ‘the *ba*, lord of Mendes’, see below).[491] Since Mendes and the fish nome are mentioned one after the other,

[483] Möller 1909: 14 no. 151 and 24 no. 257.
[484] *Pyr.* §§515a–516c.
[485] Derchain 1963: 23.
[486] Hornung 1961: 112.
[487] See Introduction.
[488] *Wb.* IV, 545.2–3.
[489] Hornung 1961: 112.
[490] Leitz 2002d: 17–18.
[491] Leitz 2002b: 683–685.

perhaps the speaker intends to name a larger group of people after a smaller one, and the translation should read: 'Mendesians, even (all) the inhabitants of the fish nome'. The settlement of Mendes is identified in the Egyptian sources by two geographical names, *Ḏd.t* and *ʿnp.t*,[492] the latter one being employed in our text. The name also occurs at two more places in the Coffin Texts (*CT* VI, 292f and 404h) but these other sources do not seem to provide any information on why the Mendesians are appealed to in spell 157. The local god of Mendes, Banebjedet – as indicated above – is associated with the other name (*Ḏd.t*), and it is perhaps his figure that justifies the appearance of this locality in *CT* 157. From line 5 we will learn that Pe was allocated to Horus by Re as a sort of compensation for his injured eye. This statement suggests that the sun god made this decision during the divine court process between Horus and Seth. In the New Kingdom story known as the Contendings of Horus and Seth (pChester Beatty I), at one point of the debate Re asks Banebdjedet to judge between the two opponents,[493] and this detail may establish a vague link between Mendes and the celestial eye of Horus (i.e. the moon).

The expression *ḥw.t-jꜣpw* does not recur elsewhere. According to Rami van der Molen, the second element of the compound is identical with the words *jꜣpj/jꜣpy/jꜣḥy* found in *CT* VI, 88f.[494] In my opinion, however, it is not impossible that *jꜣpw* ultimately comes from *jꜣf.w* on the basis of the well-known alteration between the phonemes *p* and *f*. The word *jꜣf.w* means 'discharge of the eye, tears',[495] and it seems that in spell 617 of the Coffin Texts it appears in a lunar context, too: 'Oh, Thoth, open your wing for me, because I am one of your nine *ka*s who live on the tears of your two eyes and on the hair of your armpit ... Behold, I have been commanded to you by the great encircler' (*j Ḏḥwtj wn n=j ḏnḥ=k jnk wʿ m psḏ.t=k pw kꜣ.w ʿnḫ.w m jꜣf.w n jr.tj=k m šnj jmj ḥṯṯ=k ... mk wi wḏt.w n=k jn dbn wr*).[496] The wing of Thoth was the symbol of the waxing moon,[497] so its mention supports the lunar interpretation of the text. However, in one text variant (B3Bo^{a}) the same words are spoken to Re, and not Thoth. This replacement may be explained by the fact that the spell features the dual form of the eye (*jr.tj*), so possibly a connection with both celestial eyes, the sun (Re) and the moon (Thoth), was established. In any case, the passage is quite obscure, and it is hard to determine the precise lunar connotations of the word *jꜣpw*/*jꜣf.w*, if it in fact had any.

In the next designation, 'the ones in the shade who do not know the praise of Re', the meaning of the individual elements does not pose any difficulties, but the overall message of the whole phrase – in the absence of comparable material – is harder to understand. In Asyut the phrase was reduced to *šw.tjt jꜣw* that translators render as

[492] *Wb.* V, 630.8 and I, 192.6–7.
[493] Gardiner 1932: 38; Lichtheim 1976: 215.
[494] Molen 2000: 13.
[495] *Wb.* I, 96.10 and Meeks 1980: AL 78.0152.
[496] *CT* VI, 228e–229f.
[497] Krauss 1997: 27, 31.

'sunshade-bearers of the adoration',[498] or 'femmes de l'ombre des acclamations (?)'.[499] In his note to the phrase, Raymond O. Faulkner also believes that it refers to female spirits.[500] The wording, however, is clearly different on the coffins from Deir el-Bersha. In my translation I suppose that Re precedes the words *jḫm.w j3w* due to honorific transposition and discard the possible rendering 'the ones in the shade of Re who do not know praise' (*šw.tjt Rꜥ jḫm.w j3w*), though this alternative of course cannot be ruled out categorically. Nevertheless, the description 'the ones in the shade who do not know the praise of Re' may refer to beings in the netherworld who never have the chance to meet Re or to bask in sunshine. Therefore, they also belong to the realm of the night.

The expression may be somehow connected with utterance 555 of the Pyramid Texts, too. The first part of this spell claims that Horus is crowned king in the town of Pe, so its initial topic can be linked to *CT* 157 in which Horus and the said locality also play an important role. Later the spell attains cosmic overtones, and in this part Thoth is invoked in the following way: 'Thoth, who is in the shade of his bush, put *N* on the tip of your wing on this northern side of the Winding Waterway' (*Ḏḥwtj jm.j-ḏr šw.t b3.t=f dj N tp ꜥnḏ dnḥ=k m pf gs mḥ.tj n mr-n-ḫ3*).[501] Unfortunately, the passage is rather enigmatic and the precise reference of Thoth's description as '(the one) who is in the shade of his bush' remains unclear. The mention of the celestial waterway no doubt establishes a heavenly context, and since Thoth and his wing are also named, it must involve some lunar connotations. For this it may be added that utterance 359 of the Pyramid Texts also associates the injury to the eye of Horus, the wing of Thoth, and the Winding Waterway in the sky.[502]

If the understanding of the phrase about the beings in the shade who do not know the praise of Re is problematic, the last element in the list of invocation is perhaps even more elusive. The traditional rendering of *p3sw.tjt ḥnq.t St.t* is 'brewers of Nubian beer',[503] and the expression 'Nubian beer' (*ḥnq.t St.t*) is already attested in the Pyramid Texts.[504] However, *p3sw.tjt* seems to be a hapax, occurring only in spell 157 of the Coffin Texts and its descendant, chapter 112 in the Book of Going Forth by Day. On the Asyut versions the expression indeed has the determinative of a squatting person, but this detail is missing in the Deir el-Bersha variants, where we find a hieroglyph showing a vessel (▽) as the determinative. On the basis of this, it cannot be stated with absolute certainty that *p3sw.tjt* originally – or always – referred to people; the expression may just be connected with a container of beer used in the preparation – or in the

[498] Faulkner 1973: 135.
[499] Carrier 2004: 385.
[500] Faulkner 1973: 136, n. 3.
[501] *Pyr.* §1377a–c.
[502] *Pyr.* §§594–596; Faulkner 1969: 116.
[503] cf. Faulkner 1973: 135; Carrier 2004: 385.
[504] *Pyr.* §91b.

consumption – of the beverage. This would allow for a translation as 'the ones who belong to the vessel of Nubian beer'.

The hieroglyphic writing of *pꜣsw.tjt* on the Deir el-Bersha coffins, with the determinative of the vessel, very much resembles the word denoting the water bowl of the scribes called *pꜣs*,[505] but it is unlikely that a connection with this object should be sought, because then the reference to the Nubian beer would hardly make any sense. Howsoever it is the case, the expression is really enigmatic. The allusion to an alcoholic drink perhaps refers to people celebrating the full moon. The consumption of intoxicating liquids at festivals was common practice in ancient Egypt, though again the principal sources date from the Graeco-Roman era. The best known occasion of this kind was the *tḫj*, 'the festival of intoxication' celebrated for Hathor in Dendera.[506] Though in the Egyptian documents there is no evidence for the consumption of alcoholic drinks at the monthly lunar feasts (day of invisibility, first-crescent day etc.), and the feast of *tḫj* seems to be solar in nature, since the cult statue of Hathor merged with sunshine on the roof of the temple during the festivities,[507] this wider context may be the reason for the appearance of beer or beer-brewers in spell 157 of the Coffin Texts.

Lines 3–4

jn jw⸗ṯn rḫ.tjwnj rd.t Pj n Ḥrw ḥr⸗s
n rḫ⸗ṯn st jw⸗j rḫ.kw st

Do you know why Pe was given to Horus?
You do not know it, but I know it.

The topic of special knowledge also features heavily in spells 155 and 156 of the Book of the Moon, so these lines repeat that motif. As is clear from the commentary on line 2, Horus was associated with the town of Pe already in the Pyramid Texts. While utterance 555 lays an emphasis on the royal implications of this connection, other texts suggest that Horus and Pe are also linked in the Osirian cycle of myths. From certain references in the Pyramid Texts it transpires that Isis gave birth to Horus at a location called Khemmis (Egyptian *ꜣḫ-bj.t*),[508] and according to later tradition this place was in fact near Pe.[509] The proximity of the two locations is already implied in utterance 701 of the Pyramid Texts: 'Horus comes from Khemmis and Pe is ready for him so that he could be purified there' (*prj Ḥrw m ꜣḫ-bj.t ꜥḥꜥ Pj n Ḥrw wꜥb⸗f jm*).[510] The same idea is present in the Coffin Texts: 'Oh, people, look at *N*, the son of Isis, he was

[505] *Wb.* I, 499.5.
[506] Grimm 1994: 374.
[507] Grimm 1994: 31.
[508] *Pyr.* §1204a–c, §1703c.
[509] Herodotus, *The Histories* II.156, see Godley 1920: 469.
[510] *Pyr.* §2190a–b.

conceived in Pe, he was born in Khemmis' (*rḫ.yt mꜣꜣ n N sꜣ ꜣs.t jwr[=f] m Pj ms(.w)=f m ꜣḫ-bj.t*).[511] The magical-medical Metternich stela, dated to the 4th century BCE, confirms the connection of Horus with Pe, because its inscriptions state that after having cured Horus of his scorpion bite, Thoth addresses the inhabitants of the Delta, and especially the nurses of Pe, emphasising that the child god is under their protection.[512] A stela with hieroglyphic inscriptions, most probably fashioned in Buto in the 1st century BCE, underlines the ties of the place with the moon. Buto is the name of the town that originally consisted of the twin settlements of Pe and Dep.[513] The inscriptions on the stela reveal that the Egyptians – as part of a sort of pilgrimage – travelled to Buto at the time of the full moon in order to make an oath before the goddess Hathor, and to visit the tutelary goddess of the Delta, Wadjet, who was supposed to help the pilgrims in bearing children.[514] The full moon is most probably mentioned here in association with its beneficial effects on fertility, which concept is well documented in the Egyptian sources.[515] Spell 157 of the Coffin Texts, however, is not concerned about fertility, so no direct links between it and the later stela can be inferred as regards Horus, Pe, and the full moon, but the motif of associating Buto (and thus Pe) with the full lunar disc is worth mentioning.

Line 5

jn Rʿ rdj n=f sw m jsw jꜣṯ.t m jr.t=f jw=j rḫ.kw st

It was given to him by Re in compensation for the injury to his eye, I know it.

The comments on the previous line have made it clear that Horus was associated with Pe for various reasons. The stories about Osiris and Isis locate the birth and childhood of Horus in and around Pe, and Pe is also the scene of the appearance of Horus as king. This latter event may also have been part of the myth about Osiris and his family, but it may equally have had it roots in predynastic Egypt when Pe and Dep were important cult centres in the northern sphere of the land before unification.[516] Howsoever it was the case, line 5 adds yet another dimension to the relationship of Horus with Pe, because by stating that the town was a compensation for the injured eye of Horus, it also evokes the cosmic myths related to this body part of the god. Since – as the meaning of his name 'the distant one', 'the one high up' indicates – Horus was also a god embodying the sky, his two eyes represented the two brightest celestial features, the sun and the moon.[517]

---

[511] *CT* IV, 37e–h (B1C).
[512] Scott 1951: 213.
[513] Altenmüller 1975b: 887.
[514] Rutherford 2007: 137–138.
[515] Smith 2002: 125–126.
[516] Tristant and Midant-Reynes 2011: 45–54.
[517] Wilson 1997: 286.

At the same time, the motif of compensation can also be seen to allude to the mythological episode when, after the death of Osiris, Horus and Seth vie for his inheritance – the rule over Egypt itself – through a divine legal process. This court case is alluded to for example in utterance 477 of the Pyramid Texts and spells 7–9 of the Coffin Texts,[518] but its most detailed description is preserved in the New Kingdom popular story entitled in Egyptological literature as the Contendings of Horus and Seth (or the like).[519] These sources, however, do not provide any information on the subject of line 5 of *CT* 157, that is, why Pe was given to Horus as a sort of compensation. The boasting of the speaker, and the large groups of ignorant people named at the beginning of the text, suggest that this detail of the story was not well-known, so perhaps that is the reason for the lack of other relevant references.

It should also be noted that not all researchers interpret the injury inflicted on the eye of Horus as a symbolic reference to cosmic events.[520] The adherents of this viewpoint maintain that the struggle between Horus and Seth reflects the political strife between the northern and southern parts of the land before unification, and the undeniable astral allusions, which are mostly attested from Graeco-Roman sources, were only later incorporated into the myth.[521] However, it is quite obvious that in spell 157 the injury to the eye connotes celestial – and more specifically, lunar – events, and this shows that the identification of the contestants in the story of Horus and Seth with the participants of mundane or political rivalries is oversimplifying the message and contents of the myth.

Lines 6–9

Rʿ pw ḏd.n=f n Ḥrw jmj m33=j jr.t=k ḏr ḫpr nw r=s
m33.n=f s(t) ḏd.jn=f dg r pf ʿ=k ḥbs(.w) m wḏ3.t jmj.t
wn jn Ḥrw ḥr dg.t r pf ḏd.jn Ḥrw
mk wj ḥr m33=f ḥḏ.wj ḫpr m3-ḥḏ pw

It was the case that Re said to Horus: 'Let me see your eye because this happened to it'. As he looked at it, he said: 'Take a look at this part as your hand covers the sound eye there'.
And Horus looked at that part and said:
'Behold, I see it as altogether white'. And this is how the oryx came into being.

Spell 157 describes two different injuries to the eye of Horus, and it associates both of them with an animal: the first one, which is the subject of lines 6–9, with the oryx, and the second one, as we shall see, with a black pig. On the level of natural phenomena these two injuries correspond to a lunar eclipse and the onset of the waning moon,

518 *Pyr.* §§956–959; *CT* I, 21a–27d,
519 For the hieroglyphic text, see Gardiner 1932: 37–60, for a translation Lichtheim 1976: 214–223.
520 cf. Westendorf 1980: 49.
521 Griffiths 1960: 124–127.

and the descriptions of these developments in the text comply with the chronological order in which these two events actually happen. A lunar eclipse can only occur at opposition, that is, at the time of the full moon, and waning obviously starts after this phase of the lunar cycle. A lunar eclipse lasts much shorter than the waning period, only a few hours, and the transitory nature of the phenomenon is emphasised when Re asks Horus to take a look at his eye being covered by his own hand, and Horus replies that he sees his eye still bright. The parallel with a lunar eclipse is clear: the moon first becomes totally or partially darkened, according to the type of eclipse, and then within a few hours it once more shines as a full lunar disc in the night sky.

The poetic statement about the reappearance of the full moon, 'Behold, I see it as altogether white' (*mk wj ḥr m33=f ḥḏ.wj*) is linked in the text through a wordplay to the oryx, called *m3-ḥḏ* in Egyptian. This sort of etymologising is not unique in the vast body of funerary literature. A similar example can be found in the Pyramid Texts, where the close ties of Osiris to Sokar are explained and highlighted by the desperate cry for help – *sj=k r=j* 'Go away from me!' – uttered by Osiris after Seth had attacked him.[522] The god Sokar is also interesting here because the prow of his processional barque, carrying the cult image of the divinity at his annual festival at Memphis, was adorned by the backwards-looking head of an oryx.[523] It is generally believed that the trophy of the oryx attached to the front part of the barque expressed the victory of order over chaos, because the oryx, an animal living in desert regions, was deemed to represent Seth, and the unruly world that he stood for.[524]

A series of sources from Late Period and Graeco-Roman Egypt prove that the oryx was in fact one of the general symbols of chaos, and its ritual slaying amounted to conquering the forces opposed to the establishment of order. Almost every Graeco-Roman temple has a scene on their walls showing the pharaoh killing the oryx and guaranteeing his own victory over his enemies.[525] For the same reasons on the magical and healing stelae that depict the child Horus taming dangerous animals (*Horus cippi*), he does not only overpower crocodiles, scorpions, and snakes, but in his right hand he also customarily holds an oryx.[526] Although none of the sources assigning an undoubtedly negative role to the oryx are older than the second half of the New Kingdom, it is highly likely that the animal was viewed as the symbol of the forces of disorder earlier, too.[527]

It is also clear, however, that the oldest depiction of the sacrifice of the oryx has lunar connotations. The scene is found on the northern wall of the birth chamber of the Luxor temple, together with other scenes, including notably the one that shows

[522] *Pyr.* §1256c.
[523] Kitchen 1975: 622.
[524] Wilson 1997: 406.
[525] Derchain 1962b: 39–62; Wilson 1997: 406.
[526] Kákosy 1999: 18.
[527] Kákosy 1999: 18.

Amenhotep III presenting the cult object called *šb.t* to the goddess Mut.[528] This object, which was referred to in later texts by the designations *wnšb* or *wtṯ*, usually shows a baboon sitting on top of the sign *nb* or *ḥ3b*, and leaning onto a column (the sign *ḥn*).[529] Its precise meaning is debated; on the one hand, because similar objects have in fact come down to us, they were used as water clocks,[530] while on the other, in the ritual scenes – as stylised objects lifted from their original sphere of application – they represented the cyclical nature of time.[531]

The relevant scenes in the Graeco-Roman temples reveal that when the king – either as the son of Thoth or in one of his other capacities that are related to Thoth – presents the symbol to a goddess, usually Hathor, she in return ensures that the two eyes take their appropriate places in the sky, and she hands over to the king everything that the two celestial eyes, the sun and the moon, can encompass with their vision.[532] Therefore, on the cosmic level the object *šb.t/wnšb/wtṯ* symbolises the interrelated movements of the sun and the moon. This system has two distinguished settings: conjunction (the alignment of the sun and the moon at the time of the latter one's invisibility) and opposition, that is, the time of the full moon, when the satellite of the earth is furthest from the sun. These associations may explain why the scenes showing the presentation of the *šb.t* and the slaying of the oryx are put side by side in the temple at Luxor.

The connection of the oryx with the moon is more straightforward in the pronaos of the Edfu temple, as the title of the sacrificial scene reads: 'Slaying the oryx. To be recited: The oryx is burnt and killed as the *wedjat*-eye is provided with its constituent elements. Moon, come so that you may wander through the sky and your movement could be whole and sound' (*sm3 m3-ḥḏ ḏd-mdw mḥ nsr.tw m3-ḥḏ m ds.tw wḏ3.t ʿpr.tw m r.w=s ḥr.j-j3b.t m ḫns=k m ḥ3j.t nm.t=k jr m ʿḏ wḏ3*).[533] Not only does the oryx appear together with the moon, but the full moon is also alluded to, because in the texts describing the filling of the *wedjat*-eye, the act of providing the eye with its components is often intertwined with the appearance of the full moon.[534] The association of the oryx with the full moon can also be inferred from another scene on the enclosure wall: 'Slaying the oryx. To be recited: The *wedjat*-eye is whole, oh, mighty one, lady of Bubastis (= Bastet), the robber of the *wedjat*-eye no longer exists' (*sm3 m3-ḥḏ ḏd-mdw wḏ3.t wḏ3.tj wsr.t nb.t B3s.t ḫnp wḏ3.t nn wnn=f*).[535] However, the link between the oryx and the full moon is perhaps most unambiguously stated on the propylon of the Khonsu temple at Karnak, where the sacrifice of the animal is specified to take place during the

528 Gayet 1894: pl. lxviii.
529 Sambin 1987.
530 Sambin 1987: 291–292.
531 Wilson 1997: 238.
532 Wilson 1997: 238.
533 Chassinat 1928: 138–139.
534 cf. Chassinat 1932: 139.
535 Chassinat 1932: 132.

opposition of the sun and the moon: 'Khonsu-Moon ... rises from the eastern mountain as the solar disc is on the western mountain' (*Ḫ̮ns.w-Jʿḥ ... wbn m B3ẖw jw jtn m ʿnḫ̮.t*).[536]

Also, the ties between the oryx and the full moon are apparent from the rest of the inscriptions next to the scene of slaying the animal in the pronaos of the Edfu temple. The king carrying out the ritual is described as: 'The effective god, the excellent heir of Horus, lord of Hebenu, who slays the enemy of the *wedjat*-eye, the oryx, on the sixth day of the month' (*p3 nṯr mnḫ̮ jwʿ.w mnḫ̮ n Ḥrw nb Ḥbn.w sn sbj n wḏ3.t m3-ḥḏ m sn.wt*).[537] We should not forget that the sixth day of the lunar month (*sn.wt*) signified the fullness of the moon in Heliopolitan theology.[538] The different variants of chapter 80 of the Book of Going Forth by Day clearly attest that the terms 'sixth day' (*sn.wt*) and 'fifteenth day' (*smd.t*) were used interchangeably, since there the rescue of the eye of Horus from its non-existence variously takes place on either day.[539] All this evidence associating the oryx with the full moon preclude the possibility that the horns of the animal could be the symbols of the first dark part on the lunar disc after its fullness.[540] This is also contradicted in the text of *CT* 157 by the claim of Horus that, after its temporary unease, his eye is hale again.

Much later than the New Kingdom, the oryx again appears as a symbol of the full moon and a coincidental lunar eclipse in the round Dendera zodiac that is found in the second eastern Osirian chapel on the roof of the temple there. A specific day, which happened to be not only the day of the full moon on which a lunar eclipse was observed, but also the day of the autumnal equinox, 25 September 52 BCE, was marked in the zodiac in the first place by the lunar disc encircling the *wedjat*-eye.[541] Next to this disc a rather curious figure is depicted: a squatting baboon carrying an oryx on its back. As I argued in my analysis of the Dendera zodiacs, both the baboon – which is a prime lunar symbol, anyway – and the oryx are linked to the disc containing the *wedjat*-eye, and the whole ensemble of the three figures, as a sort of paraphrase of the *wensheb*, was included in the decorative programme of the round zodiac to underline the importance of the day of 25 September 52 BCE, when the full moon coincided with the autumnal equinox.[542] The oryx is featured in the round zodiac in all probability to refer specifically to the contemporaneous lunar eclipse, just as it is referred to in connection with the same event in spell 157 of the Coffin Texts.

The oryx is also described as the enemy of the moon by the Greek writer Horapollo (4th or 5th century CE), who says that this animal – instead of greeting the rising moon – emits an unfriendly groan and fixes his eyes on the ground, while scratching the earth

[536] Sethe and Firchow 1957: 49 [61b].
[537] Chassinat 1928: 129.
[538] Smith 2002: 122.
[539] Allen 1960: 156 n. f.
[540] cf. Leitz 1994: 269.
[541] Aubourg 1995: 10, without mentioning the autumnal equinox.
[542] Priskin 2015b: 161–162.

with its hooves.[543] Since according to Horapollo the oryx is equally hostile towards the rising sun, it is not impossible that his reference to the rising moon means the full moon, because this is the moment during the lunar cycle when the moon 'copies' the movement of the sun by rising on the eastern horizon and setting in the west. This interpretation may find some backing in another claim of Horapollo, namely, that the Egyptian kings use the oryx as a sort of gnomon to determine the exact rising of the moon according to the forecast of the astrologers;[544] as we could see, in the Graeco-Roman temple scenes it is also the time of the full moon when the pharaoh, at least, symbolically, comes into contact with the oryx.

Lines 10–13

ḏd.jn Rʿ n Ḥrw dg m-dj r(rj) pf km
ʿḥʿ.n Ḥrw ḥr dg.t r(rj) pf km
ʿḥʿ.n Ḥrw ḥr kjw.t ḥr qd wr[.t] n jr.t⸗f nšn.t ḏd⸗f
m(k) jr.t⸗j mj sqr pf jrj.n Stẖ r jr.t⸗j

Then Re said to Horus: 'Now look at this black pig'.
Horus looked at the black pig.
Then he shouted because of the grave condition of his raging eye, saying:
'Behold, my eye is like the injury that Seth has inflicted on my eye'.

While the events involving the oryx are concerned with lunar eclipses, in the next part of the spell the explanation of the monthly waning of the moon features another animal, a black pig. The word *rrj* may mean pig in general,[545] but its determinative (𓂸) indicates that the animal responsible for the injury to the eye of Horus is a male. It seems that the Egyptians made a fine distinction between the malicious male pig or boar (*rrj*), and the female sow (*šꜣj*), seen as the symbol of life and death.[546] It must be noted, however, that there are some overlappings in the lexical sources concerning the different names of the pig. Both *rrj* and *šꜣj* can mean pig in general,[547] and the masculine *rrj* can be easily distinguished from its feminine counterpart, *rr.t*,[548] while *šꜣj* in itself can refer to both a male pig (or boar) and a sow.[549] The picture is further complicated by the existence of its feminine form, *šꜣj.t*, documented from the Late Period on, which obviously referred to a sow.[550] The confusion between the two expression, *rrj* and *šꜣj*, is palpable in spell 112 of the Book of Going Forth by Day, which is of course the descendant of *CT* 157. Even within one text variant, pNebseni from the

543 Horapollo, *Hieroglyphics* I.49, see Boas 1993: 65.
544 Horapollo, *Hieroglyphics* I.49, see Boas 1993: 65–66.
545 *Wb.* II, 438.7.
546 Velde 1992: 576.
547 *Wb.* II, 438.7, IV, 405.7.
548 *Wb.* II, 438.8–11.
549 *Wb.* IV, 405.9–10.
550 *Wb.* IV, 405.7–11.

18th dynasty, the two terms are used interchangeably.[551] As for *rrj*, it is in all probability an onomatopoeic word,[552] and its spelling is rather peculiar on Sen's coffin, insofar as it is written with just one *r* (the 'mouth' sign), instead of the usual two.[553]

I will analyse the relationship of Seth with the pig in the comments on lines 16–17, but here the close ties between this animal and the moon must be discussed from a more general perspective. Several Greek and Roman authors writing about Egypt report on this connection. Herodotus relates that although the pig is considered unclean by the Egyptians, at the time of the full moon they sacrifice a pig to the moon itself and Dionysus,[554] that is, Osiris, as Herodotus equated this Greek god with the ruler of the underworld.[555] Plutarch also says that in Egypt pork was consumed at the time of the full moon only once a year,[556] and he links this custom with the god Seth (see below). According to him, the animal is impure because it tends to copulate when the moon is waning. Aelian in his work about the world's fauna, written around the turn of the 2nd/3rd centuries CE, says that the pig is especially detestable for the sun and the moon, and the Egyptians only sacrifice it at the annual festival of the moon.[557]

The annual lunar festival mentioned by Plutarch and Aelian is surely identical with an entry for the first month of the third season (I *šmw*, Pachons) in the festival calendar of the Edfu temple (1st century BCE): 'the festival of the fifteenth lunar day of this month, the day of filling the *wedjat*-eye, a great festival in the whole country ... a pig is slaughtered and placed on the altar of the riverbank' (*smd.t n ꜣbd pn hrw mḥ wḏꜣ.t ḥꜣb ꜥꜣ m tꜣ ḏr≠f ... snq.tw jpḥ dj ḥr ḫꜣw.t n wḏb*).[558] It should be noted that in this Ptolemaic text yet another expression, *jpḥ*, is used for the pig, which – according to the *Wörterbuch* – first appeared under the 20th dynasty.[559] The difference that sets it apart from the other two words for the animal possibly lies in the fact that it refers to the household mammal as an offering.[560] Notably, the pig was ritually slaughtered in the month of Pachons (*pꜣ-n-Ḫ̌ns.w*), which was of course named after one of the principal lunar gods, Khonsu.[561] Therefore the calendar entry from Edfu confirms the ties between the pig and the moon not only with its contents, but also with its timing within the civil calendar.

The earlier pBrooklyn 47.218.84, the mythological manual about the cults in the Delta, dated to the 7th century BCE, also associates the pig and the moon. One of its passages reads: 'And a pig injured the eye of Re and swallowed some of its liquid' (*wn.jn šꜥj nkn.n≠f*

[551] Lapp 2004: pl. 19 (col. 5–8 – *rrj*, col. 9–11 – *šꜣj*). See also the chapter on the survival of the Book of the Moon.
[552] Velde 1992: 571.
[553] cf. for example Lapp 2004: pl. 19.
[554] Herodotus, *The Histories* II.47, see Godley 1920: 335.
[555] Herodotus, *The Histories* II.156, see Godley 1920: 469. See also Newberry 1928: 213.
[556] Plutarch, *De Iside et Osiride* 8, see Griffiths 1970: 129.
[557] Aelian, *De Natura Animalium* X.16, see Scholfield 1959: 307.
[558] Chassinat 1930: 354; Grimm 1994: 105, 197.
[559] *Wb.* I, 69.14.
[560] Meeks 2006: 82.
[561] Depuydt 1997: 126–130.

jr.t-Rʿ snnm.n=f ẖ.t m rd̠.w=s).[562] Surprisingly, the text names the moon as the eye of Re, which is usually identified with the sun.[563] This identity is stated in no uncertain terms in chapter 17 of the Book of Going Forth by Day by a gloss appended to the claim of the deceased that he has seen Re being born from the hind parts of the celestial cow, Mehetweret, explaining the whole phenomenon as 'this is the image of the eye of Re, whose birth is adored every day' (*tw.t pw n jr.t-Rʿ dwꜣ r ms.wt=f rʿ nb*).[564] However, the context of the sentence about the pig in pBrooklyn 47.218.84, later mentioning the sanctuary called 'the mansion of the net', and associated with the lunar god Thoth, clearly shows that there the expression *jr.t-Rʿ* refers to the moon, and the pig – just as in the other Egyptian sources – attacks this celestial body.[565]

In the story of pBrooklyn 47.218.84 the pig consumes the liquid or efflux of the lunar eye, so there is perhaps some remote connection between this act and the *ḥw.t-jꜣpw* appearing at the beginning of the spell, which – as I argued for it above – could be interpreted as 'the mansion of the discharge of the eye'. However, the precise connotations of the liquids or tears of the eye remain quite obscure. Therefore it is also a possibility that we should not read too much into these references. Perhaps the more abstract mythological and astral motifs are just mixed with the simpler knowledge about the anatomy of the eye.

Apart from the written accounts discussed in the previous paragraphs, some visual representations also provide evidence for the close relations of the pig with the moon. One of these is a faience container from the Middle Kingdom that is shaped as a half-cylinder and has five compartments within its interior.[566] Both ends of the object display a curious decoration: a pig and fifteen dots are inscribed into a well-formed circle. The number of these dots may allude to the days of waxing,[567] and consequently to the day of the full moon (its name in Egyptian, *smd.t*, is indeed spelled with the number fifteen), and thus the whole depiction may be related to the later accounts of the major lunar festival. When Herodotus describes it, he adds that at the time of the full moon the different parts of the pig – the tail, spleen, stomach, and the fat around it – are held together during the offering ritual.[568] It is therefore a distinct possibility that the different compartments of the half-cylindrical vessel were destined to contain the different parts of the animal's body. The partition into five spaces, on the other hand, may also stem from the fact that the numbers fifteen and thirty, which are inherently connected with the lunar month, can both be divided by five.[569]

---

[562] Meeks 2006: 14 (pBrooklyn 47.218.84 VI, 6–7).
[563] *Wb.* I, 107.8.
[564] Lapp 1997: pl. 3–9.
[565] Meeks 2006: 219–221.
[566] Friedman 1998: 137.
[567] Lieven 2007: 178 n. 987.
[568] Herodotus, *The Histories* II.47, see Godley 1920: 335
[569] Lieven 2007: 178 n. 987.

Another scene where the pig makes an appearance is found in the sixth hour of the New Kingdom Book of Gates.[570] It shows the judgement hall of Osiris with the god sitting on his throne on a slightly elevated platform. A pair of scales is in front of him, the support of which is a human mummiform figure; its pans – unlike in the vignettes of chapter 125 of the Book of Going Forth by Day – are empty.[571] A flight of stairs leads up to the platform of Osiris and the scales, and on the stairs nine figures (ennead) are approaching them. A barque is depicted above these figures in which a monkey, with a stick in its hand, seemingly tries to repel a pig. Another monkey with the same posture also appears either aboard the barque, in front of the pig, or outside the barque on the right, depending on the different variants of the scene.[572] Although the association of this scene with the moon is not straightforward, based on the assumption that the balance is meant to determine the missing part of the *wedjat*-eye, quite probably it has some lunar connotations.[573] These may be underlined by the presence of the flight of stairs, because in the Graeco-Roman temples of Edfu and Dendera the waxing period was often represented by a staircase showing the divinities filling the *wedjat*-eye, who are depicted either on the steps or poised before them.[574] The monkey driving away the pig thus may represent the same idea, that is, the repulsion of the dangers to the moon, which eventually makes waxing and the onset of the full moon possible.

Yet another pictorial attestation of the close ties between the pig and the moon comes from the much later Dendera temple. The astronomical ceiling of its pronaos was decorated in the 1st century CE, including the easternmost strip known as one half of the rectangular zodiac of Dendera.[575] Here, in the sign of Pisces we see a striding human figure, most probably Osiris himself,[576] as he is holding a pig by the hind legs. The animal is definitely a pig here, and this fact must be emphasised because a very similar depiction is also included next to the sign of Pisces in the round zodiac of Dendera.[577] Because of the state of preservation of this object, the contours of the animal are hard to make out, so there is a controversy whether it represents a pig,[578] or a baboon.[579] The seemingly corresponding depictions in the two zodiacs are, however, quite different: in the round zodiac a static female figure holds the animal by one of its rear legs, whereas in the linear zodiac, as mentioned above, the striding figure of Osiris holds both rear legs of the pig together. These differences make it highly unlikely that the figure inscribed into a disc and holding a pig represents a solar eclipse, similarly to the corresponding depiction of a woman in the round zodiac.[580]

---

[570] Hornung 1999: 62–63.
[571] Manassa 2006: 138.
[572] Manassa 2006: 122.
[573] Manassa 2006: 137–141.
[574] Derchain 1962a: 25–26; Herbin 1982: 240–243; Priskin 2016c: 132–133.
[575] Cauville 2012: pl. viii.
[576] Priskin 2015b: 170.
[577] Cauville 1997: pl. 60.
[578] Lieven 2000: 157 n. 458; Leitz 2006: 287, 302–304.
[579] Cauville 2013: 540–541.
[580] cf. Cauville 2013: 541.

It is equally implausible that the picture of Osiris holding the pig should be equated with a constellation in the vicinity of Pisces.[581] Such a view woefully disregards the Egyptian written and iconographic traditions about the astral connotations of the pig.

In my analysis of the Dendera zodiacs, I have argued that the depiction of Osiris with the pig within the lunar disc in the rectangular zodiac refers to the appearance of the full moon in the sign of Pisces on the day of the autumnal equinox (24 September) in the year 36 CE.[582] This interpretation implies that in the pronaos of the Dendera temple the pig is once more represented in connection with the full moon. While the similarly positioned depiction in the round zodiac refers to a solar eclipse, and thus the animal included in it may not be a pig, the well-discernible figure of the animal is drawn on this artefact, too, as one of the decans of Taurus. I have also analysed this feature of the round zodiac, and has established that the pig was used as an image for the middle decan of Taurus because the great annual lunar feast in the month of Pachons was celebrated at the time of the year when the sun was dwelling in the sign of Taurus (i.e. the sun was crossing Taurus during the civil month Pachons at the epoch when the zodiac was created, in the 1st century BCE).[583]

The black colour of the pig in spell 157 of the Coffin Texts may of course allude to the imminent waning of the moon, when on successive days ever larger portions of the lunar disc become darkened.[584] The colour black thus appears in the text in connection with the pig, the instigator of waning, whereas the actions of the oryx are described with the word 'cover' (*ḥbs*). The choice of words possibly reflects the actual visual observation of the moon, since during an eclipse the moon only becomes dim, usually attaining a red hue, but it does not completely turn dark. Therefore it is a mistake to amend the story about the oryx with the insertion of the adjective 'black'.[585]

Lines 14–15

ꜥḥꜥ.n Ḥrw ꜥm.n=f jb=f m-bꜣḥ=f
ḏd.jn Rꜥ dj r=ṯn sw ḥr ḥnk.wt=f j.s(n)b.t=f

Then Horus collapsed before Re.
Then Re said: 'Put him in his bed until he gets well'.

The literal translation of the reaction of Horus to the attack of the black pig is 'he swallowed his heart' (*ꜥm.n=f jb=f*). This idiomatic phrase has some diverse meanings, such as 'to be discrete', 'to keep a secret', 'to forget', and 'to lose consciousness'.[586]

581 cf. Leitz 2006: 303.
582 Priskin 2015b: 171.
583 Priskin 2016b: 86–90.
584 Leitz 1994: 269–270.
585 cf. Faulkner 1973: 135.
586 *Wb.* I, 184.14–15; Faulkner 1962: 42; Hannig 1995: 139.

My rendering 'to collapse' reflects this last translation, which – together with the penultimate one – must come from a meaning that originally connoted the loss of one's faculties to act or behave intentionally, or to use one's brain effectively. The use of the phrase with the verb *ꜥm* may be the outcome of a deliberate editorial choice. Both in the Book of Gates and pBrooklyn 47.218.84 the actions of the pig are described by the same verb. In the barque in the judgement hall of Osiris, the pig being chased by the monkey is called *ꜥm(.w)* 'the swallower',[587] while the monkey is said 'to make what has been swallowed be spat out' (*dj⸗f nẖ ꜥm*).[588] In the papyrus about the myths of the Delta, after being confronted with his act of eating from the liquid of the eye of Re, the animal replies: 'I did not swallow it' (*nn ꜥmꜣ st*).[589] So perhaps the use of the phrase *ꜥm jb⸗f* in spell 157 conjured up the deeds of the malevolent pig, too, for the knowledgeable readers.

Horus falls ill by taking a look at the black pig and this event heralds the beginning of the waning period. The illness of Horus is a motif that also appears in connection with the pig in pBrooklyn 47.218.84, and the text relates that the animal causes the disease *ḥmw.t-sꜣ* 'to come forth' from the body of Horus (*prj.n⸗s m jwf⸗f m ḥmw.t-sꜣ*).[590] From the context and demotic parallels it seems that *ḥmw.t-sꜣ* is some sort of a skin disease,[591] and not a kind of demonic obsession, as has been believed previously.[592] Though Dimitri Meeks does not mention it, the nature of the disease may be supported by the accounts of Plutarch and Aelian who say that the people making contact with the pig are prone to come out in a rash.[593]

The bodily weakness of Horus is also described in pBrooklyn 47.218.84 in connection with the period of 'covering the head' (*ḥbs tp*) that encompasses the waning and invisible phases of the moon. At this time 'Horus was sitting in his house angrily and lamented his eyes as his strength diminished' (*ḥms Ḥr.w m pr⸗f špwt jkb.n⸗f ḥr jr.wj⸗fj nḏs pḥ.tj⸗f*).[594] The same story is already included in the lunar chapter of the Fundamentals of the Course of the Stars, attested from the Osirieon at Abydos built by the 19th dynasty pharaoh Seti I, and from much later hieratic/demotic papyri.[595] The supposition that the withdrawal of Horus into his house was connected with his illness caused by a pig seems to be corroborated by the writing of the relevant name of the god 'Horus in his house' (*Ḥr.w-jmj-pr⸗f*) with the sign of the pig as the determinative on a Theban coffin, in Coffin Texts spells 67 and 839.[596]

[587] Manassa 2006: 122–123.
[588] Manassa 2006: 125.
[589] Meeks 2006: 14–15.
[590] Meeks 2006: 14.
[591] Meeks 2006: 80.
[592] cf. *Wb.* III, 85.3.
[593] Plutarch, *De Iside et Osiride* 8, see Griffiths 1970: 126–129; Aelian, *De Natura Animalium* X.16, see Scholfield 1959: 307.
[594] Meeks 2006: 14 (pBrooklyn 47.218.84, VI, 3).
[595] Lieven 2007: 97–98.
[596] *CT* I, 288h and VII, 44a; Lieven 2007: 177–178.

Lines 16–17

Sth̲ pw jrj.n=f ḫpr.w r=f m rrj km
ꜥḥꜥ.n stj.n=f sqr m jr.t=f

It was Seth who took the form of a black big,
and caused an injury to his eye.

The struggle between Horus and Seth involving serious injuries inflicted on each other is a mythological episode that is already alluded to in the Pyramid Texts.[597] Only those aspects of this myth will be discussed here that directly relate to *CT* 157, either through the identification of Seth with a pig or other tangible lunar connotations. The connection between Seth and the pig is best elaborated not in an Egyptian text, but in the treatise of Plutarch about Isis and Osiris.[598] He says that the sacrifice of the pig and the consumption of pork during the full moon at the great annual lunar feast is linked by the Egyptians to the story that Seth chanced upon the coffin of Osiris while he was chasing a pig at the light of the full moon, then cut up Osiris' body and disseminated the pieces all over the country. Osiris was thoroughly identified with the moon by Graeco-Roman times, so in this story his body represents the moon, and more precisely – when it is still intact – the full moon. Just as in spell 157 of the Coffin Texts, the appearance of the pig in the narrative leads to its downfall (waning).

There is also some iconographic evidence for the connections of the pig with Seth. About a century ago Percy Newberry suggested that the animal traditionally representing Seth was in fact a pig.[599] His idea – we may say, perhaps justifiably – did not find many followers,[600] except for Samuel Mercer,[601] and the common scholarly opinion, probably accepted by the majority of researchers, now holds that the animal of Seth is a mythical and hybrid creature that merges the characteristics of various animals such as the dog, ass, and pig.[602] It must be noted, however, that Seth can assume the identity of the pig in certain scenes, as is evidenced for example by some images on the walls of the Edfu temple.[603]

Although the conflict between Horus and Seth is one of the major themes in the Pyramid Texts, the first narrative that seems to put it, at least partly, in an expressed lunar context is the New Kingdom tale that has already been cited several times along the commentary here (the Contendings of Horus and Seth). In one of its episodes Seth invites Horus to spend a pleasant day together at his home, and then during the

597 Griffiths 1960: 1–27.
598 Plutarch, *De Iside et Osiride* 8, see Griffiths 1970: 126–129.
599 Newberry 1928: 217–219.
600 Griffiths 1960: 32; Velde 1977: 13–26.
601 Mercer 1949: 53.
602 Velde 2001: 269.
603 Newberry 1928: 214 pls 1–3; Velde 1992: 576

night he tries to make love to him.[604] However, Horus collects Seth's semen with his hands and the next day he turns to his mother, Isis, for help. Isis cuts off the hands of Horus, throws them into water, grows new hands for his son, then takes a vessel and collects Horus' semen in it. She goes to Seth's garden and spreads the sperm of Horus on the lettuce that Seth is said to eat every day. When Seth consumes the lettuce, he conceives from Horus. However, he summons Horus to the divine court again believing that with his masculine act on Horus the previous night, he has proved the unsuitability of Horus to take the inheritance of his father, Osiris. At the court Horus proposes to call out his own semen and that of Seth as well, and to see where they come forth from. So now Thoth first calls Seth's semen, which comes forth from the midst of the marshes. Next Thoth appeals to the semen of Horus, which first refuses to surface through the ears, and then grows on the top of Seth's head in the shape of a golden disc. Seth immediately attempts to remove the disc, but now Thoth grabs it and puts it on his own head.

The emphatic role of Thoth, the pre-eminent lunar deity, in the story suggests that it has to be understood within a lunar framework, but because the adornment growing from Seth's head is called a 'golden disc' (*jtn n nbw*), scholarly opinion is divided about it being the symbol of the sun or the moon.[605] However, Frédéric Servajean argues convincingly that in the story of Horus and Seth the golden disc stands for the moon. To sum up briefly the cornerstone of his arguments, he reckons that because according to the 'divine anatomy' of the Egyptians silver corresponds to the bones (the masculine side of the body), and gold to the flesh (the feminine constituent), this latter material symbolises that eventually Seth ends up having the feminine role in his relationship with Horus.[606] Servajean also associates the golden disc with the natural phenomenon that the full moon close to the horizon, at the beginning of his nocturnal orbit, may get a colouring that can be considered rather golden than silver.[607]

Another argument for equating the golden disc on the head of Seth may be derived from the name of the moon in pBrooklyn 47.218.84, 'the eye of Re', which is also a designation that was primarily reserved for the sun. The apparent confusion behind these descriptions must be due to the Egyptian perception that the full moon was basically the equal counterpart of the sun, as it copies its diurnal course during the night (rises as a full disc at dusk, crosses the whole span of the sky, and then sets in the west).[608]

At this point we have to return to lines 6–9 of our text and the description of a lunar eclipse with reference to the oryx, because another piece of evidence for the lunar connotations of the homosexual episode in the story of Horus and Seth may be the

[604] Lichtheim 1976: 219–220; hieroglyphic text in Gardiner 1932: 37–60.
[605] For bibliographic references, see Servajean 2004: 125.
[606] Servajean 2004: 136–140.
[607] Servajean 2004: 146.
[608] cf. Chassinat 1928: 211.

preceding narrative,[609] which also seems to display some lunar overtones. Here we learn that the ennead acting as the judges at the divine court wants to punish Horus because he – in his anger that the harpoon of his mother inadvertently also hit him during his underwater struggle with Seth – has cut off Isis' head and left with it to the mountains. The disappearance of the head of the goddess is perhaps a lunar allegory itself. Next, however, Seth happens to find Horus in the mountains and rips off his two eyes (*jw⸗f rwj wḏꜣ.tj⸗fj m s.t⸗w*).[610] Horus, downcast because of the loss of his eyes, is then encountered by Hathor who cures his eyes with the milk of a gazelle (*gḥs.t*), and so they heal (*mnq*) and become sound again.

There are some obvious parallels between this story and spell 157 of the Coffin Texts, since both relate that Horus loses his eye or eyes for a while, then regains his vision. In both narratives an animal from the family of antelopes and living in the semi-arid areas, an oryx or a gazelle is associated in some way with the recovery of the eye. We should not forget, however, that the New Kingdom story of Horus and Seth is perhaps intended as a caricature of the official myth, which is evidenced by the unfavourable traits of the protagonists (Horus is a physically weak but cunning 'goblin', Seth is a behemoth with limited intelligence), and several other details (for example the reputedly carnivorous Seth only eats lettuce).[611] So it is possible that the positive role of the gazelle is also a form of irony. The oryx is undeniably the symbol of chaos and disorder, so the reference to the gazelle in healing Horus' eyes may be the reversion of the traditional perception of the oryx. It is another detail worth noticing that the eyes of Horus are called 'the two sound eyes' (*wḏꜣ.tj*); the sound eye (*wedjat*-eye) of course often represented the full moon. All these niceties of the narrative underline that the story of Horus and Seth has some astral and lunar connotations.

In line 17 the reading of the verb collocating with injury (*sqr*) is problematic. On Sen's coffins, like on two other coffins from Deir el-Bersha (B2P, B1C), it is written with the brazier sign (𓊮). From the phonetic spellings of the verb as *wdn* on other coffins (B2Bo, B4Bo, B9C), it seems that it entered the text through a confusion with the hieroglyph of the pestle and mortar (𓍑) which indeed has such a phonetic value. The verb means 'to be heavy',[612] or 'to be weighty of striking power',[613] so in this case the literal translation would perhaps read: 'Seth pounded an injury' in the eye of Horus. Alternatively, perhaps a connection may be sought with another verb, also spelled *wdn*, meaning 'to pierce', but only attested from Graeco-Roman times.[614] The Asyut text variants feature the verb *stj* 'to shoot', possibly from an earlier interpretation of the sign of the brazier standing for these sounds (originally perhaps from the homophonous verb *stj* 'to set

[609] Gardiner 1932: 49–50; Lichtheim 1976: 219.
[610] Gardiner 1932: 50.
[611] Redford 2001: 294.
[612] *Wb.* I, 390.1–15.
[613] Molen 2000: 107.
[614] *Wb.* I, 389.9.

fire', 'to light').[615] This latter possibility seems to me the most plausible, so I take the brazier sign on Sen's coffin to have the phonetic value *stj*.

Lines 18–21

ḏd.jn Rꜥ bwj <rrjy n Ḥrw ḥwj snb≠f jj.n nṯr.w
ḫpr bw.t rrj pw n Ḥrw jn nṯr.w jmj.w-ḫt≠sn jsṯ
ḫr m wnn Ḥrw m ẖrd.t≠f ḫpr ḫr.wt≠f m rrj
jw.t mr.t jr.t=f

And then Re said: 'The <pig> is an abomination for Horus'. 'If only he recovered' said the gods.
This is how the pig became abominable for Horus by the gods in his retinue.
Because when he was a child, his sacrificial animal was the pig,
That is, before the injury to his eye.

These lines, similarly to the statement about the oryx in line 9, explain the taboo concerning the pig within the framework of an aetiological myth, though it is not entirely clear how the announcement of Re and the wish of the gods are connected with the development that the pig has become detestable for Horus. I have already referred above to the sources that forbid the consumption of pork with the exception of the annual lunar feast of the full moon in Pachons. The text also states that as a child Horus did not refrain from eating pork, and on the lunar level this claim may be related to the stages of the life cycle of the moon, as they are reported on the propylon of the Khonsu temple at Karnak. The relevant passage reads: 'he comes as a child, the head enduring, being mysterious, they say, in his name He-who-repeats-his-forms; the moon in his forms is, when he is young, a fiery bull, when he is old, a steer, because he is darkened' (*jw≠f m nḫn tp wꜣḥ štꜣ ḫr.tw m wḥm-qj≠f jꜥḥ m jr.w≠f ḏr sẖrd≠f kꜣ psj m kḥkḥ≠f sꜥb pw ḥr jr.t n≠f snk*).[616] The childhood of the moon is obviously the period of waxing, when it is described as 'He-who-repeats-his-forms' (*wḥm-qj≠f*).[617]

The ritual regulation that pork can only be eaten at the time of the full moon is confirmed by a gloss attached to the next chapter of the Book of the Moon, spell 158 of the Coffin Texts, on a coffin from Asyut. This spell, as we shall see, corresponds to the waning phases of the lunar cycle, and a closing formula complementing the main body of the text stipulates about the proper use of the spell: 'Not to be said when eating pork' (*n ḏd ḥr wnm rrj*).[618] This is yet another proof of the correctness of the statements made by the classical authors that the slaughter of the pig was connected with the full

615 *Wb.* IV, 330.5–12.
616 Sethe and Firchow 1957: 74 [89b].
617 Derchain 1997: 75.
618 *CT* II, 362c.

moon. As a consequence, the view that *CT* 157 is concerned with the waning phases, whereas the following *CT* 158 deals with waxing,[619] is hardly acceptable.

Lines 22–23

Jms.tj Ḥp.j <Dwꜣ-mw.t⸗f Qbḥ-sn.w⸗f>
jt⸗sn Ḥr.w-sms.w pw mw.t⸗sn ꜣs.t pw

Imseti, Hapi, <Duamutef, Qebehsenuf>!
Their father is the elder Horus, their mother is Isis.

Sen's text, just as all the other variants on the coffins from Deir el-Bersha, seems to be faulty here, because it only names the first two sons of Horus. Only the coffin of Nakht (S2P) lists all the four sons. The lack of Duamutef and Qebehsenuf is not the outcome of editorial considerations, but either a scribal error or a loss resulting from the repeated copying of the text, because line 24 of spell 157 talks about the division of the four sons into two groups, and this statement presupposes an earlier reference to the whole group. Richard O. Faulkner believes that the invocation to the four sons of Horus is out of place and was inserted awkwardly into the text, and – agreeing with Kurt Sethe – he also thinks that the listing of their names identifies the retinue of Horus (see line 19).[620] There is no doubt that here a new section of the text starts, but it seems that it is also rife with lunar connotations. The four sons of Horus – Imseti, Hapi, Duamutef, and Qebehsenuf – are a divine group that appears in a variety of roles, and the best known is perhaps their protection of the canopic containers holding the internal organs of the deceased.[621] We must suppose, however, that they appear in *CT* 157 because of their connections with astral or lunar contexts. Though they have been associated with different constellations in the northern and southern skies,[622] and also with the five falcons depicted in Graeco-Roman lunar scenes to represent the period of the moon's invisibility (Horus and his four sons),[623] to understand their significance in spell 157, we have to turn to the lists from Graeco-Roman Egypt preserving the days of the lunar month, and to their predecessors, the processional scenes of the New Kingdom astronomical diagrams. In these diagrams, two files of divine figures, with the lunar disc on their heads, approach from the two sides the images representing the northern constellations in the middle.[624]

First, however, it must be pointed out that the list in the text includes not only the four sons, but also one of the hypostases of Horus and Isis. They are said to be the parents of the four sons, and although in the text they follow their children, logically speaking

[619] Leitz 1994: 269–271.
[620] Faulkner 1973: 136 n. 12.
[621] Dodson 2001: 562.
[622] Mathieu 2008b: 11–14.
[623] Cauville 2011: 47.
[624] Neugebauer and Parker 1969: 3–4, 194.

they must head the list. This supposition is confirmed by Coffin Texts spell 404, in which they appear in the same order when the parts of the celestial ferry transporting the deceased are inventoried: 'Tell me my name, say the oars. The fingers of the elder Horus. Tell me my name, says the bailing scoop. The hand of Isis emptying the blood from the eye of Horus. Tell me my name, say the planks of the ship's body. Imseti, Hapi, Duamutef, Qebehsenuf, Haqu, Irimaua, Maanitef, Irirenefdjesef.' (*ḏd rn⸗j jn wsr.w ḏbʿ.w n.w Ḥr.w-sms.w ḏd rn⸗j jn mḏ3b.t ḏr.t pw n.t 3s.t pnq.t snf m jr.t Ḥr.w ḏd rn⸗j jn wgs.w m ẖ.t⸗s Jms.tj Ḥp.j Dw3-mw.t⸗f Qbḥ-sn.w⸗f Ḥ3q.w Jrj-m-ʿw3.y M33.n-jt⸗f Jrj-rn⸗f-ḏs⸗f*).[625]

The four divinities besides the sons of Horus – *Ḥ3q.w* 'the plunderer', *Jrj-m-ʿw3.y* 'he who acts as a robber', *M33.n-jt⸗f* 'he who sees his father', and *Jrj-rn⸗f-ḏs⸗f* 'he who makes his name himself' – also establish a direct link with the later lunar processions, because they make an appearance there, too. Already in the Pyramid Texts the celestial ferryman was identified with the moon,[626] so the parts of his ship were naturally matched with the gods that were linked to the days of the lunar month, possibly as their protectors. The information about Horus and Isis also supports the lunar origins of *CT* 404. We shall see that in the later lunar lists they stand for the second and third days of the month, that is, for days on which the first waxing crescent may appear. So the fingers of Horus may allude to filling the *wedjat*-eye that was associated with the fingers of Thoth in spell 335 of the Coffin Texts and chapter 17 of the Book of Going Forth by Day.[627] The lunar connotations are much clearer in the case of Isis, since the statement that her hand drains the blood from the eye of Horus is a direct reference to the healing of the celestial eye, and thus to the beginning of the waxing period.

To get a better understanding of the four sons of Horus in terms of their lunar associations, we can establish their precise position in the lunar lists. In line 25 another eponymous god of these lists will appear, Horus-on-his-papyrus-column, so he is also included in the comparative table that presents information from the following sources (besides spell 157): the astronomical ceiling in the tomb of Senenmut,[628] the astronomical diagrams related to Senenmut's ceiling,[629] the astronomical ceiling of the Ramesseum,[630] the procession of lunar days in the astronomical frieze in the pronaos at Edfu,[631] and the list of lunar days on the ceiling of the pronaos of the Dendera temple.[632]

From the data in Table 1 it transpires that the lists in the first two columns (Middle Kingdom), in the two middle columns (New Kingdom), and in the last two columns (Graeco-Roman Period), are understandably quite similar. The last two lists are

[625] *CT* V, 191c–192e (B9C).
[626] Krauss 1997: 67–85; Allen 2002: 63.
[627] Robins and Shute 1987: 14.
[628] Dorman 1991: 144.
[629] Neugebauer and Parker 1969: 195.
[630] Neugebauer and Parker 1969: 196–197;
[631] Brugsch 1883: 46.
[632] Cauville 2008: 32–33.

practically identical. The changes suggest that the original list – seven entries of which appear in *CT* 157 – was modified in the New Kingdom, as indicated by the appearance of a new name, *Jrj.n-ḏ.t⸗f* 'He who makes his body'. After some further alterations a different list became canonical in the Ptolemaic era that dropped Haqu and Irimaua, replaced the elder Horus with Horus-the-protector-of-his-father (*Ḥr.w-nḏ-jt⸗f*), and substituted Osiris for Isis. These changes may have been intentional, because the new figures are related to their predecessors, but they may have equally resulted from textual corruption, because the writings for the two forms of Horus and for Isis and Osiris could have easily been mixed up.

	***CT* 157**	***CT* 404**	**Senenmut**	**Ramesseum**	**Edfu**	**Dendera**
1.						
2.	[elder Horus]	elder Horus			Horus-protector-of-his-father	Horus-protector-of-his-father
3.	[Isis]	Isis	Isis		Osiris	Osiris
4.	Imseti	Imseti	Imseti	Imseti	Imseti	Imseti
5.	Hapi	Hapi	Hapi	Hapi	Hapi	Hapi
6.	Duamutef	Duamutef	Duamutef	Duamutef	Duamutef	Duamutef
7.	Qebehsenuf	Qebehsenuf	Qebehsenuf	Qebehsenuf	Qebehsenuf	Qebehsenuf
8.		Haqu	Maanitef	Maanitef	Maanitef	Maanitef
9.		Irimaua	Iriendjetef	Iriendjetef	Iriendjetef	Iriendjetef
10.		Maanitef	Irirenefdjesef	Irirenefjesef	Irirenefdjesef	Irirenefdjesef
11.		Irirenefdjesef	Haqu	Haqu		
12.			Irimaua	(Ramesses)		
13.				Irimaua		
17.	Horus-on-his-papyrus-column				Horus-on-his-papyrus-column	Horus-on-his-papyrus-column

Table 1 The divine group of Coffin Texts spell 157 in the later lunar scenes and lists.

The table shows the position of the gods of the lunar month according to the Graeco-Roman lists (numbers in first column), so in effect it projects this arrangement back onto the earlier sources (where references to specific days are missing). The first day is *psḏn.tjw*, the day of lunar invisibility protected by Thoth (not indicated in the table). Imseti is associated with the fourth day whose name is 'the going forth of the *sem*-priest' (*pr.t-sm*). As we have seen it, the appearance of the *sem*-priest on the morning of the fourth day probably celebrated the beginning of the healing process of the eye of Horus (i.e. the start of waxing).[633] The list of the group of gods in *CT* 157 starting with Imseti, but in a sense having the elder Horus as its first element, therefore once more

[633] See above and Meeks 2006: 14.

alludes to the beginning of the month, so that later it could also conjure up the full moon with the mention of another member of the lunar lists, Horus-on-his-papyrus-column (see below).

Line 24

Ḥr.w pw ḏd.n=f n Rꜥ jmj n=j 2 m Pj 2 m Nḫn m ẖ.t tn sn.wt

It was the case that Horus said to Re: 'Give me two in Pe and two in Nekhen from the group of these brothers'.

The text undeniably talks about the division of the four sons of Horus into two groups (see also the comments above), so this also strongly suggests that the absence of Duamutef and Qebehsenuf on Sen's coffin and in the Deir el-Bersha text variants resulted from a scribal mistake or textual corruption. From spell 158 it is clear that Duamutef and Qebehsenuf are assigned to the town of Nekhen. Pe and Nekhen are found in Lower and Upper Egypt, respectively, so they express the idea of duality in geographical terms; also they may be seen to allude to the unity arising from this duality (the whole of Egypt). The sons of Horus are known to embody similar concepts in other contexts. On Middle Kingdom coffins Imseti and Hapi appear on the head end, so theoretically in the north, while Duamutef and Qebehsenuf are situated at the foot end, and thus symbolically in the south.[634] In the tomb of Ay (18th dynasty) Imseti and Hapi are wearing the Red Crown of Lower Egypt, while Duamutef and Qebehsenuf the White Crown of Upper Egypt.[635] In the Book of the Moon the division of the four sons of Horus into two groups may point to the dual nature of the lunar cycle, consisting of waxing and waning, and its totality encompassing both periods. Notably, Imseti and Hapi appear in spell 157 which belongs to the first half of the lunar cycle, while Duamutef and Qebehsenuf play their role in spell 158 which is about the second half of the month (waning). However, as we have seen, all four sons of Horus belong to the first few days of the month in the lunar processions.

Line 25

wn m-ꜥ=j sjp nḥḥ wꜣḏ tꜣ ꜥḫm ḫnn.w rn=j pw Ḥr.w-ḥr-wꜣḏ=f

'Let me be the counter of eternity, the one who makes the earth verdant, the queller of disturbance in my name Horus-on-his-papyrus-column'.

In the transliteration of the first part of this line as *wn m-ꜥ=j* and translating it as a wish I follow Faulkner.[636] The name with which Horus identifies himself, Horus-on-his-papyrus-column, as I indicated above, is a direct reference to the eponymous god

634 Willems 1988: 140.
635 Mathieu 2008b: 10.
636 Faulkner 1973: 136 n. 14.

of the seventeenth day of the lunar month, since in the later lunar lists he regularly appears in that capacity. This day was significant in ancient Egypt, because – due to the complexity of the lunar cycle – in the framework of the Egyptian lunar month it signalled the latest time at which the full moon could occur.[637] In other words, the full moon could arrive between days fourteen and seventeen. That the Egyptians were aware of this fact is suggested by the identical names of these days within the lunar month.[638] Thus, towards the end of the spell that is concerned with the mythological events around the full moon, the latest possible date for the sighting of this phenomenon is alluded to through the name of Horus-on-his-papyrus-column.

The importance of the seventeenth day of the month is also underlined in Plutarch's account of the myth of Osiris. He says that Osiris died on the seventeenth day of the month because on that day the waning of the full moon becomes obvious.[639] In another passage he also states that the conspiracy against Osiris by his brother, Seth, also took place on the seventeenth day of the month of Athyr.[640] The central part of Seth's plot, the fashioning of a chest fitting the measurements of Osiris which is probed by a series of guests and then Osiris himself at the fateful banquet, has of course a distinct lunar flavour. As for the connections between the seventeenth day of the month and Horus-on-his-papyrus-column, his pictorial representation also appears among the figures that are depicted in the Dendera zodiacs.[641] My analysis of these artefacts showed that there Horus-on-his-papyrus-column likewise marked the phase of the moon on the seventeenth day of the month in the vicinity of the constellation that we now know as Gemini, and thus in fact the demise of the god exactly 770 days after he had been vivified on the day when the autumnal equinox and the full moon coincided (25 September 52).[642]

The other expressions in line 25 also seem to be connected with the full moon. As for *sjp nḥḥ* 'the counter of eternity', its second element, 'eternity', is often associated with the solar world,[643] because generally *nḥḥ* expressed the cyclical pattern of time, that is, the constant repetition of days, months, seasons, and years (as opposed to the more static aspect of eternity, *ḏ.t*).[644] Consequently, the moon could also be seen as the embodiment of *nḥḥ*-eternity. The verb *sjp*, and its root form, *jp*, is often used in a lunar context, as is well evidenced by spells 155 and 156 in the Book of the Moon. It mainly describes the counting or allotting of the constituent elements of the celestial eye (the moon). Another good example is spell 133 of the Book of Going Forth by Day, which – according to its rubric – is to be recited on the day of the first crescent (*jr.t n*

[637] Parker 1950: 13.
[638] See comments on *CT* 155 above.
[639] Plutarch, *De Iside et Osiride* 42, see Griffiths 1970: 185.
[640] Plutarch, *De Iside et Osiride* 13, see Griffiths 1970: 139.
[641] Cauville 1997: pl. 60.
[642] Priskin 2015c: 163–164.
[643] Assmann 2001: 78.
[644] Assmann 2001: 73–76.

hrw ꜣbd).[645] Later it reads: 'Oh, gods in the sky, who see *N*, praise him like Re, because he is the Great One, Thoth, who heeds the great crown of Upper Egypt on the day when its constituent elements are counted' (*nṯr.w jmj.w-p.t mꜣꜣ.w N dj=ṯn n=f jꜣ.w mj Rꜥ ntf wr ḏꜥr wrr.t hrw sjp dbḥ.w=s*).[646] The determinative of the 'Great One' (), makes an unambiguous reference to the ibis-headed lunar god, Thoth. The great crown of Upper Egypt, being equivalent with the White Crown, may stand for the full moon,[647] so in *BD* 133 the verb *sjp*, and the action it denotes, the counting of the constituent elements of the eye, also seem to refer to the full moon.

As the *nḥḥ*-eternity is undoubtedly mentioned in line 25, previous translators, based on the text of Nakht (S2P), have seen an expression involving *ḏ.t* in the next group of signs.[648] However, Sen's text – – does not support this interpretation, and the spellings on other Deir el-Bersha coffins (; B2P and B17C) make it clear that *wꜣḏ tꜣ* is the correct reading. This can be translated as 'the one who makes the earth verdant', and this expression is quite appropriate for the moon. The general connection between fertility and the moon is stated unambiguously on the propylon of the Khonsu temple: '(the moon) causes bulls to rut, impregnates cows, grows the egg in the womb' (*sṯsj kꜣ.w sbkꜣ ḥm.wt srwḏ swḥ.t m ẖ.t*).[649] Plutarch claims that the light of the moon is conducive to both the regeneration of animals and the growth of plants.[650] This concept is also hinted at by one of his other statements that the onion is detestable for the priests because it tends to grow during the waning phases of the moon.[651] The Egyptian sources usually have some obscure references in this respect,[652] though a demotic papyrus from the 2nd century CE expressly states the connection between the moon and the growth of plants.[653]

However, it must be noted that according to the *Wörterbuch* the transitive use of the verb *wꜣḏ* is only attested from the Graeco-Roman Period.[654] Then the expression *wꜣḏ tꜣ* should perhaps be understood as containing a verbal noun, with the meaning 'being verdant (on) earth'; the symbolic connotation, however, would remain largely the same. On the other hand, the parallel constructions, *sjp nḥḥ* and *ꜥḥm ẖnn.w*, both consist of verb and object, and this makes it more likely that we should seek for a similar grammatical structure with *wꜣḏ tꜣ*. The disturbance in the phrase *ꜥḥm ẖnn.w* possibly refers to cosmic disorder,[655] and the 'queller of disturbance' may be someone who sets it aright at the full moon, when a sort of equilibrium is experienced by observing that

[645] Lepsius 1842; pl. liv (pIufankh).
[646] Lepsius 1842; pl. liv (pIufankh).
[647] Goebs 2008: 140–152..
[648] Faulkner 1973: 135; Barguet 1986: 574; Carrier 2004: 386.
[649] Sethe and Firchow 1957: 74 [89b].
[650] Plutarch, *De Iside et Osiride* 41, see Griffiths 1970: 183–185.
[651] Plutarch, *De Iside et Osiride* 8, see Griffiths 1970: 129.
[652] Aufrère 1991: 282.
[653] Smith 2002: 106, 126.
[654] *Wb.* I, 265.1.
[655] *Wb.* III, 383.16.

both the sun and the moon – the latter also as a full disc – traverse through the sky from the eastern to the western horizon.

Line 26

jw=j rḫ.kw bꜣ.w Pj Ḥr.w pw Jms.tj pw Ḥpj pw

I know the *bas* of Pe. It is Horus, it is Imseti, it is Hapi.

The spell, as usual, ends with the enumeration of the *bas* of the place named at the beginning of the text. Given the contents, the listing of Horus, Imseti, and Hapi here perhaps requires no further comment.

2.5. Spell 158: the waning moon

The hieroglyphic text

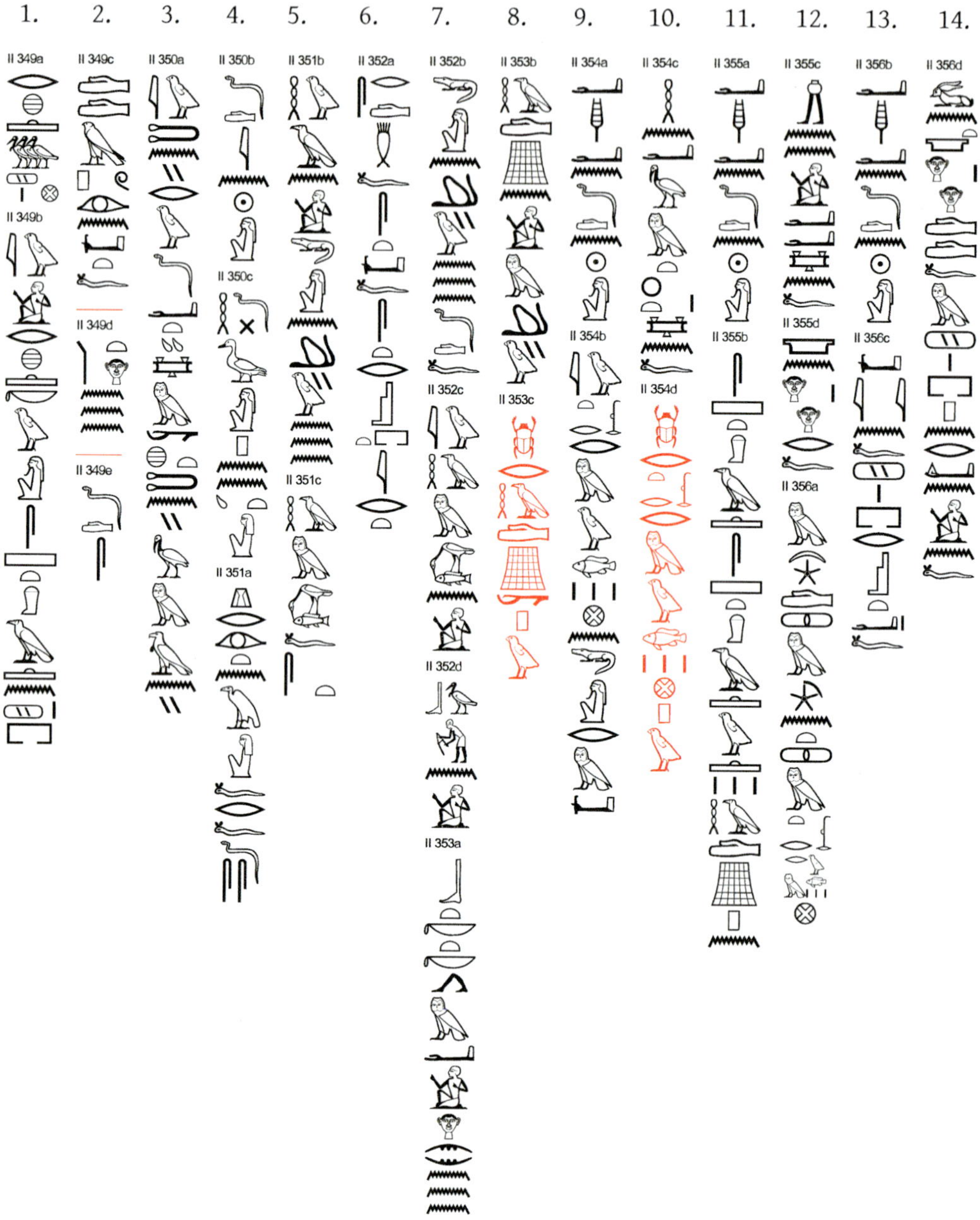

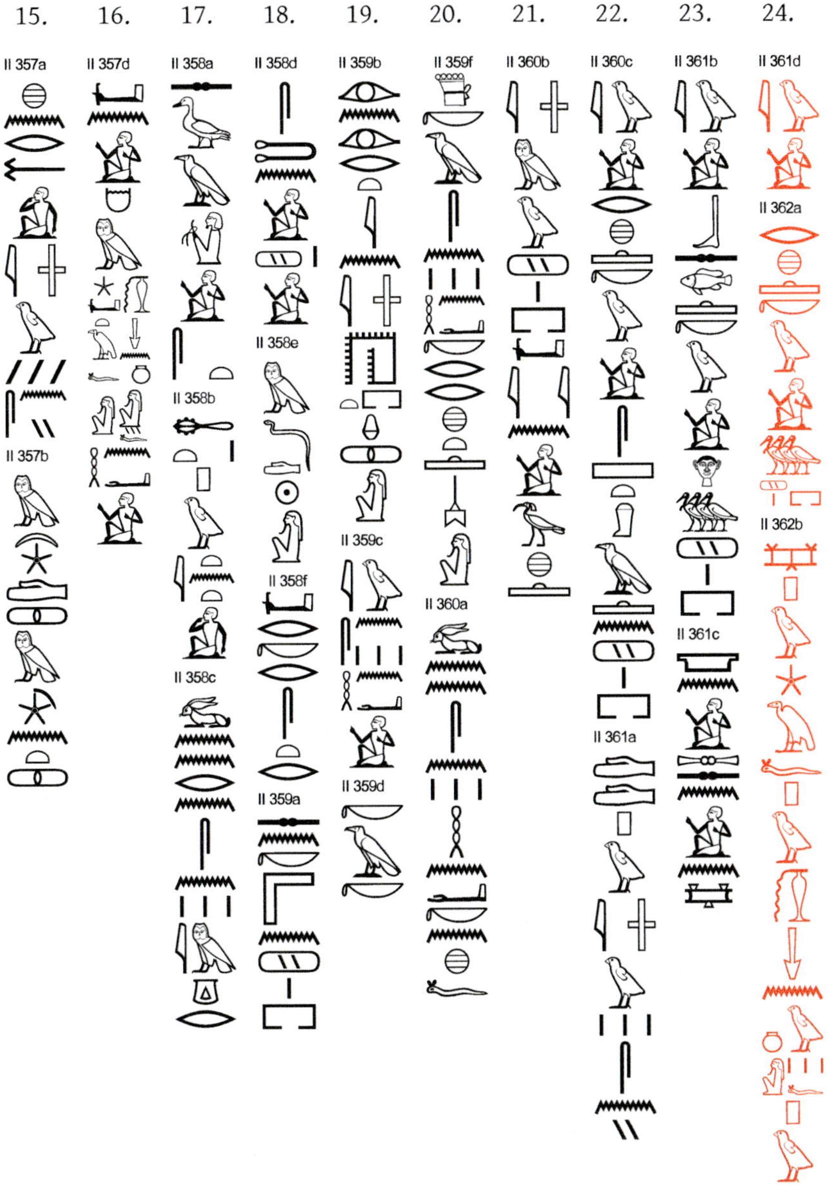
15. II 357a II 357b
16. II 357d
17. II 358a II 358b II 358c
18. II 358d II 358e II 358f II 359a
19. II 359b II 359c II 359d
20. II 359f II 360a
21. II 360b
22. II 360c II 361a
23. II 361b II 361c
24. II 361d II 362a II 362b

Transliteration and translation

1. *rḫ bꜣ.w Nḫn jw⸗j rḫ.kw sštꜣ n Nḫn*
2. *ḏr.tj Ḥr.w pw jrj.n mw.t⸗f qmꜣ.tj ḥr mw ḏd⸗s*
3. *jw⸗ṯnj r wḏꜥ.tj Ḥr.w m-ḫt ṯnj gm.tjwnj*
4. *ḏd.jn Rꜥ ḥḏ sꜣ pn n ꜣs.t ẖr jr.t.n mw.t⸗f r⸗f ḏs⸗s*
5. *ḥꜣ <jnj> n⸗j Sbk n pḥ.wj ḥꜣm⸗f st*
6. *srd⸗f st dj⸗f st r s.t jr.jt*
7. *Sbk n pḥ.wj ḏd⸗f jw ḥꜣm.n⸗j bꜣ.n⸗j btktk m ꜥ⸗j ḥr sp.tj mw*
8. *ḥꜣd.n⸗j n pḥ.wj ḫpr ḥꜣd pw*
9. *ꜥḥꜥ.n ḏd.n Rꜥ jw tr rm.w n Sbk r mj*
10. *ḥnꜥ gm.t jr.t Ḥr.w nf ḫpr Tr-rm.w pw*
11. *ꜥḥꜥ.n ḏd.n Rꜥ sštꜣ sštꜣ.w ḥꜣd pn*
12. *jnj(.w) n⸗j ꜥ.wj Ḥr.w nf wn-ḥr ḥr⸗f(j) m ꜣbd m smd.t m Tr-rm.w*
13. *ꜥḥꜥ.n ḏd.n Rꜥ dy n⸗f Nḫn r s.t ꜥ⸗f*
14. *wn.tj-ḥr ḥr ḏr.tj⸗f(j) m Nḫn pn rdj.n⸗j n⸗f*
15. *ḫnr jm.jw-snj m ꜣbd m smd.t*
16. *dj.n⸗j Dwꜣ-mw.t⸗f Qbḥ-sn.w⸗f ḥnꜥ⸗j*
17. *sꜣw⸗j st ẖ.t pw jtn.t wnn rn⸗sn jm gr*
18. *(j)sṯ n⸗j Nḫn⸗j m ḏd Rꜥ dj r⸗k r st r snk n Nḫn*
19. *jrj.n(⸗j) jrr.t jn jm.j-wsḫ.t jw⸗sn ḥnꜥ⸗j kꜣ⸗k*
20. *ḏr.kꜣ⸗sn ḥnꜥ⸗k r rḫ.t Stẖ wnn⸗sn ḥnꜥ⸗k nḫ⸗f*
21. *jm.jw Nḫn dy n⸗j ꜣḫ*
22. *jw⸗j rḫ.kw sštꜣ n Nḫn ḏr.tj pw jm.jw-snj*
23. *jw⸗j bs.kw ḥr bꜣ.w Nḫn wn n⸗j ṯs.n⸗j n Ḥr.w*
24. *jw⸗j rḫ.kw bꜣ.w Nḫn Ḥr.w pw Dwꜣ-mw.t⸗f pw Qbḥ-sn.w⸗f pw*

1. Knowing the *bas* of Nekhen. I know the secret of Nekhen.
2. It is the hands of Horus that his mother made and that were thrown into water, saying:
3. 'You are the severed body parts of Horus after you have been found'.
4. Re then said: 'This son of Isis was injured because of what his mother herself had done to him.
5. I wish Sobek of the edge of the waters <were fetched> for me
6. so that he could fish them out, grow them and put them back to their right place'.
7. Sobek of the edge of the waters said: 'I fished, I scooped (it) up, but (the catch) has slipped from my hands onto the shores of the water.
8. Finally I caught it in the edge of the waters with a cover basket'. And that is how the cover basket came into being.
9. Then Re said: 'Does Sobek have fish now
10. that he found the eye of Horus?' And that is how the town of Ter-remu came into being.

11. Re then said: 'Mysterious are the secrets of this cover basket;
12. it has brought me these hands of Horus which are revealed on the day of the first crescent and on the day of the full moon in Ter-remu'.
13. And then Re said: 'Nekhen has been given to him for the place of his hands.
14. May his two hands be revealed in Nekhen that I gave him
15. when what is in them is restrained on the day of the first crescent and on the day of the full moon'.
16. I took with myself Duamutef and Qebehsenuf,
17. so that I could protect them, they being an opposing pair. Their name exists there surely,
18. since Nekhen is mine in the words of Re: 'Put them in the darkness of Nekhen'.
19. I will have done what He-who-is-in-the-broad-hall does, and they will be with me, you will say,
20. and they will be with you until Seth learns about their being with you, and will protest about it.
21. Those who are in Nekhen, give me effectiveness!
22. I know the secret of Nekhen. It is the two hands and what is in them.
23. I have been initiated into the *bas* of Nekhen. Open to me so that I could join Horus.
24. I know the *bas* of Nekhen. It is Horus, it is Duamutef, it is Qebehsenuf.

Commentary

Line 1

rḫ bꜣ.w Nḫn jw=j rḫ.kw sštꜣ n Nḫn

Knowing the *bas* of Nekhen. I know the secret of Nekhen.

Since in spell 157 the events connected with the full moon were described in connection with Pe, now in turn the *bas* of Nekhen are introduced into the narrative. At the end of the previous spell Pe and Nekhen were mentioned together when the text claimed that from the four sons of Horus two would be in Pe with Horus, while the other two would reside in Nekhen. This theme will be further developed in the second part of the present spell. We have seen that in the previous chapters of the Book of the Moon (*CT* 154, 155, 156, and 157) the different text variants had differing titles, and especially the texts on the coffins from Asyut tended to contain longer introductory formulas. This is not the case with spell 158, and the lack of variety may be due to the fact that this text has only been preserved on one Asyut coffin (S2P). Thus the first line is almost identical on each coffin, and there are only minor variations. In some text variants the first sentence is omitted (B1C, B9C, B17C, B2P), and on two coffins (B2Bo and B4Bo) the first two statements are mixed together, because in *CT* II, 349b they start the spell with the phrase 'Knowing the secret of Nekhen' (*rḫ sštꜣ Nḫn*).

Lines 2–4

ḏr.tj Ḥr.w pw jrj.n mw.t⸗f qmꜣ.tj ḥr mw ḏd⸗s
jw⸗ṯnj r wḏʿ.tj Ḥr.w m-ẖt ṯnj gm.tjwnj
ḏd.jn Rʿ ḥḏ sꜣ pn n ꜣs.t ẖr jr.t.n mw.t⸗f r⸗f ḏs⸗s

It is the hands of Horus that his mother made and that were thrown into water, saying: 'You are the severed body parts of Horus after you have been found'.
Re then said: 'This son of Isis was injured because of what his mother herself had done to him'.

The secret of Nekhen is therefore the two hands of Horus, and these serve to refer to the moon, and more especially to the waning moon. To understand this the relevant episode from the story about the fight between Horus and Seth must again be recalled here.[656] In this episode the hands undoubtedly have lunar connotations. We must note, however, that the description of the homosexual relationship between the two combatants was already recorded in a papyrus from the Middle Kingdom,[657] and this proves that the concepts related to the hands of Horus were perhaps fairly widely known earlier. The homosexual encounter, as stated in the commentary on spell 157, was part of the story cycle about the prolonged struggle between Horus and Seth. To prove his superiority in order to gain the inheritance of Osiris' kingdom, Seth wants to tip the balance in his favour in the court case before the divine jury, so comes up with a devious plan: if he could prove that he has a sexual relationship with Horus in which he is the dominant partner, the jury would surely prefer him as the heir of Osiris. For this reason Seth invites Horus to his residence and they spend a pleasant day together, but at night Seth makes an attempt to violate Horus.[658] However, Horus collects Seth's semen with his hands and the following day he asks his mother, Isis, for help. She severs the hands of Horus, throws them into water, grows new hands for his son, and then in turn she collects Horus' semen in a vessel. She takes this vessel to Seth's garden and pours its contents on the lettuce that Seth is rumoured to eat for his breakfast day and day again. When Seth, as usual, eats the lettuce, he conceives from Horus. Unaware of the trick played on him, he cites Horus before the divine court once more in the conviction that by raping Horus the previous night, he has proved the weak character of Horus for everyone to see, which would eventually mean his unsuitability to take his father's throne. At the court Horus makes a proposal to invoke his own semen and that of Seth as well, and then those who are present can witness where the answers would come from. So first Thoth calls Seth's semen, which answers (i.e. comes forth) from the midst of the marshes, as the hands containing it had previously been thrown into the water. Then Thoth calls upon to the semen of Horus, which first refuses to come out of the ears, but then grows on the top of Seth's

656 Gardiner 1932: 51–54; Lichtheim 1976: 219–220.
657 Parkinson 1991: 120–121; Quirke 2004: 181–182.
658 Gardiner 1932: 51; Lichtheim 1976: 219.

head in the shape of a golden disc. Seth immediately tries to rip off the disc from his head, but now Thoth gets hold of it and places it on his own head. As argued in the commentary in the previous chapter, this golden disc, contrary to the claims of some researchers that it is the sun, must be the representative of the moon, as it is finally fastened to the head of Thoth, one of the major lunar gods in the Egyptian pantheon. Therefore, the severed hands of Horus in the water are directly related to the lunar disc.

Further proof for the identity of the two hands of Horus with the moon comes from Sen's text of Coffin Texts spell 158. The hands are referred to as the severed body parts of Horus, which will eventually be found (*gm.tjwnj*) in water. Later, in lines 9-10, we learn that it is Sobek who is responsible for finding (*gm.t*) the lost body parts, and while in all other text variants Sobek in fact finds the hands (*ꜥ.wj Ḥr.w*), in Sen's text the object of the verb 'find' is the eye of Horus (*jr.t Ḥr.w*), that is the moon. The equivalence of the hands with the moon will also be confirmed in line 12, because there we read that the hands become visible on the day of the first crescent and on the day of the full moon.

It is obvious then that the hands are the symbols of the moon, and what they hold, the semen of Seth, should be understood to evoke the attack against the moon and the waning period that results from it. Funerary texts express this with containing allusions to the relevant organs of the combatants: 'Seth injured the face of Horus, while Horus grabbed the testicles of Seth' (*m wd.t Sth̠ st̠ꜣ.w m ḥr n Ḥr.w m jt̠.t Ḥr.w h̠r.wj n Sth̠*).[659] The next sentence in this text, spell 335 of the Coffin Texts, then states that for the healing of the wound, that is for the filling of the eye, Thoth was responsible, because 'it was Thoth who did it with his fingers' (*jn gr.t D̠ḥwtj jrj nn m d̠bꜥ.w=f*).[660] Spell 9 of the Coffin Texts also establishes a clear connection between the moon, Seth's sperm, and Thoth: 'Hail to you, Thoth, in whom dwells the peace of the gods, together with the entire court of judges who are with you! Command that they be summoned as *N* stands before them, and they hear his speech on this day, because yours is this feather that rose from the land of the god, which was brought by Osiris to Horus to fasten it to his head as a reward for his justification against his enemies. It was him who squeezed the testicles of Seth, who did not perish and did not die. You are a star born by the beautiful west, who does not perish, nor does he die' (*jnd̠ ḥr=k D̠ḥwtj jm.j ḥtp nt̠r.w ḥnꜥ d̠ꜣd̠ꜣ.t nb.t n.tjt ḥnꜥ=k wd̠=k prr=sn m ḫsf N sd̠m=sn d̠d.t=f nb.t hrw pn ḥr-n.tjt t̠wt js šw.t tw wbn.t m tꜣ-nt̠r jn.t.n Wsjr n Ḥr.w smn=f st m tp=f r mt̠n.t mꜣꜥ-ḫrw r ḫf.tjw=f swt ꜥfꜣ h̠r.wj Sth̠ n sk=f n mt=f t̠wt sbꜣ pw msj jmn.t nfr.t n sk=f n mt=f*).[661] As I already stated it earlier, the feather in this text, rising in the land of the god (i.e. in a distant location), is the symbol of the first crescent of the waxing moon appearing over the western horizon, and this identity is accentuated in spell 9 since, through his connections with it, Thoth

659 *CT* IV, 237a–b (BH1Br and T3Be); for later variants, see chapter 17 of the Book of Going Forth by Day.
660 *CT* IV, 237c–239a (T3Be).
661 *CT* IV, 237c–239a (T3Be).

is literally said to be a star that is born in the west. This detail makes it certain that the star concerned is the moon, because it is the only celestial body that appears in the west after sunset at the beginning of its cycle. Though the exact meaning of the verb *ʿfꜣ* (*ʿfꜣ ẖr.wj Stẖ* 'squeezed the testicles of Seth') is not really known,[662] it obviously has some negative overtones in connection with the testicles, and connects the whole activity with the appearance of the first crescent in the western sky.

Thus, on the cosmic level, the eye of Horus is the moon, while Seth's testicles, or in a more indirect way, his sperm,[663] must have symbolised the dark, injured side of the moon. Seth attacks the moon with his regenerative 'organ' (his semen), and as far as natural phenomena are concerned, this detail expresses that the injury of the moon is not final and irreversible. It heals with a cyclical pattern and keeps regenerating, that is, the waning period of the moon is always followed by the waxing one. This allegory lies behind the allusions of funerary texts that link the injury to the face or eye of Horus with Seth's sexual – procreative – aspect. It should again be remembered that the New Kingdom story about Horus and Seth is the satirical and popular version of the myth,[664] so the homosexual episode – which obviously had several sociocultural aspects in ancient Egypt – was the vulgar rewriting of an official theological, we can perhaps say, philosophical concept.

The hands of Horus are said to have been created by Isis and then also cut off by her. This statement may imply the repetitive nature of these acts, and may be put in parallel with the cyclical and constant renewal of the moon. This similarity will be confirmed by the next line in the text that will talk about how the hands are fished out, and how they will have to grow and be put back in their place. This part – the search for the hands and their finding – is missing from the story known as the Contendings of Horus and Seth, because there Isis simply grows new hands for Horus. However, we could see that the episode about the hands of Horus did not lose its lunar connotations in the popular story, either; it is, on the other hand, basically a linear narrative that does not lay great emphasis on the motif of cyclical regeneration.

Re claims that the injury of Horus was caused by his own mother, Isis, because she was the one who cut off his hands. This mutilation, as spell 158 testifies to it, was surely part of the official myth that in this way symbolically referred to the ever reoccurring waning phases of the moon. In the popular story about the struggle between the two opponents the mutilation of the hands is preceded by two other gruesome episodes: Horus cuts off the head of Isis as he has been enraged by his mother's leniency towards Seth during their fight as hippopotami, and then Seth rips out the eyes of Horus.[665] Here again we may suppose that the excessive violence is a caricature-like

[662] For the meaning 'squeeze', see Molen 2000: 70.
[663] Velde 1967: 40.
[664] Redford 2001: 294.
[665] Gardiner 1932: 49–50; Lichtheim 1976: 219.

exaggeration of the official myth, with the reversal of the original roles (i.e. now not only does Isis cut off a body part of her son, but she herself also becomes the victim of a violent act).

The narrative sequence of the developments about the eye of Horus in the New Kingdom story resembles the course of events in spells 157 and 158 of the Coffin Texts.[666] First the eyes of Horus are temporarily injured when Seth cuts them out and then Hathor heals them. She uses the milk of a gazelle to relieve the pain of Horus, and this detail may directly reflect the appearance of the oryx in spell 157, and the lunar eclipse it embodies. Then follows the story about the homosexual relationship between Horus and Seth, including the mutilation of the hands. These are, in fact, the events that are linked to the inevitable monthly waning of the moon, forming the subject matter of *CT* 158.

Lines 5–6

ḥꜣ <jnj> n=j Sbk n pḥ.wj ḥꜣm=f s
srd=f st dj=f st r s.t jr.jt

'I wish Sobek of the edge of the waters <were fetched> for me
so that he could fish them out, grow them and put them back to their right place'.

The beginning of line 5, as it appears on Sen's coffin, *ḥꜣ n=j Sbk n pḥ.wj*, seems to be grammatically correct, but it differs from all the other text variants that feature the verb *jnj* after the optative particle.[667] It is quite possible then that this word was left out by a scribal oversight. There are also hieroglyphs that were inserted into the text after it had been written in lines 14 and 18,[668] and these may indicate that the copyist hired by Sen sometimes did not comply with the highest standards of his profession, or he 'had a bad day in the office'. One thing worth noticing in line 6 is that on two coffins from Deir el-Bersha (B2Bo and B4Bo), and in the sole Asyut variant (S2P), the text is quite different, because there Sobek should fish Horus' hands out 'so that his mother, Isis, grow them back to their right place (*srd mw.t=f ꜣs.t r s.t jr.jt*). Without trying to determine which text variant was the original or earlier one, we may suppose that the difference arose from the multivalence of the sign 𓂞, because this hieroglyph was used to record both the word *mw.t* 'mother' and *dj* 'to give, to place' at the time when the Coffin Texts were created.[669] The meaning 'to give' is unambiguous on the coffin marked B2P, where the hieroglyph 𓏙 appears in the relevant passage.[670] It must be noted that due to the alternative readings, the two text variants display differences in terms of content as well. In the Asyut version Isis grows back the hands of Horus

[666] cf. Gardiner 1932: 49–54; Lichtheim 1976: 219–220.
[667] Gardiner 1957a: 96.
[668] *CT* II, 356d and 359a.
[669] Gardiner 1957a: 455.
[670] *CT* II, 352a.

which were thrown into water, and this motif is repeated in the New Kingdom story about Horus and Seth, because there too she is the one who is responsible for creating new hands for his son. However, in Sen's text the consequent use of the masculine third person suffix pronoun clearly indicates that here it is Sobek's task both to grow the hands back and to reattach them into their place.

Sobek – as it follows from his name which simply means 'crocodile' – was the pre-eminent crocodile god in ancient Egypt, and because of his widespread cult and prominent position his figure was associated with a series of mythological concepts.[671] Naturally he was primarily the god of waters and marshlands, and through this he was linked with the Nile and the fertility that the river brought to Egypt. On the other hand, because of the predatory nature of the crocodile, he may be seen as a creature threatening people or other divine beings.[672] However, for the purposes of the present analysis it is more important that his figure was already attestably associated with the sun god in Middle Kingdom times, and thus in his composite form Sobek-Re he also appears as a cosmic god.[673] Several sources indicate that Sobek or Sobek-Re has especially close ties with the aspect of the solar god that embodies the rising sun.[674] A hymn to Sobek in one of the Ramesseum papyri (13th dynasty) addresses him as a god that emerged from the primaeval waters during the first sunrise.[675] The identity of Sobek with the rising sun is also attested in the Coffin Texts, since for example spell 991 – in which the deceased is assimilated to Sobek – reads: 'I am this god who rises in the east and departs in the west [...] I am the one who rises without any tiredness' (*jnk nṯr pw wbn m jꜣb.t ḫpp m jmn.t [...] jnk wbn jw.tj gnn.t≠f*).[676] In the New Kingdom royal tombs the identity of Sobek with the morning sun is also confirmed iconographically, since several scenes show the solar disc emerging above the eastern horizon as being born by a crocodile.[677] In a mythological papyrus that dates from slightly later the crocodile's name is *ḫpr*, that is the morning sun (Khepri).[678] In the Book of the Fayum, dated to the 2nd century CE, Sobek is depicted in the eastern and western liminal zones between the earth and the sky, and thus represents the rising and setting sun.[679]

Sobek thus fishes out the hands symbolising the moon in his form of the rising sun. In this way – though it is not stated explicitly in the text – the hands are also viewed as fish (in the Egyptian conceptualisation of the aquatic world the crocodile, i.e. Sobek, was likewise seen as fish).[680] Assuming the form of a fish, however, also had astronomical connotations. The Fundamentals of the Course of the Stars (Book of Nut), preserved

---

[671] Brovarski 1984: 996–998.
[672] cf. *Pyr.* §507–510.
[673] Brovarski 1984: 1001, 1007.
[674] Goebs 2008: 136 n. 337; Zecchi 2010: 23.
[675] Gardiner 1957b: 45.
[676] *CT* VII, 2002c–f.
[677] Piankoff 1953: 67–69.
[678] Kákosy 1980: 810 n. 113.
[679] Beinlich 1991: 391, pl. 9.
[680] For the crocodile as fish, see Brovarski 1984: 1000.

in one New Kingdom and several later copies,[681] gives us precise information about when celestial bodies could turn into fish. Describing the life cycle of the decans, that is the stars or groups of stars used for determining the hours of the night, it writes that these stars change into fish when after their period of invisibility they reappear in the sky immediately before sunrise.[682] For some time before this so-called heliacal rise the decans are too close to the sun to be seen; in Egyptian terms they dwell in the netherworld (*duat*) during this period. Since they reappear shortly before sunrise, this means that these stars do not have enough time to set in the west: the rays of the sun cancel out their light, and they 'fall back' into the celestial waters (i.e. disappear). The moon behaves in exactly the same way in the second half of its cycle, since after its fullness – when it copied the course of the sun by rising from the eastern horizon and setting in the west – it no longer reaches the western horizon: the waning crescent travels a lesser and lesser distance towards it each day. The rising sun also turns the waning moon into fish, as with the intensification of sunlight the lunar crescent is likewise engulfed by the waters of the celestial dome.

Lines 7–8

Sbk n pḥ.wj ḏd=f jw ḥ3m.n=j b3.n=j btktk m ʿ=j ḥr sp.tj mw
ḥ3d.n=j n pḥ.wj ḫpr ḥ3d pw

Sobek of the edge of the waters said: 'I fished, I scooped (it) up, but (the catch) has slipped from my hands onto the shores of the water.
Finally I caught it in the edge of the waters with a cover basket'. And that is how the cover basket came into being.

These lines further elaborate the theme of the identification of the waning moon with a fish. After the middle of the month the gibbous moon rises on the eastern horizon and at first it almost reaches the western one before the rays of the rising sun start to cancel out its light. As the lunation progresses and the end of the lunar cycle approaches, the lunar crescent rises later and later in the night and can travel an ever shorter distance towards the west before sunrise. This phase is described by the words of Sobek that he fishes, scoops up the catch but it repeatedly slips from his hands. In the sentence enumerating his actions the meaning of the first verb is unambiguous (*ḥ3m* – 'to fish'), but the translation of the two other ones is not so straightforward and needs some explanation. The basic meaning of *b3* is 'to hack up (the earth)', 'to open up (with a hoe)',[683] and from this derive more abstract meanings such as 'to open holes', 'to destroy'.[684] The hieroglyphic writing of the word clearly shows that the verb refers to the action by which someone removes a lump of earth from the ground with a hoe. In the fishing context of spell 158 the emphasis must be on this latter

[681] Lieven 2007.
[682] Neugebauer and Parker 1960: 68; Lieven 2007: 89.
[683] *Wb.* I, 415.12–13.
[684] Wilson 1997: 301; Molen 2000: 113.

movement, and the expression describes how a fisherman lifts or scoops up his net or other fishing device with a physical effort from the water. On one of the Deir el-Bersha coffins (B1L) and in the Asyut text (S2P), the verb *ḏꜥr* replaces *bꜣ*. It basically means 'to seek', but as has been pointed out earlier, in medical texts it signifies the act of groping with the hand or the fingers in order to feel the cause of a disease or malady. Here then *ḏꜥr* perhaps describes how the fisherman (Sobek) tries to reach for the fish with his hands.

This understanding is also suggested by the appearance of the hands in the next phrase. The verb used in it, *btktk*, is a hapax legomenon which only appears in *CT* 158 and its descendant, chapter 113 of the Book of Going Forth by Day.[685] The context – the fish gets onto the shores of the river and then later is eventually caught – suggests the meaning 'to slip', 'to escape', and all the modern translators have rendered the word in this sense.[686] The word *btktk* is obviously a reduplicating verb with five radicals that must have originated from the root *btk*; however, this verb is also very rare and thus its meaning is likewise quite obscure.[687]

On the last days of the month the ever thinner lunar crescent rises only slightly above the eastern horizon, and in the symbolic language of spell 158 it gets to the edge of the sky where the celestial waters are shallow. Then, on one day, the rising sun indeed catches the moon: the lunar crescent cannot be sighted before sunrise because it has got so close to the sun that no light is reflected from it towards the earth. The text expresses this development poetically by stating that Sobek finally catches the hands of Horus – the waning moon – by a cover basket. As already established by Pierre Lacau, the word *ḥꜣd* denotes this fishing device that is used in shallow waters.[688] It is basically a basket that is open at both ends, and the fisherman tries to place it over a fish he spots – or suspects to spot – in the shallow waters. If the basket really encloses a fish, it can be removed by the hand through the upper opening that remains above the level of the water.

The text uses the verb *ḥꜣd* to describe the conjunction of the sun and the moon (when the moon is between the earth and the sun), and through homonymy it connects it with the name of the cover basket, also called *ḥꜣd* . In spell 157, as we have seen, there is a similar wordplay with the name of the oryx. The verb was later used with a wider meaning 'to trap (fish)'.[689] The pun in spell 158 suggests that it had already had this more abstract meaning in the Middle Kingdom, since if it only meant 'to catch fish with the cover basket', then the aetiological explanation would have made little sense. In this case the meaning of the word would have been obvious for anyone, and it would not have required an explanation.

[685] Lacau 1954: 148.
[686] Speleers 1946: 90; Faulkner 1973: 136; Barguet 1986: 575; Carrier 2004: 389; see also *Wb.* I, 485.5.
[687] Gardiner 1909: 31; Faulkner 1962: 86.
[688] Lacau 1954: 146–151.
[689] Wilson 1997: 620.

Lines 9–10

ꜥḥꜥ.n ḏd.n Rꜥ jw tr rm.w n Sbk r mj
ḥnꜥ gm.t jr.t Ḥr.w nf ḫpr Tr-rm.w pw

Then Re said: 'Does Sobek have fish now
that he found the eye of Horus?' And that is how the town of Ter-remu came into being.

The identity of the eyes of Horus, or in the other text variants, the hands of Horus, with fish – which has not been so far explicitly expressed – is becoming more emphatic in these lines. In fact, it becomes clear only now why the text has refrained from referring to fish earlier, because in an untranslatable wordplay now a connection is established between the word *rm.w* 'fish' and the place name *Tr-rm.w* that also includes this word. In the question voiced in line 9, *jw tr rm.w n Sbk r mj* 'Does Sobek have fish now?',[690] the enclitic particle *tr* is put before the word *rm.w* meaning fish (plural), while in the name of the town the same word must be the first part of a direct genitival construction (possession). Most probably it is then the noun *tr* 'time',[691] and the entire name of the town stands for 'the time of fish'. From later sources we know that in the Delta there existed a settlement named *Tꜣ-rm.w* 'the land of fish', on the site of today's Tell el-Muqdam,[692] and this reaffirms that the designation *Tr-rm.w* was built around the same pattern (direct genitive). In fact, it is quite probable, as Jean Yoyotte suspects, that the two names refer to the same city.[693] On the basis of similar aetiological explanations in spells 154, 157, and in spell 158 itself, of the Book of the Moon, which give reasons for the existence of real things – the harpoon, the oryx, and the cover basket – we must suppose that *Tr-rm.w* was an actual settlement somewhere in Egypt. It was not necessarily the later *Tꜣ-rm.w*, though this seems to be the most obvious conclusion.

Surely, the name *Tr-rm.w* appears in the text as a deliberate allusion to the 'time of fish' in an astronomical context. It emphasises the similar behaviour of the waning moon to the celestial fish, that is the heliacally rising decanal stars that – likewise to the lunar crescents towards the end of the month – do not reach the western horizon but are overshone by the brightness of the rising sun. Both the waning moon and these stars eventually fade into the background of the blue sky, or – in the symbolic terminology of *CT* 158 – they fall back into the celestial waters.

Lines 11–12

ꜥḥꜥ.n ḏd.n Rꜥ sštꜣ sštꜣ.w ḥꜣd pn
jnj(.w) n=j ꜥ.wj Ḥr.w nf wn-ḥr ḥr=f(j) m ꜣbd m smd.t m Tr-rm.w

[690] Literally 'Does Sobek have fish with regard to what?', see Allen 2001b: 478.
[691] *Wb.* V, 313.12–316.11.
[692] Yoyotte 1953.
[693] Yoyotte 1953: 187–190.

Re then said: 'Mysterious are the secrets of this cover basket;
it has brought me these hands of Horus which are revealed on the day of the first crescent and on the day of the full moon in Ter-remu'.

These lines establish a connection between the mysterious secrets of the cover basket and the waxing phases of the moon that is evoked by a reference to the second day of the lunar month (day of the first crescent) and the full moon (fifteenth day of the month). As the capture by the cover basket refers to lunar invisibility, the statement really emphasises the interrelatedness of this lunar phase with waxing. Since in ancient Egypt the day of lunar invisibility was the first day of the month, such a link with the rest of the first part of a lunation – waxing – was only natural. We must also suppose that the statement implies the knowledge that during its invisibility the moon travels together with the sun in the day sky, and that is how it gets from its point of disappearance at the eastern horizon to the western one, where one or two days later it reappears as the first crescent immediately after sunset. The opinion that the Egyptians were already aware of this hidden journey of the moon at the beginning of the 2nd millennium BCE will be confirmed by spell 160 of the Coffin Texts with its description of a solar eclipse featuring the moon. As a solar eclipse can only occur during the conjunction of the sun and the moon, this also proves that the Egyptians understood that on the days of its invisibility the moon was dwelling between the earth and the sun.

The expression *wn-ḥr* literally means 'to open the face' or 'the face opens',[694] and its precise connotations are sometimes hard to grasp. It is used here in the sense 'to appear', 'to reveal', 'to be revealed', and the whole phrase *wn-ḥr ḥr=f* should perhaps be rendered as 'the face opens up on someone/something', that is 'someone/something attracts attention', 'someone/something becomes visible/noticeable'.[695] The thing that becomes visible or appears is often an image of a god that is shown to the participants of a ritual at its climax. A priest can open the sanctuaries of the gods so that they could appear, or the priests open up the face during the new year's festivities on the roof of the temple, when the cult statues are brought to sunlight through a procession around the building on the first day of the year.[696] Therefore the expression *wn-ḥr* may refer to a similar cultic activity in the town of *Tr-rm.w* that was performed on the second and fifteenth days of the month, but it is more likely that the phrase directly describes natural phenomena, that is the appearance of the first crescent and the rising of the full moon. Thus the antecedent of the suffix object *=f* of the preposition *ḥr* is not the cover basket (*ḥ3d*), but here we have a hidden dual form, and the suffix *=f(j)* refers back to the two hands. This connection once more reaffirms the identification of the arms with the moon.

---

694 *Wb.* I, 312.15–313.5.
695 *Wb.* I. 312.15.
696 Wilson 1997: 230.

Lines 13–15

ꜥḥꜥ.n ḏd.n Rꜥ dy n≠f Nḫn r s.t ꜥ≠f
wn.tj-ḥr ḥr ḏr.tj≠f(j) m Nḫn pn rdj.n≠j n≠f
ḫnr jm.jw-snj m ꜣbd m smd.t

And then Re said: 'Nekhen has been given to him for the place of his hands.
May his two hands be revealed in Nekhen that I gave him
when what is in them is restrained on the day of the first crescent and on the day of the full moon'.

According to spell 157 Pe was given to Horus as a compensation for the injury to his eye, and now we learn that Re has given Horus the town of Nekhen to keep his hands there. Unfortunately, to my knowledge, other sources do not provide further information for the better understanding of the precise role that these locations, and the concepts associated with them, play in lunar myths. The lack of such information may indicate that the motif by which the polarity embodied by the towns of Pe and Nekhen is interlaced with the moon is the invention of the author(s) of Coffin Texts spells 157 and 158, whoever they might have been either in Heliopolis or Hermopolis. A similar parallel stemming from the juxtaposition of cult places seems to exist in the Book of the Moon between Heliopolis/sun (spell 154) and Hermopolis/moon (spell 156), and also – based on geographical orientation – between the *bas* of the easterners (spell 159) and the *bas* of the westerners (spell 160). The analysis of this structure of the Book of the Moon, leaving spell 155 as the odd one out, is the subject of a separate chapter (3.2.) of the present book.

The first word of line 14 on Sen's coffin was initially written erroneously, and the scribe inserted the hieroglyph showing a loaf of bread (*t*) afterwards. The sign is recorded in all the other text variants, and the additional insertion also proves that the copyist deemed this detail important. The *t(w)* may stand for the general subject,[697] so perhaps we should read 'his two hands are seen in Nekhen that I gave him' (*wn.tw-ḥr ḥr ḏr.tj≠f(j) m Nḫn pn rdj.n≠j n≠f*).[698] On the other hand, as I interpreted it in my transliteration, the *t(j)* may be the ending of the second person stative, and in the particular context this verb form is used as an optative or to express a wish, hence my translation 'may his two hands be revealed'.[699]

Through the expression *jm.jw-snj* in line 15 we learn it for the first time in the spell that the hands of Horus hold something. I rendered *jm.jw-snj* as 'what is in them' (i.e. in the two hands), but we should note that *jm.jw* is in the plural. From the mythological parallels cited above, including the New Kingdom story about how Horus steals the

[697] cf. Carrier 2004: 388.
[698] Literally 'one turns the face towards his two hands'.
[699] Literally 'may you reveal the face to his two hands'.

semen of Seth, it seems to be obvious that the hands hide the sperm of his opponent. This interpretation is further strengthened by the statement in the text that what is in the hands are put under some form of control at the time of the first crescent and the full moon, that is, during waxing. The verb *ḫnr* basically means 'to restrain', 'to hinder',[700] and the evil – yet in some sense also regenerative – principle embodied by Seth's sperm is indeed conquered by the repeated waxing of the moon. A noticeable detail on Sen's coffin is the determinative at the end of the verb *ḫnr* , since the sitting human figure touching his mouth only features in his version. The sign may have possibly filtered through into the spelling of the verb from the related noun *ḫnr* 'prisoner', 'criminal', 'restrained person'.[701]

The emphatic statement that the two hands of Horus become visible on the days of the first crescent and the full moon may be juxtaposed by the earlier similar claim that the same event is also witnessed in the town of Ter-remu. Since this locality (possibly the later Ta-remu) is found in the Nile delta, whereas Nekhen is situated in Upper Egypt, the parallel mention of the two towns – in accordance with the characteristic dual categorisation of ancient Egyptian thought – expresses the totality and universality of the reappearance of Horus' hands, that is, the sighting of the waxing moon. The concept of duality is reflected by Pe and Nekhen in relation to spells 157 and 158 in the Book of the Moon, while in the latter spell itself Ter-remu forms in one sense the counterpart of Nekhen.

Lines 16–18

dj.n=j Dwꜣ-mw.t=f Qbḥ-sn.w=f ḥnꜥ=j
sꜣw=j st ẖ.t pw jtn.t wnn rn=sn jm gr
(j)sṯ n=j Nḫn=j m ḏd Rꜥ dj r=k r st r snk n Nḫn

I took with myself Duamutef and Qebehsenuf,
so that I could protect them, they being an opposing pair. Their name exists there surely,
since Nekhen is mine in the words of Re: 'Put them in the darkness of Nekhen'.

In the Asyut text from line 15 Horus takes over the role of the speaker, since it inserts the formula 'and then Horus said' (*ꜥḥꜥ.n ḏd.n Ḥr.w*) into the discourse.[702] This addition is lacking from all the Deir el-Bersha variants, but it seems highly likely that we should interpret lines 16–18 as uttered by Horus, since in line 18 the speaker claims Nekhen to be his. At the end of spell 157 Horus talked about the division of his four sons – Imseti, Hapi, Duamutef, and Qebehsenuf – into two groups (two in Pe, two in Nekhen), and I already suggested there that this grouping must have reflected the two

[700] *Wb.* III, 296.1–7.
[701] *Wb.* III, 296.8–11.
[702] *CT* II, 357c.

opposing phases, waxing and waning, of the lunar cycle. The four divinities, as in other contexts, may symbolise unity that is viewed as the totality of its constituent parts.[703] This interpretation is perhaps further confirmed by the presentation of Duamutef and Qebehsenuf in spell 158 as figures that oppose (*jtn*) something. At first glance this role of theirs may be a bit surprising because the four sons of Horus otherwise almost always appear as positive actors, mostly as the protectors of Osiris or Horus.[704] In the context of spells 157 and 158, where the four sons represent the lunar cycle composed of two complementing yet in a way also apposing halves, two of them inevitably must attain some negative overtones. According to the words of Re Duamutef and Qebehsenuf are put in a dark corner of Nekhen (the determinative of *snk* 'darkness' stands for a corner or nook). Other translators render *snk* as 'prison',[705] or leave it untranslated;[706] in my opininon the word is surely connected with the root *snk* 'to be dark', 'darkness',[707] and in the present text it may imply the identification of Duamutef and Qebehsenuf with the dark part of the lunar disc that gets smaller and smaller during the first half of the month. Nevertheless, the translation as prison is probably not mistaken, since also on its symbolic level the text seems to suggest that during waxing Seth's sperm is imprisoned and cannot exert its malevolent influence. Until the day of the blacked-out moon the part ripped out from the lunar disc (the eye of Horus) is growing, but this trend is reversed by the appearance of the first crescent, as now the dark part is restrained, and each day a greater portion of the moon becomes bright. This is the time when Duamutef and Qebehsenuf – and the restrained Seth evoked by them – dwell in the dark corners of Nekhen.

The word *ẖ.t* is usually translated as 'group' or 'company' in relation to a set of gods or beings,[708] but since here the group consists of two members, I use the expression 'pair' in my translation. In the sentence about the possession of Nekhen the suffix pronoun attached to the noun, *jsṯ n=j Nḫn=j*, is perhaps an example of dittography, but it may also be interpreted as a genitive suffix added for emphasis ('my Nekhen is mine'). However, it seems that a repetition of signs is responsible for the insertion of the preposition *r* before the pronominal object (*r st*), since the correct from would be *dj r=k st r snk n Nḫn*. It is also only on Sen's coffin that the same preposition *r* precedes *snk*; in all the other variants we find the phrase *m snk*.

Lines 19–20

jrj.n(=j) jrr.t jn jm.j-wsḫ.t jw=sn ḥnꜥ=j kꜣ=k
ḏr.kꜣ=sn ḥnꜥ=k r rḫ.t Stẖ wnn=sn ḥnꜥ=k nḫ=f

[703] Mathieu 2008b: 8–11.
[704] Voss 1980: 52.
[705] Faulkner 1973: 137; Barguet 1986: 575; Carrier 2004: 391.
[706] Molen 2000: 515.
[707] *Wb.* IV, 175.11–13 and 176.3.
[708] *Wb.* III, 357.18–358.3.

I will have done what He-who-is-in-the-broad-hall does, and they will be with me, you will say,
and they will be with you until Seth learns about their being with you, and will protest about it.

At this point, Sen's text, together with practically all the other versions from Deir el-Bersha, differs considerably from the Asyut text, which defines the person found in the broad hall as a female, 'She-who-is-in-the-broad-hall' (*jm.jt-wsḫ.t*), whereas at Sen this divinity is unambiguously a male. Perhaps as a result of this, existing translations take She-who-is-in-the-broad-hall to be an opponent or adversary of Horus, and thus the accomplice of Duamutef and Qebehsenuf: 'Place them in the prison(?) of Nekhen, for <they> have done what used to be done by Her who is in the Broad Hall',[709] 'Mets-les dans le cachot de Nekhen et que soit fait pour (eux) ce qui est fait habituellement par Celle-qui-est-dans-la-salle-large',[710] or 'Mets-les donc dans la prison (?) de Nekhen (afin) (qu'ils) aient fait ce qui est fait (habituellement) par Celle qui est dans la salle-ousekhet'.[711] In my opinion, however, even if the person in the broad hall is a female, she is not necessarily hostile towards Horus, and may be the designation of his mother, Isis.

The spelling on Sen's coffin makes it certain that in this version of the text He-who-is-in-the-broad-hall is a male divinity. Utterance 468 of the Pyramid Texts suggests that this designation may refer to Horus himself, as it reads: 'Oh, king, I am Horus. An offering that the king gives. You are given your bread, your beer, and your double *padj*-bread that comes forth from Horus, from He-who-is-in-the-broad-hall' (*hꜣ N jnk Ḥr.w ḥtp dj nsw dj n=k t=k ḥnq.t=k pꜣḏ.wj=k prj ḫr Ḥr.w jm.j-wsḫ.t*).[712] Since, as argued above, from line 16 the speaker of the text is very probably Horus, He-who-is-in-the-broad-hall may refer to a specific aspect of his that is somehow associated with the incarceration of Duamutef and Qebehsenuf, or more indirectly, with the second half of the lunar cycle.

However, since in Pepi's version of utterance 468 of the Pyramid Texts the speaker assumes the identity of Thoth (*jnk Ḏḥwtj*),[713] it is not entirely impossible that He-who-is-in-the-broad-hall is identical with this god. This understanding may find some support with the hieroglyphic signs of two different loaves of bread at the end of the expression *jm.j-wsḫ.t*. It is difficult to judge whether they only refer to the broad hall ('broad hall where food is offered'),[714] or to the expression *jm.j-wsḫ.t* as a whole. Howsoever it is the case, it is possible that the spelling of the word amounts to a kind of cryptography based on a visual pun which aims to display the sign ⊖, in order to evoke Thoth, since his name was written with this sign on several Middle Kingdom

[709] Faulkner 1973: 137.
[710] Barguet 1986: 575–576.
[711] Carrier 2004: 391.
[712] *Pyr.* 905a–b (Neith).
[713] *Pyr.* 905a.
[714] For the association of the broad hall with food and other goods, see also *Pyr.* 807a–b.

coffins.[715] The epithet He-who-is-in-the-broad-hall – though, to my knowledge, is not attested elsewhere with the same purpose – can aptly be used for Thoth, since he frequently appears in such a building as a judge or advocate in the court case of Horus and Seth (see for example the excerpt from Coffin Texts spell 9 above). Thoth is also always present at the judgement scene before Osiris in the netherworld, which also takes place in a broad hall ('the hall of the two truths', *wsḫ.t n mꜣꜥ.tj*).[716]

The omission of the first person singular suffix pronoun is a well-known characteristic of Egyptian written documents,[717] and I believe we encounter the same phenomenon at the beginning of line 19, rather than a missing third person plural suffix.[718] The perfect verb form, in my opinion, refers to the future and may again evoke the most important role of Thoth in a lunar context, that is, the filling of the eye of Horus. We should remember that spell 335 of the Coffin Texts and chapter 17 of the Book of Going Forth by Day clearly state this function of Thoth when they relate that Thoth used his fingers to fill the eye of Horus after it had been injured during the fight between Horus and Seth.[719] So the statement that Duamutef and Qebehsenuf will stay with the speaker, presumably Horus, in Nekhen until Seth finds out and protests about it must express the fact that the evil forces embodied by Seth cannot exert their influence during the waxing period of the lunar cycle, and naturally during full moon.

Lines 21–24

jm.jw Nḫn dy n=j ꜣḫ
jw=j rḫ.kw sštꜣ n Nḫn ḏr.tj pw jm.jw-snj
jw=j bs.kw ḥr bꜣ.w Nḫn wn n=j ṯs.n=j n Ḥr.w
jw=j rḫ.kw bꜣ.w Nḫn Ḥr.w pw Dwꜣ-mw.t=f pw Qbḥ-sn.w=f pw

Those who are in Nekhen, give me effectiveness!
I know the secret of Nekhen. It is the two hands and what is in them.
I have been initiated into the *bas* of Nekhen. Open to me so that I could join Horus.
I know the *bas* of Nekhen. It is Horus, it is Duamutef, it is Qebehsenuf.

The closing lines sum up what the text of spell 158 has been about. The effectiveness that the speaker demands from those who are in Nekhen, i.e. the *bas* of Nekhen, presumably refers to the power by which the harmful influence of Seth can be controlled and the integrity of the celestial eye – the moon – can be restored. The secret of Nekhen is once again defined as the two hands of Horus, and as the contents of the two hands, though the exact nature of what the hands hold is not expressed

[715] Gardiner 1957a: 531.
[716] Taylor 2011a: 204–206, 221.
[717] Allen 2001b: 48.
[718] cf. Faulkner 1973: 137 n. 10.
[719] *CT* IV, 233a–239a (T3Be); Lapp 1997: pl. 4.

within the spell. However, as we have seen, other sources definitely associate Seth's testicles or semen with the hands of Horus.

Though on Sen's coffin the text ends with the listing of the *bas* of Nekhen, who are understandably identified as Horus, Duamutef, and Qebehsenuf, in the Asyut variant a very interesting statement closes the discourse of spell 158. As I already discussed it to some extent above, it warns that the spell is 'not to be recited when eating pork' (*n ḏd ḥr wnm rrj*).[720] From the analysis of the relevant sources it is clear that the ritual consumption of pork in ancient Egypt was confined to the time of the full moon.[721] The instruction attached to the end of spell 158 of the Book of the Moon once more confirms that this text, unlike spell 157, does not describe the full moon, but is about the ensuing waning period of the lunar cycle.

[720] *CT* II, 362c.
[721] See comments on the previous spell.

2.6. Spell 159: the moon at the eastern horizon

The hieroglyphic text

Transliteration and translation

1. *rḫ bꜣ.w jꜣb.tjw jw=j rḫ.kw sbꜣ pw ḥr.j-jb prr.w Rꜥ jm=f m jꜣb.t*
2. *rs.j=f m š.w ḫbs.w m bw sqdd Rꜥ jm m ṯꜣw*
3. *mḥ.tj=f nw.yt sr.w m bw sqdd Rꜥ jm m ḫnj*
4. *jnk jr.j-smj.w m dp.t nṯr jnk ḫnj n wrḏ.n=f m wjꜣ Rꜥ*
5. *jw=j rḫ.kw nh.tj jptwj ntj mfkꜣ.t*
6. *pr.t Rꜥ jm.t-snj šm.tj ḥr st.t Šw r sbꜣ nb jꜣb.tj prr.w Rꜥ jm=f*
7. *jw=j rḫ.kw sḫ.t-jꜣr.w tw n.t Rꜥ*
8. *jw jnb n.tj ḥꜣ=s m bjꜣ jw qꜣw n bd.t=s m mḥ 5*
9. *jw šms=s m mḥ 1 jw mꜣw.t=f m mḥ 4*
10. *jw bd.t=s m mḥ 7 jw šms=s m mḥ 2 jw mꜣw.t=s m mḥ 5*
11. *jn ꜣḫ.tjw n.w mḥ 9 ꜣsḫ s(j) r-gs jꜣb.tjw*
12. *jw=j rḫ.kw bꜣ.w jꜣb.tjw*
13. *Ḥr.w-ꜣḫ.tj pw bḥs ḫrrw pw nṯr-dwꜣ.j pw*

1. Knowing the *bas* of the easterners. I know it is the gate in the middle, from which Re emerges in the east.
2. Its south is in the lake of the *ḫbs*-geese, which is the place where Re navigates by sailing;
3. its north is in the waters of the *sr*-geese, which is the place where Re navigates by rowing.
4. I am the one in charge of the rigging in the ship of the god, I am the one who rows and does not tire in Re's barque.
5. I know these two sycamore trees of turquoise
6. between which Re emerges, and which move on account of Shu's shooting up to every eastern gate from which Re emerges.
7. I know this Field of Reeds of Re,
8. whose surrounding wall is of iron, and the height of its emmer is five cubits,
9. its ear being one cubit, its stalk being four cubits,
10. (and then) its emmer is seven cubits, its ear being two cubits, its stalk being five cubits;
11. the nine-cubit tall horizon-dwellers reap it beside the easterners.
12. I know the *bas* of the easterners.
13. It is Harakhty, it is the solar calf, it is the Morning God.

Commentary

Line 1

rḫ bꜣ.w jꜣb.tjw jw=j rḫ.kw sbꜣ pw ḥr.j-jb prr.w Rꜥ jm=f m jꜣb.t

Knowing the *bas* of the easterners. I know it is the gate in the middle, from which Re emerges in the east.

The first sentence in line 1 is the title of the spell and, as usual, stands quite short on Sen's coffin. Longer introductory formulas are found only on two other coffins, S2P from Asyut and B1L from Deir el-Bersha. They are very similar, but the one from Asyut seems to be free of misspellings, so I quote it here:

ʿq pr.t m sbꜣ.w jꜣb.tjw n.w p.t m-m šms.w Rʿ

Entering and coming forth from the eastern gates of the sky among the followers of Re.

This extended title anticipates one of the main themes of spell 158, the description of the gate or gates from which Re emerges at sunrise. The other two major topics included in the text, the two sycamore trees in the east and the Field of Reeds (a heavenly region also in the east of the sky), as we shall see, are also concerned with the definition of the circumstances of sunrise. This great emphasis put on the behaviour of the sun in the Book of the Moon may be a bit surprising, but we have to bear in mind that spell 158 ended with describing how the rising sun, in the disguise of Sobek, caught the last crescent of the waning moon. Thus the previous chapters of the composition, spells 154 to 158, took into account the events during the course of a lunation, from the day of lunar invisibility (*psḏn.tjw*) to the last sighting of the waning crescent, and with spell 159 we have once more returned to the point in time when the moon becomes hidden in front of the sun. This, as explained above, happens when one morning the observer of the moon only sees the rising solar disc. Therefore the portrayal of sunrise is quite appropriate for evoking the invisible moon, and that is the reason why spell 159 abounds in solar references.

At the beginning of the discussion of *CT* 159 it must be pointed out that a very similar text has come down to us in the form of spell 161 of the Coffin Texts. This particular text is preserved in a sole copy on a 13th dynasty coffin originating from el-Lisht.[722] The two texts are surely related in some way, and I will discuss the possible nature of this connection in another chapter (3.2.) of the present work. The text reads:

[722] *CT* II, 388d–s; Quirke 1996: 399.

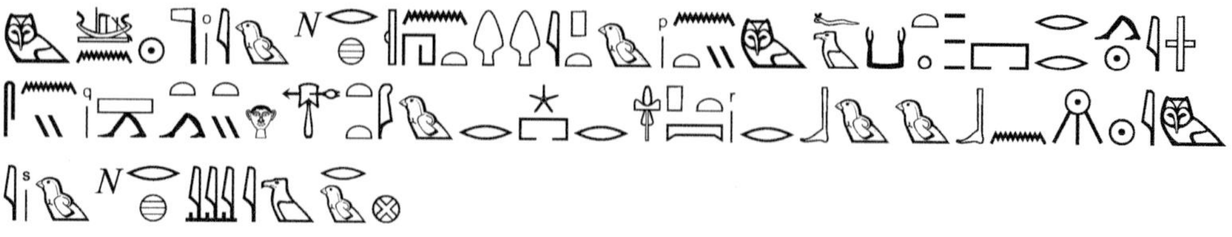

ḏd-mdw jw N rḫ sḫ.t-jꜣr.w njw.t pw n.t Rꜥ jw [...] jw šms=s m mḥ 2 jw mꜣw.t=f m mḥ 7 jn ꜣḫ n mḥ 4 ꜣsḫ st r-gs Rꜥ ḏs=f jw N rḫ sbꜣ pw ḥr.j-jb n sḫ.t-jꜣr.w prr.w Rꜥ jm=f m jꜣb.t p.t jw rs.j=f m š ḫꜣr.w [...] mḥ.tj=f m nw.yt r.w r bw sqdd.w Rꜥ jm N pw ẖnn n wrḏ.n=f m wjꜣ n Rꜥ jw N rḫ nh.tj jptw ntj mfkꜣ.t prr jm.j-snj šm.tj ḥr st.t Šw r sbꜣ r jꜣb.t p.t r bw wbn Rꜥ jm jw N rḫ sḫ.t-jꜣr.w

To be recited: *N* knows the Field of Reeds, it is the town of Re [...] its ear is two cubits, its stalk is seven cubits. The four-cubit tall effective spirit reaps it alongside with Re himself. *N* knows the gate in the middle of the Field of Reeds from which Re emerges in the east of the sky. Its south is in the lake of the *ḫꜣr*-geese, its north in the waters of the *r*-geese, as the place where Re navigates; it is *N* who rows and does not tire in Re's barque. *N* knows these two sycamore trees of turquoise between which Re emerges, and which move on account of Shu's shooting up to the eastern gate in the east of the sky, to the place where Re rises. *N* knows the Field of Reeds.

Here we should note that though the contents of the two texts are very much alike, spell 161 presents the main topics in a slightly different order, since it starts off with the description of the Field of Reeds, then continues with the gates in the east and the pair of sycamore trees. Another noticeable difference is that spell 161 does not mention the *bas* of the easterners; in other words, it lacks the title and the closing formula of spell 159 that frame the descriptions of the different features of sunrise. Spell 161 is thus just a straightforward account of the Field of Reeds, the eastern gates from which Re emerges, and the turquoise sycamore trees.

Spell 159 was recorded on coffins from Asyut and Deir el-Bersha, whereas spell 161, as stated above, has come down to us on a coffin that was manufactured in a more northerly location near the entrance to the Fayum region (el-Lisht). The relatively widespread distribution of these spells perhaps indicates that the themes contained in them were well-known throughout Egypt surely by the Middle Kingdom, but possibly even earlier. For example the Field of Reeds is mentioned quite a few times in the Pyramid Texts,[723] and it features in a number of spells in the Coffin Texts as well,[724] so it is not surprising that we come across the detailed description of the region in spells 159 and 161.

[723] Faulkner 1969: 326.
[724] Molen 2000: 530.

Lines 1–3

rḫ b3.w j3b.tjw jw=j rḫ.kw sb3 pw ḥr.j-jb prr.w Rˁ jm=f m j3b.t
rs.j=f m š.w ḫbs.w m bw sqdd Rˁ jm m t̠3w
mḥ.tj=f nw.yt sr.w m bw sqdd Rˁ jm m ẖnj

Knowing the *bas* of the easterners. I know it is the gate in the middle, from which Re emerges in the east.
Its south is in the lake of the *ḫbs*-geese, which is the place where Re navigates by sailing;
its north is in the waters of the *sr*-geese, which is the place where Re navigates by rowing.

Line 1 specifies the place of sunrise as a gate (*sb3*) in the east. There is possibly a pun behind such a definition of the location where the sun appears in the morning, because the word *sb3* 'gate' is homonymous with *sb3* 'star', and in fact the spelling of even the first word contains the hieroglyph representing a star (*). Since later the text talks about knowing every eastern gate from which Re emerges (line 6), the wordplay hinting at the equivalence of these gates with stars perhaps indicates an astronomical observation. Because the earth orbits around the sun, the latter is seemingly not set against a stationary background of the stars. Along the year, the sun moves through a distinct band of the sky, the ecliptic, and from time to time it masks a different group of stars, that is, for example in the middle of the winter it cancels out the light of certain stars, while in the middle of the summer it blots out a totally different set of stars.

Later classical astronomy, based on Babylonian and Hellenic notions, grouped these stars into the signs of the zodiac in accordance with the partition of the year into twelve months.[725] This scheme was certainly not known to the Egyptians until Ptolemaic times, and possibly only in the 1st millennium BCE was it devised in a systematic manner in Mesopotamia itself.[726] Nevertheless, the information about the gates in the east, and the wordplay involving these heavenly gates and stars in spell 159 seem to imply that the Egyptians also understood the yearly wandering of the sun through the starry regions of a specific band of the celestial dome. The zodiac and the ecliptic are of course modern concepts; in no way do I want to imply that the Egyptians used these notional frameworks at the beginning of the 2nd millennium BCE. I only wish to highlight that the gates in the east may have some astronomical connotations. There is of course evidence from the Pyramid Texts that the ancient Egyptians identified the path of the sun among the stars as the Winding Waterway (*mr-n-ḫ3*).[727]

To understand the message of the first few lines of the text, the yearly movement of the sun must also be tracked down within another framework, which basically means the eastern horizon. Since the earth's axis is slightly tilted from its plane of orbit

[725] Waerden 1953.
[726] Waerden 1953: 218–224.
[727] Krauss 1997: 49–63.

around the sun, the place of sunrise on the eastern horizon does not remain constant but varies according to a well-definable pattern. In summer, when the northern hemisphere is tilted towards the sun, the sun rises more to the north on the horizon. As time progresses, the sun wanders southward along the eastern horizon until, at a certain point in winter (in modern terms, at winter solstice), it reaches its most southerly point. Then the trend changes and the solar disc starts to move northwards until, in the middle of summer (summer solstice), it gets to its northernmost point. Then the cycle starts to repeat itself.

In the symbolic language of spell 159 the two extremities of this apparent movement of the sun along the eastern horizon are defined as watery regions where different kinds of bird reside, and where Re travels by means of his barque. The southern region belongs to the *ḫbs*-geese; the species of bird called *ḫbs* has been interpreted to denote the cormorant.[728] It is possible that this bird was chosen to mark the southern limit of Re's journey with a pun in mind, because the name of the animal resembled the expression *ḫꜣ-bꜣ=s* 'starry sky',[729] sometimes simply spelled *ḫbs*.[730] Re travels to this region by sailing, since this was the ordinary mode of transport towards the south due to the dominant north-south wind direction in Egypt.[731] The bird of the northern watery region in the path of Re is the *sr*-goose (grey goose),[732] and Re reaches its territory by rowing, which was of course the way to travel north in the Nile.

In modern terms we would say that these watery limits in the south and north correspond to the winter and summer solstices, respectively. In fact, from Ptolemaic times, when the scheme of the zodiacal signs was adopted in Egypt, we do have some evidence to suggest that the *sr*-goose – more precisely, its female form, the *sr.t*-goose – was associated with the winter solstice. By this time the decans, that is the stars or star clusters that signalled the hours of the night, were often represented as a procession of human and zoomorphic figures.[733] In a parallel development three decans were assigned to each of the signs of the zodiac, due to the fact that one decan was supposed to mark a particular hour of the night for ten days (so three decans roughly corresponded to thirty days).[734]

Different traditions existed about the decans, both in terms of nomenclature and iconography,[735] but in the group that has been customarily called the Tanis family,[736] shown for example in the temple at Esna and in the round zodiac of the Dendera

[728] Vernus and Yoyotte 2005: 85.
[729] The term literally means 'a thousand are her (that is, the sky goddess Nut's) *bas*', see Wilson 1997: 704.
[730] *Wb.* III, 230.1.
[731] Partridge 2010: 371.
[732] Behrens 1975: 504.
[733] Neugebauer and Parker 1969: 153–174.
[734] Neugebauer and Parker 1969: 168–174.
[735] Neugebauer and Parker 1969: 105–174.
[736] Neugebauer and Parker 1969: 140–149.

temple,[737] the three decans of Capricorn were called *smd* ('eyebrow'?), *sr.t* ('grey goose'), and *s3-sr.t* ('son of the grey goose').[738] The decan was indeed represented by the figure of the bird (though the images of the two other decans did not correspond to their names). Capricorn was of course the sign in which the sun dwelled at the time of the winter solstice during the epoch when the decan lists were matched with the zodiac in ancient Egypt.

That the pairing of the decan *sr.t* ('grey goose'), and its derivative *s3-sr.t* ('son of the grey goose'), with Capricorn, and consequently with the winter solstice, was not fortuitous is suggested by the iconographic programme of the round Dendera zodiac. As I argued in my analysis of this artefact,[739] its images – a mixture of pictorial representations of actual constellations and cultic events – record the celestial birth myth of Horus that was tied to three key points in the year: the conjunction of the sun and the moon after the autumnal equinox, the winter solstice, and the appearance of the first lunar crescent after the vernal equinox.[740] To mark the winter solstice – the time of gestation for Horus in the womb – the inner frame of the round zodiac once more shows the figure of the grey goose, together with the slightly modified images of the two other decans of Capricorn.[741]

Therefore in these late sources the *sr.t* decan signifies the winter solstice, that is the southernmost point of the sun along the eastern horizon. In spell 159 the male equivalent of this bird belongs to the opposite, northern extremity of the solar path. It is not impossible that this dichotomy between the male and female forms of the grey goose, corresponding to the end points of the sun's wandering in the east, already existed when the Coffin Texts were written, though – admittedly – no evidence to this effect has been preserved. Alternatively, the appearance of the *sr.t* decan marking the winter solstice may be the late reflection of the original northerly region belonging to the *sr*-goose, but in the meantime its original role was somehow reversed. Such a confusion, it seems, could have easily arisen, because the southern and northern waters of the eastern horizon were associated with other species of waterfowl (*ḫ3r.w* and *r.w*) in chapters 107 and 109 of the Book of Going Forth by Day,[742] the descendants of spell 159 of the Book of the Moon. The alternative naming of these waters – as spell 752 of the Coffin Texts testifies to it – was already known at the beginning of the 2nd millennium BCE.[743]

The text of spell 159 defines the *bas* of the easterners as the gate in the middle of the east, which is flanked in the south and the north by watery regions that – as has

[737] Sauneron 1969: 14; Cauville 1997: pl. 60.
[738] For the correspondences between the decans and zodiacal signs, see Priskin 2015b: 166–170.
[739] Priskin 2015b.
[740] Priskin 2015b: 142–152.
[741] Priskin 2015b: 147–149.
[742] Allen 1974: 85–86.
[743] *CT* VI, 381a.

been argued – in all probability correspond to the winter and summer solstice points marked along the horizon. This description lends itself to two interpretations as to the exact nature of the gate in the middle. On the one hand, this gate may be understood as that stretch of the eastern horizon that the rising sun wanders through during its yearly movement. However, there is also room for another interpretation, because the introductory formula on the Asyut coffin talks about gates, and not one gate (see above), and also the expression in line 6 'every eastern gate' implies that more than one gate signify the place or places where the sun rises. Obviously, all of these gates would be found between the realms of the *ḫbs*-geese and the *sr*-geese. Within this framework, then, the gate in the middle would define the mid-point between the southern and northern extremities. In modern terms, as these latter mark the winter and summer solstices, the gate in the middle would stand for the equinoctial point, either in the autumn or spring.

This is of course largely conjecture, but I think we cannot categorically rule out that with its description of the gate in the middle spell 159 wants to refer to an equinox. From my analyses of the depiction of the constellation of the boat on the astronomical diagram of the Ramesseum and the Graeco-Roman zodiacs, it transpired that the ancient Egyptians indeed observed the equinoxes, and especially those autumnal equinoxes that corresponded with the day of the full moon.[744] Such a day, in my opinion, was viewed in ancient Egypt as the expression of perfect cosmic harmony: both the sun and the moon spent the same amount of time in the sky, crossing it from the east to the west, the latter as the full lunar disc, the worthy counterpart of its diurnal companion.[745] From the context of spell 159, however, it is clear that it does not describe the day of the full moon, but – as argued – rather its opposite, the day of the invisible moon. We may suppose that if the coincidence of the full moon with the autumnal equinox was a marked occasion, its reversal, the coincidence of the blacked-out moon with the equinox was also seen as somehow special, and perhaps that is why a reference to the middle gate in the sun's yearly shuttle along the eastern horizon is included in *CT* 159.

Line 4

jnk jr.j-smj.w m dp.t nṯr jnk ḫnj n wrḏ.n=f m wjꜣ Rꜥ

I am the one in charge of the rigging in the ship of the god, I am the one who rows and does not tire in Re's barque.

In the previous lines it was described how Re moved both to the south and the north along the imagined eastern water route corresponding to the span of the horizon from which the morning sun could appear. From line 4 we learn that the speaker –

[744] Priskin 2015b: 149–152; Priskin 2016b: 101–104.
[745] Priskin 2015b: 163.

the deceased – also takes part in this journey as a member of the crew in the divine barque. The sentence emphasises that he equally busies himself when the barque is travelling south, as he handles the sails on this leg of the journey, and when the ship is heading north, as he tirelessly rows to propel it to its other destination. The dual nature of his job reflects the opposing directions of the solar barque.

Line 4 thus basically tells us that the speaker is on board the solar barque, and we of course know it from a number of sources that this was one of the principal wishes of the deceased in ancient Egypt.[746] Spell 159 is about the invisible moon, and certain texts seem to connect the joining of Re's barque with this moment of the lunar cycle. Spell 176 of the Coffin Texts expresses this action with the following words: 'May the god come in peace, say those who are in the moon, the Great One; they have given me glorious appearances together with Re. To go forth to the sky, to the place where Re is' (*jj nṯr m ḥtp jn≈sn jmj.w jꜥḥ wr rdj.n≈sn n≈j ḫꜥ.w ḥna Rꜥ pr.t r p.t r bw ntj Rꜥ jm*).[747] Whereas in this text it is tempting to see the expression *jꜥḥ wr* 'the moon, the Great One' or 'the great moon' as a reference to the full moon,[748] the assertion that the beings associated with it assisted in glorious appearances with Re suggests the time of conjunction, when the invisible moon does in fact emerge together with the sun. This meaning is further supported by the rubric at the end, which specifies the purpose of the spell as going to the place in the sky where Re is. Furthermore, a very similar statement is made in spell 853,[749] preserved in a single copy on a coffin from Saqqara, and there the next spell (854) is about becoming Khepri, the rising sun.[750]

The idea of the deceased and the moon being on board the barque of Re is also recorded in one of the vignettes of the Book of Going Forth by Day. It is actually known as chapter 143 of the composition and belongs to chapters 141 and 142,[751] two initiation spells. Crucially, chapter 141 starts with the instruction that it should be recited on the day of the blacked-out moon (*ḏd.t hrw psḏn.tjw jn N*).[752] The vignettes in the individual papyrus rolls containing the Book of Going Forth by Day may vary slightly,[753] but for example in the papyrus of Iufankh (Ptolemaic Period) we see five registers, and in one of them a barque is shown carrying a human figure (the deceased) and two discs.[754] The bigger one of these must represent the sun, while the smaller one next to it is in my opinion the depiction of the invisible moon in Re's morning barque. The whole image thus records how the deceased joins Re on the day of lunar invisibility. Although the statement in spell 159 implies that the deceased is constantly part of the crew on the

[746] *CT* VII, 258a–261b (*CT* 1030); see also for example chapters 100–102 of the Book of Going Forth by Day, Allen 1974: 82–84.
[747] *CT* III, 62f–i.
[748] Faulkner 1973: 151; Barguet 1986: 382; Carrier 2004: 437.
[749] *CT* VII, 56l–p.
[750] *CT* VII, 57f–l.
[751] Allen 1974: 117–120.
[752] Lepsius 1842: pl. lviii.
[753] cf. Mosher 2001: pl. 22.
[754] Lepsius 1842: pl. lix.

solar barque, when it fares both upstream and downstream, the cited written and visual references suggest that the time of the invisible moon was especially propitious for stepping on the barque of Re, and this corresponds well with the wider context of the spell, the disappearance of the last crescent on the day of lunar invisibility.

Lines 5–6

jw=j rḫ.kw nh.tj jptwj n.tj mfkꜣ.t
pr.t Rꜥ jm.t-snj šm.tj ḥr st.t Šw r sbꜣ nb jꜣb.tj prr.w Rꜥ jm=f

I know these two sycamore trees of turquoise
between which Re emerges, and which move on account of Shu's shooting up to every eastern gate from which Re emerges.

This is the first written description of the motif of two sycamore trees flanking the rising sun in the east.[755] The idea was possibly older, as is suggested by a statement in utterance 568 of the Pyramid Texts: 'The king will seize for himself the two sycamore trees that are on the other side of the sky. "Ferry him over!" So they place him on the other, eastern side of the sky' (*nḏr n=f N pn nh.tj jm.tj gs pf n p.t ḏꜣj sw dj=sn sw m gs pf jꜣb.tj n p.t*).[756] In this passage, too, the twin sycamores are located on the eastern side of the sky. Since the preceding part of utterance 568 describes how the king and a divinity embodying the two celestial eyes, Mekhentiirti,[757] go to their *kas* by ferrying over the sky, it may well be that the twin sycamores also appear in a lunar context in the Pyramid Texts, since the moon was often seen as the pre-eminent celestial ferryman.[758] Perhaps it is directly evoked in utterance 568 by the claim that 'the bull of the sky has bent down its horn so that he (the king) may pass there to the lakes of the netherworld' (*qꜥḥ.n kꜣ p.t ꜥb=f swꜣ=f jm jr š.w dꜣ.t*).[759] These lakes are perhaps identical with the ones mentioned in spell 159 of the Book of the Moon. It must be said, however, that while the moon is perhaps only alluded to in utterance 568, the imperishable stars are explicitly named as the entities responsible for making the celestial ferryboat cross the sky.[760]

From the New Kingdom onwards, pictorial representations of the two sycamore trees in the east frequently occur in private tombs and in papyri, as vignettes to chapter 109 of the Book of Going Forth by Day, the descendant of spell 159 of the Coffin Texts.[761] They usually show the representation of the sun, either the figure of Re in his barque or the solar disc, together with a calf, another symbol of the rising sun (see

[755] Refai 2000: 384.
[756] *Pyr.* §1433b–c.
[757] Leitz 2002c: 394–396.
[758] Krauss 1997: 67–79.
[759] *Pyr.* §1432b.
[760] *Pyr.* §1432a.
[761] Wilkinson 1992: 116–117.

below).[762] The Egyptians often depicted the rising solar disc surrounded on the two sides by the two Meret-goddesses (*uraei*), baboons, two lions, two *wedjat*-eyes, or other divinities.[763] Whether the two sycamores originated this iconographic tradition, or simply conformed to this pattern, is difficult to tell. The different motifs could later be combined with each other, when for example the two sycamores appear together with Isis and Nephthys,[764] who from the New Kingdom onwards also frequently assisted at the birth of the morning sun in the east.[765]

The sycamore tree, besides its cosmic significance, was especially closely associated with the goddesses Nut and Hathor.[766] According to the written accounts and vignettes in the Book of Going Forth by Day, these tree goddesses – as they were in fact depicted residing in the sycamore tree – provided nourishment for the deceased.[767] Sometimes these mythological concepts were intertwined, as for example in a scene found in the new year's court (*wꜥb.t*) of the Dendera temple.[768] This temple was of course dedicated to Hathor, and one of the epithets of this goddess was 'Mistress of the Sycamore' (*nb.t-nh.t*).[769] The scene shows the sky goddess Nut arching over a large hieroglyph of the horizon (*ꜣḫ.t*) that supports the emblem of Hathor (a bovine female head). She here clearly stands for the rising sun as Nut overhead is in fact giving birth to the solar disc, and its rays shine directly on Hathor's head. Two trees, planted into the hills of the *akhet*-hieroglyph at both ends, flank the symbol of Hathor, and this detail once more emphasises the connection of the scene with sunrise on the one hand, and the cosmic significance of the two sycamore trees on the other.

In line 6 we learn two important things about the two sycamores on the two sides of the eastern gate of sunrise. The first one is that they move, or more literally, 'go about' (*šm.tj* – the ending indicates that the verb refers to the two trees). This is of course a surprising piece of information, because trees are generally fixed and stationary, and to put it sarcastically, hardly ever change their place on their own initative. The movement of the trees is again most probably due to the fact that the place of sunrise wanders along the eastern horizon as time progresses. Consequently, the trees must also follow the displacement of the emerging solar disc. The description of the sycamores as shuffling along is yet another argument in favour of the interpretation that the gate in the east does not stand for a particular stretch of the eastern horizon, but for the individual spots that represent the rising sun on different days.

The other notable thing is that it is Shu, the god of the air and the atmosphere, who is ultimately responsible for the movement of the trees. The verb that denotes his

[762] Billing 2002: 330–347 figs. A.1–31.
[763] Refai 2000: 386.
[764] Refai 2000: 386, 391 fig. 12, 392 figs. 13–14.
[765] Hornung 2002: 307–308.
[766] Buhl 1947: 91.
[767] Buhl 1947: 91–92.
[768] Refai 2000: 391 fig. 11; Cauville 1990: 61.
[769] Leitz 2002d: 79.

relevant activity, *stj*, has been interpreted as 'to strew',[770] or 'to seed', 'to throw seeds'.[771] In my opinion, the word used here is *stj* 'to shoot', 'to throw', 'to pour',[772] and the whole expression evokes how at dawn, before the solar disc actually appears on the horizon, the hue of the sky in the east changes to foreshadow the arrival of the rising sun. Spell 75 of the Coffin Texts, which is a transformation text used by the deceased to turn themselves into Shu, clearly specifies the role of the god in this respect: 'I am the one who foretells him as he comes forth from the horizon' (*jnk sr sw prj=f m ꜣḫ.t*),[773] where 'he' obviously refers to the sun god.[774] Now it also makes sense why the two sycamores are said to be of turquoise: this is a material that through its colour is inherently associated with the blue sky of the day.[775] In short, the two sycamore trees are the symbols of the part of the sky that lightens up in the east before sunrise, and for the ancient Egyptians this phenomenon was a manifestation of the air god Shu.[776]

Lines 7–11

jw=j rḫ.kw sḫ.t-jꜣr.w tw n.t Rꜥ
jw jnb n.tj ḥꜣ=s m bjꜣ jw qꜣw n bd.t=s m mḥ 5
jw šms=s m mḥ 1 jw mꜣw.t=f m mḥ 4
jw bd.t=s m mḥ 7 jw šms=s m mḥ 2 jw mꜣw.t=s m mḥ 5
jn ꜣḫ.tjw n.w mḥ 9 ꜣsḫ s(j) r-gs jꜣb.tjw

I know this Field of Reeds of Re,
whose surrounding wall is of iron, and the height of its emmer is five cubits,
its ear being one cubit, its stalk being four cubits,
(and then) its emmer is seven cubits, its ear being two cubits, its stalk being five cubits;
the nine-cubit tall horizon-dwellers reap it beside the easterners.

The third major theme of spell 158 is the knowledge about the Field of Reeds. It directly relates to the two previous themes – the gate in the east and the two sycamore trees – because the Field of Reeds is another name for the location where sunrise takes place. This role of the mythical region called the Field of Reeds is already attested for example in utterance 479 of the Pyramid Texts that connects it with the emergence of the sun – alluded to in the texts as the different forms of Horus, Osiris, and the king – in the morning: 'The two door leaves of the sky open as the two door leaves of the celestial waters open for Horus of the Gods. He comes forth at dawn and he is purified in the Field of Reeds' (*wn ꜥꜣ.wj p.t j.sn ꜥꜣ.wj qbḥ n Ḥr.w-nṯr.w prj=f m tp-dwꜣ wꜥb=f*

[770] Faulkner 1973: 138. Faulkner misunderstands the name of Shu as the object of the infinitive and a reference to shading (from the homonymy between the divine name and an expression with that meaning, see *Wb.* IV, 429.1–4 and 432.1–5).
[771] Barguet 1986: 386?; Carrier 2004: 393.
[772] *Wb.* IV, 326.1–327.14.
[773] *CT* I, 321d–322a.
[774] Faulkner 1973: 75 n. 8.
[775] Lucas and Harris 1999: 404.
[776] cf. Faulkner 1973: 75 n. 8.

m sḫ.t-j3r.w).[777] In utterance 253 it is Re himself who is purified in the Field of Reeds: 'Re has been purified in the Field of Reeds, who has been purified has purified himself in the Field of Reeds, the king has been purified in the Field of Reeds; the king's arm is the arm of Re, oh, Nut, take his arm, oh, Shu, lift him up' (*wꜥb.n Rꜥ m sḫ.t-j3r.w wꜥb.n wꜥb.n m sḫ.t-j3r.w wꜥb.n N m sḫ.t-j3r.w ꜥ n N pn m ꜥ Rꜥ Nw.t šsp ꜥ=f Šw sšwj sw)*.[778] This passage is also interesting because Shu once more appears in connection with sunrise, as he is supposed to lift up Re.

The cited excerpts from the Pyramid Texts prove that the Field of Reeds was closely associated with the eastern region of the sky. However, most researchers believe that in this oldest corpus of funerary literature the Field of Reeds corresponded to the region of the sky that was situated south of the Winding Waterway, the band of the sky across which the sun, moon, and the planets traversed the watery celestial expanses.[779] It had its northern counterpart – the area north of the Winding Waterway – called the Field of Rest (or Offerings, *sḫ.t-ḥtp.w*). Due to the non-exclusive logic of Egyptian thought, it may have been that the Field of Reeds sometimes referred to the southern sky and sometimes to its eastern regions. Howsoever it was the case, from the Coffin Texts onwards it was increasingly seen to be situated in the east, as a destination for the deceased where they could attain a blissful, bucolic life,[780] and spell 159 is one of the earliest texts that marks this shift of meaning, with its references to the reaping of corn of gigantic proportions (though these allusions are perhaps rather symbolic, see below).

The vision of the Field of Reeds as the place of idyllic netherworldly existence is best evidenced in the Book of Going Forth by Day. Three chapters of this composition provide information on the Field of Reeds. Chapter 109 is the direct descendant of *CT* 159, so it links the description of the Field of Reeds – and of the eastern gates and twin sycamores – with the *bas* of the easterners.[781] Chapter 149 takes account of the mounds in the Field of Reeds, and its second mound is essentially described with the words of chapter 109.[782] Chapter 110 not only describes the Field of Reeds in words as the place where the pursuits of earthly existence – ploughing, reaping, eating, drinking, making love – can be continued, but it is also appended by a vignette that visually represents the ideal landscape of the netherworld.[783] This illustration shows the deceased as they perform agricultural work or meet different divinities within an elaborate network of waterways surrounding a few islands. Interestingly enough, this diagram of the Field of Reeds originates from a drawing in the Coffin Texts, attached to spells 466 and 467,

[777] *Pyr.* §981a–b. Similar statements are made in utterances 325, 510, and 563.
[778] *Pyr.* §275b–f.
[779] Krauss 1997: 14–66; Allen 2002: 63; Taylor 2011b: 242.
[780] Taylor 2011b: 242.
[781] Allen 1974: 86. See also chapter 3.4.
[782] Allen 1974: 142.
[783] Allen 1974: 87–90; Lapp 2004: pls 49–53.

the forerunners of Book of the Going Forth by Day chapter 110, though there the texts identify the illustration as showing the Field of Rest, and not the Field of Reeds.[784]

As the history of the vignette of chapter 110 shows, when we look at all the evidence pertaining to the Field of Reeds, it is difficult to project a clear-cut image of this region of the netherworld. Perhaps its definition was already loose originally, allowing for different interpretations; then it got entangled with other concepts such as the Field of Rest/Field of Offerings, and its meaning shifted towards being the perfect location of netherworldly existence. However, it seems to be a constant trait that it had something to do with the eastern region of the sky and with sunrise, and these aspects explain why spell 159, offering a catalogue of the phenomena connected with the emergence of the sun in the morning, also includes the description of the Field of Reeds.

In line 8 we learn that the Field of Reeds is surrounded by a wall made of iron, and this detail emphasises the heavenly nature of the region, because the word *bjꜣ* was used to refer to meteoric iron.[785] After the short reference to the enclosure wall, a relatively detailed description informs us about the emmer (wheat) that grows in the Field of Reeds. While based on the Asyut version of the text it is customary to render the two expressions denoting corn in lines 8 and 10 as barley and emmer,[786] on Sen's coffin and in the Deir el-Bersha variants there is no difference in their spelling, apart from the reversion of the first few signs (the loaf, the strokes, and the ear of emmer). This means, in my opinion, that they refer to the same thing, and the different dimensions assigned to them want to evoke the idea of growth. First the emmer is said to be five cubits tall, its ear being one cubit and its stalk reaching four cubits, then – although it is not stated explicitly – it grows to the height of seven cubits, its ear being two cubits and its stalk being five cubits. It is worth noting that the measurements correspond to a simple pattern of addition: the ear grows one cubit, and the stalk also grows one cubit, and that results in an overall difference of two cubits (five cubits as opposed to seven cubits).

The measurements are of course also unrealistic; no actual emmer can grow to reach a height of approximately two and a half metres (five cubits), not to mention three and a half metres (seven cubits). The exaggerated size of the plants may express the extraordinary conditions of the netherworld in general, or – as I conjectured earlier – may allude to the proximity of the moon,[787] since there is some evidence from Egypt showing that the moon had a beneficial effect on the growth of vegetation.[788] However, as spell 159 is about the rising sun in the east, it is not impossible that the growing measurements of the emmer simply allude to one thing that can in fact be

[784] *CT* V, 352–380d.
[785] *Wb.* I, 438.8–11.
[786] Faulkner 1973: 138; Barguet 1986: 576; Carrier 2004: 393.
[787] Priskin 2016a: 109.
[788] Smith 2002: 126.

seen getting bigger and bigger in the Field of Reeds, in the eastern region of the sky: the emerging solar disc. In this interpretational framework the ears of the emmer symbolise the part of the solar disc that is above the horizon, first only one cubit and then two cubits, while the stalks refer to the unseen parts growing from four cubits to five cubits. When the solar disc lifts up and is severed from the horizon, it is reaped; the horizon-dwellers who do this are described as nine cubits tall, which is possibly a reference to the full extent of the sun's disc, in accordance with the symbolic connotations of the number nine expressing totality.[789]

This is of course not to deny that the Field of Reeds had strong agricultural connotations. Utterance 461 of the Pyramid Texts already described it as a land where corn is grown: 'The two door leaves of the sky open as the two door leaves of the celestial waters open. You will begin your journey by boat to the Field of Reeds, and you will cultivate barley and reap emmer there' (*wn ꜥꜣ.wj p.t j.sn ꜥꜣ.wj qbḥ.w jṯj=k ḥjp.t r sḫ.t-jꜣr.w skꜣ=k jtj ꜣsḫ=k bd.t*).[790] Unlike the Deir el-Bersha versions of spell 159, this text also juxtaposes barley with emmer. Spell 159 builds upon this agricultural imagery of the Field of Reeds, and through a matrix of dimensions that describe the emmer growing there possibly also evokes the emerging solar disc. The equivalence between the sun and emmer could have easily been imagined, as the yellow colour of the latter may have been likened to the bright colour of the solar disc.

Lines 12–13

jw=j rḫ.kw bꜣ.w jꜣb.tjw
Ḥr.w-ꜣḫ.tj pw bḥs ḫrrw pw nṯr-dwꜣ.j pw

I know the *bas* of the easterners.
It is Harakhty, it is the solar calf, it is the Morning God.

The final lines of spell 159, as usual in the chapters of the Book of the Moon, list the *bas* of the place, phenomenon, or beings the particular text deals with. The list always consists of three members. In the previous chapters these *bas* were mostly divinities that already appeared in some form or another in the body of the spells themselves. Spell 159 deviates from this pattern because the *bas* of the easterners named here, Harakhty, the solar calf, and the Morning God, did not play a part in the preceding discussion. Nonetheless, they are closely associated with the major topic of the spell, the emergence of the sun in the east, because these three beings are further symbols of the rising solar disc. The sharp contrast between the main body of the spell, with its descriptions of the eastern gate(s), the two sycamores, and the Field of Reeds, and the three – only indirectly related – *bas* may be made sense of if we remember that the body of spell 159, without the references to the *bas* in the title and the closing formula,

[789] Wilkinson 1994: 136.
[790] *Pyr.* §873c–874a.

also existed as a separate spell (*CT* 161). Very probably, this description was borrowed by the editors of the Book of the Moon, and to fit it into the composition, they added the title and the colophon to make the spell similar to the other chapters.[791] This procedure then resulted in the apparent incongruity of the *bas* with the described features of sunrise.

Harakhty's name (*Ḥr.w-ꜣḫ.tj*) literally means 'Horus of the horizon',[792] and while the usual translation of *ꜣḫ.t* is horizon, we should not forget that it is really the name of the region around the horizon – the land of light – where the sun god emerges.[793] Thus Harakhty's connection with the beginning of the day is quite obvious. He is also one of the hypostases of Horus who is addressed in the lustration spells of the Pyramid Texts, so he is also a divinity for whom the doors of the sky open at dawn and who is purified in the Field of Reeds.[794] The close connections of Harakhty with the sun god are of course also indicated by his syncretistic form, Re-Harakhty, often associated with the morning and diurnal sun.[795]

The name of the next being identified as one of the *bas* of the easterners is a bit problematic. It is certainly introduced by the noun *bḥs* 'calf', but what follows is a real enigma. The word has been interpreted as *ḫwrr*,[796] possibly the same expression that is used in connection with the divine ennead in utterance 218 of the Pyramid Texts (*ḫwrr psḏ.t*, 'the *ḫwrr* of the ennead').[797] As practically all the text variants spell the word as *ḫwrr*, the form *ḫrrw* on Sen's coffin seems to be a scribal mistake. In any case, the expression is a hapax legomenon, the precise meaning of which eludes me. As an approximation, I render the phrase *bḥs ḫwrr* 'the solar calf',[798] mainly on the evidence provided by the later vignettes to chapter 109 of the Book of Going Forth by Day. These illustrations, besides the two sycamores and the representation of the solar disc or the sun god, also show a calf that is either white or spotted.[799] This animal is yet another symbol of the young sun, since the sky – sometimes imagined as a cow (the heavenly cow) – was thought to give birth to the sun in the form of a cow. This idea is already present in the Pyramid Texts, as utterance 485A says: 'The king has come to you, Re, a calf of gold born of the sky' (*jw.n N pn ḫr≠k Rʿ bḥs n nbw ms.w p.t*).[800]

The third *ba* of the easterners, and the third symbol of the rising sun, is the Morning God, whose name (*nṯr-dwꜣ.j*) is often translated as the Morning Star. The Morning God has been equated with Venus when it appears as a herald of sunrise just before

[791] For further remarks on this topic, see chapter 3.2.
[792] Leitz 2002e: 239.
[793] Allen 1994: 26–27.
[794] See for example *Pyr.* §526a–c.
[795] cf. chapter 15 of the Book of Going Forth by Day, Allen 1974: 12–26.
[796] Faulkner 1973: 138 n.3; Barguet 1986: 576; Carrier 2004: 392.
[797] *Pyr.* §163a. See also Faulkner 1973: 138 n.3.
[798] cf. Hodel-Hoenes 2000: 264.
[799] Billing 2002: 330–331 figs. A.1–4.
[800] *Pyr.* §1029a–b.

dawn,[801] and indeed in demotic – and some late hieroglyphic – texts the name *nṯr-dwꜣ.j* denotes the planet Venus.[802] However, it seems that in certain contexts the term was used more widely, and it could refer to any star rising heliacally and thus foretelling the arrival of the rising sun.[803] It is even possible that the Morning God was envisioned as the emerging solar disc, perhaps in constellation with a bright star at dawn or the planet Venus.[804] Howsoever it was the case, one thing is for certain: the Morning God was a celestial phenomenon at dawn with inherent links to the rising of the solar disc in the east, and thus could be counted among the *bas* of the easterners in spell 159 of the Coffin Texts. It may be added that a passage in utterance 437 of the Pyramid Texts joins two of the major themes of the spell, as it states that 'he (Re) places you as the Morning Star in the middle of the Field of Reeds' (*dj≠f ṯw m nṯr-dwꜣ ḥr.j-jb sḫ.t-jꜣr.w*).[805]

[801] Krauss 1997: 216–226.
[802] Neugebauer and Parker 1969: 181.
[803] Goebs 2008: 20–21.
[804] Goebs 2008: 21.
[805] *Pyr.* §805a.

2.7. Spell 160: a solar eclipse

The hieroglyphic text

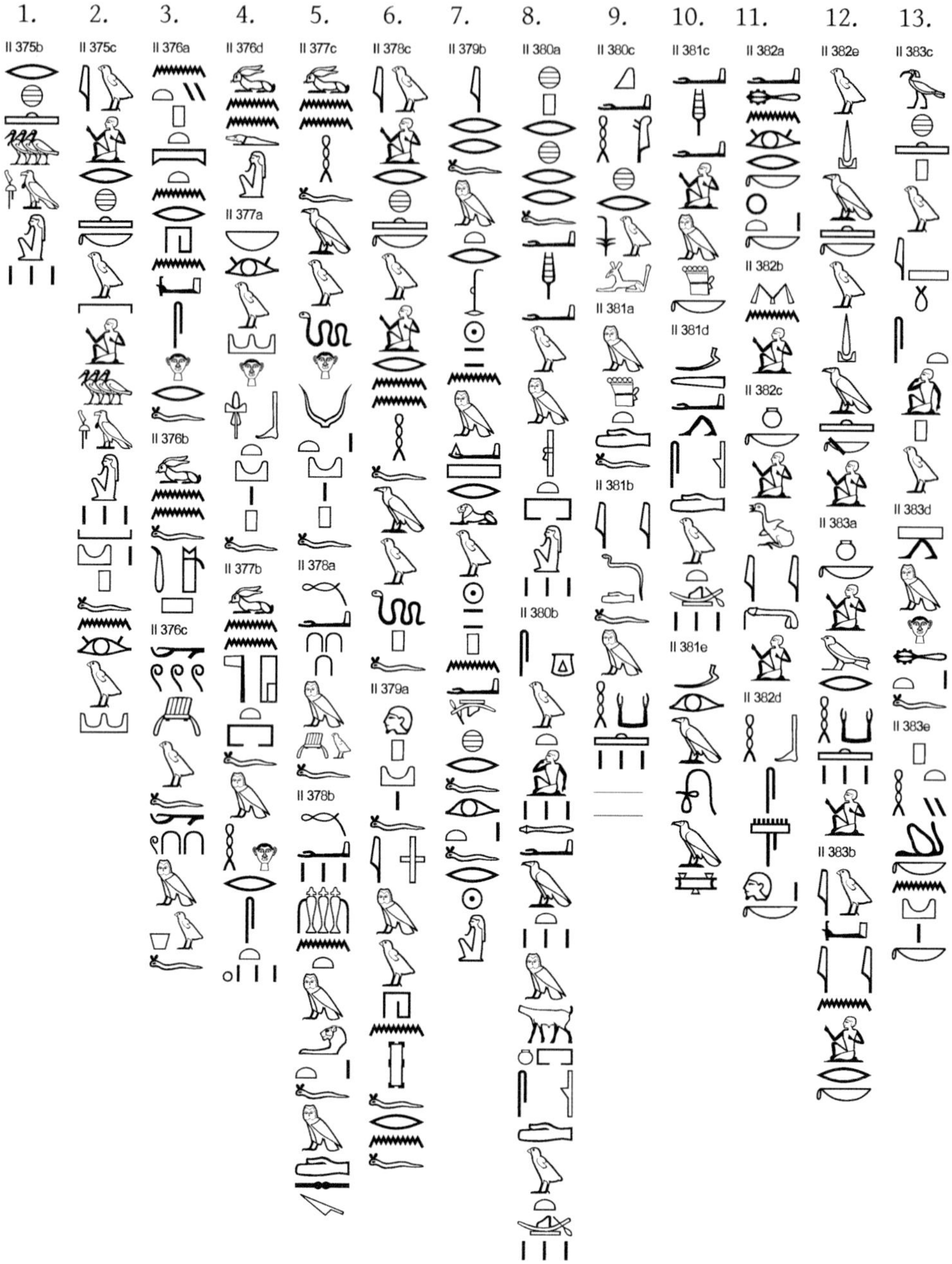

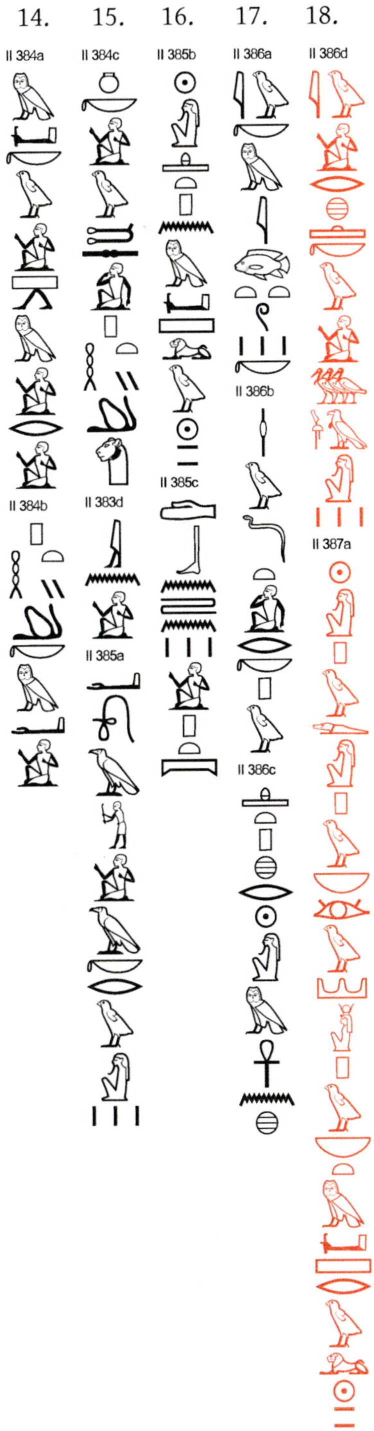
14. 15. 16. 17. 18.
II 384a
II 384b
II 384c
II 383d
II 385a
II 385b
II 385c
II 386a
II 386b
II 386c
II 386d
II 387a

Transliteration and translation

1. *rḫ bꜣ.w jmn.tjw*
2. *jw⸗j rḫ.kw [bꜣ.w jmn.tjw] ḏw pf n Bꜣẖ.w*
3. *ntj p.t tn rhn⸗s ḥr⸗f wnn⸗f ṯḥn ḫt 300 ꜣw⸗f ḫt 120 m wsḫ.t⸗f*
4. *wnn Sbk nb Bꜣẖ.w ḥr jꜣb.t ḏw pf wnn ḥw.t-nṯr⸗f m ḥrs.t*
5. *wnn ḥfꜣ.w ḥr wp.t ḏw pf mḥ 30 m ꜣw⸗f mḥ 3 ḫnt m ḥꜣ.t⸗f m ds*
6. *jw⸗j rḫ.kw rn n ḥfꜣ.w pf tp ḏw⸗f Jm.j-whm⸗f rn⸗f*
7. *jr r⸗f m tr n mšr.w pnꜥ.ḫr⸗f jr.t⸗f r Rꜥ*
8. *ḫpr.ḫr⸗f ꜥḥꜥ.w m js.t sg.wt ꜥꜣ.wt m-ẖnw sqd.wt*
9. *qꜥḥ.ḫr Swtj m ḏr.tj⸗fj ḏd⸗f m ḥkꜣ.w*
10. *ꜥḥꜥ⸗j m-ḏr⸗k mꜣꜥ sqd.wt mꜣꜣ wꜣ*
11. *ꜥẖn r⸗k jr.t⸗k ṯmꜣ.n⸗j jnk ṯꜣ.y ḥbs tp⸗k*
12. *wḏꜣ⸗k wḏꜣ⸗j jnk wr ḥkꜣ.w⸗j jw rdj.n⸗j r⸗k*
13. *ꜣḫ pw jšst pw šm ḥr ḫ.t⸗f pḥtj⸗k n ḏw⸗k*
14. *mk wj šm⸗j r⸗j pḥtj⸗k m ꜥ⸗j*
15. *jnk wṯs pḥtj jj.n⸗j ꜥwꜣ⸗j ꜣkr.w*
16. *ḥtp.n Rꜥ mšr.w dbn⸗n p.t*
17. *jw⸗k m jnt.wt⸗k wḏ.t r⸗k pw ḥtp.ḫr Rꜥ m ꜥnḫ*
18. *jw⸗j rḫ.kw bꜣ.w jmn.tjw Rꜥ pw Sbk pw nb Bꜣẖ.w pw nb.t mšrw*

1. Knowing the *bas* of the westerners.
2. I know [the *bas* of the westerners] the mountain of Bakhu
3. on which the sky leans; it is of crystal, 300 rods in length and 120 rods in width.
4. Sobek, the Lord of Bakhu is on the east of the mountain, and his temple is made of carnelian.
5. There is a snake on the top of the mountain, 30 cubits in length and three cubits of its forepart are of flint.
6. I know the name of the serpent dwelling on the mountain: He-who-is-in-his-fire is its name.
7. Now, as if it was the time of evening, it (the snake) turns its eye against Re,
8. and there occurs a stoppage in the crew, and a great astonishment within the journey.
9. Seth will then bend down with his hands, saying his words of magic:
10. 'I stand against you, setting the journey right and seeing far.
11. Shut your eye, for I am strong, for I am a male who covers your head.
12. If you are hale, I am hale; I am one great of my magic powers that I have placed against you'.
13. 'What is this power?' 'You who move on your belly, your strength belongs to your mountain.
14. Behold, me, I go as I wish, with your strength restrained in my arm.
15. I am the one who shows strength, I have come and gathered the land serpents.
16. Re will have set in the evening after we circle the sky,

17. while you are in your fetters, this is the decree against you, and Re will set in the west'.
18. I know the *bas* of the westerners. It is Re, it is Sobek, Lord of Bakhu, it is the Lady of the Evening.

Commentary

Line 1

rḫ bꜣ.w jmn.tjw

Knowing the *bas* of the westerners.

The title is laconic on Sen's coffin, but – as usual – other text variants have longer introductory formulas. On the inner coffin of Nakht (S2P), coming from Asyut, we read:

wꜣḥ tp tꜣ tm wnm ḥs m ẖr.t-nṯr tm mt n ḥfꜣ.w wḏꜣ.w tp tꜣ ʿq pr.t m sbꜣ.w jꜣb.tjw n.w p.t

Enduring on earth, not eating excrement in the necropolis, not dying because of a snake, being sound on earth, entering and going forth from the eastern gates of the sky.

Two coffins from Deir el-Bersha (B2Bo and B1L) also add:

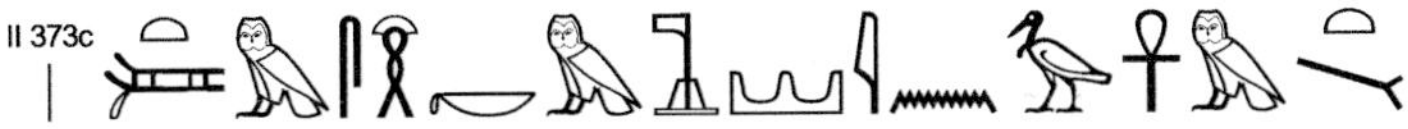

tm sk m ẖr.t-nṯr jn bꜣ ʿnḫ mt

Not perishing in the necropolis by a living and dead *ba*.

The coffin B3C[a] continues with the statement:

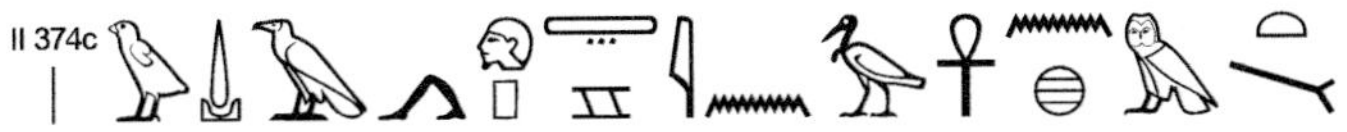

wḏꜣ tp tꜣ jn bꜣ ʿnḫ mt

Going around in procession on earth by a living and dead *ba*.

There is also another formula found on the coffin B1L:

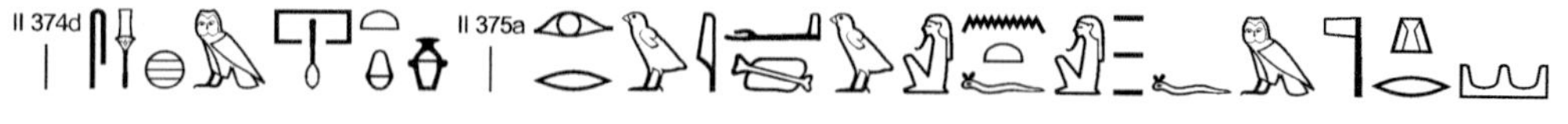

sḫm pr.t-ḫrw jr.w jwꜥ.w n jt⸗f m ẖr.t-nṯr

Having power (over) the invocation offerings made by the heir to his father in the necropolis.

As we can see, most of these statements voice general wishes about the conditions of the deceased in the netherworld. Perhaps the only interesting detail is the repetition of one of the main topics of the previous spell (159) about entering and going forth from the eastern gates of the sky. Since spell 160 is basically about the *bas* of the westerners, at first sight there seems to be some contradiction with an emphasis on the eastern gates of the sky. We shall see, however, that the spell is about a solar eclipse, so again the sun – and its meeting with the moon at the eastern horizon – plays an important role in the text, and this can explain the reference to the eastern regions of the sky, to the places from where Re customarily emerges in the morning (see commentary on the relevant part of spell 159). The statement on Nakht's coffin that the spell prevents dying from a snake is also noteworthy, because it anticipates one of the main themes of spell 160: the encounter of the moon, in the disguise of a snake, with the sun at the time of conjunction, when a solar eclipse occurs.

Lines 2–3

jw⸗j rḫ.kw [bꜣ.w jmn.tjw] ḏw pf n Bꜣḫ.w
ntj p.t tn rhn⸗s ḥr⸗f wnn⸗f ṯḥn ḫt 300 ꜣw⸗f ḫt 120 m wsḫ.t⸗f

I know [the *bas* of the westerners] the mountain of Bakhu
on which the sky leans; it is of crystal, 300 rods in length and 120 rods in width.

Line 2 of spell 160 provides yet another example for the sloppiness of the scribe preparing the inscriptions on the coffin of Sen. After the introductory verbal phrase 'I know' (*jw⸗j rḫ.kw*) he repeated the object of the title, 'the *bas* of the westerners', instead of the correct 'mountain of Bakhu', but then he realised his mistake and crossed out the faulty words by red strokes (the cancelled part of the text appears between square brackets in my hieroglyphic transcription). These lines thus, eventually, boast about the knowledge on the mountain of Bakhu that is described from a cosmic perspective: this mountain is said to support the sky. It seems that originally Bakhu was a mountain in the west,[806] but this claim is essentially based on the association of the place with Sobek – already recorded in the Pyramid Texts[807] – whose main cult area was the Fayum situated west of the main branch of the Nile. Furthermore, in the Coffin Texts, in the

[806] Wilson 1997: 302–303.
[807] *Pyr.* §456a.

present spell and in spell 752 (see below), Sobek, Lord of Bakhu, appears in connection with the *bas* of the westerners, which again vouches for its place in that direction.[808]

However, as time went by, and certainly from the New Kingdom onwards, Bakhu became to signify the mythological eastern mountain from which the sun rose, as opposed to the mountain of Manu (*Mꜣnw*) in the west where it set.[809] This much is already clear from chapter 15 of the Book of Going Forth by Day in which the rising of Re is associated with the mountain of Bakhu, whereas its setting is linked with Manu.[810] Spell 160 also mentions Bakhu in its cosmic role, and – though it may have already connoted the eastern regions of the sky to some extent – it defines it as a mountain that seems to hold up the entirety of the celestial dome. Two details in the description of Bakhu underline its cosmic connotations. Firstly, it is said to be made of crystal ('glass', *ṯḥn*),[811] a material that may forcefully evoke the brightness of the sky, as it is connected with the root *ṯḥn* 'to dazzle', 'to shine'.[812] It must be added that *ṯḥn* may alternatively be interpreted as 'faience' (i.e. Egyptian faience),[813] which with its most common blueish-greenish colour may also symbolise the appearance of the sky.[814] Secondly, the dimensions of Bakhu likewise seem to be meaningful from a cosmic – and lunar – point of view. It is 300 rods long and 120 rods wide, and these figures, as simple multiples of the numbers 30 (ten times 30 equals 300) and twelve (ten times twelve equals 120), allude to the number of days in a full lunar month, and the usual number of months in a year. This lunar numbers game, as shall be argued soon, is continued in the next lines of the spell.

Just as in the case of spell 159, at the beginning of the commentary on spell 160 it must be pointed out that a very similar text, repeating some of the major topics of both spells (159 and 160) and known as spell 752 of the Coffin Texts, has come down to us from the coffin of Sepi (B1C):

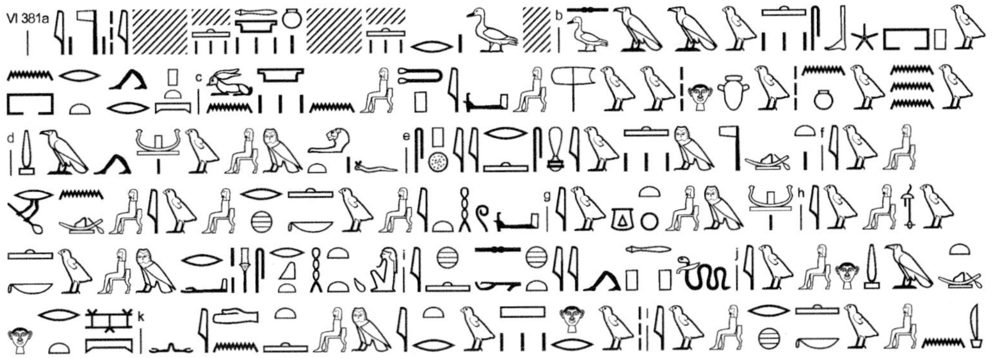

808 Otto 1975: 594.
809 Wilson 1997: 303.
810 Allen 1974: 19–20.
811 *Wb.* V, 390.13; Nicholson 2009: 1.
812 *Wb.* V, 391–392.16; Nicholson 2009: 1.
813 *Wb.* V, 390.12.
814 Nicholson 2009: 1.

j nṯr.w j[r.j]w ꜥꜣ.w n.w [...] r.w sꜣꜣ.w sbꜣ pw n pr.t r p.t wn n⸗j ṯpj⸗j ṯꜣw.w ḥr.jw-jb.w nw.w ḏꜣ wjꜣ wj m ḥꜣ.t⸗f Spj jr.j smj.w m dp.t nṯr jw⸗j ẖnj⸗j jw⸗j rḫ.kw jtḥ jw ns.t⸗j m wjꜣ jw⸗j ḥmw.kw m-r-ꜥ ḫrp Srq.t-ḥty.t jḫ sḫtj ꜥꜣpp jw⸗j ḥr ḏꜣ.t ḥr.t n jdn.t⸗j m jtr.w ḥr.w jw⸗j rḫ.kw nmj-š n š Ḥtp sr.n⸗j sw n nṯr.w bꜣ.w jmn.tjw ntj.w ḥr ḏw pf n Bꜣẖ.w jw ḫt 300 m ꜣw⸗f jw ḫt 120 m wsḫ⸗f r n ꜥq r jmn.t m šms.w n Rꜥ rꜥ nb

Oh, gods in charge of the doors of [...] the *r*-geese guarding the gate for entering the sky, open to me so that I may catch the air in the midst of the celestial waters, and so the solar barque in its bow may take me across, (that is me) Sepi who is in charge of the rigging of the god's ship; I row (in it), even I know how to tow (it). My seat is in the solar barque, because I am skilled also in controlling She-who-lets-the-throat-breathe (= Serqet), and therefore I can repel Apep. I cross the heaven without being replaced in the waterways above, because I know how to ferry to the lake of He-who-is-setting (= the setting sun), having visited it for the gods, (that is, for) the *bas* of the westerners who are on the mountain of Bakhu that has a length of 300 rods and a width of 120 rods. Spell for entering the west among the followers of Re every day.[815]

As we can see, the similarities between spells 160 and 752 are somewhat weaker than those between spells 159 and 161. In fact, the first part of spell 752 touches upon themes – the doors of the heaven, the waterfowl in the east, the gates of sunrise, the deceased in charge of the sails and rowing in the solar barque – that prominently feature in spell 159 of the Book of the Moon. Then, towards the end of the spell, the mountain of Bakhu is described in the same way as it is in spell 160, being 300 rods long and 120 rods wide. Also, the *bas* of the westerners are said to dwell on this mountain, and the rubric states that the spell is about entering the west with the followers of Re, that is, about being present when Re, the sun god, sets in the evening. Notwithstanding this claim, the text as a whole encompasses the rising of the sun in the east (note the mention of doors, waterfowl, the gates of entering the sky at the beginning of the spell), the crossing of the celestial expanses (the deceased as a skilful crewman, also well versed in driving off Apep by commanding the scorpion goddess Serqet), and the arrival in the region where He-who-is-setting dips below the horizon.[816] Therefore the dimensions of the mountain of Bakhu in spell 752 of the Coffin Texts may again allude to the entire sky, not just particularly the eastern or western part of it.

[815] *CT* VI, 281a–p.

[816] For *Ḥtp* 'He-who-is-setting' as the designation of the setting sun, see Leitz 2002e: 566.

Line 4

wnn Sbk nb Bꜣẖ.w ḥr jꜣb.t ḏw pf wnn ḥw.t-nṯr⸗f m ḥrs.t

Sobek, the Lord of Bakhu is on the east of the mountain, and his temple is made of carnelian.

This line provides further evidence for the claim that the mountain of Bakhu should be interpreted – at least in the context of spell 160 – as referring to the entire sky, because its lord, Sobek, is said to dwell on the eastern side of it. Sobek, as we have seen in the analysis of spell 158, symbolically represented the rising sun, and therefore it befits him just right that he is found on the eastern part of the celestial mountain. His association with the morning sun is once more reinforced by the detail that his temple – which, by the logic of the text, is in the east – is made of carnelian. This semi-precious stone, which was widely used in jewellery in ancient Egypt,[817] had of course the colour of red, and consequently was often associated with the sun, and more particularly, with the emerging solar disc in the east.[818] Alternatively, the material of Sobek's temple and its red colour may allude to the reddish hue of the sky that foreshadows the emergence of the sun, its disc also being red in the vicinity of the horizon due to atmospheric refraction.

Lines 5–6

wnn ḥfꜣ.w ḥr wp.t ḏw pf mḥ 30 m ꜣw⸗f mḥ 3 ḫnt m ḥꜣ.t⸗f m ds
jw⸗j rḫ.kw rn n ḥfꜣ.w pf tp ḏw⸗f Jm.j-whm⸗f rn⸗f

There is a snake on the top of the mountain, 30 cubits in length and three cubits of its forepart are of flint.
I know the name of the serpent dwelling on the mountain: He-who-is-in-his-fire is its name.

Now we learn that the top of the mountain of Bakhu is the home of a snake that is clearly described with some lunar allusions. The dimensions once again seem to be meaningful: the serpent is 30 cubits long, corresponding to the number of days in a full lunar month (and in a month of the civil calendar, for that matter). The forepart of the creature equals three cubits, and this number possibly evokes the period of lunar invisibility since, for the Egyptians, as has been argued in the commentary on spell 155, its maximum length encompassed three days (i.e. the first crescent could be sighted at the latest on the evening of the third day of the lunar month). It is also significant that the forepart of the snake is of flint. This material certainly had lunar connotations,[819] and the best evidence for this is the fact that Thoth, the pre-eminent lunar deity, was

[817] Hussein 2010: 185.
[818] Hussein 2010: 186–187.
[819] Graves-Brown 2006: 55–57.

said to carry a flint-knife, which was the symbol of the crescent moon.[820] This is quite clear for example from spell 246 of the Coffin Texts, giving an elaborate description of the period of lunar invisibility, in which the deceased – entering and going forth from the sun's fire in the sky – claims to be the flint-knife (*ds*) and flint-sickle (*mds*) in the hands of Thoth.[821] These cutting tools in my opinion represent the last crescent of the waning moon and the first crescent of the waxing moon, that is, the visible shapes of the moon that frame the period when it is invisible in front of the sun.[822]

Line 6 identifies the snake on the mountain as He-who-is-in-his-fire, the same being that featured as the opponent of the sun god in spell 154 of the Book of the Moon. His name is slightly misspelled on the coffin of Sen, *Jm.j-whn⸗f* as opposed to *Jm.j-whm⸗f*, but the correct orthography is preserved on coffins B17C, B1C, and B3C[a],[823] so we can be absolutely sure that the same serpent is meant in Sen's text as well. The second element of the name in Sen's version resembles the writing of the verb *whn* 'to overturn', 'to fall into ruin',[824] but it is difficult to make out what could have caused the confusion of the two words, *whm* and *whn*. In any case, with the introduction of He-who-is-in-his-fire in the narrative, the two protagonists of a solar eclipse are named: Sobek, as before, stands for the morning sun, while the serpent named He-who-is-in-his-fire represents the invisible moon. It once more appears in the disguise of a serpent because the eclipse is seen as a hostile act towards the sun god.

Lines 7–8

jr r⸗f m tr n mšr.w pnꜥ.ḫr⸗f jr.t⸗f r Rꜥ
ḫpr.ḫr⸗f ꜥḥꜥ.w m js.t sg.wt ꜥꜣ.wt m-ẖnw sqd.w

Now, as if it was the time of evening, it (the snake) turns its eye against Re,
and there occurs a stoppage in the crew, and a great astonishment within the journey.

The plane of the moon's orbit around the earth is slightly tilted from the plane of the earth's orbit around the sun, which means that – although the two planes are always close enough to make the moon invisible when it travels between the earth and the sun – a solar eclipse only occurs when the two planes also meet during the time of lunar invisibility (conjunction), so the moon gets directly between the earth and the sun. Due to the complexities of the orbits of the moon and the earth, a solar eclipse can be (1) partial, when the lunar disc covers only a part of the sun, (2) annular, when the moon is farther from the earth in its orbit, so it does not totally cover the sun, but leaves a ring of light around the black lunar disc, and (3) total, when the lunar disc perfectly fits the disc of the sun (it must be noted, however, that a total solar eclipse is

---

[820] Kees 1925: 2–5; Derchain 1962a: 41.
[821] *CT* III, 337g. For the translation arguing that both names derive from ds 'flint', see Priskin 2018: 166.
[822] Priskin 2018: 166.
[823] *CT* II, 379a.
[824] *Wb.* I, 345.6–13.

observed as a partial one from the locations that do not entirely fall into the moon's shadow).[825] Quite obviously, from the different types of eclipses the last one is the most spectacular, because only during a total eclipse does the light of the sun fade sufficiently to create the eerie atmosphere as if day turned into night, and there were a glitch in the usual course of celestial cycles.

Spell 160 of the Book of the Moon describes such a situation, the total eclipse of the sun, as the meeting between the lunar serpent and Re. When He-who-is-in-his-fire turns his eye towards Re, i.e. when the moon 'turns its back' on its earthbound observers, the crew of the solar barque stops. The stoppage of the barque (when it grinds to a halt on a sandbank in the Lake of Knives) is associated with a solar eclipse in two Ptolemaic papyri,[826] and therefore a similar incident must also refer to an event of that kind here. The serpent turns his eye towards Re, and this detail possibly indicates that the Egyptians understood that at the time of conjunction the bright part of the moon was facing the sun, and not the earth (i.e. light was only reflected from the other side of the moon). Another characteristic feature of a total eclipse, the darkening of the sky, is indicated by the statement that the encounter between the snake and Re takes place when the light of day dims (*mšr.w* 'evening', 'twilight'). The generally extraordinary nature of the eclipse is emphasised by the statement that a great astonishment occurs in the journey of the solar barque.

Spell 160 is no doubt the oldest description of a solar eclipse not only in ancient Egypt, but possibly also in the whole world. It is a mythological account, but its connections with the relevant natural phenomena are easily recognisable. Perhaps surprisingly, however, there are only a few sources from later times regarding how the Egyptians recorded or perceived solar eclipses.[827] The lack of records in Egypt is in sharp contrast to other ancient high cultures, such as Mesopotamia and China, that preserved ample documentation on these unruly occurrences in the sky.[828] What little evidence we have on the subject from Egypt is dated to the Graeco-Roman era. As already mentioned above, two very similar Ptolemaic papyri, written in the late 4th/early 3rd century BCE,[829] about the violations that Seth commits against the order of the world, contain a description of a solar eclipse.[830] The phenomenon itself is understood as the darkening of the solar disc on the sandbank of the mythical place called the Lake of Knives, and there is no mention of the moon in the short passage that deals with the solar eclipse.[831] However, the account of the solar eclipse is immediately followed by the description of a lunar eclipse (when 'the sky swallows the moon'),[832] and this possibly

[825] For a simple explanation of these phenomena, see Seeds and Backman 2011: 37–46.
[826] Altmann 2010: 91–92.
[827] Ray and Gilmore 2006: 191.
[828] Ray and Gilmore 2006: 191.
[829] Altmann 2010: 3–4.
[830] Altmann 2010.
[831] Altmann 2010: 91.
[832] Altmann 2010: 93.

indicates that the authors of these late papyri were also aware of the agency of the moon in a solar eclipse.

From Roman times a demotic papyrus dated to the 2nd century CE explains the omens that can be inferred from both lunar and solar eclipses, according to their time and date, and also their particular appearance in the sky.[833] It is quite likely that this document is based on a 6th century BCE original that was an import from Mesopotamia adjusted to the Egyptian context of celestial divination.[834] It then implies that eclipse phenomena was already closely followed in dynastic times. This conclusion is also prompted by the claim of another papyrus dated to the 1st century BCE that during the mummification process of the pharaoh Psammetichus I, who reigned between 664–610 BCE, a solar eclipse took place.[835] Now we can add that spell 160 of the Book of the Moon indicates that – even if the Egyptians did not systematically record the occurrences of solar eclipses, though they may in fact have done so – they were certainly familiar with the phenomenon and could write a mythological account of it which was, nevertheless, based on some facts of nature, too (such as the involvement of the moon in the event).

Apart from the few written documents, a pictorial representation of a solar eclipse has also come down to us from ancient Egypt. Éric Aubourg was the first researcher to realise that in the round zodiac of Dendera a figure next to the sign of Pisces refers to an annular solar eclipse, observed as partial in Dendera, on 7 March 51 BCE.[836] The symbol of the eclipse shows a disc encircling a goddess as she is holding in her left hand an animal by its hind legs.[837] Since a comparable depiction exists in the rectangular zodiac in the pronaos of the temple, where the animal is recognisably a pig,[838] some experts believe that the animal in the round zodiac is also a pig.[839] However, there are some notable differences in the rectangular zodiac, because there the pig is held by a male figure, who – judged by his green skin – is apparently Osiris.[840] The depiction of Osiris with the pig in the rectangular zodiac, in accordance with spell 157 and a host of other sources that indicate a very strong connection between this animal and the full moon,[841] alludes to the coincidence of the full moon with the autumnal equinox, so if the disc containing the goddess with the animal in the round zodiac records a solar eclipse, then the animal in question is definitely not a pig. Aubourg and Sylvie Cauville think it is a baboon, a prime representative of the moon in its form as Thoth.[842]

[833] Parker 1959.
[834] Ray and Gilmore 2006: 191.
[835] Hornung 1965.
[836] Aubourg 1995: 10.
[837] Aubourg 1995: 4 fig. 2.
[838] Cauville 2012: pl. viii.
[839] Lieven 2000: 157 n. 458; Leitz 2006: 287, 302–304.
[840] Robins 2001: 291.
[841] See comments on spell 157.
[842] Aubourg 1995: 10; Aubourg and Cauville 1998: 768; Cauville 2013: 540–541.

They are probably right, and there is also evidence that the baboon could sometimes symbolise the moon at its time of invisibility.[843]

Discussing the issue of eclipses in ancient Egypt, we should also mention that according to the Greek author Plutarch (end of 1st/beginning of 2nd century CE) some people regarded the myth of Osiris – and especially the episode in which he was murdered by Seth using a coffin custom-made to the size of his victim – as a story that was inspired by eclipses, both lunar and solar.[844] While we have good reasons to believe that Plutarch was really familiar with the myth of Osiris as it was narrated in Roman times in Egypt itself,[845] and in fact his account preserved many indigenous elements of the story at a time when the mysteries of Osiris' wife, Isis, were increasingly appropriated by an international audience in the Hellenic world,[846] it is difficult to ascertain whether the connection between the myth of Osiris and the eclipses was a late invention, or it was established earlier in pharaonic times, but the pertinent evidence was either lost, or is so obscure that we simply do not recognise it. In any case, we can see that spell 160 of the Book of the Moon does not place the description of a solar eclipse in an Osirian context, and neither does so the account of the lunar eclipse – involving the oryx – in spell 157. This does not necessarily mean of course that the Egyptians saw no links between Osiris and the eclipses at the beginning of the 2nd millennium BCE, but possibly the concerns of the author or authors of the Book of the Moon lay elsewhere.

Line 9

qꜥḥ.ḫr Swtj m ḏr.tj=fj ḏd=f m ḥkꜣ.w

Seth will then bend down with his hands, saying his words of magic:

Seth, just like other members of the Egyptian pantheon, was a complex deity who could appear in a variety of roles. One of these was of course his figure as the archenemy and murderer of Osiris, and then the rival of Horus in the quest for the legacy of the deceased Osiris. In spells 157 and 158 we could see that the Book of the Moon evoked these mythical episodes with its references to the injury that Seth caused to the eye of Horus (the moon), and to the peaceful stay of Horus, Duamutef, and Qebehsenuf in Nekhen until Seth finds out about their presence there. In spell 160, however, Seth features for another characteristic role of his, as the divine crew member of the solar barque who – standing in the prow of the ship – repels the enemies of the sun god. It is in fact in the Coffin Texts that Seth is first described as the protector of Re, and – apart from spell 160 – the best evidence for it comes from spell 1128: 'The entourage of the fire (thrice), (that is) the fire of the day barque. The entourage in the prow: Isis, Seth,

843 See for example my arguments in Priskin 2016c: 124–125.
844 Plutarch, *De Iside et Osiride* 44, see Griffiths 1970: 187.
845 Priskin 2016c: 137.
846 Bøgh 2013.

and Horus. The entourage in the stern: Hu, Sia, and Re' (*šnw.t n.t sḏ.t šnw.t n.t sḏ.t šnw.t n.t sḏ.t sḏ.t mʿnḏ.t šnw.t jm.jt ḥꜣ.t ꜣs.t Stš Ḥr.w šnw.t jm.jt pḥ.wj Ḥw Sjꜣ Rʿ*).[847]

From the New Kingdom onwards not only do we have a series of written sources that present Seth as standing in the prow of the solar barque defending Re,[848] but he also often appears in the visual representations of the barque. For example in an oft-cited depiction in the mythological papyrus of Herytwebekhet (21st dynasty) we see the barque of the sun god Re-Harakhty situated on the elongated sign of the sky that is supported by the coils of a long serpent.[849] The ship is towed by four jackals and four human-armed *uraei* that are arranged in two registers at the front. The head of the giant serpent rises up in front of the barque, between its tip and the creatures towing it, and Seth is shown in the prow, legs astride, as he is piercing the snake with a harpoon. The scene, with the coils of the serpent underneath the barque, clearly reflects the idea that the danger threatening its voyage was running aground on a sandbank, the home of the inimical snake, in the celestial waters (the stretch of water posing the danger was known as the Lake of Knives, or Lake of Two Knives).[850]

Though the serpent is not named in the papyrus of Herytwebekhet, from parallel scenes where its name is written out (for example in the tomb of Ramesses I)[851] it is clear that it represents Apep, who was seen as the symbol of utter chaos and the archenemy of the sun god.[852] However, the hostile serpent was known by other names as well, for example Nehaher (*Nḥꜣ-ḥr* 'He-with-fierce-face') in the New Kingdom netherworld books,[853] and from spell 160 of the Book of the Moon it is also obvious that the hostile snake – as He-who-is-in-his-fire (*Jm.j-whm⸗f*) – could acquire certain lunar characteristics. It is difficult to tell whether these differently named creatures are identical or they stand for various manifestations of Apep. As for the lunar connotations of the fight against the snake, a very interesting depiction is preserved on the New Kingdom stela of Taqayna.[854] It shows Seth in his human form, named 'He-from-Ombos, the great god' (*Nbw.tj nṯr ʿꜣ*), as he pierces a snake with human arms and head. Above them, in the lunette of the stela and below an arching hieroglyph of the sky, are depicted the symbols of the sun and the moon, a solar disc enveloped by two *uraei* and the lunar disc resting on the crescent moon. If the sun and the moon side by side are not an early example of the cryptic writing for *rʿ nb* 'every day',[855] meaning that the slaying of Apep is effected each day, then the scene on this stela may provide evidence that the occasional lunar character of the serpent enemy of the sun god was still recognised in New Kingdom times. In fact, the depiction may be an illustration to

[847] *CT* VII, 458a–l (synoptic version based on the existing text variants).
[848] Velde 1967: 99.
[849] Nagel 1928: 35 fig. 1; Piankoff : pl. 2; DuQuesne 1998: 616 fig. 4.
[850] Quirke 2001: 36–37, 45.
[851] Piankoff 1956: pl. iv.
[852] Quirke 2001: 36–37.
[853] Leitz 2002d: 271–273.
[854] Nagel 1928: 38 fig. 2.
[855] cf. *Wb.* II, 402.5.

spell 108 of the Book of Going Forth by Day, the descendant of spell 160 of the Coffin Texts, and in that case the proximity of the solar and lunar discs perhaps refers to a solar eclipse, too.

Seth was probably cast in the role of the slayer of the Apep snake because of his physical strength. This aspect of his personality, as we shall see, is also apparent in spell 160, and line 9 refers to it by picturing Seth as bending down with his arms to tackle the serpent He-who-is-in-his-fire. However, to gain victory over the enemy of Re the show of physical violence is not enough in itself, and it must be augmented by the utterance of magic words, as Seth also claims to say the necessary spells. Indeed, numerous compositions were written in ancient Egypt that were recited during rituals intended to fend off Apep,[856] such as the one known as the Book of Overthrowing Apep from the beginning of the Ptolemaic Period (end of 4th century BCE).[857] From the example of spell 752 of the Coffin Text above we could see that other divine beings – in the particular case, the scorpion goddess Serqet – could also be responsible for warding off Apep, just as in fact she is later depicted in the seventh hour of the Amduat restraining the serpent.[858] She – as her epithet She-who-lets-the-throat-breathe shows – could also be effective in fighting the snake because she could cause bodily harm through her sting. On the other hand, another goddess, Isis, was able to take part in the battle because her magic utterances dispelled the raging of the snake.[859] These examples illustrate that strength and magic words were equally important in overcoming the enemies of Re, and Seth has recourse to both of them in spell 160 of the Book of the Moon.

Line 10

ꜥḥꜥ=j m-ḏr=k mꜣꜥ sqd.wt mꜣꜣ wꜣ

'I stand against you, setting the journey right and seeing far'.

These are the first words of magic that Seth speaks and he declares that he will oppose the serpent of the invisible moon 'attacking' Re during a solar eclipse, and he will correct the journey of the solar barque, apparently by removing the danger that threatens it. Line 10 ends a bit differently on Nakht's coffin (S2P) with the phrase *mꜣꜣ.n=j wꜣ*, and this prompted previous translators to interpret it as a vocative addressed to the serpent and designating it as 'you whom I have seen from afar',[860] or the like.[861] In my opinion, the phrase refers to Seth, and symbolically to the regained

[856] Quirke 2001: 60–61.
[857] Faulkner 1937.
[858] Hornung 1999: 38–39 fig. 13.
[859] Faulkner 1937: 169.
[860] Faulkner 1973: 138.
[861] Barguet 1986: 577; Carrier 2004: 395.

vision of the solar eye – i.e the newly visible, intact solar disc – after the lunar serpent has been thrown back.

Line 11

ꜥẖn r=k jr.t=k ṯmꜢ.n=j jnk ṯꜢ.y ḥbs tp=k

'Shut your eye, for I am strong, for I am a male who covers your head'.

In contrast to the anticipated unobstructed vision that he, and Re, will possess, Seth calls on the serpent to shut its eye. Again, this imperative may stem from the understanding that during an eclipse the moon turns its bright part – its eye – towards the sun. Seth emphasises his strength and his dominance by stating that he is a male covering his enemy's head. The act of covering the head, as we have seen, has strong lunar connotations, because the sixteenth day of the lunar month bore this name. It certainly referred to the fact that after total baldness – the full moon, putatively on the fifteenth day – the lunar disc started to dwindle and the waning period began. The eclipse of the sun could be seen to mirror this event, and now the covering of the head could mean the passing by of the lunar disc after the few minutes of totality, that is, its gradual disappearance from sight as it moves on its orbit. To make sense of the statement about the covering of the head we must again suppose that the event is seen from the viewpoint of the sun. During an eclipse, as expounded above, the 'bald head' of the moon – the full lunar disc – is facing away from the earthbound observers, but to make things right, Seth could rightfully refer to its covering, alluding to its disappearance.

Line 12

wḏꜢ=k wḏꜢ=j jnk wr ḥkꜢ.w=j jw rdj.n=j r=k

'If you are hale, I am hale; I am one great of my magic powers that I have placed against you'.

Although in spell 160 the moon appears as the enemy of the sun god, a solar eclipse was an extraordinary event, and usually the sun and the moon are seen as equal counterparts, especially during full moon, when the solar disc copies the movement of the sun, crossing the sky from the eastern horizon to the western one. The description of the lunar cycle on the eastern and western walls of the pronaos of the Edfu temple (1st century BCE),[862] or the claim of Clement of Alexandria (2nd century CE) that the Egyptian priests carried books about the conjoined movements of the sun and the moon during the processions of Osirian festivals,[863] all testify to the Egyptians'

[862] Chassinat 1928: 207–208, 211–212.
[863] Aelian, *Stromateia* 6.4.35, see Stählin 1906: 449.

acknowledgement of the general equality of the two brightest celestial bodies, which they in fact in Ptolemaic inscriptions labelled as 'the two lights' (*ḥꜣy.tj*).[864] The balanced sentence introducing line 12, 'if you are hale, I am hale' (*wḏꜣ=k wḏꜣ=j*), also alludes to this equal status of the two major cosmic actors, though the general tone of Seth's speech lays an emphasis on his superiority over the lunar snake.

The same formula features in another text that very probably contains another account of a solar eclipse. This is spell 101 of the Book of Going Forth by Day that in its title promises to offer protection for the barque of Re.[865] As usual, the spell slightly varies in the individual papyri; below I cite the version found in the papyrus that was prepared for Iufankh at the beginning of the Ptolemaic Period:[866]

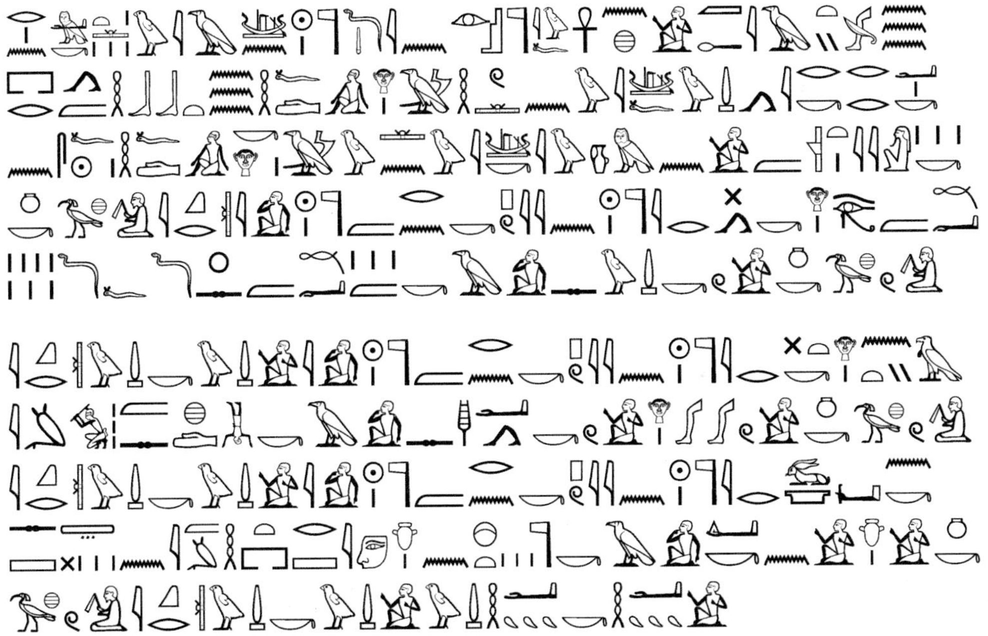

r n mk.t wjꜣ n Rꜥ ḏd mdw jn Wsjr Jw=f-ꜥnḫ mꜣꜥ-ḫrw j ꜣ.tj mw prj m ḥbb.t ḥfd ḥr mꜣhw n wjꜣ=f wḏꜣ jr=k r r-ꜥ=k n sf ḥfd=k ḥr mꜣḥw n wjꜣ=k jw ḫnm.n=j m js.yt=k jnk ꜣḫ jqr j Rꜥ m rn=k pwy n Rꜥ jr swꜣ=k ḥr wḏꜣ.t m mḥ 7 ḏfḏ=s m mḥ 3 gs kꜣ swḏꜣ=k wj jnk ꜣḫ jqr wḏꜣ=k wḏꜣ=j j Rꜥ m rn=k pwy n Rꜥ jr swꜣ=k ḥr ntjw-jm.w m sḫd kꜣ sꜥḥꜥ=k wj ḥr rd.wj=j jnk ꜣḫ jqr wḏꜣ=k wḏꜣ=j j Rꜥ m rn=k pwy n Rꜥ jr wn n=k sštꜣ.w n jmḥ.t ršj jb n pšd.t kꜣ rdj=k n=j jb=j jnk ꜣḫ jqr wḏꜣ=k wḏꜣ=j wḏꜣ ḥꜥ.w=k ḥꜥ.w=j

Spell for protecting the barque of Re. To be recited by *N*: Oh, he who treads the celestial waters, he who goes forth from the inundation water, he who sits on the prow of his barque, may you proceed to your state of yesterday! May you sit on the prow of your

[864] Wilson 1997: 613.
[865] Allen 1974: 82–83.
[866] Lepsius 1846: pl. xxxvii.

barque! Indeed, I have joined your crew, for I am an excellent and effective spirit. Oh, Re, in your name of Re, when you pass by the seven-cubit *wedjat*-eye, whose pupil is three and a half cubits, you make me hale, for I am an excellent and effective spirit. If you are hale, I am hale! Oh, Re, in your name of Re, when you pass by those who are with their head downwards, you make me upright on my feet, for I am an excellent and effective spirit. If you are hale, I am hale! Oh, Re, in your name of Re, when the secrets of the netherworld open for you, and the heart of the divine ennead rejoices, you give me my heart, for I am an excellent and effective spirit. If you are hale, I am hale! If your limbs are hale, my limbs are hale!

The spell starts with an invocation to Re who is identified by three of his characteristics. He traverses the celestial waters, he rises from the inundation waters, that is from the waters near the horizon that flood before the emergence of the sun (or, alternatively, from the primordial waters), and he sits in the prow of his barque. The wish that the sun god should proceed to his place of yesterday is intended to ensure the unhindered advance of the solar barque. Then three potential dangers are alluded to, the first one concerns the day leg of the journey, while the two others are connected with the voyage through the netherworld. The description of the sun passing the seven-cubit *wedjat*-eye with a pupil half of its size quite probably refers to a solar eclipse, when the corona of the sun, a delicate veil of light centred around the black disc of the moon, could occasionally be seen. An eclipse is a threat that does not occur frequently, but the sun has to cross the netherworld every night, and that is why its perils are referred to twice, once with the beings turned upside down, and once with the opening of its secrets. Clearly, in spell 101 of the Book of Going Forth by Day the phrase 'if you are hale, I am hale' is used differently, because it is spoken by the deceased, himself part of the crew of the solar barque, to the sun god, but the context, at least with the elaborate *wedjat*-eye pointing to a solar eclipse, is quite similar.

Lines 13-15

ꜣẖ pw jšst pw šm ḥr ẖ.t=f pḥtj=k n ḏw=k
mk wj šm=j r=j pḥtj=k m ꜥ=j
jnk wṯs pḥtj jj.n=j ꜥwꜣ=j ꜣkr.w

'What is this power?' 'You who move on your belly, your strength belongs to your mountain.
Behold, me, I go as I wish, with your strength restrained in my arm.
I am the one who shows strength, I have come and gathered the land serpents.

The question at the beginning of line 13 is surely asked by the lunar serpent,[867] and since it is inserted in the text, it takes the form of a dialogue at this point. In his response Seth states that the strength of the snake enemy of the sun derives from its

[867] Faulkner 1973: 139 n. 15.

mountain. Since this mountain, the mountain of Bakhu, was described earlier in lunar terms – its dimensions being based on the numbers twelve and thirty – the statement may imply that though a solar eclipse was a real threat to the voyage of the sun, it was a relatively rare occurrence. The moon repeated its cycle endlessly, but due to the inherent complexity of its orbit in relation to the sun and the earth (as briefly explained above), it only occasionally resulted in a state of affairs that led to a solar eclipse. There is no way of knowing whether the ancient Egyptians recognised any patterns in the solar – or lunar – eclipses, though some classical authors have claimed that they had kept records of them.[868] Even if there is a kernel of truth in this claim, it may not necessarily apply to the beginning of the 2nd millennium BCE, the era when the Book of the Moon was created. However, the Egyptians need not have been aware of any sophisticated patterns of eclipses to see that the lunar cycle was the ultimate cause of these – regularly but rarely occurring – phenomena.

Lines 16-17

ḥtp.n Rʿ mšr.w dbn=n p.t
jw=k m jnt.wt=k wḏ.t r=k pw ḥtp.ḫr Rʿ m ʿnḫʿ

Re will have set in the evening after we circle the sky,
while you are in your fetters, this is the decree against you, and Re will set in the west'.

While at the beginning of the text the mountain of Bakhu, and the serpent on its east side, certainly pointed to the eastern direction, alluding to the fact that the invisible moon causing a solar eclipse is – so to speak – observed there (when only the solar disc is seen after the day of the last crescent), in lines 16–17 it finally becomes clear that the purpose of the spell is to ensure the setting of the sun god in the west, and that of course also explains why it deals with the *bas* of the westerners. Seth's words make it unambiguous that spell 160 describes the encounter of Re with the serpent He-who-is-in-his-fire while he is travelling through the day sky, and not through the netherworld. We should not forget that the later sources, especially the netherworld books of the New Kingdom, set the meeting of Re with Apep in that region, that is, during the time when the sun god crosses it from the west to the east each night. This implies that though He-who-is-in-his-fire and Apep were probably fundamentally the same beings, they were also somehow different: the former represented the temporary darkness that occurred during a total solar eclipse, while the latter stood for darkness in general, i.e. the darkness of the night that was a regular feature of the solar cycle.

Line 18

jw=j rḫ.kw bꜣ.w jmn.tjw Rʿ pw Sbk pw nb Bꜣḫ.w pw nb.t mšrw

---

[868] Neugebauer 1975: 572 n. 4; 666 n. 13.

I know the *bas* of the westerners. It is Re, it is Sobek, Lord of Bakhu, it is the Lady of the Evening.

As usual, the last line of the spell names the *bas* that have been its main subject. Since the text is the description of a solar eclipse, not surprisingly the first *ba* of the westerners is Re himself. The second one is Sobek, Lord of Bakhu. The spell in fact starts with the description of this mythical mountain, with the temple of Sobek on its east, so the appearance of this god – who is, as mentioned before, the embodiment of the morning sun – among the *bas* of spell 160 is also quite understandable. The third *ba* is defined as the Lady of the Evening, and from the descendants of the spell, chapter 108 of the Book of Going Forth by Day, it is clear that this female divinity is Hathor.[869] Since spell 160 basically concerns the unhindered passage of the sun through the day sky, and its eventual setting in the west, Hathor is included among the *bas* of the westerners because of her obvious connections with that cardinal direction,[870] and with – as her epithet indicates – the major event of the west, the setting of the sun in the evening. Her association with the west is quite apparent from visual representations that show her with the headdress of the hieroglyphic sign 'west' (also often worn by the goddess of the west, Imentet), as for example in the tomb of Horemheb (18th dynasty).[871] Furthermore, other scenes depict her as the goddess that each day receives the dying sun.[872]

[869] Allen 1974: 86.
[870] Vischak 2001: 82.
[871] Wilkinson 2003: 142.
[872] Vischak 2001: 82.

3. General Commentary

In the previous section of the book the individual spells of the Book of the Moon were discussed. The focus there lied on understanding what the phrases and sentences of the composition meant, and what lunar connotations they may have had. However, in order to fully appreciate the relevance of the Book of the Moon in ancient Egyptian lunar ideology, and in broader terms, in Egyptian mythological thinking in general, it seems desirable to look at the work as a whole, and examine its internal contents and structures on the one hand, and its wider external context on the other. So, in this part of my presentation of the Book of the Moon, I will first give a summary of the major themes of the individual spells. This will highlight the chronological line – the period from one conjunction of the sun and the moon to the next one – on which the composition is based, and make the logic of the succession of the spells more intelligible. Although the Book of the Moon is a finished and unified composition, in terms of content it – as shall be argued in the following chapter – is made up of different textual layers that were created at different times and at different locations. Understanding the various levels of meaning of the book tells us a lot about the circumstances that prompted the learned elite of Hermopolis to compile it around the end of the First Intermediate Period or beginning of the Middle Kingdom. As I indicated it in the introduction, I believe that the Book of the Moon was written at that locality, and my claim is underlined by the fact that with the exception of one specimen its extant copies all originate from Deir el-Bersha, the burial ground of Hermopolis. Therefore I will also examine how the different text versions on the Deir el-Bersha coffins relate to each other and in what chronological order they were created. Possibly because the composition represented the special knowledge of those who participated in the lunar cult of Hermopolis, when the Coffin Texts were superseded by the Book of Going Forth by Day at the beginning of the New Kingdom, the Book of the Moon was not included in this new corpus of magical spells. However, we should note that this statement is true insofar as the Book of the Moon was not taken over as a whole: with the exception of one spell (155) the other texts did survive and were incorporated in the Book of Going Forth by Day papyri until Ptolemaic and Roman times. Therefore, in the final chapter of my general commentary I will examine what was preserved and what was lost during this process.

3.1. The major themes of the spells

Spell 154: the origins of the month

Spell 154 is about the origins of the month and it explains why months are not of uniform length in nature. Any steadfast observer of the moon is bound to discover that in some lunations 30 days elapse between two identical phases of the moon, whereas in other months only 29 days do. In the language of modern astronomy we express this irregularity by saying that the synodic month – the period between two successive full moons, or any other phases – lasts an average of 29.53059 days.

jw=j rḫ.kw jr.t Jwn.w tmm.t bsj wr-mꜣ.w ḥr=s
ḫb.t r m sn.wt ḏA.t ʿjn ḥtm r jwʿ Jwn.w jw=j rḫ.kw jry.t ḥnk.t n ṯA.y ḥr=s

I know the eye of Heliopolis into which not even the greatest of seers has been initiated, the diminishing of the part in the *senut*, and how the destroyer extends the arm against the heir of Heliopolis. I know how a braided lock of hair of a man is made upon it.[873]

The allusion to a lock of hair at the end of this passage is juxtaposed later in the text by the mention of a shorn man (*fꜣk*).[874] These images surely evoke the waxing and waning of the moon, stemming from an old concept that likened the different phases of the earth's satellite to a bald head (the full moon) with hair gradually beginning to cover it.[875] Another key phrase here is *sn.wt*, the name of the sixth day of the month,[876] which in Heliopolitan doctrine symbolised the fullness of the moon.[877] In later texts this expression was often used interchangeably with *smd.t*, the designation of the fifteenth of the lunar month, on which day the full moon takes place in most lunations..[878] The sixth day could be associated with the fullness of the moon because according to a related mytheme the lunar eye consisted of six parts.[879] The six fractions corresponding to these parts – the dimidiated series starting with 1/2 – fail to add up to unity by a tiny margin (1/64), such that they expressed the idea of near completeness at the same time.[880] Furthermore, this arithmetic exercise of the fractions may have actually been connected with the average length of the synodic month.[881] The 'diminishing of the part in the *senut*' would therefore refer to a month that is somewhat shorter than the ideal 30 days, the period that was the basis for the twelve equally measured monthly units of the civil calendar. This length of time is alluded to in spell 154 by the mention of the *mʿbꜣ*-harpoon, which was written with the number 30.[882] The harpoon belongs to He-who-is-in-his-fire, a creature – a snake according to the hieroglyphic determinative – that acts as the enemy of the sun god Re.

Rʿ pw ḥr mdw.t ḥnʿ Jm.j-whm=f ḥr psš.t Jwn.w
ʿḥʿ.n r=f jꜣṯ ḫpr ḫb.t pw m ꜣbd

It was the case that Re had a discussion with He-who-is-in-his-fire over the division of Heliopolis.

[873] *CT* II, 272a–274b.
[874] *CT* II, 282c–4b.
[875] Derchain 1962: 20; Eaton 2011: 236.
[876] Parker 1950: 11; Winter 1970: 152.
[877] Smith 2002: 122.
[878] Lieven 2000: 75.
[879] Junker 1911: 101; Meeks 2006: 220.
[880] Robins and Shute 1987: 14–15.
[881] Priskin 2002.
[882] *CT* II, 278a–b; Arquier 2013: 123.

Then his part was injured and that is how the diminishing of the month came into being.[883]

Thus we learn that the reduction in the length of the month resulted from a dispute between Re and He-who-is-in-his-fire. This name must be a designation of the moon in conjunction, that is when the moon is between the sun and the earth. During this period of lunar invisibility, when the waning crescent can no longer be seen before sunrise at the eastern horizon and the first crescent has not yet appeared in the western sky after sunset – the moon apparently dwells in the vicinity of the sun, i.e. in the sun god's fire. In other words, the moon is invisible because it moves conjointly with the sun.[884] That the name He-who-is-in-his-fire describes the moon in conjunction is further reinforced by spell 160 in which the serpent once more makes an appearance as a hostile entity towards the sun, this time responsible for a solar eclipse. The ancient Egyptians started the lunar month with the onset of lunar invisibility,[885] so this was the time when the months were really reckoned. Consequently, it is quite appropriate for the invisible moon to feature in a description that is trying to come to terms with the different lengths of the month. The serpent injures and takes away a part of Re, and the recognition that the moon reflects the light of the sun may lie behind this statement. The motif may also be a distant relative or predecessor of Plutarch's story of how Thoth won a part of each day from the moon through playing draughts to form the five epagomenal days .[886]

Spell 155: the period of lunar invisibility

The title of spell 155 (*CT* II, 290a) leaves absolutely no doubt about which phase of the lunar cycle this text describes, because, unlike the other spells, it connects the *bas* not with a place or cardinal direction, but with *psḏn.tjw*, the invisibility of the moon. The reciter of the spell boasts about his duties concerning the lunar eye, including being in charge of its fractional components in the room where the eye itself is stored. This may be a direct allusion to the cult practices in Hermopolis, and to a store room where the ritual objects used in the cult were kept. However, the speaker's familiarity with the eye does not only encompass the tangible paraphernalia of the lunar cult, but also such facts that we would now call scientific knowledge.

jw⸗j rḫ.kw jꜣṯ.t m jr.t Tby jp r.w⸗s
wꜣš ꜥnḏw r wšꜣ.w wḫ.w
r 5-nw n gs twt n jp r.w⸗s m jmj.t mḥ.t r ẖqs.t

I know what is missing from the eye of Tebi when its parts are counted,

[883] *CT* II, 274c–276c.
[884] For possible iconographic and textual references to this union of the sun and the moon from the New Kingdom onwards, see Depuydt 1998: 76–85.
[885] Parker 1950: 9–23.
[886] Plutarch, *De Iside et Osiride* 12, see Griffiths 1970: 135.

and when dawn is stronger than the glow of the darkened night.
The fifth part of an entire half for counting its parts between what is in the filling eye and the ailing eye.[887]

The filling eye and the ailing eye are definitions of the waxing and waning moon, respectively, and the cryptic definition of a number, 'the fifth part of an entire half', refers to the period that separates them. The entire half means the half of a full month, and thus equals fifteen; consequently its fifth part equals three, and thus the whole expression defines the length of the period of lunar invisibility as lasting for three days. In some months the new crescent of the waxing moon appeared on the evening of the third day of the lunar month,[888] and in all probability this observation prompted the statement in the Book of the Moon. Other sources also suggest that the ancient Egyptians regarded the maximum length of the time of the moon's absence from the sky as three days. The Fundamentals of the Course of the Stars,[889] and a passage in a mythological manual about the cults in the Delta claim that when Horus regains the vision of his eyes (i.e. the waxing crescent appears in the west), he goes forth on the morning of the fourth day of the month.[890] This occasion is also called *pr.t-sm*, 'the going forth of the *sem*-priest', and indeed designates the fourth day in the lists of the lunar days that have come down to us from the Graeco-Roman Period.[891] The act of the *sem*-priest ritually expressed that the moon passed before the sun, was – after three days – surely and irrevocably 'released' by the sun, and could again be seen in the night sky.

The reciter of the spell now compares his knowledge to that of the embalmer priest, and defines the invisibility of the moon in concrete anatomical terms, by likening this phenomenon to the appearance of an eyeball. Then he provides yet another description of *psḏn.tjw*, referring to the mysterious lack of Osiris.

jw m jwtt ḫnt Wsjr
ṯs.n.tw ḥꜣ.t=f n pḥ.wj=f
m mḏḥ.t n.t sꜣw

It is a void out of Osiris,
when one has joined his front with his back
as the hewn out part of the beam.[892]

This passage probably has some links with the type of objects that from later periods are known as Osiris beds and Osiris bricks.[893] The silhouette of Osiris was sunk into

[887] *CT* II, 294d–298a.
[888] Parker 1950: 13.
[889] Lieven 2007: 97–101, 177–184, 455–463.
[890] Meeks 2006: 14 (pBrooklyn 47.218.84, IV, 5–6).
[891] Parker 1950: 11.
[892] *CT* II, 302c–304a.
[893] Carter 1933: 81 and pl. lxii;

wood or pottery and this space was filled with soil and seeds, so that the latter could sprout and the emerging green vegetation could re-enact the resurrection of the god.[894] The invisibility of the moon is associated with the empty void of the figure of Osiris: he is there but at the same time unseen and non-existent. He only comes to life when the seeds start to produce the green foliage, just as the moon is invisibly present in front of the sun and only springs to life after it is sufficiently distant from it.

After stressing the point that the speaker of the spell has been initiated into lunar matters, the text closes with an allusion to the end of the period of invisibility.

wn n⸗j ntjw m psḏn.tjw
jw mꜣꜣ.n⸗j wp.w pr(.w) m sẖ.w n.w Wr.t

Open to me, those in the moon's invisibility.
I have seen the gelder come out of the slaughterhouse of the Great Eye.[895]

Written sources that have come down to us from Graeco-Roman times indicate that the two halves of the lunar cycle were envisioned as bulls with different temperaments.[896] The waxing moon was thus seen as a fiery, vigorous bull (*kꜣ psj*), whereas the waning moon was equated with an ox, a castrated bull (*sꜥb*).[897] So, when the person responsible for the castration of the lunar bull (*wp.w* 'someone who cuts, a gelder') leaves the slaughterhouse, it means that the period of waning and invisibility is about to end, and the waxing of the moon can begin.

Spell 156: waxing

It is at this point, at the very end of lunar invisibility, that spell 156 joins in and provides an all-encompassing description of the waxing period by identifying two of its key moments.

ṯwn šw.t ẖnt qꜥḥ
wbn dšr.t m mnṯꜣ.t

The feather is thrust into the shoulder,
and then the Red Crown rises in the *mentjat*-bowl.[898]

It is clear from a number of other sources, including notably other Coffin Texts (spells 6 and 9),[899] that the feather was a symbol of the first lunar crescent appearing over

[894] Tooley 1996.
[895] *CT* II, 306a–b.
[896] Derchain 1962: 43; Leitz 1994: 268–9; Lieven 2000: 86.
[897] Sethe and Firchow 1957: 54.
[898] *CT* II, 312f–4b.
[899] *CT* I, 16c–9a, 29a–31a.

the western horizon just after sunset,[900] which in turn led to its close association with this cardinal direction.[901] In this context then the shoulder must refer to the relevant body part of the arching sky goddess, Nut, which is in fact situated in the west. The signification of the Red Crown in the next line is less certain, not negligibly because of the obscurity of the word *mnṯꜣ.t*,[902] but most probably it denotes the full moon rising from the eastern horizon (the connotations of the verb *wbn* hint at this meaning). Due to the atmospheric scattering of light, the full moon when close to the horizon – just like the sun near the horizon – may appear to have a red hue.[903] The two lines thus demarcate the starting and end points of the waxing period: the first crescent above the western horizon and the full lunar disc over the eastern horizon. Such an interpretation finds strong support towards the final lines of the spell where the same two antithetic lunar events framing the first half of the month are named again in more certain terms.[904]

jw⸗j rḫ.kw bꜣ.w Ḫmnw
šr.t m ꜣbd pw ꜥꜣ.t m smd.t pw

I know the *bas* of Hermopolis.
It is the small eye on the second day of the lunar month, it is the great eye on the fifteenth day of the lunar month.[905]

Spell 157: full moon

Spell 157 introduces a new context into the Book of the Moon with the struggle between Horus and Seth. It is about the two different kinds of injury that the full moon – the intact eye of Horus – can suffer.

Rꜥ pw ḏd.n⸗f n Ḥr.w jmj mꜣꜣ⸗j jr.t⸗k ḏr ḫpr nw r⸗s
mꜣꜣ.n⸗f s(t) ḏd.jn⸗f dg r pf ꜥ⸗k ḥbs(.w) m wḏꜣ.t jmj.t
wn.jn Ḥr.w ḥr dg.t r pf ḏd.jn Ḥr.w
mk wj ḥr mꜣꜣ⸗f ḥḏ.wj ḫpr mꜣ-ḥḏ pw

It was the case that Re said to Horus: ‘Let me see your eye because this happened to it’.
As he looked at it, he said: ‘Take a look at this part as your hand covers the sound eye there’.
And Horus looked at that part and said:
‘Behold, I see it as altogether white’. And this is how the oryx came into being.[906]

900 Kees 1980: 282; Goedicke 1989: 61; Willems 2005: 210.
901 Willems 2005; Meeks 2006: 32, 292.
902 Willems 1996: 215.
903 For the association of redness and the full moon, see Goebs 2008: 158–159.
904 Parker 1950: 12.
905 *CT* II, 322c–334a.
906 *CT* II, 334b–338b.

Through a pun between the expressions *ḥr m33=f ḥḏ.wj* and *m3-ḥḏ* the oryx plays a crucial role in this story. Its connection with the time of the full moon is intimated in some of the inscriptions that accompany the scenes of the slaying of this animal on the walls of Graeco-Roman temples: 'The oryx is burnt and killed as the *wedjat*-eye is provided with its constituent elements. Moon, come so that you may wander through the sky and your movement could be whole and sound!' (*sm3 m3-ḥḏ ḏd-mdw mḥ nsr.tw m3-ḥḏ m ds.tw wḏ3.t ʿpr.tw m r.w=s ḥr.j-j3b.t m ḫns=k m ḥ3j.t nm.t=k jr(.t) m ʿḏ wḏ3*).[907] Horapollo, the Greek author who penned down often enigmatic descriptions of a series of hieroglyphic signs in the 4th or 5th century CE, also connects the oryx with the moon, and most probably with the full moon, when he says that it could foretell the rising of the sun and the moon.[908] He also speaks of this animal as somewhat inimical to the moon.[909] These two strands of tradition are intermingled in spell 157 of the Coffin Texts as well. The oryx is included in a context that deals with a temporary covering of the moon given that, after Re warned Horus of some overcast part to his celestial eye, Horus replied that it was still shining unblemished. The whole episode must then denote a lunar eclipse during which one part, or the entirety, of the lunar disc is temporarily dimmed as the shadow of the earth falls on it. Lunar eclipses, as a matter of fact, can only happen during full moon, at the time of opposition when the sun, earth, and moon are aligned.

The second injury involves the pig as a Sethian animal knocking Horus unconscious, thus presaging the regular monthly waning of the moon.

ḏd.jn Rʿ n Ḥr.w dg m-dj r(rj) pf km
ʿḥʿ.n Ḥr.w ḥr dg.t r(rj) pf km
ʿḥʿ.n Ḥr.w ḥr kjw.t ḥr qd wr[.t] n jr.t=f nšn.t ḏd=f
m(k) jr.t=j mj sqr pf jrj.n Stḫ r jr.t=j

Then Re said to Horus: 'Now look at this black pig'.
Horus looked at the black pig.
Then Horus shouted because of the grave condition of his raging eye, saying:
'Behold, my eye is like the injury that Seth has inflicted on my eye'.[910]

The pig was closely associated with the full moon and, once again, there is plenty of evidence from later times that support this notion. A hieroglyphic inscription from the temple of Edfu,[911] as well as the writings of classical authors testify to the fact that the ancient Egyptians sacrificed pigs and consumed pork on the day of the full moon.[912] According to Plutarch, furthermore, Seth discovers the body of Osiris when

[907] Chassinat 1928: 138–139.
[908] Horapollo, *Hieroglyohics* I.49; Boas 1993: 65–66.
[909] Horapollo, *Hieroglyphics* I.49; Boas 1993: 65.
[910] *CT* II, 338c–341b.
[911] Chassinat 1930: 354.
[912] Meeks 2006: 219.

he is chasing a pig in the light of the full moon.[913] The pig is also portrayed as a threat to the moon – a repugnant animal that is ready to swallow the lunar disc – in, for instance, the Book of Gates,[914] or in a 7th century BCE mythological manual from the Delta.[915] As a consequence, we must assume that the mention of the pig in Coffin Texts spell 157 refers to the regular injury suffered by the lunar eye, i.e. the beginning of the monthly waning of the moon.

Spell 158: waning

The period of waning itself is evoked in the following spell through subtle, but still intelligible, allusions.

rḫ bꜣ.w Nḫn jw=j rḫ.kw sštꜣ n Nḫn
ḏr.tj Ḥr.w pw jrj.n mw.t=f qmꜣ.tj ḥr mw

Knowing the *bas* of Nekhen. I know the secret of Nekhen.
It is the hands of Horus that his mother made and that were thrown into water.[916]

From a story that was already known in Middle Kingdom times,[917] but has survived in its fullest form in a Ramesside papyrus recounting the strife between Horus and Seth,[918] we know that Isis cuts off and replaces Horus' hands because he used them to collect the semen of Seth who had tried to force a sexual intercourse with him. At a later point of the narrative, it is Horus' semen that eventually prevails over Seth, leading to the creation of a disc on the head of Thoth that must be the moon itself.[919] The hands of Horus being made by his mother therefore surely refers to this mythological episode and symbolises the waning of the moon in the lunar cycle, when it is feeble and vulnerable, but still carries its inherent capacity of rejuvenation. The statement that Horus' hands are thrown into water metaphorically describes the second half of the lunar cycle because the waning crescent, after having risen from the eastern horizon and travelled some distance towards the west, never reaches the western horizon and is never able to set. Each day in the second half of the monthly cycle, the rising sun starts to cancel out the moon's light at dawn, and as the light of the sun intensifies, the lunar crescent fades away into the blue background of the sky; it is, in effect, 'thrown into the celestial waters'.

ḏd.jn Rꜥ ḥḏ sꜣ pn n ꜣs.t ẖr jr.t.n mw.t=f r=f ḏs=s
ḥꜣ (jnj) n=j Sbk n pḥ.wj ḥꜣm=f st srd=f st dj=f st r s.t jr.jt
Sbk n pḥ.wj ḏd=f jw ḥꜣm.n=j bꜣ.n=j btktk m ꜥ=j ḥr sp.tj mw

[913] Griffiths 1970: 129.
[914] Manassa 2006: 122–125, 137–141.
[915] Meeks 2006: 14–15, 218–219.
[916] *CT* II, 349a–d.
[917] Quirke 2004: 181–182.
[918] Gardiner 1932: 49–54; Lichtheim 1976: 219–220.
[919] Servajean 2004: 125.

ḥꜣd.n=j m pḥ.wj ḫpr ḥꜣd pw

Re then said: 'This son of Isis was injured because of what his mother herself had done to him.
I wish Sobek of the edge of the waters were fetched for me so that he could fish them out, grow them and put them back to their right place'.
Sobek of the edge of the waters said: 'I fished, I scooped (it) up, but (the catch) has slipped from my hands onto the shores of the water.
Finally I caught it in the edge of the waters with a cover basket'. And that is how the cover basket came into being.[920]

This passage further refines the description of the waning moon. The crocodile god Sobek is the embodiment of the rising sun,[921] the emerging solar disc that eventually causes the concealment of the waning crescent. In some of the netherworld books of the New Kingdom a crocodile gives birth to the morning sun.[922] Also, in the much later Book of the Fayum (2nd century CE) Sobek is depicted as the sun dwelling around the liminal zones of the eastern and western horizons;[923] in the context of spell 158, he must be the rising sun in the east (he also appears in this role in spell 160). His epithet, 'Sobek of the edge of the waters', also implies that he lingers around the horizon, close to the shore of the celestial waters (just as real crocodiles habitually lurk at the edge of waters waiting for they prey). He tries to fish out the hands but they keep slipping from his grasp. This describes how the dwindling crescent still continues to elude the sun on the successive days of the waning period, even though it rises closer and closer to dawn and travels shorter and shorter distances towards the west. Sobek finally catches his fish (the hands/moon) with a device that is used in shallow waters: a cover basket (a wickerwork basket with no bottom that is placed over a fish, which could thus be grabbed by hand through the upper opening remaining above the level of the water).[924] In astronomical terms this act corresponds to the meeting of the sun and the moon at the eastern horizon, and consequently to the eventual capture of the moon by the sun (i.e. the disappearance of the waning crescent).

Spell 159: the arrival of the last crescent at the eastern horizon

Spell 159 is also concerned with the beginning of the period of lunar invisibility. It further elaborates the theme of the encounter of the moon and the sun at the eastern horizon, in the realm that was known to the ancient Egyptians as the Field of Reeds (*sḫ.t jꜣr.w*).[925]

---

920 *CT* II, 350b–353c.
921 Zecchi 2010: 23.
922 Piankoff 1953: 67–69.
923 Beinlich 1991: 319, pl. 9.
924 Lacau 1954: 137–151.
925 *CT* II, 368c; Hays 2008: 177 n. 14; Taylor 2011b: 241–243.

rḫ bȝ.w jȝb.tjw rḫ.kw sbȝ pw ḥrj-jb prr.w Rʿ jm⸗f m jȝb.t
rs.j⸗f m š.w ḫbs.w m bw sqdd Rʿ jm m tʿw
mḥ.tj⸗f nw.yt sr.w m bw sqdd Rʿ jm m ẖnj

Knowing the *bas* of the easterners. I know it is the gate in the middle, from which Re emerges in the east.
Its south is in the lake of the *ḫbs*-geese, which is the place where Re navigates by sailing;
its north is in the waters of the *sr*-geese, which is the place where Re navigates by rowing.[926]

Whereas spell 155 is about the invisible moon in the evening anticipating the appearance of the first crescent in the west, this spell is connected with the east and the morning sun. Because the moon becomes hidden in the light of the sun, the text refers to it through the description of the latter. The southern and northern limits of the sun's yearly path along the eastern horizon are specified; this part of the text perhaps emphasises the fact that, although the moon slightly strays off the trajectory of the sun (the ecliptic) during its monthly cycle, they are always close enough for the moon to become invisible when the two meet at the eastern end of the sky. The enormous dimensions of the vegetation in the Field of Reeds that are cited in the second part of the spell – emmer five cubits tall, and then reaching seven cubits[927] – possibly allude to the closeness of the moon and its beneficial effects on the growth of plants,[928] or to the emerging solar disc that reveals ever greater parts of itself as dawn turns into day.

Spell 160: a solar eclipse

The last chapter of the Book of the Moon, Coffin Texts spell 160, describes the situation when the invisible moon in conjunction travels with the sun through the day sky and a solar eclipse occurs.

rḫ bȝ.w jmn.tjw jw⸗j rḫ.kw bȝ.w jmn.tjw ḏw pf n Bȝḫ.w
ntj p.t tn rhn⸗s ḥr⸗s wnn⸗f thn ḥt 300 ȝw⸗f ḥt 120 m wsḫ.t⸗f
wnn Sbk nb Bȝḫ.w ḥr jȝb.t ḏw pf wnn ḥw.t-nṯr⸗f m ḥrs.t
wnn ḥfȝ.w ḥr wp.t ḏw pf mḥ 30 m ȝw⸗f mḥ 3 ẖnt m hȝ.t⸗f m ds
jw⸗j rḫ.kw rn n ḥfȝ.w pf tp ḏw⸗f Jm.j-whm⸗f rn⸗f

Knowing the *bas* of the westerners. I know the *bas* of the westerners, the mountain of Bakhu
on which the sky leans; it is of crystal, 300 rods in length and 120 rods in width.

---

[926] *CT* II, 363c–366a.
[927] *CT* II, 369b–370d.
[928] Smith 2002: 126.

Sobek, the Lord of Bakhu is on the east of the mountain, and his temple is made of carnelian. There is a snake on the top of the mountain, 30 cubits in length and the three cubits of its forepart are of flint.
I know the name of the serpent dwelling on the mountain: He-who-is-in-his-fire is its name.[929]

The two protagonists of an eclipse are named: Sobek once more stands for the morning sun in the east, whereas the moon reappears as He-who-is-in-his-fire – cast again in the role of the enemy of the solar deity (his name, however, is slightly misspelled on Sen's coffin; for the correct orthography see coffins B17C, B1C, and B3C[a]).[930] The lunar connotations of the passage are also evident from the dimensions: the celestial mountain is 300 rods long (ten times 30) and 120 rods wide (ten times twelve), and the lunar serpent itself is meaningfully 30 cubits long. Quite in keeping with the contents of the spell, the three-cubit-long forepart possibly represents the period of invisibility since, for the Egyptians, its maximum length – as explained above – equalled three days.[931]

jr r=f m tr n mšr.w pnʿ.ḫr=f jr.t=f r Rʿ
ḫpr.ḫr=f ʿḥʿ.w m js.t sg.wt ꜥ3.wt m-ẖnw sqd.wt

Now, as if it was the time of evening, it (the snake) turns its eye against Re,
and there occurs a stoppage in the crew, and a great astonishment within the journey.[932]

When He-who-is-in-his-fire turns his eye towards Re, i.e. when the moon 'turns its back' on its earthbound observers, the crew of the solar barque stops. The stoppage of the barque (when it grinds to a halt on the sandbank in the Lake of Knives) is associated with a solar eclipse in two Ptolemaic papyri,[933] and therefore a similar incident must also refer to such an event here. The darkening of the sky that is characteristic of a total solar eclipse is indicated by the statement that the meeting of the serpent and Re happens when the light of day dims (*mšr.w*,, 'evening', 'twilight'). According to the rest of the spell Seth, in his capacity of defender of the solar barque, springs into action and after he utters a magic spell and displays his strength to repel the lunar serpent, the voyage of the sun continues and Re can set in the west.[934] The moon presumably also emerges from the encounter unscathed, and thus the endless cycle of lunar withering and renewal can be perpetuated.

[929] *CT* II, 375b–379a.
[930] *CT* II, 379a (B17C, B1C, B3Ca).
[931] See my discussion in Priskin 2013: 36.
[932] *CT* II, 379b–380b.
[933] Altmann 2010: 91–92.
[934] *CT* II, 380c–386c.

3.2. Textual layers in the Book of the Moon

The claim that Coffin Texts spells 154–160 give a mythicised account of the lunar cycle is strongly supported by the place from which they originate. In all, eleven complete versions of the composition have come down to us, out of which ten are found on coffins that were unearthed at Deir el-Bersha and only one is from another location in Middle Egypt, Asyut; fragmentary copies that lack some parts or entire spells exist on yet another coffin from Deir el-Bersha and six coffins from Asyut (plus a short fragment of spell 154 from Meir).[935] Deir el-Bersha was the Middle Kingdom burial ground of Hermopolis, the chief cult centre of the pre-eminent lunar god of ancient Egypt, Thoth.[936] Since a considerable number of Coffin Texts are only attested from Deir el-Bersha, we know that the local scribes there were very actively contributing to this new text corpus of mortuary literature.[937] All these details suggest that the Book of the Moon was created in Hermopolis, from where it was later 'exported' to the not too distant cult centre of Asyut.[938] The next chapter will compare the available manuscripts and will try to establish how they are interrelated and how the different versions had developed from one another. By doing so, it will reveal a great deal about the scribal transmission of the composition within the two localities mentioned.

In this chapter, however, I am more interested in the ideological background and considerations that led to the writing of the Book of the Moon in the first place, that is the initial phase by which the Book of the Moon – as a distinct textual unit, elaborating on a specific topic and distinguished by the identically formulated rubrics of the spells – was created. In this respect general guidance is offered by what we know about the transition from the earlier group of mortuary spells, the Pyramid Texts, to the later Coffin Texts. Whereas for a long time scholarship saw a sharp divide between these two great text corpora – Pyramid Texts as the exclusive prerogative of the king versus Coffin Texts as offering participation in the afterlife for a wider section of society; a concept often summarised by the term 'the democratisation of the afterlife' – nowadays researchers tend to advocate a much less accentuated contrast between the two great collections of spells.[939] Already in the Old Kingdom both royal and private individuals resorted to the same body of knowledge to ensure their continued existence, though the means with which they recorded or made use of it may have been different (inscriptions in pyramids as opposed to oral recitation or perishable media – papyri – in elite tombs).[940] The material seems to suggest that the spells of Old Kingdom mortuary literature, Pyramid Texts including, are only a selection from a larger corpus that was created, looked after, and maintained in the

935 *CT* II, 266a–388c.
936 Stadler 2009: 96, 200–218.
937 Gestermann 2008: 201–203; Morales 2013: 343–344; Stadler 2009: 96–99; Willems 2014: 176.
938 cf. Gestermann 2008: 213–214; Lapp 1990: 229–230.
939 Hays 2011; Mathieu 2008; Morales 2013; Smith 2009; Willems 2008. For a recent overview of the subject, see Willems 2014: 124–135.
940 Baines 2008: 38–39; Smith 2009: 4.

administrative and religious heartland of the time, that is in the area around Memphis and Heliopolis.[941]

With the break-up of the Old Kingdom state, from the First Intermediate Period onwards socio-cultural and ideological changes resulted in the local production of texts in such outstanding centres as Asyut, Beni Hasan, Deir el-Bersha, el-Lisht, Meir, and several other places.[942] However, the great prestige of the older texts that had been recorded under royal patronage during the Old Kingdom was still recognised and these spells continued to be in use, especially after the reunification of the country, when access to the central archives was made increasingly possible.[943] Thus, in relation to the older textual corpus, the Coffin Texts emerged along a threefold process: (1) there was a verbatim transmission of texts, for example certain Pyramid Texts passages made their way into the Coffin Texts in an unchanged form, (2) Middle Kingdom variants of Old Kingdom texts were written, that is older texts were reworded or changed, and (3) new texts were composed that in tone, content, and style imitated the products of Old Kingdom mortuary literature.[944]

The Book of the Moon comprising Coffin Texts spells 154–160 can serve as a very good example to illustrate these developments, and I believe that its examination here in this chapter, based on traditional content analysis, will give us a valuable insight into the processes that characterised the transition from the Pyramid Texts to the Coffin Texts, especially in connection with points (2) and (3) outlined above. The careful reading of the texts will lead to the conclusion that – although spells 154–160 form a clear unity – they certainly represent a compilation that stems from different sources.

The core text: spells 154, 157, and 158

While the titles of the seven spells making up the whole composition are sometimes summarily described as connected with localities,[945] when we take a closer look at the headings of the texts, this generalising statement does not really stand up to scrutiny. One title, that of spell 155, is an obvious odd-one out because it refers to the *bꜣ.w psḏn.tjw*, that is, the *bas* of lunar invisibility. As for the remaining six spells, at face value two sub-groups can be distinguished. One consists of spells 159 and 160, which according to their titles describe the *bas* of the easterners and westerners (*bꜣ.w jꜣb.tjw, bꜣ.w jmn.tjw*). Although these are not localities in the strict sense, but rather beings that dwell in particular places, they still strongly connote spatial arrangement and form a meaningful pair of opposites. Thus, under the classification that is based on the titles, the remaining sub-group is made up of the spells that are about the *bas* of genuine localities: Heliopolis (spell 154), Hermopolis (spell 156), Pe (spell 157), and

[941] Baines 2008: 21, 31; Mathieu 2008: 256; Morales 2013: 40; Smith 2009: 6.
[942] Morales 2013: 100–104.
[943] Gestermann 2008: 214–215.
[944] Hays 2011: 118; Smith 2009: 5–6.
[945] Sethe 1922; Assmann 2005: 203; Lieven 2016: 67.

Nekhen (spell 158). When we look at the contents of these texts, however, we will see that spells 154, 157, and 158 share a number of common features that are entirely absent from spell 156.

First of all, in all three spells the solar god, Re, is one of the chief protagonists. Spell 154 relates the animosity between Re and the serpent called He-who-is-in-his-fire (*Jm.j-whm=f*), representing the moon in conjunction, and describes how their quarrel led to the irregularity of the months. In spell 157 we read about the injuries that Horus suffered to his eyes (i.e. lunar eclipses and the monthly waning of the moon), and how Re compensated him for his losses. Spell 158 puts Re in the company of Sobek, who himself is the representative of the rising sun catching with its rays the waning moon in the morning; Re and Sobek interact in order to help the moon through its period of strife. So in all three spells Re appears as one of the main characters and through dialogues with various other gods he propels the story forward.

Another recurring feature of the three spells is the aetiological motif, that is the explanations that are embedded in the text to expound on the existence of certain things. These aetiologies are only found in these three spells and are missing from the other four texts that make up the rest of the composition. Three examples may be cited here to recall the general nature of these explanatory passages:

Spell 154

Rʿ pw ḥr mdw.t ḥnʿ Jm.j-whm=f ḥr psš.t Jwn.w ʿḥʿ.n r=f jꜣṯ ḫpr ḫb.t pw m ꜣbd

It was the case that Re had a discussion with He-who-is-in-his-fire over the division in Heliopolis. Then his part was injured and that is how the diminishing of the month came into being.[946]

Spell 157

Rʿ pw ḏd.n=f n Ḥr.w jmj mꜣꜣ=j jr.t=k ḏr ḫpr nw r=s mꜣꜣ.n=f s(t) ḏd.jn=f dg r pf ʿ=k ḥbs(.w) m wḏꜣ.t jmj.t wn jn Ḥr.w ḥr dg.t r pf ḏd.jn Ḥr.w mk wj ḥr mꜣꜣ=f ḥḏ.wj ḫpr mꜣ-ḥḏ pw

It was the case that Re said to Horus: 'Let me see your eye because this happened to it'. As he looked at it, he said: 'Take a look at this part as your hand covers the sound eye there'. And Horus looked at that part and said: 'Behold, I see it as altogether white'. And this is how the oryx came into being.[947]

Spell 158

ḥꜣ <jnj> n=j Sbk n pḥ.wj ḥꜣm=f st srd=f st dj=f st r s.t jr.jt Sbk n pḥ.wj ḏd=f jw ḥꜣm.n=j bꜣ.n=j btktk m ʿ=j ḥr sp.tj mw ḥꜣd.n=j m pḥ.wj ḫpr ḥꜣd pw

[946] *CT* II, 274c–276c.
[947] *CT* II, 334b–338b.

(Re about the severed hands of Horus:) 'I wish Sobek from the edge of the waters <were fetched> for me so that he could fish them out, grow them and put them back to their right place'. Sobek of the edge of the waters said: 'I fished, I scooped (it) up, but (the catch) has slipped from my hands onto the shores of the water. Finally I caught it in the edge of the waters with a cover basket'. And that is how the cover basket came into being.[948]

The close-knit nature of the three spells may be underlined by the fact that the *bas* of the three places referred to in their titles – Heliopolis, Pe, and Nekhen – are already grouped together in utterance 468 of the Pyramid Texts. Since the *bas* of Pe and Nekhen often appear together in Egyptian sources,[949] the interesting detail here is the addition of Heliopolis to the two towns: 'May your *ba* take after the *bas* of Heliopolis, / May your *ba* take after the *bas* of Nekhen, / May your *ba* take after the *bas* of Pe, / May your *ba* take after a living star in front of its brother!' (*bꜣ⸗k bꜣ.w Jwn.w js bꜣ⸗k bꜣ.w Nḫn js bꜣ⸗k bꜣ.w Pj js bꜣ⸗k sbꜣ ʿnḫ js ḫnt.j sn.w⸗f*).[950] Utterance 468 is a collection of short spells, so it is difficult to draw further conclusions as to what exactly dictated the grouping of these three localities together. Nevertheless, it is perhaps not without significance that in an earlier passage of the utterance two monthly festivals are referred to and the closing paragraph identifies the interlocutor with Thoth. It is quite possible then that the original linkage of the three places was already somehow connected with lunar concepts. It must also be noted, however, that Heliopolis, Pe, and Nekhen are mentioned together in utterance 365 without any apparent lunar context.[951]

The ubiquitous presence of Re, the shared aetiological motif, and the earlier association of Heliopolis, Pe, and Nekhen in the Pyramid Texts all seem to suggest that Coffin Texts spells 154, 157, and 158 make up the oldest layer of the Book of the Moon, a core text that was in all probability produced by the scribal workshops in the religious capital of the Old Kingdom, Heliopolis. It must have been part of the larger corpus of earlier mortuary literature, though it itself had not been recorded in tombs or on funerary equipment until it was disseminated from the royal archives around the beginning of the Middle Kingdom (unless of course such records were lost due to the ravages of time).

Texts from Hermopolis: spells 155 and 156

In sharp contrast to the three spells forming the core part of the Book of the Moon, in which Re is mentioned fifteen times, the chief solar god is entirely absent from spell 155 and only appears once or twice in spell 156, depending on the particular version of the text. Also, there is a significant stylistic difference. Whereas in the three core spells narrative and dialogue are the dominant forms of discourse, the two

948 *CT* II, 351b–353c.
949 cf. for contemporary examples *Pyr.* §478a, §942a, §1253a, §1549c.
950 *Pyr.* §904a–c.
951 *Pyr.* §622a–625d.

spells under discussion now are written in the first person singular, which is a more commonly employed communicative technique in the mortuary literature.[952] Since, however, we hear the voice of a speaker who boasts about his knowledge concerning lunar invisibility (spell 155) and the waxing moon (spell 156), these texts, with their great emphasis on acquired skills and personal abilities, also display close affinities with the biographical inscriptions of high officials that are found on stelae or tomb walls.[953]

Besides the extreme scarcity of references to Re, the lack of the aetiological motif, and the monologous speech, spells 155 and 156 share one more common trait: the speaker in both texts identifies himself with the lunar god Thoth. In spell 155 this identity is stated both in connection with Thoth's role as the divine physician of the eye,[954] and as the god who manipulates the fractions of the eye of Horus and determines the lunar phases:

wn n=j jnk tr(.w) sm.y jnk ḥbs(.w) ẖ.t n pr Wsjr jnk nṯr jr.j sjꜣ m ꜥ.t ẖr dbḥ.w

Open to me because I am one who respects the observed one, because I am one who makes the covering in the house of Osiris, and because I am the god in charge of the full moon period in the room where the vessel containing the fractional components of the eye is stored.[955]

In the following spell the speaker asserts: 'I have come as a divine image on account of what I know, I have not repeated it to men, nor have I told it to the gods' (*jj.n=j m sḫm ḥr rḫ.t.n=j n wḥm=j n rmṯ n ḏd=j n nṯr.w*).[956] Because Thoth is frequently identified as a divine image or power (*sḫm*) both textually and iconographically,[957] in the lunar context of spell 156 we can have little doubt about the reference of the statement.[958]

Having looked at the distinctive features of the two texts in terms of their style and content, we may reasonably suppose that spells 155 and 156 of the Book of the Moon were composed in the chief cult centre of lunar ideology, Hermopolis. With this assumption, it is not difficult to give an explanation for the choice of the titles. If spell 156 was written by scribes working in Hermopolis, it was of course only natural for them to name their own city in the title. As they now used up the only meaningful locality in the series of lunar spells they wanted to create, in the case of spell 155 they had no choice but to break off from the regular pattern and opt for a somewhat different title that nevertheless fitted into the chronological scheme of the composition.

[952] Baines 2008: 16.
[953] Gnirs 1996: 195–196, 204.
[954] Priskin 2013: 46–47.
[955] *CT* II, 292d–294c.
[956] *CT* II, 318d–320b.
[957] Stadler 2009: 399–403.
[958] Stadler 2009: 402.

Further texts from the central archive: spells 159 and 160

As noted above, these two spells form a group of their own since their titles make a contrastive pair. Spell 159 describes the Field of Reeds located at the eastern horizon, and how the moon at the end of its cycle arrives at this region (i.e. how the waning crescent becomes totally absorbed by the light of the sun at the very end of the month). That this work was also originally part of the Old Kingdom royal archives is strongly suggested by the existence of a variant of the text which – it seems – has no links whatsoever with the Book of the Moon or Hermopolis. This variant is of course spell 161 of the Coffin Texts which has come down to us in only one copy preserved on a coffin that was found in el-Lisht and dated to the 13th dynasty.[959] The description of the Field of Reeds is almost identical to the one in spell 159, especially concerning the gate in the east from which Re emerges,[960] but crucially spell 161 does not have a title talking about the *bas* of the easterners; it is simply introduced by the phrase '*N* knows the Field of Reeds' (*jw N rḫ sḫ.t jꜣr.w*).[961] Since el-Lisht lies closer to the Memphite area than Hermopolis, we may reasonably suppose that – instead of being a Hermopolitan composition – the source text for both spells 159 and 161 had been kept in the royal archives, and when it became available for the scribes at the two locations, they – at different times – appropriated and adjusted it for their own use.

The last spell of the composition (spell 160) is possibly the oldest written account of a solar eclipse. Since such an event can only occur when the sun and the moon are in conjunction, the main protagonists of spell 154 – Re and the serpent called He-who-is-in-his-fire – reappear in the narrative. They also engage in a dialogue with each other, so this text shows close similarities with the core texts of the Book of the Moon, with one significant exception – the aetiological motif is missing from the discourse. This prompts us to believe that spell 160 also originated from the pool of wisdom that had previously been kept in the Old Kingdom royal archives. At the same time, the lack of the explanatory element suggests that it was possibly not part of the proto-composition – the predecessors of spells 154, 157, and 158 – that formed the nucleus of the Book of the Moon. Again, in the case of spell 160 a parallel text exists in the form of spell 752 of the Coffin Texts which at the same time also reiterates some of the themes of spell 159.[962] Since this spell is found on a coffin from Deir el-Bersha (B1C), the existence of this variant carries less force in terms of arguing for the possibility of an original text coming from the central royal archives, since spell 752 may have been based on the locally available manuscripts of spells 159 and 160. However, we should note that the bird associated with the northern limits of the sun's path along the eastern horizon is named differently from the designation in spell 159,[963] and this perhaps after all indicates that spell 752 belongs to a textual tradition that has

[959] *CT* II, 388d–s; Quirke 1996: 399.
[960] Compare *CT* II 364a–368c and 388i–r.
[961] *CT* II, 388d.
[962] *CT* VI, 281a–p.
[963] *CT* II, 356b sr-geese vs *CT* VI, 381a *r*-geese.

no immediate connections with the Book of the Moon. Still, it is impossible to tell whether the text was a local development, or represents links with a wider pool of texts or the manuscripts of central archives.

The creation of the spell sequence 154–160

After analysing the contents and stylistic features of the spells making up the Book of the Moon, we may set up a plausible scenario by which this spell sequence of the Coffin Texts was created. When the documents that had been stored in the central archives of the Memphite area became newly accessible after the reunification of the country at the beginning of the Middle Kingdom, three spells – which were very probably viewed already in Old Kingdom times as belonging together and dealt with the mythicised descriptions of lunar phenomena – reached Hermopolis. Although their lunar content no doubt reflected and was screened by the dominant, solar ideology of Heliopolis, the Hermopolitan scribes – themselves being officiants of the lunar cult centred around Thoth – recognised the immediate relevance of the texts. To give a more thorough account of the moon's behaviour, they augmented this core composition (spells 154, 157, and 158) with four more spells. On the one hand, they wrote two spells locally, or picked two already existing spells from their own repertoire (spells 155 and 156), and inserted them into the original series of spells at the position that was dictated by their wish to make a chronologically ordered description of the lunar month, after spell 154. On the other hand, they borrowed two more texts from the old royal archives, slightly modified them and appended them at the end of the composition (spells 159 and 160). During this editing process, they titled all the spells to refer to *bas* (possibly the rubrics of the three core spells already mentioned them).

3.3. The text variants from Deir el-Bersha and Asyut

As I argued in the previous chapter, I believe that the Book of the Moon was created in Hermopolis, the town that was home to the cult of the lunar deity Thoth. It is from the Middle Kingdom burial site of this town, Deir el-Bersha, that the majority of the coffins recording the entire composition originate (nine coffins with ten text variants as opposed to a single whole copy from Asyut). From among these ten versions I chose to present the text of the Book of the Moon as it is written on the coffin of Sen, based on the assumption that it best displays the lunar connotations of the composition. However, as shall become obvious from the following analysis, Sen's text is not the oldest one. We know that he lived and fulfilled his duties in Hermopolis around the middle of the 12th dynasty, under the reigns of Senwosret II and Senwosret III,[964] and copies of the lunar spells (*CT* 154–160) have come down to us from at least a generation earlier (see below). In other words, it is not self-evident that Sen's text should be given priority in the translation of the Book of the Moon. Perhaps an equally justified choice would be to use the oldest manuscript originating from Deir el-Bersha. Instead of doing

[964] Willems 1988: 76–77.

so, I opted to translate Sen's text, and below I will gather some arguments in favour of my approach. In order to do so, first the chronological order of the text versions from Deir el-Bersha must be determined with the help of external archaeological and other historical data. Then this chronological order can be compared with the philological evidence provided by the texts themselves, and in this way conclusions can be drawn about the absolute and relative positions of the different texts in the development of the Book of the Moon.

The chronology of the Deir el-Bersha coffins

The lunar (or *rḫ-bꜣ.w*) spells of the Coffin Texts are recorded on nine coffins that originate from Deir el-Bersha. These coffins can be arranged into a chronological order by considering a number of criteria.[965] One of these is the family relations between the owners of the coffins that can be reconstructed from inscriptions indicating filiations in the tombs or at other places. The similarities or differences of stylistic elements on the coffins may provide other clues, and this of course means that the coffins displaying the same style are more likely to be contemporaneous. Archaeological evidence is also important, for example the location of a tomb in relation to another one. This type of data is especially useful with the burial places of high officials working under a nomarch, who positioned their final resting places around the tomb complex of their superior.

Coffin sigla according to CT and its type (i: inner; o: outer; n/a: data not available)	*Owner's name*	*Owner's title or other description*
B2Bo (i)	Djehutinakht	nomarch
B4Bo (i)	Djehutinakht	female, wife of the owner of B2Bo
B9C (i)	Amenemhat	nomarch
B2P (i)	Sepi	overseer (*jm.j-r pr*)
B4L (i)	Sen	chief physician (*wr swnw*)
B1Y (n/a)	Djehutinakht	seal bearer (*ḫtmw-bjtj*)
B1L (i)	Gua	chief physician (*wr swnw*)
B17C (i)	Neferi	overseer (*jm.j-r pr wr*)
B1C (o)	Sepi	general (*jmj-r mšꜥ*)

Table 2 The coffins recording the Book of the Moon in the order as they appear in the synoptic edition of the Coffin Texts (*CT*). In the sigla the letter B before the number refers to Deir el-Bersha, while the letters after the number define the places where the coffins are now found (Bo – Boston; C – Cairo; L – London; P – Paris; Y – Yale University, New Haven).

Before taking all these criteria into consideration, first I present a list of the relevant coffins as they appear in Adriaan de Buck's publication of the Coffin Texts (Table

[965] Willems 1988: 51–57.

2). It is clear from the table that the spells describing the lunar cycle are recorded, among others, on the coffins of two nomarchs (Djehutinakht and Amenemhat). The chronological seriation should start with their coffins, since the most prosopographical data have been preserved in connection with these high-ranking individuals. Despite this, it must be added, the absolute chronological framework which the nomarchs of Deir el-Bersha should be fitted into is still a hotly debated issue in Egyptology. Absolute chronology here means that the researchers try to establish the dynasty or more precisely the reign under which a particular nomarch fulfilled his office. Since this absolute chronology has little relevance to the relative sequence of the coffins, it perhaps suffices to say here that according to the most commonly accepted view the owner of B2Bo, the nomarch identified as either Djehutinakht IV or V, lived and worked towards the end of the 11th dynasty and the beginning of the 12th dynasty.[966]

Fortunately, the relative chronology of the nomarchs – the order in which they succeeded each other – is more straightforward, though, as indicated above, there is some ambiguity concerning the owner of the coffin B2Bo, since this person can either be the son of Ahanakht I (Djehutinakht IV), or the son of Nefri I (Djehutinakht V), who lived a generation later.[967] However, this uncertainty does not pose any difficulties for the purposes of the present analysis, since the other nomarch featuring in table 2, Amenemhat, took office after either of the two possible Djehutinakhts.[968] On the basis of this information we can put three coffins into a chronological order: B2Bo and B4Bo are roughly contemporaneous, since the latter was made for the wife of the owner of B2Bo (Djehutinakht IV or V), who was also called Djehutinakht, while the coffin of Amenemhat (B9C) is definitely of a later date.

Some of the stylistic elements of the coffins B2Bo and B4Bo suggest that they are the oldest artefacts recording the Book of the Moon. One of the main characteristics of the First Intermediate Period and Middle Kingdom coffins is a picture strip showing the objects used during interment or the funerary rites and needed in the netherworld, the so-called object frieze. On the coffins B2Bo and B4Bo the depictions of these objects closely resemble the style of the coffins that were produced in Heracleopolis prior to the emergence of the 11th dynasty.[969] It logically follows from this that these coffins were decorated not long after the Heracleopolitan precedents. We may add that the overall analysis of the coffins, considering all the stylistic features of them and not just the appearance of the object frieze, also assigns the wooden caskets of Djehutinakht IV/V and his wife to the earliest generation of Deir el-Bersha coffins.[970]

The chronology of the nomarchs at Deir el-Bersha helps us to determine the relative age of five more coffins, though they were not made for nomarchs. However, the

[966] Brovarski 1981: 29; Willems 1988: 70; Gestermann 2008: 11–13.
[967] Willems 1988: 70; Gestermann 2008: 11–13.
[968] Brovarski 1981: 29; Willems 1988: 71.
[969] Brovarski 1981: 24 n. 75.
[970] Willems 1988: 73.

tombs of Sepi (overseer), Sen, Gua, Neferi, and Sepi (general) were all located in the forecourt of the tomb complex that belonged to the nomarch called Djehutihotep, and quite obviously could not have been completed earlier than the main funerary complex of their superior.[971] Since Djehutihotep – again, depending on whether the owner of B2Bo was the fourth or fifth Djehutinakht – came three or four generations later than his predecessor, and followed Amenemhat in the position of nomarch,[972] the coffins of the five officials named above date from a later period than the coffins of Djehutinakht, his wife, and Amenemhat. Unfortunately, there is insufficient data to put the owners of the five coffins into a precise chronological order. For example, since both Sen and Gua bore the same title (*wr swnw*), it is possible that they represent the two succeeding generations of the same family, so they are father and son, but even in this case it cannot be determined with absolute certainty who of the two came earlier and was the father, and who was the child.[973]

Thus, on their own, archaeological and epigraphic evidence do not provide sufficient information to establish the sequence of the coffins that come from the tombs in the forecourt of Djehutihotep's funerary complex. However, in this case also the seriation of the coffins based on their style may offer a clue. The stylistic features suggest that the earliest coffin belongs to general Sepi (B1C), the overseer Sepi's coffin (B2P) is in all probability almost contemporaneous, from a little later next come in close succession the coffins of Neferi and Sen (B17C and B4L), and finally the last member of the group, also close in time, is Gua's coffin (B1L).[974]

This sort of stylistic seriation can also help to fit in the coffin of the seal bearer Djehutinakht (B1Y), which has been ignored so far. In the case of this coffin even such external clues are lacking as was the positioning of the tombs with the five previously discussed coffins. Although the title 'seal bearer' was borne by several nomarchs, the owner of B1Y in all probability did not hold the highest office in the nome, because his titulary in other respects differed considerably from the usual ranks of a nomarch.[975] Judged from its stylistic features, the seal bearer Djehutinakht's coffin is positioned between the coffins of Amenemhat and general Sepi, and perhaps it displays slightly more similarities with the former than the latter.[976]

On the basis of all the information thus gathered, we can reconstruct the relative chronological order of the coffins on which copies of the Book of the Moon were written (table 3), which in fact has been established by Harco Willems as part of his work to determine the sequence of all the coffins from Deir el-Bersha.[977] From the

[971] Willems 1988: 75–77.
[972] Willems 1988: 70.
[973] Willems 1988: 76 n. 87.
[974] Willems 1988: 73.
[975] Willems 1988: 80.
[976] Willems 1988: 80.
[977] Willems 1988: 73.

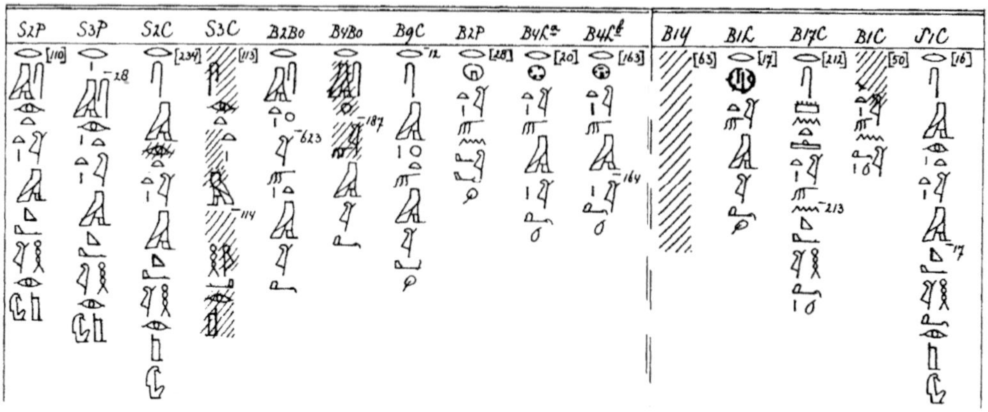

Figure 1 The hieroglyphic passage in *CT* II, 318a/319a on the various coffins (© The Oriental Institute of The University of Chicago).

table it becomes immediately clear that Sen's coffin, which I deem to display the most authentic version of the Book of the Moon, was – far from being the carrier of the oldest text variant – one of the latest objects recording the lunar spells. Despite the undoubtedly late date of Sen's text, I still opted for using it as the source for my presentation of the Book of the Moon, and my choice basically rests on several observations which suggest that his text on the one hand best preserved the lunar character of the composition, and on the other its language and vocabulary may predate other text variants that had been recorded earlier, notably the oldest one of them, the text on Djehutinakht's coffin (B2Bo).

Relative order	*Coffin sigla*	*Owner's name*
1	B2Bo	Djehutinakht
2	B4Bo	Djehutinakht (female)
3	B9C	Amenemhat
4	B1Y	Djehutinakht (seal bearer)
5	B1C	Sepi (general)
6	B2P	Sepi (overseer)
7	B17C	Neferi
8	B4L	Sen
9	B1L	Gua

Table 3 Relative chronology of the coffins recording the Book of the Moon based on historical/archaeological data and stylistic seriation.

Philological remarks on the chronological sequence of the text versions

When we compare Sen's version of the Book of the Moon with Djehutinakht's text, the first noticeable thing is that the latter has much longer introductory passages. Whereas Sen's spells start with the uniform statement 'knowing the *bas*' (*rḫ bꜣ.w*), the spells on Djehutinakht's coffin regularly insert statements before it to describe the general wishes of the deceased or to add some other extra information at the beginning of the text. In my opinion, the titles of the spells originally only consisted of the short formula 'knowing the *bas*', and these titles were devised to edit – possibly already existing – spells into a sequence in order to describe the lunar cycle. Although of course a reverse scenario is not absolutely impossible, I think that the longer titles in Djehutinakht's copy of the Book of the Moon are a later development: if they had been part of the composition right from the outset, it is highly likely that they would have been kept in later versions, too, at least in some instances (i.e. at least some of the statements in the case of some of the spells). Unless of course the brevity of the titles on Sen's coffin is a deliberate element of the discourse to imitate the terser style of older texts (i.e. texts that originally came from the central royal archives of the Old Kingdom).

Another clue for the possible antiquity of Sen's text can be found in the description of the full moon in spell 156. Towards the end of the spell we learn that the symbols representing the waxing moon have reached their state of completion, 'the feather has grown and the Red Crown is whole' (*šw.t rd.t dšr.t km.t*), and with the arrival of the full moon 'now there is rejoicing over what has had to be counted has been counted' (*nẖ m jp.w jp.t*).[978] To express the joy over this moment of the lunar cycle, six texts use the verb *ršw* (B2Bo, B4Bo, B9C, B1C, B2P, and B17C), three texts – including that of Sen's – feature the verb *nẖ* (B4L^{a}, B4L^{b}, and B1L), whereas on one coffin there is a lacuna at the particular place (B1Y). The verb *nẖ* undoubtedly derives from the duplicated stem *nẖnẖ*, an expression that is attested in the Pyramid Texts.[979] The use of the longer form was confined to the Pyramid Texts, and with time it seems that both *nẖnẖ* and *nẖ* were dropped from everyday usage. The appearance of the expression in the place of *ršw* on the coffins of Sen and Gua suggests that these copies of the Book of the Moon were more archaic than the ones that used the most common word for expressing the joy around the full moon. The question, however, remains whether the appearance of this word was intentional and is proof for an archaising style, or it genuinely reflects the older age of the manuscripts concerned.

There is yet another passage in spell 156 that easily lends itself for a comparison trying to determine the possible chronological order of the manuscripts on philological grounds. This is the line stating the purpose of the errand the speaker does for Re: 'to establish the feather in the shoulder' (*r smn.t šw.t m qꜥḥ*).[980] Although I take the

[978] *CT* II, 322b.
[979] *Wb.* II, 312.11.
[980] *CT* II, 318a.

infinitive in this phrase to be the verb *smn* 'to establish', this reading is far from being certain, due to the fact that on Sen's coffin – similarly to some other coffins – the word is recorded with a cryptographic sign that eludes easy interpretation (see figure 1). The copies on four other coffins spell out the word (B2Bo, B4Bo, B9C, and B17C), but only one of them (B17C) gives the meaningful lexeme *smn.t*. On B2Bo, B4Bo, and B9C we encounter a sequence of hieroglyphic signs, *s* + *m* + *jr.t*, which is a hapax and does not make sense, and in fact seems to be an attempt to interpret the unique cryptic sign that is used in some of the other text versions.[981] This implies that the copies of the Book of the Moon in which the cryptographic sign appears to denote the action concerning the lunar feather predate those that contain a (partly) phonetic – yet still enigmatic – spelling of the particular verb.

It has now become customary in studies of the Coffin Texts to establish the genealogical relations between the manuscripts of given spells by drawing up a stemma which is essentially based on the observation of meaningful differences between the available copies of the same text.[982] The application of these text critical methods, focusing originally on classical and mediaeval works, is not without problems in ancient Egyptian philology, because it always involves questionable judgements of originality.[983] So, while we can see that well-discernible differences show up in the various text versions of the Book of the Moon, I will not attempt to present a stemma for the individual spells included in it, or in fact for the entirety of the composition. I refrain from doing so mainly for two main reasons. First, none of the master copies – recorded on papyrus and kept in the local archives (see below) – that were used in transferring the Book of the Moon from one generation to the next one have been preserved, which is of course generally the case with the compositions of Egyptian mortuary literature. The lack of these manuscripts creates such huge gaps in our knowledge about editorial processes that bridging them inevitably requires a series of subjective judgements that in the end make the whole enterprise rather pointless.[984] Second, as I implied above, textual features that may seem to indicate the greater antiquity of a given manuscript may in fact be deliberate stylistic elements that are employed to create the impression of the archaic nature of a text. The attempts to give greater prestige to a composition in this way, or through pseudoepigraphy, is not an uncommon practice in ancient Egypt.[985]

The transmission of the manuscripts of the Book of the Moon: the House of Life in Hermopolis

When we compare the chronological sequence of the coffins recording the Book of the Moon with the textual characteristics of the copies, we can see that the two analyses yield entirely different conclusions. The coffin B2Bo is the oldest object that

[981] Thausing 1941.
[982] Backes 2011.
[983] Peust 2012: 209–210.
[984] cf. Peust 2012: 210–211.
[985] Loprieno 1996: 53.

preserved the composition, yet the text written on it has some features that suggest it had developed from earlier versions which seem to have influenced the texts of later copies (in which for example the cryptic sign in *CT* II, 318a was retained). This dichotomy can of course be resolved if we bear in mind that the copies of the Book of the Moon were not directly copied from one coffin to another one. Quite obviously, after the interment of the deceased their coffins were sealed in the tomb and became unavailable for further use. There must have been master copies recorded on papyrus that allowed the makers of funerary equipment to consult them when their customers desired to include the lunar spells in the mortuary texts written on their coffins.[986] The cases of textual corruption that can be explained by the confusion of hieratic signs suggest that these master copies, or at least some of them, were written in that script.[987]

The available sources seem to indicate that there existed a place in Hermopolis, the House of Life (*pr-ꜥnḫ*), where the Book of the Moon could have been written, preserved, and transmitted. One of the high officials buried in Deir el-Bersha, Iha – according to an inscription in his tomb – was the overseer of the scribes working in the House of Life (*jmj-r sš.w m pr-ꜥnḫ*).[988] Since Iha undoubtedly had some connections with the royal residence, there is some uncertainty as to where this House of Life was found precisely, in the royal court or in Iha's own nome, but there is some firm ground to believe that the House of Life Iha talks about was in fact situated in Hermopolis.[989]

Therefore this House of Life in Hermopolis must have been the institution in which the master copy – or, judged from the widely differing text versions – master copies of the Book of the Moon were kept, re-copied and updated or augmented from time to time. Relevant evidence clearly shows that one of the main functions of the House of Life was the preservation of written knowledge and the care of sacred texts.[990] It should neither be forgotten, however, that the House of Life was also the centre of healing and medicine.[991] Two of the owners of the coffins with the Book of the Moon, Sen and Gua, bore the title of chief physician (*wr swnw*), and they could also have been part of the staff working in the House of Life in Hermopolis. In addition, as is well-known and has also been stressed in my commentary, the waxing moon was seen as the healing of the injured eye of Horus, and this medical context, both in tangible and mythological terms, is referred to in the spells of the Book of the Moon.

Finally, it may perhaps be tentatively suggested that the unusual listing of the *bas* of Hermopolis at the end of spell 156 contains an indirect reference to the House of Life. One of the *bas* is defined as the knowledge that has been acquired in the house

[986] Baines 2004: 30–31.
[987] Faulkner 1981: 173.
[988] Willems 2007: 66.
[989] Morenz 1996: 84–86; Nordh 1996: 200–201; Willems 2007: 99; Willems 2014: 182.
[990] Gardiner 1938: 175; Jasnow and Zauzich 2005: 34.
[991] Gardiner 1938: 176.

of the night (*rḫ.n=ṯ m pr-grḥ pw*).[992] The expression *pr-grḥ* 'the house of the night' is not attested elsewhere, but can possibly be put in parallel with a much later similar name. In the demotic composition that its publishers prefer to call the Book of Thoth (1st/2nd century CE),[993] the text often refers to a 'room of darkness' (*ʿ.t-kky*), which place is on the one hand undoubtedly one of the regions of the netherworld, but on the other may denote a certain part of the House of Life, or even the expression *ʿ.t-kky* is an alternative designation of the House of Life as a whole.[994] Undeniably there is a great distance both in terms of time and lexical elements between the names *pr-grḥ* and *ʿ.t-kky*, but it may perhaps be argued that the house of the night and the room of darkness can easily be associated with each other, since they both connote the absence of sunlight. This connection may further be strengthened if we remember that both the Book of Thoth and the definition of the house of the night is concerned with some learning process (*rḫ*). So it is not altogether impossible that the expression *pr-grḥ* relates to the House of Life in Hermopolis, though in three text versions the place is named as the house of the day (*pr-hrw*).[995]

The Book of the Moon in Asyut

Six fragmentary versions and one complete copy of the Book of the Moon have come down to us from Asyut. The complete version is found on Nakht's coffin (S2P), which was in all probability produced for its owner during the 12th dynasty, though unfortunately – because of their peculiar local style – the coffins of Asyut cannot be seriated in the same way as the ones originating from Deir el-Bersha.[996] Since Nakht's version shows close affinities with the text of Djehutinakht (B2Bo), even with the placement of spells 154–160 on the lid of the coffin,[997] it was possibly recorded around the same time or later than Djehutinakht's manuscript; in any case, both texts must have shared a common master copy. The direction of the flow of manuscripts, from Hermopolis/Deir el-Bersha to Asyut, is indicated by the fact that ornamental texts on some coffins from Asyut invoke the Hermopolitan gods.[998] On the other hand, perhaps the best-known characteristic of Asyut coffins, the diagonal star tables listing the decans, are not found on coffins coming from Deir el-Bersha.[999] The significance of the presence of the Book of the Moon in Asyut is the fact that it made possible the transition of the composition into the Book of Going Forth by Day around the middle of the 2nd millennium BCE (see next chapter).[1000]

---

992 *CT* II, 324d.
993 Jasnow and Zauzich 2005: 77.
994 Jasnow and Zauzich 2005: 37.
995 *CT* II, 324d/325d (B2P, B17C, B1C).
996 Willems 1988: 102–103.
997 Arquier 2013: 130.
998 Willems 1988: 103 n. 203.
999 Arquier 2013: 7879.
1000 Kahl 1999: 283–291.

3.4. The survival of the spells in the Book of Going Forth by Day

Around the middle of the 2nd millennium BCE a new collection of spells superseded the Coffin Texts, which became known as the Book of Going Forth by Day (alternatively called – especially in earlier literature – the Book of the Dead).[1001] This change was partly prompted by historical circumstances: the emerging elite in the southern centre of power, Thebes, did not have access to the royal archives in the north, in Memphis, since Lower Egypt and the northern part of Upper Egypt, down to the point of Cusae, was occupied by the rival Hyksos dynasty.[1002] Nevertheless, since Coffin Texts were produced in a series of regional capitals around Egypt, including areas that fell outside the sphere of influence of the Hyksos rulers, many of the earlier spells made it into the new corpus of funerary literature. The same fate awaited the spells of the Book of the Moon, but the transmission was – so to speak – not perfect: while the individual spells, with the exception of Coffin Texts spell 155, were included in the Book of Going Forth by Day, their order – especially in the long term – was not retained, so the composition as a whole was gradually lost. This loss is perhaps a bit surprising, given that at the end of the 17th and at the beginning of the 18th dynasty there surely must have been an upsurge in the lunar cult, as the increased number of royal and common names associated with the moon (Jahhotep, Jahmes, Thothmes [i.e. Djehutimes], Djehuti) indicate.[1003]

The Book of Going Forth by Day, just as the Coffin Texts, is a general term that denotes a large group of spells not all of which were recorded continuously and simultaneously.[1004] In other words, the individual manuscripts of the Book of Going Forth by Day, typically written on papyri, represent a selection of spells from an available corpus that was significantly larger than the series of texts actually recorded at one time. This implies that the statement that with the exception of Coffin Texts spell 155 all the other spells of the Book of the Moon were transmitted into the Book of Going Forth by Day is not necessarily true for a particular manuscript: it may only contain some of the chapters of the original lunar composition, as is for example the case with the papyrus of Nu (18th dynasty) that has a string of four spells about the origins of the month, the waxing moon, the full moon, and the waning moon (chapters 115–116–112–113, see below), and then the descriptions of the *bas* of the easterners and westerners (chapters 108 and 109) located at other parts of the papyrus.[1005] In order to understand the survival of the Book of the Moon, first a concordance between the two text corpora can be established (Table 4), using the designation of the Coffin Texts spells as it was introduced in de Buck's synoptic edition of them,[1006] and the

[1001] Hornung 1999: 13.
[1002] Bourriau 2000: 193.
[1003] Bryan 2000: 209.
[1004] Hornung 1999: 13–14.
[1005] Lapp 1997: 68.
[1006] See *CT* II, 266a–388c.

traditional numbering of the spells (chapters) of the Book of Going Forth by Day, based on how a late edition of this composition was published in the 19th century.[1007]

Coffin Texts spell	*Book of Going Forth by Day spell*
154	115
155	-
156	114, 116
157	112
158	113
159	107, 109, 149
160	108, 111

Table 4 Concordance of spells in the Book of the Moon (Coffin Texts) and the Book of Going Forth by Day.

Although the individual manuscripts of the Book of Going Forth by Day were selections from a larger corpus of spells, there were – similarly to the case of the Coffin Texts – some sequences that regularly appeared together in the same order.[1008] Not surprisingly, one of these sequences consisted of the descendants of the spells of the Book of the Moon, that is the spells that promised the knowledge of the *bas*. In its fullest form this sequence included all of the spells from the Book of the Moon with the exception of Coffin Texts spell 155 (for the complete neglect of this spell 155, see my comments below).[1009] The chapters of the Book of Going Forth by Day followed one another in the order 115–116–112–113–108–109, so even the original order of the spells was retained to a large extent, with only the last two being swapped. Since both of these last two spells are concerned with the conjunction of the sun and the moon (the period of lunar invisibility), it may be said that their reversed order did not fundamentally change the overall message of the shortened composition about the lunar cycle embedded in the newly developed corpus of funerary texts. It may be added that since the first spell (chapter 115) of the sequence about the origins of the month also made references to the period of lunar invisibility, neither the lack of the spell about the *bas* of *psḏn.tjw* (Coffin Texts spell 155) broke entirely the original chronological scheme of the composition.

Another frequently occurring sequence during the New Kingdom included five chapters of the Book of Going Forth by Day in the order: 114–112–113–108–109.[1010] This meant that the original order of the spells of the Book of the Moon, with the omission

[1007] Lepsius 1842; Hornung 1999: 15.
[1008] Munro 1988: 140–143; Gee 2010: 26; Lapp 2004: 45–51.
[1009] Munro 1988: 156, 220; Lapp 1997: 40.
[1010] Lapp 2004: 45, 49.

of the first two spells, was maintained for three spells, while the last two were once again swapped. In other words, the sequence started with the description of the *bas* of Hermopolis (the waxing moon), continued with the *bas* of Pe (full moon) and the *bas* of Nekhen (waning moon), but the description of the *bas* of the westerners (solar eclipse) preceded the spell about the *bas* of the easterners (the moon at the eastern horizon). The omission of the first two spells about the origins of the month and lunar invisibility was perhaps driven by a desire to start with the description of the waxing phases of the moon that perhaps – in the judgement of the Theban editors – better expressed the concept of rebirth after death.

The description of the waxing moon, in the from of chapter 116 of the Book of Going Forth by Day, was also included in another sequence in which it was preceded by chapter 65 and followed by chapter 91.[1011] Chapter 65 is basically a short hymn to the sole one who rises as the moon,[1012] possibly the designation of the blacked-out moon, so it is quite evident why it appears immediately before chapter 116 describing the waxing moon. The connection between chapter 116 and the ensuing chapter 91 is not so obvious, but this text – a short hymn addressed to the lofty one (*qꜣ*)[1013] – perhaps refers to the moon or the full moon without naming it. The lofty one is urged to make way for the deceased to the place where Re and Hathor are, and this is perhaps a reference to the setting sun and the west, so the full moon – travelling from the eastern horizon to the western one – may well be disguised under the name of the lofty one. Admittedly, however, this interpretation of the spell is mostly based on speculation.

By the time when the group of spells that were to be included in the Book of Going Forth by Day began to be canonised during the 26th dynasty,[1014] the chronological order of the spells had disappeared. Since the modern numbering of the chapters of the Book of Going Forth by Day reflects this so-called Saite recension,[1015] we can basically distinguish two sequences that are the descendants of the Book of the Moon, chapters 107–108–109 and 111–112–113–114–115–116, the two being separated by the lengthy description of the Field of Reeds and Field of Rest (chapter 110).[1016] Thus the shorter sequence begins with the short and jumbled description of the *bas* of the westerners and the eastern gates of the sky (chapter 107), continues with the spell about the *bas* of the westerners (chapter 108), and then closes with the *bas* of the easterners associated with the Field of Reeds (chapter 109). The longer sequence kicks off with a shortened description of the mountain of Bakhu and the meeting between Re and the hostile snake (chapter 111), and then follow the texts about the *bas* of Pe/ full moon (chapter 112), the *bas* of Nekhen/waning moon (chapter 113), the *bas* of Hermopolis/waxing moon (chapter 114), the *bas* of Heliopolis/origins of the month

[1011] Lapp 2004: 46.
[1012] See Allen 1974: 60.
[1013] Allen 1974: 75.
[1014] Hornung 1999: 17.
[1015] Hornung 1999: 15.
[1016] Lepsius 1842: pls. xxxix–xliv.

(chapter 115), and then again the *bas* of Hermopolis/waxing moon (chapter 116). In this way the order of the original composition was completely rearranged, which possibly indicates that the knowledge about the ultimate editorial principle and logic behind it – the chronologically sequenced description of the lunar cycle – had also disappeared.

Not only did the sequence of the spells change, especially over the long run, but the texts themselves were often significantly altered. The term Book of Going Forth by Day of course encompasses a huge text corpus ranging well over more than a thousand years and including about 3500 copies,[1017] so it is impossible to take a look at all the individual manuscripts and detect every single difference. Such an undertaking – using even only a fairly large selection of manuscripts – would vouch for its own monograph (i.e. falls outside the scope of the present study), and would significantly exceed my capabilities and means at the moment, since many of these manuscripts are still unpublished. Instead, to track down the textual changes that occurred in the lunar spells during the transition from the Coffin Texts to the Book of Going Forth by Day, and then along the history of the latter collection, I adopted a simplified approach. Below I present the relevant spells from the Book of Going Forth by Day from three manuscripts that stand roughly at the two extreme points of the history of the text corpus, the 18th dynasty and early Ptolemaic times. These copies of the spells are available in modern transcriptions or facsimile publications, so they can be easily consulted by other researchers, too. For the formative period of the Book of Going Forth by Day I use the papyrus of Nebseni,[1018] produced most probably under Thutmose IV, and when a spell is missing there (chapters 115 and 116), the papyrus of Nu,[1019] also dated to the 18th dynasty. For the Ptolemaic times, I have chosen the well-known papyrus of Iufankh from the beginning of the 3rd century BCE.[1020] After the transliteration and translation of each spell, I summarise the most significant developments and innovations of the texts.

Spell 154: chapter 115 of the Book of Going Forth by Day

pNu

There is no accompanying vignette.

r n pr.t r p.t wbꜣ jmḥ.t rḫ bꜣ.w Jwn.w
ḏd-mdw jn N jw wrš.n⸗j m sf m-m wr.w
ḫpr.n⸗j m(-m) Ḫpr.j wn-ḥr ḥr jr.t wꜥ.t wn qd kk.w
jnk wꜥ jm⸗tn jw⸗j rḫ.kw pꜣ bꜣ.w Jwn.w tm bsj wr-mꜣ.w ḥr⸗f m sn.t ḏꜣj.t
n ntj⸗j n ḏd⸗j n nṯr.w jn ḥtm jwꜥ.t Jwn.w

[1017] Kockelmann 2006: 161–162.
[1018] Lapp 2004.
[1019] Lapp 1997.
[1020] Lepsius 1842.

jw⸗j rḫ.kw jr.y ḥnsk.t n ṯꜣy ḥr⸗s
Rꜥ ḥr mdw.t n Jm.j-<w>hm⸗f ꜥḥꜥ.n r⸗f <j>ꜣt ḫpr ḫb.t pw m ꜣbd
ḏd.jn Rꜥ n Jm.j-<whm>⸗f šsp mꜥbꜣ jwꜥ.t rmṯ ḫpr mꜥbꜣ.yt pw jn Jm.j-<w>hm⸗f
ḫpr sn.tj ḫpr sn.t Rꜥ pw
ḫpr sḏm jns.j⸗f n ḫn<.t> ꜥ⸗f
ꜥḥꜥ.n jrj.n⸗f ḫpr.w⸗f m s.t-ḥm.t ḥnsk.t ḫpr ḥnsk.<tj> pw n Jwn.w
kfꜣ sḫm m r-pr pn ḫpr kfꜣ pw n Jwn.w
ḫpr jwꜥ.t jwꜥ.t⸗f
wr mꜣꜣ.t⸗f ḫpr.ḫr⸗f m wr-mꜣ.w n Jwn.w
jw⸗j rḫ.kw bꜣ.w Jwn.w Rꜥ pw Šw Tfnw.t pw

Spell for coming forth to the sky and opening up the netherworld. Knowing the *bas* of Heliopolis.
To be recited by *N*: I spent yesterday among the great ones, and I became Khepri – looking at the sole eye and revealing the form of darkness.
I am one of you because I know the *bas* of Heliopolis into which not even the greatest of seers has been initiated when going out (with) extended (arms).
I will not be in distress, for I do not tell the gods of the destroyer of the heir of Heliopolis.
I know how a braided lock of hair of a man is made upon it (= the eye).
Re had a discussion with He-who-is-in-his-fire, and then his part was injured. That is how the diminishing of the month came into being.
Then Re said to He-who-is-in-his-fire: 'Take the harpoon, the inheritance of people!', and that is how the tribunal of 30 came into being by He-who-is-in-his-fire.
The two sisters came into being, and that is how the passing of Re came into being.
The servant of his red linen came into being before his arm alighted.
Then he assumed his form as a woman with braided hair, and that is how She-with-braided-hair came into being in Heliopolis.
The divine power was uncovered in the temple, and that is how the uncovering in Heliopolis came into being.
The heir of his inheritance came into being.
What he saw was great, so he became the greatest of seers in Heliopolis.
I know the *bas* of Heliopolis. It is Re, it is Shu and Tefnut.[1021]

In the New Kingdom descendant of spell 154 of the Coffin Texts the title is slightly augmented by adding a statement about coming forth to the sky and opening up the netherworld. The speaker claims to have become Khepri – the rising sun – and in connection with him reference is made to the sole eye and the revealing of a form of darkness, which expressions possibly describe the unseen manifestation of the moon in front of the solar disc, so the knowledge that this spell was about the encounter between the two major celestial bodies may not have been entirely lost at this time.

[1021] Lapp 1997: pl. 52.

As for the aetiological motif about the harpoon, it changed completely, because now a comparison is made between the harpoon (*mꜥbꜣ*) and the tribunal of 30 (*mꜥbꜣ.yt*). This alteration was certainly based on the similarity of the two words, resembling – and in the second case, originating from – the expression denoting the number 30. The original comparison between the flagpoles of Re (*sn.wt*) and the *senut*-festival (*sn.wt*) has also disappeared, and it has been replaced by a simile between the two sisters (*sn.tj*) and the passing (*sn.t*) of Re. The original expression *fꜣk* ('shorn man') has metamorphosed into *kfꜣ* ('uncover'), which possibly resulted from the misreading of the first word by a scribe copying an older manuscript.

pIufankh

The vignette shows the deceased adoring Re, Shu, and Tefnut.

r n prj n p.t wbꜣ jmḥ.t rḫ bꜣ.w Jwn.w
ḏd-mdw jn N jw wr.n⸗j m sf m-ꜥ wr.w ḫpr.n⸗j m-ꜥ ẖpr.w
wn.n⸗j-ḥr ḥr jr.t wꜥ.t wn qd kk.w
jnk wꜥ jm⸗tn jw⸗j rḫ.kw pꜣ bꜣ.w Jwn.w tm bsj wr pḥ.tj ḥr⸗f m sn.t ḏꜣj
n ntj⸗j n ḏdt n nṯr.w jn sḥtm jwꜥ Jwn.w
jw⸗j rḫ.kw jr.tyw ḥnsk.t n ṯꜣy ḥr⸗s
Rꜥ ḥr mdw n nswt m hꜣw⸗f ꜥḥꜥ.n r⸗f jꜣt ḫpr ḫb.t pw m ꜣbd
ḏd.jn Rꜥ n Jm.j-hꜣw⸗f šsp mꜥbꜣ jwꜥ.t rmṯ ḫpr mꜥbꜣ pw jn Jm.j-hꜣw⸗f
ḫpr sn.tj ḫpr sn.wt Rꜥ pw
ḫpr sḏm jns.j⸗f n ḫn ꜥ⸗f
ꜥḥꜥ.n jrj.n⸗f ḫpr.w⸗f m s-ḥm.t ḥnsk.t ḫpr ḥnsk.tj pw m Jwn.w
kfꜣ sḫm jwꜥ n r-pr pn ḫpr kfꜣ pw n Jwn.w
ḫpr jwꜥ n jwꜥ⸗f wr mꜣw⸗f ḫpr.ḫr⸗f m pḥ.tj nṯr m sꜣ jr.t n jt⸗f
ḫpr ẖr.t⸗f m pḥ.tj n Jwn.w
jw⸗j rḫ.kw bꜣ.w Jwn.w Rꜥ pw Šw Tfnw.t pw

Spell for coming forth to the sky and opening up the netherworld. Knowing the *bas* of Heliopolis.
To be recited by *N*: I became great yesterday among the great ones, and I became (one of their) beings.
I have looked at the sole eye revealing the form of darkness.
I am one of you because I know the *bas* of Heliopolis into which not even he with great strength has been initiated when going out (with) extended (arms).
I will not be in distress for the saying of the gods by the destroyer of the heir of Heliopolis. I know how a braided lock of hair of a man is made upon it (= the eye).
Re had a discussion with a king in his neighbourhood, and then his part was injured. That is how the diminishing of the month came into being.

Then Re said to He-who-is-in-his-neighbourhood: 'Take the harpoon, the inheritance of people!', and that is how the harpoon came into being by He-who-is-in-his-neighbourhood.
The two sisters came into being, and that is how the *senut*-festival of Re came into being.
The servant of his red linen came into being before his arm alighted.
Then he assumed his form as a woman with braided hair, and that is how She-with-braided-hair came into being in Heliopolis.
The divine power was uncovered in the temple, and that is how the uncovering in Heliopolis came into being.
The heir of his inheritance came into being, his greatest of seers, and then he would come into being as divine strength, as the son acting for his father.
His belongings came into being as strength in Heliopolis.
I know the *bas* of Heliopolis. It is Re, it is Shu and Tefnut.[1022]

The beginning of the Ptolemaic version of chapter 115 of the Book of Going Forth by Day closely follows its New Kingdom forerunner. The first significant alteration occurs in the claim that the speaker knows the *bas* of Heliopolis into which not even 'the one with great strength' (*wr pḥ.tj*) has been initiated into. With this change the text loses its reference to the greatest of seers, a priestly title that in all probability involved the observation of celestial phenomena, and most certainly, the observation of the sun. Re does not have a discussion with the serpent He-who-is-in-his-fire, but with a king around him, a change that is difficult to explain, but possibly occurred through mistaking the first sign of *jm.j*, showing a papyrus reed, with the first sign of the word for king, *nswt*, which was the similar hieroglyph – especially in cursive hieroglyphic or hieratic texts – depicting the stalk of a plant.[1023] Later in the text Re's adversary is defined as He-who-is-in-his-neighbourhood. The creation of the harpoon is explained tautologically, and in this detail the Ptolemaic version of chapter 115 of the Book of Going Forth by Day resembles more closely Coffin Texts spell 155 than its earlier version from the New Kingdom. The wordplay with the two sisters now involves the *senut*-festival, so here again Iufankh's composition seems to display more lunar characteristics. Towards the end of the spell the strength that exists or works in Heliopolis is once more mentioned, so it must have played an important role in the contemporaneous image of the seat of the solar cult.

Spell 155

This spell was not transmitted into the Book of Going Forth by Day, but we should perhaps be cautious with this statement. Since this funerary composition, at least around the time of its conception, was – just like its predecessors, the Pyramid Texts and the Coffin Texts – a variable selection of magical spells, theoretically it is not impossible

1022 Lepsius 1842: pl. lxiv.
1023 cf. Möller 1909: 27 (nos. 282 and 289).

that some of the manuscripts contained the spell about the *bas* of lunar invisibility. On the other hand, a significant number of copies of the Book of Going Forth by Day have come down to us, and therefore – chances of preservation notwithstanding – if this spell had been included in some collections of New Kingdom funerary spells, at least one copy would have surely made it to our day. Consequently, I believe that it is best to assume that spell 155 of the Coffin Texts was neglected deliberately when the texts for the new collections of funerary spells were compiled. Since this spell was most definitely written in Hermopolis, at first glance we may suspect some historical circumstances behind its omission. Hermopolis lied north of Cusae, the border town between the Hyksos territories and those under the influence of the emerging 17th dynasty, so its archives were not available for the scribes composing the nascent Book of Going Forth by Day. However, spell 155 has also been preserved on coffins originating from Asyut,[1024] and we know that this town had a major intellectual influence on the religious compositions of the New Kingdom.[1025] So it is unlikely that the unavailability of the text was a factor. Neither can the omission be attributed to a supposed reluctance to take over a text with strong ties to a location lying in hostile territory, since spell 156 of the Coffin Texts about the *bas* of Hermopolis was selected to be perpetuated.

Another point that may be raised about the disappearance of spell 155 concerns its contents. Perhaps, after all, as lunar invisibility was a kind of non-event, it was just an unimportant phase of the lunar cycle, and while it may have carried some weight for the adherents of the lunar cult in Hermopolis, it was not considered worth mentioning by the Theban intellectual elite. Two arguments may be recalled to refute this reasoning. Firstly, as emphasised quite a few times in this work, the Egyptians started their lunar month with the disappearance of the last crescent, so the invisible period of the moon was of utmost importance for them at all times and in all places.[1026] Secondly, what is perhaps even more important, it seems that the Egyptians devised a new sign for *psḏn.tjw*, the period of lunar invisibility, showing the merger of the lunar and solar discs, just around the beginning of the New Kingdom,[1027] and this also testifies to the recognition of this phase of the lunar cycle around the time when the Book of Going Forth by Day came into use. Then perhaps the obvious conclusion is that spell 155 was left out from the new corpus because it originally was also the odd-one out in the Book of the Moon: its title referring to the *bas* of lunar invisibility was quite dissimilar to the other titles connected with locations or beings strongly associated with the specific locations of east and west. This – coupled with the inherent arcane nature of the text that was probably quite enigmatic to any educated person outside Hermopolis – must have been the main reason for the elimination of spell 155.

1024 *CT* II, 290a–309b (S2P, S3P, S1Ta, S1Ca, S1Cb, S2C, S3C, S9C).
1025 Kahl 1999.
1026 I have collected textual evidence for the importance of *psḏn.tjw* in Priskin (forthcoming).
1027 Depuydt 1998.

Spell 156: chapters 114 and 116 of the Book of Going Forth by Day

Chapter 114 (pNebseni)

The vignette shows three ibis-headed squatting figures.

r n rḫ bꜣ.w Ḫmn.w jn N
jšš šw.t m rmn wbn n.t m mnṯꜣ.t
sḥḏ.w jr.t m wḏꜥ sj
jw=j bs=kw ḥr=s jw=j rḫ.kw jnn st m Qjs
n ḏd=j n rmṯ n wḥm=j n nṯr.w
jj.n=j m wpw.t n.t Rꜥ r smn šw.t m rmn r wbn n.t m mnṯꜣ.t r sjp jr.t n jp sj
jj.n=j m sḫm ḥr rḫ bꜣ.w Ḫmn.w
mrr.jw rḫ mrj=ṯn mrr.jw rḫ mrj=ṯn
jw=j rḫ.kw šw.t rwḏ.tj km.tj jp sj
ršj=j ḥr jp jp.t
jnḏ ḥr=ṯn bꜣ.w Ḫmn.w
jw=j rḫ.kw šr.t m ꜣbd <wr.t> m smd.t
sjꜣ Rꜥ štꜣ.w grḥ rḫ n=ṯn sjꜣ.n wj Ḏḥwtj pwj
jnḏ ḥr=ṯn bꜣ.w Ḫmn.w mj rḫ=j ṯn rꜥ-nb

Spell for knowing the *bas* of Hermopolis by *N*.
The feather is carried in the shoulder, and then the Red Crown rises in the *mentjat*-bowl.
The eye is made to shine by separating it.
I have been initiated into it, I know the one who brings it in Cusae.
I have not told it to men, nor have I repeated it to the gods.
I come on an errand for Re to establish the feather in the shoulder, to make the Red Crown rise in the *mentjat*-bowl, and to take count of the eye for him who counts it.
I come as a divine power for I know the *bas* of Hermopolis.
Oh, those who love the knowing one, love (me, too), oh, those who love the knowing one, love (me, too).
I know that the feather has grown and been completed, and that it has been counted.
I rejoice because what has to be counted has been counted.
Hail to you, the *bas* of Hermopolis!
I know what is small on the second day of the lunar month, and (what is big) on the fifteenth day.
Re knows the secrets of the night that are known to you, and Thoth knows me.
Hail to you, the *bas* of Hermopolis, as I know you every day.[1028]

[1028] Lapp 2004: pl. 19.

Perhaps the most important novelty of chapter 114 of the Book of Going Forth by Day is the appearance of the verb *jšš* 'to carry'[1029] collocating with its object, the lunar feather. The verb was in all probability chosen to replace the enigmatic expression written with a cryptic sign or its derivatives in the Middle Kingdom copies of the text for its similarity to the verb *jšš* 'to spit out'.[1030] This verb described the act by which the creator god Atum brought Shu to life, as for example in utterance 660 of the Pyramid Texts,[1031] and I believe that this already existing collocation – and the similarity of the expressions *Šw* (Shu) and *šw.t* (feather) – prompted the editors of the spells of the Book of Going Forth by Day to pick the verb *jšš*. In the continuation of the sentence about the appearance of the feather, the full moon is described as the Red Crown rising from the *mentjat*-bowl, and here the Red Crown is spelled out as *n.t*, not *dšr.t*.

The meaning of the geographical reference made in connection with the eye – i.e. that it is brought in, or perhaps from, Cusae – eludes me. Once again, perhaps the fact that this town lied at the frontier of the two opposing parts of the country under the 17th dynasty may have had something to do with its appearance in the spell under discussion. Nonetheless, it should be noted that the mention of Cusae replaces the earlier reference to the initiation of the speaker of the spell by the *sem*-priest.

After we learn that the deceased comes as a divine power, the text continues with an obscure exhortation to 'those who love the knowing one', which part was also newly inserted into the spell. The ending of the spell has been rewritten, and in fact there is no orderly listing of the *bas* of Hermopolis. Instead, as an entirely new element, Re is given prominence, because we learn that he knows the secrets that are also known to the *bas* of Hermopolis. Then Thoth is mentioned, and the perpetual knowledge of the speaker about the *bas* of Hermopolis is emphasised.

Chapter 114 (pIufankh)

The vignette shows the deceased adoring Thoth, Sia, and Atum.

r n rḫ bꜣ.w Ḫmn.w
ḏd-mdw jn N jšš šw.t m rmn wbn Nj.t m ṯꜣr.t
nḏ jr.t n wḏꜥ sj
jw⸗j bs⸗kw ḥr⸗s jw⸗j rḫ.kw jnn s<j> m Qjs
nn ḏd<⸗j> n rmṯ n wḥm<⸗j> n nṯr.w
jj.n⸗j m wpw.t n Rꜥ smn mꜣꜥ.t r⸗j n wbn Nj.t m ṯꜣr.t r sjp s<j>
jj<⸗j> m sḫm ḥr rḫ bꜣ.w Ḫmn.w
mrj n rḫ mrj⸗tn jw⸗j
rḫ.kw mꜣꜥ.t jp.t<j> km.tj rwḏ.tj ršj<⸗j> ḥr jp

[1029] *Wb.* I, 136.1.
[1030] *Wb.* I, 135.14–15.
[1031] *Pyr.* §1871a.

jnḏ ḥr⸗tn bꜣ.w Ḫmn.w mj rḫ<⸗j> tn Ḏhwtj Sjꜣ Tm pw

Spell for knowing the *bas* of Hermopolis.
To be recited by *N*. (The feather) is carried in the shoulder, and then Neith rises in the shelter. The eye is protected by him who separates it.
I have been initiated into it, I know the one who brings it in Cusae.
I have not told it to men, nor have I repeated it to the gods.
I come on an errand for Re; *maat* is established for me, and Neith rises in the shelter for him who takes count of it.
I come as a divine power for I know the *bas* of Hermopolis.
The love of the knowing one is what you love.
I know that *maat* has been counted, completed, and grown. I rejoice for the counting.
Hail to you, the *bas* of Hermopolis as I know you. It is Thoth, Sia, and Atum.[1032]

By the time of the Ptolemaic era, it seems, the entire message about the Red Crown rising from the *mentjat*-bowl was lost. The Red Crown, spelled as *n.t* in pNebseni, transformed into the divine name *Nj.t* (Neith) – a development already present in pNu in chapter 116 of the Book of Going Forth by Day (see below) – whereas the word *mnṯꜣ.t* was replaced by *ṯꜣr.t* (shelter). Also, the hieroglyph of the feather was at some point misread as *mꜣꜥ.t*, so the text talks about the establishment of *maat*, and it is also the *maat* that is counted, completed, and grown towards the end of the spell. In this case, too, the same change was already effected in chapter 116 in the papyrus of Nu (see also below).

Chapter 116 (pNu)

There is no accompanying vignette.

ky r n rḫ bꜣ.w Ḫmn.w
ḏd-mdw jn N mꜣꜥ-ḫrw wbn Nj.t m Mꜣꜣṯꜣ.t stꜣ Mꜥꜣ.t ḫnt.t qꜥḥ wnm jr.t jn jp-sj
<jw⸗j bsj>⸗kw ḥr⸗s jn sm
n ḏd⸗j n rmṯ n wḥm⸗j n nṯr.w ṯs-pḫr
ꜥq.n⸗j m ḫm mꜣꜣ.n⸗j štꜣ.w
jnḏ ḥr⸗ṯn nṯr.w jm.jw Ḫmn.w rḫ⸗ṯn wj mj rḫ⸗j n.t r srwd jr.t km.t rš m jp jp.wt
jw⸗j rḫ.kw bꜣ.w Jwn.w ꜥꜣ.t m ꜣbd ḫb.t m smd.t
Ḏḥwtj pw štꜣ Sjꜣ pw rḫ Tm pw

Another spell for knowing the *bas* of Hermopolis.
To be recited by *N* true of voice: Neith rises in Matjat, and Maat moves in front of the shoulder while the eye is consumed by He-who-counts-it.
I have been initiated into it by the *sem*-priest;
I have not told it to other people, nor have I repeated it to the gods, and *vice versa*.

[1032] Lepsius 1842: pl. xliii.

I have entered as an ignorant one, and then I saw secrets.
Hail to you, gods who are in Hermopolis, know me as I know the Red Crown, with respect to growing the eye complete, when there is rejoicing over what has had to be counted has been counted.
I know the *bas* of Heliopolis, what is great on the second day of the lunar month and what is reduced on the fifteenth day.
It is Thoth, it is the secret of Sia, it is the knowledge of Atum.[1033]

In chapter 116 not only the Red Crown and the feather are replaced with other words – Matjat and the divine name Maat, respectively – but also the order of the statements about them have been reversed. Nonetheless, the initiation is once more accredited to the *sem*-priest. The speaker stresses the point that he has entered as an ignorant one and then saw secrets. This statement is lacking in the corresponding spell of the Book of the Moon. In a curious twist – which is perhaps only the mistake of a careless scribe – at the end of the spell the *bas* of Heliopolis are mentioned, instead of the *bas* of Hermopolis. On the other hand, this statement may not be a simple slip of the pen, because the parallel mention of the *bas* of Heliopolis and Hermopolis reappears in pIufankh (see below).

Quite remarkably, the spell at the end defines the *bas* of Heliopolis as what is great on the second day of the lunar month and what is small (reduced) on the fifteenth day. If this is not an inadvertent or careless swap of the adjectives, then the statement perhaps refers to the dark part of the lunar disc, as suspected by other researchers.[1034] The listing of the *bas* at the end follows the pattern of the kindred spells more closely, because it mentions three divinities with only minor embellishments (secret of Sia, knowledge of Atum).

Chapter 116 (pIufankh)

The vignette shows the deceased adoring Thoth, Sia, and Atum.

r n rḫ bꜣ.w Jwn.w
ḏd-mdw jn N mꜥꜣ-ḫrw wbn m Mꜣṯꜣ stꜣ m-ꜥ ḫnt.t qꜥḥ wnm jr.t jn jp-sj
jw⸗j bsj⸗kw ḥr⸗s jn sm
nn ḏd<⸗j> n rmṯ nn wḥm<⸗j> n nṯr.w ṯs-pḫr
ꜥq.n⸗j m ḫm mꜣꜣ.n⸗j štꜣ.w
jnḏ ḥr⸗tn nṯr.w jpw n.w Ḫmn.w
ꜥꜣ.t m ꜣbd ḫbꜣ m smd.t
Ḏḥwtj pw štꜣ Sjꜣ pw rḫ Tm pw

Spell for knowing the *bas* of Heliopolis.

[1033] Lapp 1997: pl. 53.
[1034] Allen 1974: 93 n. 201.

To be recited by *N*: Rising in Matja, and moving in front of the shoulder while the eye is consumed by He-who-counts-it.
I have been initiated into it by the *sem*-priest;
I have not told it to other people, nor have I repeated it to the gods, and *vice versa.*
I have entered as an ignorant one, and then I saw secrets.
Hail to you, the gods of Hermopolis.
Being great on the second day of the lunar month and being reduced on the fifteenth day.
It is Thoth, it is Sia, it is Atum.[1035]

In this version the *bas* that the spell will describe are identified as the ones of Heliopolis. What moves in front of the shoulder is not specified, but perhaps the subject of this statement was simply omitted through error. The statement about being great on the second day of the lunar month and being reduced on the fifteenth day is repeated here, and the listing of the *bas* in the final sentence now only includes three divine names.

Spell 157: chapter 112 of the Book of Going Forth by Day

pNebseni

The vignette shows the squatting figures of Horus (falcon-headed), Imseti, and Hapi (both human-headed).

r n rḫ bꜣ.w Pj jn N
ḏd⸗f ẖꜣ.tjw jm.jw ẖꜣ.tjw ꜥnp.tjw Ḥꜣ.t-mḥj.tjw sḫt.y jm.jw Pj šw.tjw jḫm.w jw pꜣs.wt ḥnq.t qn.tj t.w
jn-jw⸗tn rḫ⸗tn rdj Pj n Ḥr.w ḥr⸗s
jw⸗j rḫ.kw st n rḫ⸗tn st
jn Rꜥ rdj n⸗f sw m jsw jꜣṯ m jr.t⸗f m nw
ḏd.n Rꜥ n Ḥr.w dj⸗k mꜣꜣ⸗j nn ḫpr m jr.tj⸗k mjn
mꜣꜣ.n⸗f ḏd.jn Rꜥ n Ḥr.w dgꜣ mj r pfj rrj km
wn.jn⸗f ḥr dgꜣ ꜥḥꜥ.n <n>ky jr.t⸗f nšnj wr
ḏd.jn Ḥr.w n Rꜥ mk jr.t⸗j mj sqr pf jrj.n Stš r jr.t⸗j
ꜥḥꜥ.n ꜥm.n⸗f jb⸗f
ḏd.jn Rꜥ n nṯr.w dy.w sw ḥnk.yt⸗f jḫ snb⸗f
Stš pw jrj.n⸗f ḫpr.w r⸗f m rrj km
ꜥḥꜥ.n pfs.n⸗f sqr jm.j jr.t⸗f
ḏd.jn Rꜥ n nṯr.w bw šꜣj n Ḥr.w jḫ snb⸗f ḫpr bw pw šꜣj n Ḥr.w jn psḏ.t jm.jw-ḫt⸗f
wnn Ḥr.w ẖrdw⸗f ḫpr ḫry⸗f m jḥ.w⸗f m šꜣj.w⸗f
jw bw jm.jw ḫt⸗f
Jms.tj Ḥpj Dwꜣ-mw.t⸗f Qbḥ-sn.w⸗f jt⸗sn <Ḥr.w> mw.t⸗sn ꜣs.t

[1035] Lepsius 1842: pl. xliv.

ḏd.jn Ḥr.w n Rꜥ dj=k jr=f n=j 2 m Pj 2 m Nḫn m ẖ.t tn ḥnꜥ wnn m-ꜥ=j m sjp nḥḥ wꜣḏ tꜣ ꜥḫm ẖnn.w
ḫpr rn=f pw Ḥr.w-ḥr-wꜣḏ=f
jw=j rḫ.kw bꜣ.w Pj Ḥr.w pw Jms.tj pw Ḥpj pw
fꜣj ḥr.w=ṯn nṯr.w jm.jw dwꜣ.t
jj.n=j ḫr=ṯn mꜣꜣ=ṯn sw ḫpr m nṯr ꜥꜣ

Spell for knowing the *bas* of Pe by *N*.
He says: Oh, swamp-dwellers in swamp-dwellers, Mendesians, those of the fish nome, bird-catchers in Pe, the ones in the shade who do not know coming (back), brewers of beer kneading dough!
Do you know why Pe was given to Horus?
I know it, but you do not know it.
It was given to him by Re in compensation for the injury to his eye as this.
Re said to Horus: 'Let me see what happened to your eye today!'.
As he looked, Re said to Horus: 'Look at this black pig!'
Then he looked at it, and the injury in his eye was very painful.
Then Horus said to Re: 'Look, my eye is like the injury that Seth has inflicted on my eye'. Then he collapsed.
Re said to the gods: 'Put him on his bedchamber until he recovers'.
It was Seth who took the form of a black big.
Then he burned the injury in his eye.
Then Re said to the gods: 'The pig is abominable for Horus until he recovers'.
And that is how the abomination of the pig for Horus came into being by the gods in his retinue.
For when Horus was a child, his sacrificial animals were his cattle and his pigs.
Now it is an abomination (for) his retinue.
Imseti, Hapi, Duamutef, Qebehsenuf, their father (is Horus), their mother is Isis.
Then Horus said to Re: 'Give two in Pe, two in Nekhen as my company, so that they are with me as the counters of eternity, the rejuvenators of man, and quellers of disturbance'. And this is how his name Horus-on-his-papyrus-column came being.
I know the *bas* of Pe. It is Horus, it is Imseti, it is Hapi.
Lift your faces, gods in the netherworld, for *N*.
I have come to you, so that you may see he has become a great god.[1036]

While the group of beings addressed at the beginning of the text have also changed to some extent, the biggest modification in chapter 112 of the Book of Going Forth by Day is undoubtedly the fact that the entire episode about the oryx has been left out. Consequently, the veiled reference to a lunar eclipse disappeared. The encounter between Horus and Seth in his form of a pig is described along the same lines as previously, the only innovative element perhaps being the statement that the sacrificial animals of Horus in his childhood included not only pigs, but also some

[1036] Lapp 2004: pls. 19–20.

cattle. The expression 'the one who makes the earth verdant' has been replaced by 'rejuvenator of man' (literally, 'the one who makes man verdant'), but I cannot fathom the exact rationale behind this alteration. At the end of the spell a new line appears exhorting the gods of the netherworld to lift their faces and recognise the deceased as a being who has become a great god, that is, someone who has attained a successful netherworldly existence.

pIufankh

The vignette shows the deceased adoring Horus (falcon-headed), Imseti (human-headed), and Hapi (ape-headed).

k<y> r n rḫ bꜣ.w Pj
ḏd-mdw jn N ẖꜣ.tj jm.j Ḥꜣ.t-mḥj.t ꜥnp sḫt.y jrf m Pj sms.w jw.ḫm.w jw pꜣs.wt qrḥ.w qn.tj dq jn-jw=tn rḫ=tn rdj.yt Pj n Ḥr.w ḥr=s
jw=j rḫ.kw <sj>
jn Rꜥ rdj n=f sw m jsw <j>ꜣṯ m jr.t=f m nw
ḏd Rꜥ n Ḥr.w dj=k mꜣꜣ=j nn ḫpr m jr.tj=k mj
mꜣꜣ=f ḏd.jn Rꜥ n Ḥr.w dgꜣ mj r pfj rrj km
wnn=f ḥr dgꜣ=f ꜥḥꜥ<.n n>ky n jr.t=f nšnj wr
ḏd.jn Ḥr.w n Rꜥ mk jr.t=j mj sqr pw jr.t.n Jnp.w r jr.t=j
ꜥḥꜥ.n ꜥm.n=f jb=f
ḏd.jn Rꜥ n nn n nṯr.w bw.t šꜣj n Ḥr.w jḫ snb=f
ḫpr bw.t šꜣj ꜥꜣ
ḏd.jn Ḥr.w n nn n nṯr.w ntj m-ḫt=f m-ḫt wn Ḥr.w m nḫn=f ḫpr ḫr.y m nṯr.w m jḥ.w=f m ꜥw.wt=f m šꜣ.w=f
jr Jms.tj Ḥpj Dwꜣ-mw.t=f Qbḥ-sn.w=f jtj=sn pw Ḥr.w mw.t=sn pw ꜣs.t
ḏd.jn Ḥr.w n Rꜥ dj=k n=j snj m Pj snj m Nḫn m ẖ.t=j ḥnꜥ wn ḥnꜥ=j m sjp-nḥḥ wꜣḏ s ꜥḫm ḫnnj ḫpr rn=f n Ḥr.w-ḥr-wꜣḏ=f
jw=j rḫ.kw bꜣ.w Pj Ḥr.w pw Jms.tj Ḥpj pw
fꜣj ḥr.w=tn nṯr.w jm.jw dwꜣ.t n N pn m sw ḫpr m nṯr ꜥꜣ

Another spell for knowing the *bas* of Pe.
To be recited by N. Oh, swamp-dweller of the fish nome, Mendesian, bird-catcher in Pe, old ones who do not know coming (back), brewers of pots (of beer) kneading dough! Do you know why Pe was given to Horus?
I know it.
It was given to him by Re in compensation for the injury to his eye as this.
Re said to Horus: 'Let me see what happened to your eye'.
As he looked, Re said to Horus: 'Look at this black pig!'
Then he looked at it, and the injury in his eye was very painful.
Then Horus said to Re: 'Look, my eye is like the injury that Anubis has inflicted on my eye'. Then he collapsed.

Re said to the gods: 'The pig is abominable for Horus until he recovers'.
And that is how the great abomination of the pig came into being.
Then Horus said to the gods in his retinue: 'When Horus was a child, his sacrificial animals were his cattle, his flocks, and his pigs'.
As for Imseti, Hapi, Duamutef, Qebehsenuf, their father is Horus, their mother is Isis.
Then Horus said to Re: 'Give two in Pe, two in Nekhen as my company, so that they are with me as the counters of eternity, the rejuvenators of man, and quellers of disturbance'. And this is how his name Horus-on-his-papyrus-column came into being.
I know the *bas* of Pe. It is Horus, It is Imseti and Hapi.
Lift your faces, gods in the netherworld, for *N*. Look, he has become a great god.[1037]

The Ptolemaic version of the spell follows pretty closely its New Kingdom antecedent, with one remarkable exception. The injury to the eye of Horus is said to have been inflicted not by Seth but by Anubis. This attribution is quite unusual and possibly resulted from a misreading of Seth's name starting with the sign of the typical Upper Egyptian plant (𓇓) as the name of Anubis, the first sign of which is the flowering reed (𓇋); the cursive hieroglyphic or hieratic forms of the two signs – as stated earlier – can easily be confused.[1038]

Spell 158: chapter 113 of the Book of Going Forth by Day

pNebseni

The vignette shows the squatting figures of Horus (falcon-headed), Duamutef, and Qebehsenuf (both human-headed).

r n rḫ bꜣ.w Nḫn jn N
ḏd⸗f jw⸗j rḫ.kw sštꜣ.w Nḫn
Ḥr.w pw nw pw jrj.n mw.t⸗f qmꜣ.tjw ḥr mw m ḏd⸗s
jw ḏd⸗tn n⸗j r wḏꜥ.tj r⸗j wꜣ.t m-ḫt tn gmgm.<tjw>nj
ḏd.jn Rꜥ ḥḏ.(j)w sꜣ pn ꜣs.t ḥr nw jrj.n mw.t⸗f r⸗f ḏs⸗s
ḥwj jnj.tw⸗f n⸗n Sbk nb pḥ.wj ḥꜣm⸗f st gm.n⸗f st rd.n st mw.t⸗f ꜣs.t
ḏd.jn Sbk nb pḥ.wj jw ḏꜥr.n⸗j gm.n⸗j btktk⸗sn ḫr ḏbꜥ.w⸗j ḥr sp.tj mw ḥꜣd.n⸗j st m ḥꜣd
ḫpr ḥꜣd pw
ḏd.jn Rꜥ jw tr rm.w m-dj n Sbk ḥnꜥ gm.t⸗f ꜥ.wj n Ḥr.w n⸗f
ḫpr Tr-rm.w pw
ḏd.jn Rꜥ sštꜣ.w sp sn ḥr ḥꜣd jnj.n ḏr.tj Ḥr.w n⸗f wn rdj.tw ḥr ḥr⸗f<j> m ꜣbd smd.t ḥꜣm.tj rm.w ꜥḥꜥ.n
ḏd.n Rꜥ rdj⸗j Nḫn n Ḥr.w r s.t ꜥ.wj⸗fj ḥr ḥr⸗f ḏr.tj⸗f m Nḫn pn rdj.n⸗j n⸗f ḫnr jm.jw⸗sn m ꜣbd smd.t
ḏd.jn Ḥr,w nḥm.n dj Dwꜣ-mw.t⸗f Qbḥ-sn.w⸗f ḥnꜥ sꜣ.y dj⸗j st ḫ.t⸗j pw jtn.t wn rdj⸗sn ḫr nṯr Nḫn
ḏd.jn Rꜥ jmj jr⸗k st jm m snk.t jrj⸗sn jr.t n jm.jw Nḫn kꜣ ḫꜣꜣ⸗sn r wnn ḥnꜥ⸗k

[1037] Lepsius 1842: pl. xliii.
[1038] cf. Möller 1909: 27 (nos. 282 and 289).

ḏd.jn Ḥr.w jw=sn ḥnʿ=k wn ḥnʿ=j r sḏm=j Stš nẖj
bꜣ.w Nẖn dj=j n=j jw=j bsj.kw ḥr bꜣ.w Nẖn wn dj=w n=j ṯs Ḥr.w
jw=j rẖ.kw bꜣ.w Nẖn Ḥr.w pw Dwꜣ-mw.t=f pw Qbḥ-sn.w=f pw

Spell for knowing the *bas* of Nekhen by *N*.
He says: I know the secrets of Nekhen.
It is Horus and these which his mother has done and were thrown into water, she saying, 'You are named to me as the severed body parts that are away from me after they have been torn'.
Then Re said: 'The son of Isis has been injured on account of this which his mother herself has done to him.
I wish Sobek, lord of the edge of the waters, were brought to us, so that he could fish them out and find them, and his mother, Isis, could grow them'.
Then Sobek, lord of the edge of the waters, said: 'I groped for them, I found them, but they slipped from my fingers onto the shores of the water. Finally, I caught them with a cover basket'.
And that is how the cover basket came into being.
Then Re said: 'Does Sobek have fish with what he has found for himself, the hands of Horus?'
And that is how the town of Ter-remu came into being.
Then Re said: 'Mysterious are the secrets of the cover basket that bring the hands of Horus to him, which are made to be seen on the second and fifteenth days of the lunar month when fish is caught'.
Then Re said: 'I gave Nekhen to Horus as the place of his hands, so that he could see his hands in Nekhen that I gave him, what is restrained in them on the second and fifteenth days of the lunar month'.
Then Horus said: 'Surely, place Duamutef and Qebehsenuf with the guardian that I provide, for they are my opposing company, they being put in the possession of the god of Nekhen'. Then Re said: 'Put them there in darkness, so that they do what is the doing of those in Nekhen. Then they will decide to be with you'.
Then Horus said: 'They are with you (as well as) they are with me until I hear Seth complaining'.
Oh, the *bas* of Nekhen, I have given to me; I have been initiated into the *bas* of Nekhen who make the knot of Horus open for me.
I know the *bas* of Nekhen. It is Horus, it is Duamutef, it is Qebehsenuf.[1039]

The first part of the spell generally follows the pattern of its predecessor, although initially the texts fails to name the hands of Horus as the secrets of Nekhen. Another notable difference is that the body parts of Horus being severed by his mother, Isis, are identified as torn (*gmgm*), rather than being found (*gm*). The similarity of the two words is surely responsible for this change, and because in fact the meaning of the

[1039] Lapp 2004: pls. 20–21.

first verb seems to suit the context better, we may wonder whether this New Kingdom emendation is a return to an unattested Middle Kingdom original which also featured the verb *gmgm*. While Sobek is urged to find and fish out the hands of Horus, according to the text now Isis is responsible for growing them back – in spell 158 of the Coffin Texts this action was also attributed to Sobek. From the second part the mention of He-who-is-in-the-broad-hall disappears and is replaced with a reference to 'those in Nekhen' (*jm.jw Nẖn*). Furthermore, a sentence is added stating that the initiation into the *bas* of Nekhen is connected with opening the knot of Horus. This claim possibly stems from the idea that the knot is a magical device often employed in healing practices, as when Isis ties seven strings of knots around the neck of the child Horus to dispel his headache.[1040]

pIufankh

The vignette shows the deceased adoring Horus (falcon-headed), Duamutef (jackal-headed), and Qebehsenuf (falcon-headed).

rẖ bꜣ.w Nẖn
ḏd-mdw jn N jw=j rẖ.kw sštꜣ.w n Nẖn
Ḥr.w pw nw jrj.n mw.t=f r=f ḏd=s ḥwj jnj.tw n=n Sbk nb pḥ.wj ḥꜣm=f s<j> gm.n=f s<j> rd.n mw.t=f r s.t jr=w
ḏd.jn Sbk nb pḥ.wj jw ḏʿr.n=j gm.n=j btktk=sn ẖr ḏbʿ.w=j ḥr sp.tj mw ḥꜣd.n=j s<j> m ḥꜣd pḥ.tj ẖpr ḥꜣd pw
ḏd.jn Rʿ jw tr rm.w m-dj n Sbk ḥnʿ gm ʿ.wj=f Ḥr.w n=f m Tꜣ-rm.w pw
ḏd.jn Rʿ n štꜣ sp sn ḥꜣd pn jnj.n ḏr.tj n Ḥr.w n=f wn.tw ḥr ḥr=f m ꜣbd smd.t m Tꜣ-rm.w ʿḥʿ.n ḏd.jn Rʿ rdj.n=j Nẖn n Ḥr.w r s.t ʿ.wj=f wn.tw ḥr ḏr.tj=f m Nẖn ẖrp.tw n=f ẖnj.w jm=sn m ꜣbd smd.t
ḏd.jn Ḥr,w dj n=j ḥm Dwꜣ-mw.t=f Qbḥ-sn.w=f ḥnʿ=j sꜣw=sn ẖ.t=j pw jr m wnn jm ẖr js nṯr Nẖn
ḏd.jn Rʿ jmj jr=k sj m-m snk.t jrj.tw n=sn jr.yw n jm.jw Nẖn kꜣ ẖꜣꜣ=sn ḥnʿ=k
ḏd.jn Ḥr.w jw=sn ḥnʿ=k wnn=sn ḥnʿ=j r sḏm=j Stš nẖj
bꜣ.w Nẖn dj n=j
jw=j rẖ.kw bꜣ.w Nẖn Ḥr.w pw Dwꜣ-mw.t=f Qbḥ-sn.w=f pw

Spell for knowing the *bas* of Nekhen.
To be recited by *N*. I know the secrets of Nekhen.
It is Horus and this which his mother has done against him, she saying, 'I wish Sobek, lord of the edge of the waters, were brought to us, so that he could fish them out and find them, and his mother could grow them to their proper place'.
Then Sobek, lord of the edge of the waters, said: 'I groped for them, I found them, but they slipped from my fingers onto the shores of the water. Finally, I caught them with a strong cover basket'.
And that is how the cover basket came into being.

[1040] Wendrich 2006: 250–251.

Then Re said: 'Does Sobek have fish with finding for himself the hands of Horus in Ta-remu?'
Then Re said: 'There is no mystery about the secret of the cover basket that bring the hands of Horus to him, which are seen on the second and fifteenth days of the lunar month in Ta-remu'.
Then Re said: 'I gave Nekhen to Horus as the place of his hands, and his hands are revealed in Nekhen. What is in them are provided as prisoners for him on the second and fifteenth days of the lunar month'.
Then Horus said: 'Surely, place Duamutef and Qebehsenuf with me so that they could guard my body, being under the god of Nekhen'.
Then Re said: 'Put them there in darkness, so that what is the doing of those in Nekhen is done to them. Then they will decide to be with you'.
Then Horus said: 'They are with you (as well as) they are with me until I hear Seth complaining'.
Oh, the *bas* of Nekhen, give to me!
I know the *bas* of Nekhen. It is Horus, it is Duamutef and Qebehsenuf.[1041]

The beginning of the spell is more laconic than in the New Kingdom version, only mentioning the wrongdoing of Isis once. The cover basket with which Sobek finally catches the hand of Horus is said to be strong, and this is a detail that is lacking from earlier versions. In disagreement with earlier texts, Re now announces that there is no mystery about the secrets of this cover basket. Whether making this statement negative is a result of the deterioration of the text or a deliberate change is hard to judge. The reference to the knot of Horus is missing from this version of the text.

Spell 159: chapters 107, 109, and 149 of the Book of Going Forth by Day

Spell 159 of the Coffin Texts was the source for three chapters of the Book of Going Forth by Day, and among these chapter 109 is the most important one, because it was part of the sequence that was the direct descendant of the Book of the Moon (115–116–112–113–108–109). Chapter 107 is an abridged version containing only the description of the eastern gate, not attested before the 19th dynasty. As for its Ptolemaic version in pIufankh, the only thing that should be noted is perhaps the curious reference to the western gate, instead of the eastern one; the body of the text, however refers to this latter one.[1042] In chapter 149 the information on the Field of Reeds serves as the description of the second mound of Osiris, and contains no additional or innovative elements in comparison with chapter 109.[1043]

[1041] Lepsius 1842: pl. xliii.
[1042] Lepsius 1842: pl. xixxx.
[1043] Lepsius 1842: pl. lxxi; Lapp 2004: pl. 79.

Chapter 109 (pNebseni)

The vignette shows the deceased adoring the squatting figure of Re-Harakhty; the depiction of the spotted solar calf is placed between them.

r n rḫ bꜣ.w jꜣb.tjw jn N
ḏd⸗f jw⸗j rḫ.kw sbꜣ pf jꜣb.tj pn p.t ntj rs.j⸗f m š ḫꜣr.w
mḥ.tj⸗f m nw.yt r.w m bw sqdd Rꜥ jm m ṯꜣ.w m ḫn.t
jnk jr.j-smj.w m dp.t nṯr jnk ḫnn n wrḏ.n⸗f m wjꜣ Rꜥ
jw⸗j rḫ.kw nh.tj twy n.t mfkꜣ.t prr.t Rꜥ jm.wtj⸗snj šm.yw <ḥr sṯs Šw> r sbꜣ nb prr.t Rꜥ jm
jw⸗j rḫ.kw sḫ.t-jꜣr.w jw jnb⸗s m bjꜣ jw bd.t⸗s m mḥ 5 jw šms.w⸗s m mḥ 2 jw mꜣw.yt⸗f m mḥ 3 jw bd.t⸗s m mḥ 3 jw šms.w⸗s m mḥ 3 jw mꜣw.yt⸗f m mḥ 3
jn ꜣḫ.w n mḥ 9 m ꜣw n wꜥ-nb jm ꜣsḫ st r-gs bꜣ.w jꜣb.tjw
jw⸗j rḫ.kw <bꜣ.w jꜣb.tjw> Rꜥ-Ḥr.w-ꜣḫ.tj pw bḥs ḫwrr.tj pw dwꜣ nṯr Rꜥ rꜥ-nb
jw qd.n N njw.t nṯr jw⸗j rḫ.kw sj rḫ.kw rn⸗s sḫ.t-jꜣr.w rn⸗s

Spell for knowing the *bas* of the easterners by *N*.
He says: I know the eastern gate of the sky whose south is in the lake of the *ḫꜣr*-geese, and its north in the waters of the *r*-geese, which is the place where Re navigates by sailing and rowing.
I am the one in charge of the rigging in the ship of the god, I am the one who rows and does not tire in Re's barque.
I know these two sycamore trees of turquoise between which Re emerges, and which move (on account of Shu's lifting up) to every eastern gate from which Re emerges.
I know this Field of Reeds whose surrounding wall is of iron, and its emmer is five cubits, its ear being two cubits, its stalk being three cubits, (and then) its emmer is three cubits, its ear being three cubits, its stalk being three cubits.
The effective spirits, each of whom is nine cubits tall, reap it alongside the *bas* of the easterners.
I know (the *bas* of the easterners). It is Re-Harakhty, it is the solar calf; adoring Re every day.
N has built the town of the god. I know it, and I know its name. The Field of Reeds is its name.[1044]

Instead of the gate in the middle from which Re emerges in the east, the text simply speaks of the eastern gate. The watery boundaries of the gate are associated with different birds from those in spell 159 of the Coffin Texts, the south here connected with the *ḫꜣr*-geese, and the north with the *r*-geese. However, we should remember that the latter kind of waterfowl already appears in spell 752 of the Coffin Texts in connection with the eastern gate of the sky,[1045] and possibly – if there was no lacuna in the texts – the *ḫꜣr*-geese would have also been mentioned. The dimensions of the emmer are slightly

[1044] Lapp 2004: pl. 22.
[1045] See my comments on spell 159.

different, too. At its second mention the copyist must have made a mistake, because presumably instead of three cubits, the overall height of the emmer should have read six cubits. The horizon-dwellers are replaced by the effective spirits as the main group of reapers of the ethereal emmer, and this change surely stems from the similarity of the two expressions (*ꜣḫ.tjw* versus *ꜣḫ.w*). The ending of the spell differs greatly from its predecessor, but in all probability also results from the poor understanding of the original text. The third *ba* of the easterners in the Middle Kingdom spell is defined as the Morning God (*nṯr-dwꜣ*), and the same sequence of signs could be taken to mean 'to adore (the god)'. So one ancient copyist made this mistake, and inserted the name of Re as the suitable object of the phrase expressing adoration. In addition, he possibly copied the first few lines of a hymn to Re, and that is how the final sentences of the spell, with references to building the town of god and the Field of Reeds, were formed.

pIufankh

The vignette shows the deceased adoring the solar barque as it sails towards two sycamore trees. The solar calf, Re, and a human steersman are on board the barque.

r n rḫ bꜣ.w jꜣb.tjw
ḏd-mdw jn N jw=j rḫ.kw sbꜣ pfj jꜣb.tj n.t p.t ntj rs.j=f m š ḫꜣr.w
mḥ.tj=f m nw r.w m bw sqd.t Rꜥ jm m ṯꜣ.w n ẖnn.w
jnk jr.j-smj.w m dp.t nṯr jnk ẖnn nn wrḏ.n=f m wj<ꜣ> Rꜥ
jw=j rḫ.kw nh.t<j> twy n.t mfk<ꜣ.t> prj Rꜥ jm.tw=s šm ḥr sṯs Šw
jw=j rḫ.kw sbꜣ nb prj Rꜥ jm=f
jw=j rḫ.kw sḫ.t-jꜣr.w twy ntj jnb=s m bjꜣ jw qꜥ n bd.t=s m mḥ 7 jw wšm.w=s m mḥ 3 jw mꜣw.y=f m mḥ 4
jn ꜣḫ.w n mḥ 8 m ꜣw wꜥ-nb jm ꜣsḫ sn r-gs bꜣ.w jꜣb.tjw
jw=j rḫ.kw bꜣ.w jꜣb.tjw Rꜥ-Ḥr.w-ꜣẖ.tj pw bḥs.w ḫr nṯr pn dwꜣ nṯr-dwꜣ pw
jw qdj.n N wḏꜣ r=k ḥnꜥ=j jn mḥ.y tḫ pw n.t ḥnk mtw.t kꜣ r jm.j šs ns.t=k pꜣ bꜣ ḫnt wnn.w=f mḫꜣ
sḫr.w=k m ḥw.t jbt.j r jbt.jw ḥr šfd.w
qbḥ r=s ḥr ḏꜣjs mrw.t=k ḥr-nb
bjk nṯr ḥr jr.t jꜣb<.t> km ḥr qꜥḥ=f mj.tt prj r p.t mj ḫꜣbs.w
ẖr qrs.t pw sqdd ḥr mtnw nn tḥꜣ tš.w šd.ywt n.t nṯr.w
sẖꜣ.w ḥnꜥ=k r dd ꜣw ꜣh.wt ḫndš šꜣꜥ.tw nfr.y jm m rḏw nw ꜣw<-ḥnb>
qꜥ n.t bd.t=s m mḥ 5 wšm.w=s m mḥ 2
jsḫ.n=k js ḥnꜥ ꜣḫ.w r-gs bꜣ.w jꜣb.tjw
ꜥq.tw m wstn.w r sbḫ.wt štꜣ.w wꜥb=k jn jm.jw=sn
spr.w pr=k m-ꜥ kꜣ.w ḥr snḏm jb n.t ṯꜣ.wj
bw.t=k pw mt m-wḥm
ḏ.t n=k m ꜥḥꜥ.w mtn.w rdj m fqꜣ.w sꜥꜣ fꜣw n N

Spell for knowing the *bas* of the easterners.
To be recited by N. I know the eastern gate of the sky whose south is in the lake of the *ḫꜣr*-geese,

and its north in the waters of the *r*-geese, which is the place where Re navigates by the wind of disturbance.
I am the one in charge of the rigging in the ship of the god, I am the one who rows and does not tire in Re's barque.
I know these two sycamore trees of turquoise between which Re emerges, and which move on account of Shu's lifting up.
I know every gate from which Re emerges.
I know this Field of Reeds whose surrounding wall is of iron, and the height of its emmer is seven cubits, its awn being three cubits, its stalk being four cubits.
The effective spirits, each of whom is eight cubits tall, reap it alongside the *bas* of the easterners.
I know the *bas* of the easterners. It is Re-Harakhty, it is the calf near the god, it is the Morning God.
N has been building. Be in procession with me by He-who-fills (= Thoth), the plummet of the balance, the semen of the bull for what is in the linen, your tongue, the balance of your plans in the mansion of the net for the fowlers on papyrus.
A libation for the sake of spelling out your love of everyone.
The divine falcon on the blacked-out left eye on its similar shoulder emerges to the sky like the starry firmament.
The one with a funeral goes on the way, for there is no going astray of the limits of the field of the gods.
The writings are with you to place the offerings of the fields and lots, you start (cultivating) grain there from the efflux of He-with-wide-fields.
The height of its emmer is five cubits, its awn being two cubits.
You have reaped with the effective spirits alongside the *bas* of the easterners.
As you enter the secret portals unhindered, you are purified in them.
You reach your house with the *kas* while you make the two fledglings rejoice.
Your abomination is to die again.
Eternity belongs to you as (your) lifetime, reward is given as a gift to expand the magnificence of *N*.[1046]

By Ptolemaic times, the reference to the act of rowing (*ẖn.t*) deteriorated into the expression 'disturbance' (*ẖnn.w*). The description of the emmer is simplified, and instead of its ear (*šms*), its awn (*wšm*) is mentioned. The effective spirits are only eight cubits tall. The second *ba*, the solar calf, is reinterpreted as a a calf around an unspecified god, who should surely be understood as Re. While the third *ba* is again the Morning God, a substantial text is added at the end of the spell that makes references to Thoth, the blacked-out left eye which must be the invisible moon, and again the netherworldly fields.

[1046] Lepsius 1842: pls. xxxix–xl.

Spell 160: chapters 108 and 111 of the Book of Going Forth by Day

Chapter 108 (pNebseni)

The vignette shows the squatting figures of Atum (human-headed), Sobek (crocodile-headed), and Hathor (human-headed).

r n rḫ bꜣ.w jmn.tjw jn N
ḏd⸗f jr ḏw pf Bꜣẖ.w ntj p.t t<n> rhn.tj ḥr⸗f wn jnb jw mḥ n šsp 7 gs n mḫꜣ.t n.t tꜣ m ꜣw⸗f mḥ 300 m wsḫ 200
jw Sbk nb Bꜣẖ.w m jꜣb.tj ḏw pf jw ḥw.t-nṯr⸗f m ẖ.t
jw ḥfꜣw ḥr wp.t ḏw pf mḥ 50 m ꜣw⸗f mḥ 3 m ds m ḥꜣ.t⸗f
jw⸗j rḫ.kw rn n ḥfꜣ.w pn tp ḏw⸗f Jm.j-hh⸗f rn⸗f
jr m-ḫt ꜥḥꜥ.y pnꜥ.ḫr⸗f jr.t⸗f r Rꜥ ḫpr.ḫr ꜥḥꜥ.w m wjꜣ sg.wt ꜥꜣ.t m-ẖnw sqd.wt
sẖb.ḫr⸗f mḥ <7> m mw ꜥꜣ.w
rdj.ḫr Stš wꜥr mtꜣ.yt r⸗f n.t bjꜣ rdj.ḫr⸗f bšj⸗f sẖb.n⸗f nb.t
rdj.ḫr sw Stš m-ḏr.j⸗f ḏd.ḫr⸗f m ḥkꜣ.w ḥmj jr⸗k bjꜣ spd jm.j ꜥ⸗j ꜥḥꜥ⸗j m-ḏr.j⸗k mꜣꜥ sqd.wt wjꜣ mꜣꜣ wꜣ.w ꜥẖn
rdj.n⸗j jr.t⸗k ḥbs tp⸗k ḏꜣ.t ḥmj.n⸗j jnk ṯꜣ.y ḥbs dj ḥr⸗k qbḥ.w šsp⸗k
wḏꜣ⸗j wḏꜣ⸗k(wj) jnk wr-ḥkꜣ.w
jw rdj.n⸗j r jšst pwy ꜣḫ
šm ḥr ẖ.t⸗f pḥ<.tj>⸗f <n> ṯs.w⸗f
mk šm⸗j jr⸗f pḥ.tj⸗kj m-ꜥ⸗j jnk wṯs pḥ.tj
jj.n⸗j ꜥwꜣ⸗j ꜣkr.yw n Rꜥ
ḥtp⸗f n⸗j m mšr.w dbn⸗f p.t tn
jw⸗k m jnt.t wḏḏ.t pw r⸗k m-bꜣḥ
ḥtp.ḫr⸗f Rꜥ m ꜥnḫ r ꜣḫ.t⸗f
jw⸗j rḫ.kw sšm n rḫ.w ḫsf.t n ꜥꜣpp ḥr⸗s
jw⸗j rḫ.kw bꜣ.w jmn.tjw Tm pw Sbk pw nb Bꜣẖ.w Ḥw.t-Ḥr.w <pw> nb.t mšr,w

Spell for knowing the *bas* of the westerners by *N*.
He says: As for the mountain of Bakhu on which the sky leans, whose wall is 30 cubits at the balance of the land (= in the middle of the land); its length is 300 cubits, and the width is 200.
Sobek, lord of Bakhu, is on the eastern side of the mountain, his temple being made of carnelian.
There is a snake on the top of the mountain, its length is 50 cubits, and three cubits of its forepart are of flint.
I know the name of the serpent dwelling on the mountain: He-who-is-in-his-flame is its name.
As for after midday, it turns its eye against Re, and there occurs a stoppage in the barque, and a great astonishment within the journey.
Then it swallows seven cubits of the great water.

Seth will then brandish (his) forked iron staff against it, causing it to spit out all that it has swallowed.
Then Seth puts himself against it, and says his magic words: 'Turn back, (my) sharp iron is in my hand, I stand against you, making the journey right and seeing far.
I will make your eyes shut and your head covered, having the journey turned back on its course. I am a male who makes your face covered and your lips cooled.
If I am hale, you are hale. I am great of magic'.
'What effective spirit am I put against?'
'Oh, you who move on your belly, your power (belongs to) your vertebrae.
Look, I go against you, your powers in my hand, for I am the one who shows strength.
I have come and gathered the land serpents for Re.
He sets for me in the evening, after he circles the sky.
You are in your fetters, that is what has been commanded against you beforehand.
Re will set as a living one in his horizon'.
I know the guidance of the knowledge for repelling Apep.
I know the *bas* of the westerners. It is Atum, it is Sobek, lord of Bakhu, it is Hathor, Lady of the Evening.[1047]

As a new piece of information that was absent from spell 160 of the Coffin Texts, we learn that – presumably – the height of the wall surrounding the mountain of Bakhu is 30 cubits. This dimension is given cryptically as the expression *mḥ n šsp 7 gs* 'cubit of seven and half palms', where the palm stands for the number four, since it consists of four fingers. Consequently, seven and a half times four equals 30 cubits. The overall dimensions of the mountain of Bakhu, specified in cubits and not rods, and the dimensions of the snake on top of it are different from those cited in the corresponding Coffin Texts spell. The name of the serpent is also slightly different, as it is now called He-who-is-in-his-flame (*Jm.j-hh=f*). Instead of the conditional reference to the evening, the stoppage of the solar barque takes place after midday, which is in harmony with the general message of the spell about a solar eclipse. As an addition, the lunar snake is now said to swallow the water that makes the celestial voyage of the solar barque possible. Seth then makes the snake regurgitate this water. In the question asked by the snake Seth is referred to as an effective spirit, rather than the more general expression 'might'. At the end of the spell the knowledge about repelling Apep is expressly mentioned, so in the New Kingdom the attack of the lunar snake on the sun at the time of an eclipse was surely equated with the actions of Apep, the primordial enemy of the sun god. The Lady of the Evening as the third *ba* of the westerners is named as Hathor.

pIufankh

The vignette shows the deceased adoring Atum, Sobek, and Hathor.

[1047] Lapp 2004: pl. 21.

r n rḫ bꜣ.w jmn.tjw
ḏd-mdw jn N jr ḏw pwy n Bꜣẖ.w n.t p.t tn rhꜣ.tw ḥr⸗f wnn⸗f m jꜣb.t n.t p.t
nsw ẖt 370 m ꜣw⸗f mḥ 140 m wsḫ⸗f
jw Sbk nb Bꜣẖ.w m jꜣb.tj ḏw pfj jw ḥw.t⸗f m ḥr(d)s<.t>
jw ḥfꜣw ḥr wp.t ḏw pfj nsw mḥ 30 m ꜣw⸗f mḥ 10 m wsḫ⸗f jw mḥ 3 ḥꜣ.t⸗f m ds m
jw⸗j rḫ.kw rn n ḥfꜣ.w pn ḥr ḏw⸗f Jm.j-hh⸗f rn⸗f
jr m-ḫt ꜥḥꜥ.y n hrw pnꜥ.ḫr⸗f jr.tj⸗f r Rꜥ ḫpr.ḫr ꜥḥꜥ.w m wj<ꜣ> sdgꜣ ꜥꜣ m-ẖnw sqd.wt
sḫ(t)p.ḫr⸗f mḥ 7 m mw⸗s
rdj.ḫr Swtj m-ḏr⸗f rdj.ḫr⸗f mtꜣ.yt⸗f n.t bjꜣ⸗f ḥr nḥb.t⸗f rdj.ḫr⸗f bšj⸗f ꜥm.n⸗f nb
ḏd.ḫr⸗f m ḥkꜣ.w ḥmj jr⸗k bjꜣ spd jm.j ꜥ⸗j m-ḏr⸗k mꜣꜥ sqd.wt m wj<ꜣ>
wꜣj ꜥḫn jr.tj⸗k ḥbs tp⸗k ḏꜣj⸗f
ḥmj n N ntf ṯꜣ.y m ẖ.t n mw.t⸗f ḥbs tp⸗k qbḥ šsp⸗k
wḏꜣ⸗j wḏꜣ⸗k jnk wr-ḥkꜣ.w sꜣ Nw.t
jw rdj.n⸗j ꜣḫ.w pn r⸗k
jšst pwy
šm ḥr ẖ.t⸗f pḥ.tj⸗f n ṯs.w⸗f
mk N šm pḥ.tj⸗k m-ꜥ⸗f ntf wṯs pḥ.tj
jj.n⸗j ꜥwꜣ.n⸗j ꜣkr n Rꜥ
ḥtp⸗f n⸗f m mšr.w pḫr.n⸗f p.t
jw⸗k m jnt.w⸗k ky-ḏd r<wj> wḏḏ.t pw r⸗k m-bꜣḥ Rꜥ
ḥtp.ḫr⸗f Rꜥ m ꜥnḫ.t r ꜣḫ.t⸗f
jw⸗j rḫ.kw sšm n ẖ.t ḥsf n ꜥꜣpp ḥr⸗s
jw⸗j rḫ.kw bꜣ.w jmn.tjw Tm pw Sbk pw nb Bꜣẖ.w Ḥw.t-Ḥr.w <pw> ḥnw.t mšr,w ḏd<.tw> r ꜣs.t

Spell for knowing the *bas* of the westerners.
To be recited by N. As for the mountain of Bakhu on which the sky leans, it is in the east of the sky.
It is 370 rods in its length and 140 cubits in its width.
Sobek, lord of Bakhu, is on the eastern side of the mountain, his temple being made of carnelian.
There is a snake on the top of the mountain, it is 30 cubits in its length and ten cubits in its width, and three cubits of its forepart are of flint.
I know the name of the serpent dwelling on the mountain: He-who-is-in-his-flame is its name.
As for after midday, it turns its two eyes against Re, and there occurs a stoppage in the barque, and a great astonishment within the journey.
Then it swallows seven cubits of the water.
Seth will then oppose it and place his forked staff of his iron on its neck, causing it to spit out all that it has swallowed.
Then Seth says his magic: 'Turn back, (my) sharp iron is in my hand against you, making the journey right.

Distance yourself, shut your eyes and cover your head, so that he (Re) could ferry across. Turn back for *N*, for he is a male from the womb of his mother who makes your face covered and your lips cooled.
If I am hale, you are hale. I am great of magic, the son of Nut.
I have placed these powers against you'.
'What is it?'
'Oh, you who move on your belly, your power (belongs to) your sandbank.
Look, *N* goes with your powers in his hand, for he is the one who shows strength.
I have come and gathered the land serpent for Re.
He sets in the evening, after he has gone around the sky.
You are in your fetters – in other words, go away – that is what has been commanded against you before Re.
Re will set in the living west in his horizon'.
I know the guidance of the things for repelling Apep.
I know the *bas* of the westerners. It is Atum, it is Sobek, lord of Bakhu, it is Hathor, Mistress of the Evening, also said to be Isis.[1048]

The dimensions of the mountain of Bakhu are different from those cited either in the original Coffin Texts spell or the New Kingdom variant. There also seems to be some confusion regarding them because the length is described in rods, whereas the width is in cubits. For the snake not only is its length given, but also its width is specified as ten cubits. The snake turns both its eyes towards Re (i.e. the dual form of the word is used). The figure of Seth and that of the deceased is merged, so the latter himself plays an active role in repelling the hostile snake. The decree against the snake, condemning it to be in fetters, is augmented with a short gloss ('go away'). The third *ba*, Hathor, is called Mistress of the Evening (*ḥnw.t mšr,w*), instead of Lady in the Evening (*nb.t mšr,w*), and it is stated that in this capacity she is also known as Isis.

Chapter 111 (pIufankh)

r n rḫ bꜣw Pj
ḏd-mdw jn N jr ḏw pfj Bꜣẖ.w n.t p.t dhn.tw ḥr=f wnn Sbk nb Bꜣẖ.w m wp.t n.t ḏw pwj
jw ḥw.t-nṯr=f m-ḥr=f n tp dhn.n=f ḏw rn=f jw mḥ šsp [ky=s] 120 m ꜣw=f mḥ 30 ky=s 3 m wsḫ=f jw mḥ 4 m ḥꜣ.t=f m ds
jr m-ḫ.t ʿḥʿ.w n.t hrw pnʿ.ḫr=f jr.tj=f r Rʿ ḫpr ʿḥʿ.w pw
sgꜣgꜣ jm.jw-ẖn.w wj<ꜣ> rdj.ḫr Swtj m-ḏr.j=f ḏd=f mꜣʿ sqd.wt
ḏd.ḫr=f m ḥkꜣ.t mꜣꜣ wꜣj ʿḫn jr.tj=k ʿʿw n=j jnk ṯꜣ.y ḥbs tp=k
wḏꜣ=k wḏꜣ=j jnk wṯs pḥ.tj
jw rdj.n=j ꜣḫ pn r[n]=k
jj.n=j ʿwꜣ.n=j ꜣkr n Rʿ m mšr.w
hꜣ N ṯs.tw ḥr gs=k jꜣb ʿnḫ.tw mꜣwj.tw rnp.tw mj Rʿ rʿ-nb nn mt=k ḏ.t nḥḥ

[1048] Lepsius 1842: pl. xxxix.

Spell for knowing the *bas* of Pe.
To be recited by *N*. As for the mountain of Bakhu on which the sky leans, Sobek, lord of Bakhu, is on the top of the mountain,
and his temple is in his view to the head (of the snake), He-who-leans-on-the-mountain is his name, its length is 120 cubits, and its width is thirty or three cubits; four cubits of its forepart are made of flint.
As for after midday, it turns its two eyes against Re. That is how midday came into being. The ones in the barque become confused, and then Seth will oppose it, saying, 'The journey will be made right!'.
Then he will say as magic, seeing far: 'Shut your eyes, be fearful of me, for I am a male that covers your head.
If you are hale, I am hale. (I) show strength'.
'I am put against this effective spirit?'
'I have come and gathered the land serpent for Re in the evening'.
Oh, *N*, be raised from your left side, be alive, be renewed and rejuvenated like Re, never ever die!

The earliest copy of chapter 111 of the Book of Going Forth by Day dates from the 19th dynasty. Compared to Coffin Texts spell 160, a significant change occurs in the title, because it concerns the *bas* of Pe. Its text is also shortened, as for example the measurements of the mountain of Bakhu are not mentioned. The information that there is a snake on the mountain is somewhat veiled, and is only apparent from the serpent determinative of the name He-who-leans-on-the-mountain, the name itself being an innovation. The dimensions of the snake are partly cryptic (see my remarks above about chapter 108 in pNebseni). An aetiological statement about the origins of midday is inserted in the text, possibly on the influence of the other similar spells. A formula is appended to the end to ensure the existence of the deceased in the netherworld.

4. Conclusion

While there were sporadic references to the moon in the Pyramid Texts, especially in connection with monthly feasts and the figure of the celestial ferryman, Coffin Texts spells 154–160, that is the Book of the Moon, elevated the description of the moon to a whole new level. In fact, in the vast body of ancient Egyptian textual sources we can hardly find anything that is comparable with it, the only exception perhaps being the long inscriptions about the conjoined movements of the sun and the moon in the pronaos of the much later Edfu temple. The differences between the two compositions, however, are not negligible. The Book of the Moon belonged to the genre of funerary literature, and was no doubt aimed at increasing the chances of the deceased for a successful afterlife, while the treatise at Edfu was in all probability copied onto the walls from a book (papyrus roll) in the temple archive, and was thus more of a 'technical manual' for the observation of the two brightest celestial bodies, though nevertheless it also contained some mythological allusions. Furthermore, the Edfu text is a continuous narrative which seems to have had a proper title, 'Knowing the course of the two celestial lights, the sun and the moon' (*rḫ nmt.t ḥ3y.tj*),[1049] while the Book of the Moon was a collection of similarly titled, relatively short spells. As such, it was a sort of proto-composition: it surely had a plot, the chronological description of the lunar month, but because of its fragmented structure, it was still prone to alteration and disintegration, which in fact happened after the demise of the Middle Kingdom, when the new text corpus of the Book of Going Forth by Day was developed.

Since the overall majority of the complete manuscripts of the Book of the Moon – ten out of eleven – were recorded on coffins that originate from Deir el-Bersha, it is quite clear that the book was compiled in nearby Hermopolis, which was in fact the location that contributed the biggest number of spells to the collection known as the Coffin Texts. Hermopolis, ancient Egyptian *Ḫmn.w* 'the town of the eight', was of course the primary cult centre of the pre-eminent lunar god Thoth, so it is not surprising that the oldest composition about the moon in ancient Egypt, and in fact, in the whole world, was written there, though some of its spells must have been part of the wider inventory of magical texts that had been created in the religious centre of the Old Kingdom, Heliopolis. It included references to all the phenomena that could be observed about the moon by the naked eye: its absence from the sky lasting for one or two days (or, in the Egyptians' perception, three days), the appearance and waxing of the lunar crescent in the first half of the month, the onset of the full moon with a possible lunar eclipse, the waning during the second half of the month, and then the disappearance of the moon once again, with the possibility of a solar eclipse. The references to these celestial developments mostly take the form of mythological

[1049] Chassinat 1928: 351.

allusions that are sometimes easy to grasp, whereas at other times are really difficult – or nigh impossible – to understand, in accordance with the usual arcane nature of the mortuary spells.

The Book of the Moon is thus a real treasure trove of the myths and mythological concepts that were circulated in ancient Egypt. Some of them are in fact easier to understand because they were very widely known and often repeated elsewhere. The prime example of this category is the equation of the moon with the eye of Horus, which of course implied the corollary association of the developments during a lunation with the injuries to the eye inflicted by Horus' archenemy, Seth. This was a myth that was often referred to in a wide variety of sources, and in the Book of the Moon it first surfaces in spell 157. While the motif that the waning of the moon was caused by a pig, being in fact the disguise of Seth, is attested – or, at least, alluded to – elsewhere, for example in the Book of Gates (as part of the scene showing the judgement hall of Osiris), or in Plutarch's account of the myth of Osiris, a new detail about the eye of Horus that we learn in the spell, which seems to have no parallels, is that the town of Pe was given to Horus in compensation for the injury that he had suffered to his eye.

The case is different with the oryx, another animal that is featured in connection with the full moon, as a veiled reference to a lunar eclipse. From the descendants of Coffin Texts spell 157, the copies of chapter 112 of the Book of Going Forth by Day, the description of the oryx and how Horus temporarily covers his eye with his hand is missing, while the knowledge that the oryx had something to do with the full moon was not entirely lost, since the temple scenes showing the slaughter of the animal time this event to the full moon. In addition, the oryx seems to make a reference to the lunar eclipse that happened on a special day in the middle of the 1st century BCE in the round zodiac of Dendera (when the full moon coincided with the day of the autumnal equinox), and even the late author Horapollo (4th/5th century CE) stresses the links of the oryx with the moon.

At the end of spell 156 the waxing moon is likewise described by establishing the identity of the moon with the eye, when it is stated that the *bas* of Hermopolis refer to what is small on the second day of the lunar month and what is big on the fifteenth day (the adjectives are matched with determinatives showing the *wedjat*-eye). While the symbol of the first crescent of the waxing moon, the feather of the west, is well-known from other sources, including other Coffin Texts spells, the pictorial representations of the western direction, and later from the treatise on the lunar cycle in the Edfu temple, the imagery concocted about the full moon, the rising of the Red Crown from the *mentjat*-bowl is again a motif that is virtually unrecorded elsewhere (excluding of course chapters 114 and 116 of the Book of Going Forth by Day). Some passages in the Pyramid Texts and later mortuary literature can be interpreted as identifying the Red Crown with the full moon, and it also appears in the late tomb of Petubastis on the head of the cobra under a *wedjat*-eye standing for the full moon, but the *mentjat*-bowl is a real enigma. Perhaps it is just a reference to the primordial waters, and to the rise of the full lunar disc from them in the same manner as the sun emerges from the celestial waters every morning.

From spell 158 it transpires that the waning moon was essentially identical with the hands of Horus that his own mother, Isis, cut off. The same gruesome act is part of the plot of the famous New Kingdom story (though with some Middle Kingdom antecedents), the Contendings of Horus and Seth, in which it eventually leads to the appearance of the lunar disc on the head of Thoth. The Contendings of Horus and Seth was in all probability a subversive or satirical rewriting of the 'official' myth, but the fact that the mutilation of Horus' hands is mentioned in it implies that this development was a well-known part of the story, even if it seems not to have been recorded in other literary works. Another detail about the waning moon that lacks other mentions is the role of Sobek, the crocodile god, in fishing out the hands, figuratively describing how the rising sun eventually 'catches' the waning lunar crescent when it gets so close to it that it no longer reflects any light towards the earth (i.e. the moon becomes invisible). There is some evidence to support the association of Sobek with the rising sun, but his relation to the moon is not stressed elsewhere.

One thing that should be noted about the overall contents of the Book of the Moon is the various allusions to the invisibility of the moon. In the first spell about the origins of the month (154) the blacked-out moon assumes the form of a serpent called He-who-is-in-his-fire, because it acts as the enemy of the sun god that manages to injure him ('his part') to create the major lunar event of the month in Heliopolis, the *senut*, and eventually the month itself. It may be added that although this narrative is not embellished elsewhere, it unfolds along the same lines as the much later description of how Thoth created the epagomenal days for the births of the gods by chipping away from the light of the moon. The serpent He-who-is-in-his-fire (i.e. the invisible moon) reappears in the final spell, being similarly hostile towards the sun god and this time responsible for stopping his barque momentarily during a solar eclipse. Seth comes to the rescue of the solar barque, and this motif – in connection with the repulsion of Apep – is well-attested in later pictorial representations, implying that He-who-is-in-his-fire is an avatar of Apep itself.

The importance of the phase of invisibility is of course underlined by the existence of spell 155, which is entirely devoted to the description of the *bas* of *psḏn.tjw*, and which was – besides spell 156 – one of the chapters of the Book of the Moon that was written in Hermopolis. The lunar eye is also mentioned here in a cryptic reference to the maximum length of time – three days in the view of the Egyptians – during which the moon is absent from the sky. This is the only text within the composition in which Osiris makes an appearance, possibly foreshadowing his later thorough identification with the moon, especially in the Graeco-Roman Period. He was, in my opinion, closely associated with the moon earlier in his mysteries, but these links were not propagated widely until the Late Period. With the statement that the gelder leaves the slaughterhouse of the lunar eye, spell 155 evokes another motif that is well-documented from late sources: the identification of the waxing moon with a fiery bull, and the waning one with a castrated bull. Despite its rich imagery, spell 155 was discarded when the Book of Going Forth by Day replaced the Coffin Texts as the collection of texts deemed necessary for a blessed existence in the netherworld.

The penultimate spell (159) is also concerned with the encounter between the moon and the sun at the time of lunar invisibility. Since at this time the lunar disc is hidden in the overwhelming brightness of the sun, the text basically describes the behaviour of the rising sun on the eastern horizon, which is a shuttle from the north to the south and then from the south to the north on the celestial waters between two regions that are homes to different types of goose. Some of the associated motifs, such as the two sycamore trees and the solar calf marking the place of sunrise were popular in later visual representations (mostly vignettes to the relevant chapters of the Book of Going Forth by Day). The eastern region from which the sun emerges is furthermore equated with the Field of Reeds, and the written and pictorial representations of this netherworldly realm became one of the central themes in later concepts about the afterlife (spell 110 of the Book of Going Forth by Day, which in the later versions of the composition was in fact inserted between the chapters descending from the Book of the Moon).

The frequent allusions to the invisible moon may at first seem surprising, because it is generally thought that the Egyptians preferred to make references to the waxing phase of the lunar cycle. This misconception, however, is for a large part based on our view of lunations, which is rooted in Greek and Near Eastern calendars that started the month with the appearance of the first crescent in the evening. The Egyptians began their month with the day of lunar invisibility, so being the very first day of a new lunation, the day of the blacked-out moon could just as well express the idea of a new beginning and regeneration as the spectacular waxing of its crescent. Far from being relegated into neglect or having ominous connotations, the day on which the thin waning crescent could no longer be seen just before sunrise was accorded great importance by the Egyptians. We may just want to recall once more that the odd-one-out spell of the composition bore the title 'Knowing the *bas* of *psḏn.tjw*'.

With its numerous references and allusions to lunar myths, not all of which of course can be highlighted in these summary remarks, the Book of the Moon can further our understanding of how the ancient Egyptians viewed the earth's satellite, and what stories and symbols they deemed fit to describe its continually changing forms. Grasping the meaning of ancient texts, we may say, is a delight in itself, but the realisation that Coffin Texts spells 154–160 constitute a 'treatise' about the moon has already brought some other fruits. For example when I was working on spell 157 and researching the various references and sources connected with the oryx, I came across the depictions of this animal in the Dendera zodiacs. Then with time I realised that it was probably included in the iconographic programme of the round zodiac for the very same reason that it appears in the Book of the Moon: to mark a lunar eclipse. This single piece of discovery – later of course coupled with detecting the presence of yet another character from the spell, Horus-on-his-papyrus-column, among the depicted figures – eventually had a snowball effect, and launched me on a train of thought that resulted in the radical reinterpretation of the Graeco-Roman zodiacs. While of course scholarly opinion may be divided for the moment whether my analysis of the zodiacs is a step in the right direction that takes us closer to the correct interpretation of these ancient artefacts, the obvious parallels between them and the much earlier Book of the Moon provide more evidence for how much in fact this latter is embedded in Egyptian thought, and how important a role it may play in furthering our knowledge about the place and importance of the moon in ancient Egypt.

Bibliography

Allen, J. P. 1994. Reading a Pyramid, in C. Berger (ed.), *Hommages à Jean Leclant* I: 5–28. Cairo: Institut Français d'Archéologie Orientale

Allen, J. P. 2001a. Ba, in D. B. Redford (ed.), *The Oxford Encyclopedia of Ancient Egypt* I: 161–162. Oxford: Oxford University Press.

Allen, J. P. 2001b. *Middle Egyptian: An Introduction to the Language and Culture of Hieroglyphs.* Cambridge: Cambridge University Press.

Allen, J. P. 2002. Review of 'Astronomische Konzepte und Jenseitsvorstellungen in den Pyramidentexten by Rolf Krauss'. *Journal of Near Eastern Studies* 61: 62–68.

Allen, J. P. 2005. *The Ancient Egyptian Pyramid Texts.* Writings from the Ancient World 23. Atlanta: Society of Biblical Literature.

Allen, T. G. 1960. *The Egyptian Book of the Dead Documents in the Oriental Institute Museum at the University of Chicago.* Oriental Institute Publications 82. Chicago: The University of Chicago Press.

Allen, T. G. 1974. *The Book of the Dead or Going Forth by Day: Ideas of the Ancient Egyptians Concerning the Hereafter as Expressed in Their Own Terms.* Studies in Ancient Oriental Civilizations 37. Chicago: The University of Chicago Press.

Altenmüller, B. 1975a. Anubis, in W. Helck and E. Otto (eds), *Lexikon der Ägyptologie* I: 327–333. Wiesbaden: Harrassowitz.

Altenmüller, B. 1975b. Buto, in W. Helck and E. Otto (eds), *Lexikon der Ägyptologie* I: 887–889. Wiesbaden: Harrassowitz.

Altmann, V. 2010. *Die Kultfrevel des Seth. Die Gefährdung der göttlichen Ordnung in zwei Vernichtungsritualen der ägyptischen Spätzeit (Urk. VI).* Studien zur spätagyptischen Religion 1. Wiesbaden: Harrassowitz.

Arquier, B. 2013. *Le double sarcophage de Mésehti S1C (CG 28118)-S2C (CG 28119). Recherches sur l'organisation du décor iconographique et textuel.* Unpublished PhD thesis, Université Paul Valéry Montpellier III.

Assmann, J. 2001. *The Search for God in Ancient Egypt.* (transl. D. Lorton). Ithaca: Cornell University Press.

Assmann, J. 2005. *Death and Salvation in Ancient Egypt* (transl. D. Lorton). Ithaca: Cornell University Press.

Aubourg, É. 1995. La date de conception du zodiaque du temple d'Hathor à Dendera. *Bulletin de l'Institut Français d'Archéologie Orientale* 95: 1–10.

Aubourg, É. and Cauville, S. 1998. En ce matin du 28 décembre 48..., in W. Clarysse, A. Schoors and H. Willems (eds), *Egyptian Religion: The Last Thousand Years. Studies Dedicated to the Memory of Jan Quaegebeur*: 767–772. Orientalia Lovaniensia Analecta 85. Leuven: Peeters.

Aufrère, S. 1991. *L'univers minéral dans la pensée égyptienne.* Bibliothèque d'Étude 105. Cairo: Institut Français d'Archéologie Orientale.

Backes, B. 2011. Zur Anwendung der Textkritik in der Ägyptologie. Ziele, Grenzen und Akzeptanz, in A. Verbovsek, B. Backes, and C. Jones (eds), *Methodik und Didaktik in der Ägyptologie. Herausforderungen eines kulturwissenschaftlichen paradigmenwechsels in den Altertumswissenschaften:* 451–479. Ägyptologie und Kulturwissenschaft 4. Munich: Wilhelm Fink.

Baines, J. 1990. Restricted Knowledge, Hierarchy, and Decorum: Modern Perceptions and Ancient Institutions. *Journal of the American Research Center in Egypt* 27: 1–23.

Baines, J. 2004. Modelling Sources, Processes, and Locations of Early Mortuary Texts, in S. Bickel & B. Mathieu (eds), *D'un monde à l'autre. Textes des Pyramides & Textes des Sarcophages. Actes de la table ronde internationale «Textes des Pyramides* versus *Textes des Sarcophages» Ifao - 24-26 septembre 2001:* 15–41. Bibliothèque d'Études 139. Cairo: Institut Français d'Archéologie Orientale.

Baines, J. 2007. *Visual and Written Culture in Ancient Egypt*. Oxford: Oxford University Press.

Baines, J. and Malek, J. 2002. *Atlas of Ancient Egypt*. Revised edition. Cairo: The American University in Cairo Press.

Barguet, P. 1986. *Les Textes des sarcophages égyptiens du Moyen Empire*. Paris: Éditions du Cerf.

Behrens, P. 1975. Geflügel, in W. Helck és E. Otto (eds), *Lexikon der Ägyptologie* II: 503–505. Wiesbaden: Harrassowitz.

Beinlich, H. 1991. *Das Buch vom Fayum. Zum religiösen Eigenverständnis einer ägyptischen Landschaft*. Ägyptologische Abhandlungen 51. Wiesbaden: Harrassowitz.

Bickel, S. 1994. *La cosmogonie égyptienne avant le Nouvel Empire*. Orbis Biblicus et Orientalis 134. Fribourg: Editions Universitaires.

Billing, N. 2002. *Nut: The Goddess of Life in Text and Iconography*. Uppsala Studies in Egyptology 5. Uppsala: Department of Archaeology and Ancient History.

Boas, G. (transl.). 1993. *The Hieroglyphics of Horapollo*. Bollingen Series 23. Princeton: Princeton University Press.

Borchardt, L. 1935. *Die Mittel zur zeitlichen Festlegung von Punkten der ägyptischen Geschichte und ihre Anwendung*. Quellen und Forschungen zur Zeitbestimmung der ägyptischen Geschichte 2. Cairo: Self-Published.

Borghouts, J. F. 1971. The Magical Texts of Papyrus Leiden I 348. *Oudheidkundige Mededelingen uit het Rijksmuseum van Oudheden te Leiden* 51: 1–248.

Bosse-Griffiths, K. 2001. *Amarna Studies and Other Selected Papers*. Fribourg: University Press.

Bourriau, J. 2000. The Second Intermediate Period, in I. Shaw (ed.), *The Oxford History of Ancient Egypt:* 172–206. Oxford: Oxford University Press.

Boylan, P. 1922. *Thoth: The Hermes of Egypt*. London: H. Milford–Oxford University Press.

Bøgh, B. 2013. The Graeco-Roman Cult of Isis, in L. B. Christensen, O. Hammer, and D. A. Warburton (eds), *The Handbook of Religions in Ancient Europe:* 228–241. Cambridge: Cambridge University Press.

Breasted, J. H. 1912. *Development of Religion and Thought in Ancient Egypt: Lectures Delivered on the Morse Foundation at Union Theological Seminary*. New York: Charles Scribner's Sons.

Breasted, J. H. 1930. *The Edwin Smith Surgical Papyrus* I. Oriental Institute Publications 3. Chicago: Oriental Institute.

Brovarski, E. 1981. Ahanakht of Bersheh and the Hare Nome in the First Intermediate Period, in W. K. Simpson and W. M. Davis (eds), *Studies in Ancient Egypt, the Aegean, and the Sudan: Essays in Honor of Dows Dunham on the Occasion of His 90th Birthday, June 1, 1980:* 14–30. Boston: Museum of Fine Arts.

Brovarski, E. 1984. Sobek, in W. Helck and E. Otto (eds), *Lexikon der Ägyptologie* V: 995–1031. Wiesbaden: Harrassowitz.

Brugsch, H. 1883. *Thesaurus Inscriptionum Aegyptiacarum* I. Leipzig: Hinrichs'sche Buchhandlung.
Bryan, B. M. 2000. The 18th Dynasty before the Amarna Period, in I. Shaw (ed.), *The Oxford History of Ancient Egypt*: 207–264. Oxford: Oxford University Press.
Budge, E. A. W. 1912. *The Greenfield Papyrus of the British Museum*. London: British Museum.
Budge, E. A. W. 1913. *The Papyrus of Ani* III. *The Papyrus of Ani Reproduced in 37 Coloured Plates*. London: Philip Lee Warner.
Buhl, M.-L. 1947. The Goddesses of the Egyptian Tree Cult. *Journal of Near Eastern Studies* 6: 80–97.
Caminos, R. A. 1958. *The Chronicle of Prince Osorkon*. Analecta Orientalia 37. Rome: Pontificium Institutum Biblicum.
Carrier, C. 2004. *Textes des sarcophages du Moyen Empire égyptien*. Monaco: Éditions du Rocher.
Carter, H. 1933. *The Tomb of Tut.ankh.Amen* III. London: Cassell.
Cauville, S. 1990. *Le temple de Dendera. Guide archéologique*. Bibliothèque Générale XII. Cairo: Institut Français d'Archéologie Orientale.
Cauville, S. 1997. *Le temple de Dendara. Les chapelles osiriennes*. Dendara X/2. Cairo: Institut Français d'Archéologie Orientale.
Cauville, S. 2008. *Le temple de Dendara. Pronaos: plafond et parois extérieurs*. Dendara XV/1. Published by the author on the Internet: http://www.dendara.net/download/Dendara-XV.pdf [23 June 2010]
Cauville, S. 2011. Le pronaos d'Edfou: une voûte étoilée. *Revue d'Égyptologie* 62: 41–55.
Cauville, S. 2012. *Dendara XV: Traduction. Le pronaos du temple d'Hathor: Plafond et parois extérieures*. Orientalia Lovaniensia Analecta 213. Leuven: Peeters.
Cauville, S. 2013. *Dendara. Le pronaos du temple d'Hathor: Analyse de la décoration*. Orientalia Lovaniensia Analecta 221. Leuven: Peeters.
Chassinat, E. 1928. *Le temple d'Edfou* III. Mémoires publiés par les membres de l'Institut Français d'Archéologie Orientale 20. Cairo: Institut Français d'Archéologie Orientale.
Chassinat, E. 1929. *Le temple d'Edfou* IX. Mémoires publiés par les membres de l'Institut Français d'Archéologie Orientale 26. Cairo: Institut Français d'Archéologie Orientale.
Chassinat, E. 1930. *Le temple d'Edfou* V. Mémoires publiés par les membres de l'Institut Français d'Archéologie Orientale 22. Cairo: Institut Français d'Archéologie Orientale.
Chassinat, E. 1931. *Le temple d'Edfou* VI. Mémoires publiés par les membres de la Mission archéologique française au Caire 23. Cairo: Institut Français d'Archéologie Orientale.
Chassinat, E. 1932. *Le temple d'Edfou* VII. Mémoires publiés par les membres de la Mission archéologique française au Caire 24. Cairo: Institut Français d'Archéologie Orientale.
Chassinat, E. 1935. *Le temple de Dendara* IV. Cairo: Institut Français d'Archéologie Orientale.
Chassinat, E. 1966. *Le mystère d'Osiris au mois de khoiak* 1. Cairo: Institut Français d'Archéologie Orientale.

Clagett, M. 1995. *Ancient Egyptian Science* II: *Calendars, Clocks, and Astronomy*. Memoirs of the American Philosophical Society 214. Philadelphia: American Philosophical Society.

Clère, P. 1961. *La Porte d'Evergète à Karnak*. Mémoires publiés par les membres de l'Institut Français d'Archéologie Orientale 84. Cairo: Institut Français d'Archéologie Orientale.

CT = Buck, A. de. 1935–1961. *The Egyptian Coffin Texts* I–VII. Chicago: The University of Chicago Press.

Darnell, J. C. 2004. *The Enigmatic Netherworld Books of the Solar-Osirian Unity: Cryptographic Compositions in the Tombs of Tutankhamon, Ramesses VI and Ramesses IX*. Fribourg: Academic Press.

Daumas, F. 1988. *Valeurs phonétiques des signes hiéroglyphiques d'époque gréco-romaine*. Montpellier: Université de Montpellier.

David. R. 2002. *Religion and Magic in Ancient Egypt*. London: Penguin Books.

Depuydt, L. 1997. *Civil Calendar and Lunar Calendar in Ancient Egypt*. Orientalia Lovaniensia Analecta 77. Leuven: Peeters.

Depuydt, L. 1998. The Hieroglyphic Representation of the Moon's Absence (*Psḏntyw*), in L. H. Lesko (ed.), *Ancient Egyptian and Mediterranean Studies in Memory of William A. Ward*: 71–89. Providence: Brown University Press.

Depuydt, L. 2001. What Is Certain about the Origin of the Egyptian Civil Calendar?, in H. Győry (ed.), *Le lotus qui sort de terre. Mélanges offerts à Edith Varga*: 81–94. Bulletin du Musée hongrois des beaux-arts, Supplément 2001. Budapest: Musée Hongrois des Beaux-Arts.

Derchain, P. 1962a. Mythes et dieux lunaires en Égypte, in *La lune. Mythes et Rites*: 19–68. Paris: Éditions du Seuil.

Derchain, P. 1962b. *Le sacrifice de l'oryx*. Rites égyptiens 1. Bruxelles: Fondation Égyptologique Reine Élisabeth.

Derchain, P. 1963. Nouveaux documents relatifs à Bébon (*Bꜣbꜣwj*). *Zeitschrift für ägyptische Sprache und Altertumskunde* 90: 22–25.

Derchain, P. 1996. Auteur et société, in A. Loprieno (ed.), *Ancient Egyptian Literature: History and Forms*: 83–94. Probleme der Ägyptologie 10. Leiden: Brill.

Derchain, P. 1997. Miettes (IV). *Revue d'Egyptologie* 48: 71–80.

Dodson, A. 2001. Four Sons of Horus, in D. B. Redford, (ed.), *The Oxford Encyclopaedia of Ancient Egypt* I: 561–563. Oxford: Oxford University Press.

Dorman, P. F. 1991. *The Tombs of Senenmut: The Architecture and Decoration of Tombs 71 and 353*. New York: Metropolitan Museum of Art.

DuQuesne, T. 1998. Seth and the Jackals, in W. Clarysse, A. Schoors and H. Willems (eds), *Egyptian Religion: The Last Thousand Years. Studies Dedicated to the Memory of Jan Quaegebeur*: 613–627. Orientalia Lovaniensia Analecta 85. Leuven: Peeters.

DuQuesne, T. 2001. Concealing and Revealing: The Problem of Ritual Masking in Ancient Egypt. *Discussions in Egyptology* 51: 5–31.

Eaton, K. 2011. Monthly Lunar Festivals in the Mortuary Realm: Historical Patterns and Symbolic Motifs. *Journal of Near Eastern Studies* 70: 229–245.

Faulkner, R. O. 1937. The Bremner-Rhind Papyrus III: The Book of Overthrowing ʿApep. *Journal of Egyptian Archaeology* 23: 166–185.

Faulkner, R. O. 1962. *A Concise Dictionary of Middle Egyptian*. Oxford: Griffith Institute.

Faulkner, R. O. 1969. *The Ancient Egyptian Pyramid Texts*. Oxford: Oxford University Press.

Faulkner, R. O. 1973. *The Ancient Egyptian Coffin Texts* I: *Spells 1-354*. Warminster: Aris & Phillips.

Faulkner, R. O. 1977. *The Ancient Egyptian Coffin Texts* II: *Spells 355-787*. Warminster: Aris & Phillips.

Faulkner, R. O. 1978. *The Ancient Egyptian Coffin Texts* III: *Spells 788-1185 & Indexes*. Warminster: Aris & Phillips.

Faulkner, R. O. 1981. Abnormal or Cryptic Writings in the Coffin Texts. *Journal of Egyptian Archaeology* 67: 173–174.

Faulkner, R. O. 1982. A Coffin Text Miscellany. *Journal of Egyptian Archaeology* 68: 27–30.

Faulkner, R. O. 1994. *The Egyptian Book of the Dead: the Book of Going Forth by Day*. San Francisco: Chronicle Books.

Finnestad, R. B. 1997. Temples of the Ptolemaic and Roman Periods: Ancient Traditions in New Contexts, in B. E. Shafer (ed.), *Temples of Ancient Egypt*: 185–237. Ithaca: Cornell University Press.

Fischer-Elfert, H-W. 1983. *Die satirische Streitschrift des Papyrus Anastasi I*. Wiesbaden: Harrassowitz.

Friedman, F. D. 1998. *Gifts of the Nile: Ancient Egyptian Faience*. London: Thames & Hudson.

Galán, J. M. 2000. The Ancient Egyptian *Sed*-festival and the Exemption from Corvée. *Journal of Near Eastern Studies* 59: 255–264.

Gardiner, A. H. 1909. *The Admonitions of an Egyptian Sage from a Hieratic Papyrus in Leiden (Pap. Leiden 344 recto)*. Leipzig: J. C. Hinrichs.

Gardiner, A. H. 1932. *Late Egyptian Stories*. Bibliotheca Aegyptiaca I. Brussels: Fondation Égyptologique Reine Élisabeth.

Gardiner, A. H. 1938. The House of Life. *Journal of Egyptian Archaeology* 24: 157–179.

Gardiner, A. H. 1947. *Ancient Egyptian Onomastica* II. Oxford: Oxford University Press.

Gardiner, A. H. 1957a. *Egyptian Grammar: Being an Introduction to the Study of Hieroglyphs*. (Third Edition). Oxford: Griffith Institute.

Gardiner, A. H. 1957b. Hymns to Sobk in a Ramesseum Papyrus. *Revue d'Egyptologie* 11: 41–56.

Gauthier, H. 1927. *Dictionnaire des noms géograpiques contenus dans les textes hiéroglyphiques* IV. Cairo: Société Royale de Géographie d'Égypte.

Gayet, A. 1894. *Le temple de Louxor. Constructions d'Aménophis III*. Paris: E. Leroux.

Gee, J. 2010. The Book of the Dead as Canon. *British Museum Studies in Ancient Egypt and Sudan* 15: 23–33.

Gestermann, L. 2004. Sargtexte aus Dair al-Biršā, in S. Bickel & B. Mathieu (eds), *D'un monde à l'autre. Textes des Pyramides & Textes des Sarcophages. Actes de la table ronde internationale «Textes des Pyramides* versus *Textes des Sarcophages» Ifao - 24-26 septembre 2001*: 201–217. Bibliothèque d'Études 139. Cairo: Institut Français d'Archéologie Orientale.

Gestermann, L. 2008. Die Datierung der Nomarchen von Hermopolis aus dem frühen Mittleren Reich: Eine Phantomdebatte? *Zeitschrift für ägyptische Sprache und Altertumskunde* 135: 1–15.

Gnirs, A. M. 1996. Die ägyptische Autobiographie, in A. Loprieno (ed.), *Ancient Egyptian Literature: History and Forms*: 191–241. Probleme der Ägyptologie 10. Leiden: Brill.

Godley, A. D. (transl.). 1920. *Herodotus* I. London: Heinemann.

Goebs, K. 2003. Zerstörung als Erneuerung in der Totenliteratur. Ein kosmische Interpretation des Kannibalenspruchs. *Göttinger Miszellen* 194: 29–50.
Goebs, K. 2008. *Crowns in Egyptian Funerary Literature: Royalty, Rebirth, and Destruction.* Oxford: Griffith Institute.
Goedicke, H. 1989. Coffin Text Spell 6. *Bulletin de la Société d'Égyptologie Genève* 13: 57–64.
Goyon, J.-C. 1965, Le cérémonial de glorification d'Osiris du papyrus du Louvre I. 3079 (colonnes 110 à 112). *Bulletin de l'Institut Français d'Archéologie Orientale* 65: 89–156.
Goyon, J.-C. 1983. Aspects thébains de la confirmation du pouvoir royal. Les rites lunaires. *Journal of the Society for the Study of Egyptian Antiquities* 13: 2–9.
Graves-Brown, C. 2006. Emergent Flints, in K. Szpakowska (ed.), *Through a Glass Darkly: Magic, Dreams & Prophecy in Ancient Egypt*: 47–62. Swansea: The Classical Press of Wales.
Gray, H. 1918. *Anatomy of the Human Body.* (Twentieth Edition). Philadelphia: Lea & Febiger.
Grieshammer, R. 1977. Flammeninsel, in W. Helck, E. Otto and W. Westendorf (eds), *Lexikon der Ägyptologie* II: 258–9. Wiesbaden: Otto Harrassowitz.
Griffiths, J. G. 1960. *The Conflict of Horus and Seth from Egyptian and Classical Sources.* Liverpool: Liverpool University Press.
Griffiths, J. G. 1970. *Plutarch's De Iside et Osiride.* Swansea: University of Wales Press.
Griffiths, J. G. 1976. Osiris and the Moon in Iconography. *Journal of Egyptian Archaeology* 82: 153–159.
Griffiths, J. G. 1980. *The Origins of Osiris and His Cult.* Leiden: Brill.
Grimm, A. 1994. *Die altägyptischen Festkalender in den Tempeln der griechisch-römischen Epoche.* Ägypten und Altes Testament 15. Wiesbaden: Harrassowitz.
Guglielmi, W. and Buroh, K. 1997. Die Eingangssprüche des Täglichen Tempelrituals nach Papyrus Berlin 3055 (I, 1–VI, 3), in J. van Dijk (ed.), *Essays on Ancient Egypt in Honour of Herman te Velde*: 101–166. Groningen: Styx Publications.
Hannig, R. 1995. *Großes Handwörterbuch Ägyptisch-Deutsch. Die Sprache der Pharaonen (2800-950 v. Chr.).* Kulturgeschichte der Antiken Welt 64. Mainz: Philipp von Zabern.
Hassan, S. 1948. *Excavations at Gîza VI/2: The Offering List in the Old Kingdom.* Cairo: Government Press:.
Hays, H. M. 2008. Transformation of Context: The Field of Rushes in Old and Middle Kingdom Mortuary Literature, in S. Bickel and B. Mathieu (eds), *D'un monde à l'autre. Textes des Pyramides & Textes des Sarcophages. Actes de la table ronde internationale «Textes des Pyramides* versus *Textes des Sarcophages» Ifao - 24-26 septembre 2001*: 175–200. Bibliothèque d'Études 139. Cairo: Institut Français d'Archéologie Orientale.
Hays, H. M. 2011. The Death of the Democratisation of the Afterlife, in N. Strudwick and H. Strudwick (eds), *Old Kingdom: New Perspectives. Egyptian Art and Archaeology 2750-2150 BC*: 115–130. Oxford: Oxbow Books.
Herbin, F-R. 1982. Un hymne à la lune croissante. *Bulletin de l'Institut Français d'Archéologie Orientale* 82: 237–282.
Hodel-Hoenes, S. 2000. *Life and Death in Ancient Egypt: Scenes from Private Tombs in New Kingdom Thebes.* Translated by D. Warburton. Ithaca: Cornell University Press.
Hornung, E. 1961. Lexikalische Studien I. *Zeitschrift für ägyptische Sprache und Altertumskunde* 86: 106–114.
Hornung, E. 1965. Die Sonnenfinsternis nach dem Tode Psammetichs I. *Zeitschrift für ägyptische Sprache und Altertumskunde* 92: 38–39.

Hornung, E. 1999. *The Ancient Egyptian Books of the Afterlife*. (transl. D. Lorton). Ithaca: Cornell University Press.

Hornung, E. 2002. *Die Unterweltsbücher der Ägypter*. Düsseldorf: Patmos Verlag.

Hornung, E., Krauss, R., and Warburton, D. A. 2006. Methods of Dating and the Egyptian Calendar, in E. Hornung, R. Krauss and R. A. Warburton (eds), *Ancient Egyptian Chronology:* 45–51. Handbook der Orientalistik 83. Leiden: Brill.

Hussein, A. M. 2010. Beware of the Red-Eyed Horus: The Significance of Carnelian in Egyptian Royal Jewelry, in Z. Hawass, P. Der Manuelian, and R. B. Hussein (eds), *Perspectives on Ancient Egypt: Studies in Honor of Edward Brovarski:* 185–190. Supplément aux Annales du Service des Antiquités de l'Égypte, Cahier 40. Cairo: Conseil Suprême des Antiquités de l'Égypte.

James, T. G. H. 2000. *Tutankhamun: The Eternal Splendour of the Boy Pharaoh*. London: Tauris Parke.

Jasnow, R. and Zauzich, K.-T. 2005. *The Ancient Egyptian Book of Thoth: A Demotic Discourse on Knowledge and Pendant to the Classical Hermetica* I: *Text*. Wiesbaden: Harrassowitz.

Jones, D. 2000. *An Index of Ancient Egyptian Titles, Epithets and Phrases of the Old Kingdom*. BAR International Series 866. Oxford: Archaeopress.

Josephson, J. A. 2001. Amasis, in D. B. Redford (ed.), *The Oxford Encyclopedia of Ancient Egypt* I: 66–67. Oxford: Oxford University Press.

Junker, H. 1911. Die sechs Teile des Horusauges und der 'sechste Tag'. *Zeitschrift für ägyptische Sprache und Altertumskunde* 48: 101–106.

Junker, H. 1940. Der Tanz der Mww und das Butische Begräbnis im Alten Reich. *Mitteilungen des Deutschen Archäologischen Instituts Kairo* 9: 1–39.

Kahl, J. 1999. *Siut-Theben. Zur Wertschätzung von Traditionen im alten Ägypten*. Probleme der Ägyptologie 13. Leiden: Brill.

Kahl, J. 2007. *'Ra Is My Lord': Searching for the Rise of the Sun God at the Dawn of Egyptian History*. MENES, Studien zur Kultur und Sprache der ägyptischen Frühzeit und des Altes Reiches 1. Wiesbaden: Harrassowitz Verlag.

Kákosy, L. 1980. Krokodilskulte, in W. Helck and E. Otto (eds), *Lexikon der Ägyptologie* III: 802–811. Wiesbaden: Harrassowitz:.

Kákosy L. 1999. *Egyptian Healing Statues in Three Museums in Italy (Turin, Florence, Naples)*. Torino: Soprintendenza al Museo delle Antichità Egizie.

Kees, H. 1922. Die Schlangensteine und ihre Beziehungen zu den Reichsheiligtümern. *Zeitschrift für ägyptische Sprache und Altertumskunde* 57: 120–136.

Kees, H. 1925. Zu den ägyptischen Mondsagen. *Zeitschrift für ägyptische Sprache und Altertumskunde* 60: 1–15.

Kees, H. 1956. *Totenglauben und Jenseitsvorstellungen der alten Ägypter. Grundlagen und Entwicklung bis zum Ende des Mittleren Reiches*. Berlin: Akademie-Verlag.

Kemp, B. J. 1991. *Ancient Egypt: Anatomy of a Civilization*. London: Routledge.

Kitchen, K. A. 1975. Barke, in W. Helck and E. Otto (eds), *Lexikon der Ägyptologie* I: 619–625. Wiesbaden: Harrassowitz.

Kockelmann, H. 2006. From One to Ten: The Book of the Dead Project after Its First Decade, in B. Backes, I. Munro, and S. Stöhr (eds), *Gesammelte Beitrage des 2. Internationale Totenbuch-Symposiums, Bonn, 25. bis 29. September 2005:* 161–165. Wiesbaden: Harrassowitz.

Koemoth, P. P. 1996. Osiris-Lune, l'horizon et l'œil *oudjat*. *Chronique d'Égypte* 71: 203–220.

Krauss, R. 1997. *Astronomische Konzepte und Jenseitsvorstellungen in den Pyramidentexten*. Ägyptologische Abhandlungen 59. Wiesbaden: Harrassowitz Verlag.

Krauss, R. 2006. Lunar Days, Lunar Months, and the Question of the Civil Based Lunar Calendar, in E. Hornung, R. Krauss and R. A. Warburton (eds), *Ancient Egyptian Chronology:* 386–391. Handbook der Orientalistik 83. Leiden: Brill.

Lacau, P. 1954. Le panier de pêche égyptien. *Bulletin de l'Institut Français d'Archéologie Orientale* 54: 137–163.

Lapp, G. 1990. Die Spruchkompositionen der Sargtexte. *Studien zur altägyptischen Kultur* 17: 221–234.

Lapp, G. 1997. *The Papyrus of Nu (BM EA 10477)*. Catalogue of the Books of the Dead in the British Museum 1. London: British Museum Press.

Lapp, G. 2004. *The Papyrus of Nebseni (BM EA 9900)*. Catalogue of the Books of the Dead in the British Museum 8. London: British Museum Press.

Leahy, A. and Mathieson, I. 2001. The Tomb of Nyankhnesut (Re)discovered. *Journal of Egyptian Archaeology* 87: 33–42.

Leitz, C. 1994. *Tagewählerei. Das Buch ḥꜣt nḥḥ pḥ.wy ḏt und verwandte Texte*. Ägyptologische Abhandlungen 55. Wiesbaden: Harrassowitz.

Leitz, C. 2002a. *Lexikon der ägyptischen Götter und Götterbezeichnungen* I. Orientalia Lovaniensia Analecta 110. Leuven: Peeters.

Leitz, C. 2002b. *Lexikon der ägyptischen Götter und Götterbezeichnungen* II. Orientalia Lovaniensia Analecta 111. Leuven: Peeters.

Leitz, C. 2002c. *Lexikon der ägyptischen Götter und Götterbezeichnungen* III. Orientalia Lovaniensia Analecta 112. Leuven: Peeters.

Leitz, C. 2002d. *Lexikon der ägyptischen Götter und Götterbezeichnungen* IV. Orientalia Lovaniensia Analecta 113. Leuven: Peeters.

Leitz, C. 2002e. *Lexikon der ägyptischen Götter und Götterbezeichnungen* V. Orientalia Lovaniensia Analecta 114. Leuven: Peeters.

Leitz, C. 2006. Die Sternbilder auf den rechteckigen und runden Tierkreis von Dendera. *Studien zur Altägyptischen Kultur* 34: 285–318.

Lepsius, R. 1842. *Das Todtenbuch der Ägypter nach dem hieroglyphischen Papyrus in Turin*. Leipzig: Georg Wigand.

Lichtheim, M. 1975. *Ancient Egyptian Literature* I: *The Old and Middle Kingdoms*. Berkeley: University of California Press.

Lichtheim, M. 1976. *Ancient Egyptian Literature* II: *The New Kingdom*. Berkeley: University of California Press.

Lieven, A. von. 2000. *Der Himmel über Esna. Eine Fallstudie zur Religiösen Astronomie in Ägypten am Beispiel der kosmologischen Decken- und Architravinschriften im Tempel von Esna*. Ägyptologische Abhandlungen 64. Wiesbaden: Harrassowitz Verlag.

Lieven, A. von. 2007. *The Carlsberg Papyri 8: Grundriss des Laufes der Sterne. Das sogennante Nutbuch*. Carsten Niebuhr Institute Publications 31. Copenhagen: Museum Tusculanum Press.

Lieven, A. von. 2016. Closed Canon vs. Creative Chaos, in K. Ryholt and G. Barjamovic (eds), *Problems of Canonicity and Identity Formation in Ancient Egypt and Mesopotamia:* 51–78. CNI Publications 43. Copenhagen: Museum Tusculanum Press.

Loprieno, A. 1996. Defining Egyptian Literature: Ancient Texts and Modern Theories, in A. Loprieno (ed.), *Ancient Egyptian Literature: History and Forms:* 39–58. Probleme der Ägyptologie 10. Leiden: Brill.

Lucas, A. and Harris, J. A. 1999. *Ancient Egyptian Materials and Industries.* (Reprint of the 1962 edition.) Mineola: Dover Publications.

Luft, U. 1992. *Die chronologische Fixierung des ägyptischen mittleren Reiches nach den Tempelarchiv von Illahun.* Vienna: Österrechischen Akademie der Wissenschaften.

Luiselli, M. 2003. The Colophone as an Indication of the Attitudes towards the Literary Tradition in Egypt and Mesopotamia, in S. Bickel and A. Loprieno (eds), *Basel Egyptology Prize: Junior Research in Egyptian History:* 343–360. Aegyptiaca Helvetica 17. Basel: Schwabe & Co. AG Verlag.

Manassa, C. 2006. The Judgment Hall of Osiris in the Book of Gates. *Revue d'Egyptologie* 57: 109–150.

Mathieu, B. 2008a. La distinction entre Textes des Pyramides et Textes des Sarcophages est-elle légitime?, in S. Bickel and B. Mathieu (eds), *D'un monde à l'autre. Textes des Pyramides & Textes des Sarcophages. Actes de la table ronde internationale «Textes des Pyramides* versus *Textes des Sarcophages» Ifao - 24-26 septembre 2001:* 247–262. Bibliothèque d'Études 139. Cairo: Institut Français d'Archéologie Orientale.

Mathieu, B. 2008b. Les Enfants d'Horus, théologie et astronomie. *Égypte Nilotique et Méditérranéenne* 1: 7–14.

Meeks, D. 1980. *Année lexicographique. Égypte ancienne* I. Paris: Cybele.

Meeks, D. 1998. L'Horus de *Tby*, in W. Clarysse, A. Schoors and H. Willems (eds), *Egyptian Religion: The Last Thousand Years. Studies Dedicated to the Memory of Jan Quaegebeur:* 1181–1190. Orientalia Lovaniensia Analecta 85. Leuven: Peeters.

Meeks, D. 2000. Locating Punt, in D. O'Connor and S. Quirke (eds), *Encounters with Ancient Egypt: Mysterious Lands:* 53–80. London: UCL Press.

Meeks, D. 2006. *Mythes et légendes du Delta d'après le papyrus Brooklyn 47.218.84.* Mémoires publiés par les membres de l'Institut Français d'Archéologie Orientale 125. Cairo: Institut Français d'Archéologie Orientale.

Mercer, S. 1949. *The Religion of Ancient Egypt.* London: Luzac.

Molen, R. van der. 2000. *A Hieroglyphic Dictionary of Egyptian Coffin Texts.* Probleme der Ägyptologie 15. Brill: Leiden.

Morales, A. J. 2013. *The Transmission of Pyramid Texts into the Middle Kingdom: Philological Aspects of a Continuous Tradition in Egyptian Literature.* Unpublished PhD thesis, University of Pennsylvania.

Morenz, L. D. 1996. *Beiträge zur Schriflichkeitskultur im Mittleren Reich und in der 2. Zwischenzeit.* Ägypten und Altes Testament 29. Wiesbaden: Harrassowitz.

Mosher, M. 2001. *The Papyrus of Hor (BM EA 10479) with Papyrus MacGregor: The Late Period Tradition at Akhmim.* Catalogue of the Books of the Dead in the British Museum 2. London: British Museum.

Möller, G. 1909. *Hieratische Paläographie* 1. Leipzig: J. C. Hinrichs.

Mueller, D. 1972. An Early Egyptian Guide to the Hereafter. *Journal of Egyptian Archaeology* 58: 99–125.

Munro, I. 1988. *Untersuchungen zu den Totenbuch-Papyri der 18. Dynastie.* London: Kegan Paul.

Nagel, G. 1928. Set dans la barque solaire. *Bulletin de l'Institut Français d'Archéologie Orientale* 28: 33–39.

Neugebauer, O. 1975. *A History of Ancient Mathematical Astronomy.* Berlin: Sringer-Verlag.

Neugebauer, O. and Parker, R. A. 1960. *Egyptian Astronomical Texts I: The Early Decans.* Providence: Brown University Press.

Neugebauer, O. and Parker, R. A. 1969. *Egyptian Astronomical Texts* III: *Decans, Planets, Constellations and Zodiacs.* Providence: Brown University Press.

Newberry, P. E. 1928. The Pig and the Cult-Animal of Set. *Journal of Egyptian Archaeology* 14: 211–225.

Nicholson, P. T. 2009. Faience Technology, in J. Dieleman and W. Wendrich (eds), *UCLA Encyclopedia of Egyptology.* Los Angeles, http://escholarship.org/uc/item/9cs9x41z#page-1 [30 September 2017].

Nordh, K. 1996. *Aspects of Ancient Egyptian Curses and Blessings: Conceptual Background and Transmission.* Boreas 26. Stockholm: Almqvist & Wiksell International.

Nyord, R. 2003. Spittle, Lies and Regeneration: Some Religious Expressions on a Stela from the First Intermediate Period. *Göttinger Miszellen* 197: 73–91.

Nunn, J. F. 2002. *Ancient Egyptian Medicine.* Norman: University of Oklahoma Press.

O'Connor, D. 2001. The City and the World: Worldview and Built Forms in the Reign of Amenhotep III, in D. O'Connor and E. H. Cline (eds), *Amenhotep III: Perspectives on His Reign:* 125–172. Ann Arbor: The University of Michigan Press.

Osing, J., Moursi, M., Arnold, D. O., Neugebauer, O., Parker, R. A., Pingree, D., and Nur-el-Din, M. A. 1982. *Denkmäler der Oase Dachla aus dem Nachlass von Ahmed Fakhry.* Mainz: Philipp von Zabern.

Otto, E. 1975. Bachu, in W. Helck and E. Otto (eds), *Lexikon der Ägyptologie* I: 594. Wiesbaden: Harrassowitz.

Parker, R. A. 1950. *The Calendars of Ancient Egypt.* Studies in Ancient Oriental Civilization 26. Chicago: University of Chicago Press.

Parker, R. A. 1953. The Names of the Sixteenth Day of the Month. *Journal of Near Eastern Studies* 12: 50.

Parker, R. A. 1959. *A Vienna Demotic Papyrus on Eclipse- and Lunar-Omina.* Providence: Brown University Press.

Parkinson, R. B. 1991. *Voices from Ancient Egypt: An Anthology of Middle Kingdom Writings.* London: British Museum Press.

Parkinson, R. B. 2002. *Poetry and Culture in Middle Kingdom Egypt: A Dark Side to Perfection.* London: Continuum.

Partridge, R. B. 2010. Transport in Ancient Egypt, in A. B. Lloyd (ed.), *A Companion to Ancient Egypt* I: 370–389. Chichester: Wiley-Blackwell.

Peet, T. E. 1923. *The Rhind Mathematical Papyrus: British Museum 10057 and 10158.* London: Hodder & Stoughton.

Peust, C. 2012. The Stemma of the Story of Sinuhe or: How to Use an Unrooted Phylogenetic Tree in Textual Criticism. *Lingua Aegyptia* 20: 209–220.

Piankoff, A. 1953. *La création du disque solaire.* Bibliothèque d'étude 19. Cairo: Institut Français d'Archéologie Orientale.

Piankoff, A. 1954. *The Tomb of Ramesses VI: Texts.* Bollingen Series XL/1. New York: Pantheon Books.

Piankoff, A. 1956. La tombe de Ramsès Ier. *Bulletin de l'Institut Français d'Archéologie Orientale* 56: 189–200.

Piankoff, A. 1957. *Mythological Papyri* I–II. Bollingen Series XL/3. New York: Pantheon Books.

Plas, D. van der, and Borghouts, J. F. 1998. *Coffin Texts Word Index.* Utrecht/Paris: CCER.

Pommerening, T. 2005. *Die altägyptischen Hohlmaße.* Beihefte Studien zur altägyptischen Kultur 10. Hamburg: Helmut Buske Verlag.

Porter, B. and Moss, R. I. B. 1960. *Topographical Bibliography of Ancient Egyptian Hieroglyphic Texts, Reliefs, and Paintings* I: *The Theban Necropolis*. Oxford: Griffith Institute.

Priskin, G. 2002. The Eye of Horus and the Synodic Month. *Discussions in Egyptology* 53: 75–81.

Priskin, G. 2013. Coffin Texts Spell 155 on the Moon. *Birmingham Egyptology Journal* 1: 25–63.

Priskin, G. 2015a. The Encounter between the Sun and the Moon on Hypocephali. *Birmingham Egyptology Journal* 3: 24–41.

Priskin, G. 2015b. The Dendera Zodiacs as Narratives of the Myth of Osiris, Isis, and the Child Horus. *Égypte Nilotique et Méditérranéenne* 8: 133–185.

Priskin, G. 2016a. The Ancient Egyptian Book of the Moon: Coffin Texts Spells 154–160, in C. Alvarez, A. Belekdanian, A.-K. Gill, and S. Klein (eds), *Current Research in Egyptology 2015: Proceedings of the Sixteenth Annual Symposium:* 102–113. Oxford: Oxbow Books.

Priskin, G. 2016b. The Astral Myth of Osiris: The Decans of Taurus and Libra. *Égypte Nilotique et Méditérranéenne* 9: 79–111.

Priskin, G. 2016c. The Depictions of the Entire Lunar Cycle in Graeco-Roman Temples. *Journal of Egyptian Archaeology* 102: 111–144.

Priskin, G. 2017a. Textual Layers in Coffin Texts Spells 154–160, in G. Rosati and M. C. Guidotti (eds), *Proceedings of the XI International Congress of Egyptologists, Florence Egyptian Museum, Florence 23-30 August 2015:* 527–531. Archaeopress Egyptology 19. Oxford: Archaeopress.

Priskin, G. 2017b. The Description of the Invisible Moon at Edfu, in B. Németh (ed.), *Now Behold My Spacious Kingdom: Studies Presented to Zoltán Imre Fábián on the Occasion of His 63rd Birthday:* 303–316. Budapest: L'Harmattan.

Priskin, G. 2018. Coffin Texts Spell 246: A Description of the Moon in Conjunction with the Sun, in I. Incordino, S. Manieri, E. D'Itria, M. D. Pubblico, F. M. Rega, and A. Salsano (eds), *Current Research in Egyptology 2017: Proceedings of the Eighteenth Annual Symposium:* 161–171. Oxford: Archaeopress

Priskin, G. (forthcoming). 'Mythological Associations of Lunar Invisibility in Ancient Egypt'.

Pyr. = Sethe, K. 1908–1910. *Die Altaegyptischen Pyramidentexte nach den Papierabdrücken und Photographien des Berliner Museums*. Leipzig: J. C. Hinirichs'sche Buchhandlung.

Quack, J. F. 2013. Conceptions of Purity in Egyptian Religion, in C. Frevel and C. Nihan (eds), *Purity and the Forming of Religious Traditions in the Ancient Mediterranean World and Ancient Judaism:* 115–158. Dynamics in the History of Religions 3. Leiden: Brill.

Quirke, S. 1996. Archive, in A. Loprieno (ed.), *Ancient Egyptian Literature: History and Forms:* 379–401. Probleme der Ägyptologie 10. Leiden: Brill.

Quirke, S. 2001. *The Cult of Ra: Sun-worship in Ancient Egypt*. London: Thames & Hudson.

Quirke, S. 2003. Measuring the Underworld, in D. O'Connor and S. Quirke (eds), *Mysterious Lands: Encounters with Ancient Egypt:* 161–181. London: UCL Press.

Quirke, S. 2004. *Egyptian Literature 1800 BC: Questions and Readings*. GH Egyptology 2. London: Golden House Publications.

Ray, J. and Gilmore, G. 2006. A Fixed Point in Coptic Chronology: The Solar Eclipse of 10 March, 601. *Zeitschrift für Papyrologie ind Epigraphik* 158: 189–193.

Redford, D. B. 2001. Contendings of Horus and Seth, in D. B. Redford, (ed.), *The Oxford Encyclopaedia of Ancient Egypt* I: 294–295. Oxford: Oxford University Press.

Refai, H. 2000. Überlegungen zur Baumgöttin. *Bulletin de l'Institut Français d'Archéologie Orientale* 100: 383–392.

Reisner, G. A. 1905. *The Hearst Medical Papyrus: Hieratic Text in 17 Facsimile Plates in Collotype with Introduction and Vocabulary*. Leipzig: J. C. Hinrichs.

Ritner, R. K. 1985. Anubis and the Lunar Disc. *Journal of Egyptian Archaeology* 71: 149–155.

Ritner, R. K. 2008. *The Mechanics of Ancient Egyptian Magical Practice*. (Fourth Printing). Studies in Ancient Oriental Civilisation 54. Chicago: Oriental Institute.

Ritter, J. 2002. Closing the Eye of Horus: The Rise and Fall of 'Horus-eye Fractions', in J. M. Steele and A. Imhausen (eds), *Under One Sky: Astronomy and Mathematics in the Ancient Near East*: 297–323. Münster: Ugarit-Verlag.

Robins, G. 2001. Color Symbolism, in D. B. Redford (ed.), *The Oxford Encyclopedia of Ancient Egypt* I: 291–294. Oxford: Oxford University Press.

Robins, G. and Shute, C. C. D. 1987. *The Rhind Mathematical Papyrus: An Ancient Egyptian Text*. London: British Museum Publications.

Robinson, P. 2008. Book of the Dead Chapters 149 & 150 and Their Coffin Texts Origins, in K. Griffin (ed.), *Current Research in Egyptology 2007: Proceedings of the Eighth Annual Symposium*: 123–140. Oxford: Oxbow Books.

Russmann, E. R. 2001. *Eternal Egypt: Masterworks of Ancient Art from the British Museum*. London: British Museum Press.

Rutherford, I. 2010. Down-Stream to the Cat Goddess: Herodotus on Egyptian Pilgrimage, in J. Elsner and I. Rutherford (eds), *Pilgrimage in Graeco-Roman and Early Christian Antiquity: Seeing the Gods*: 131–150. Oxford: Oxford University Press.

Sambin, C. 1987. Les objets *šbt* des musées. *Bulletin de l'Institut Français d'Archéologie Orientale* 87: 275–292.

Sauneron, S. 1952. *Rituel de l'embaumement*. Cairo: Service des Antiquites de l'Egypte.

Sauneron, S. 1960. *The Priests of Ancient Egypt*. Evergreen Profile Book 12. New York: Grove Press.

Sauneron, S. 1969. *Le temple d'Esna Nos 399–472*. Cairo: Institut Français d'Archéologie Orientale.

Schmitz, B. 1987. Sem(priester), in W. Helck and E. Otto (eds), *Lexikon der Ägyptologie* V: 833–836. Wiesbaden: Harrassowitz.

Scholfield, A. F. (transl.). 1959. *Aelian: On the Characteristics of Animals* II. London: Heinemann.

Schott, S. 1929. *Urkunden mythologischen Inhalts*. Urkunden des ägyptischen Altertums 6. Leipzig: J. C. Hinrichs'sche Buchhandlung.

Scott, N. 1951. The Metternich Stela. *Bulletin of the Metropolitan Museum of Arts* 9: 201–217.

Seeber, C. 1980. Maske, in W. Helck and E. Otto (eds), *Lexikon der Ägyptologie* III: 1196–1199. Wiesbaden: Harrassowitz.

Seeds, M. A. and Backman, D. E. 2011. *The Solar System*. Boston: Brooks/Cole.

Servajean, F. 2003. L'étoffe *sjꜣ.t* et la régénération du défunt. *Bulletin de l'Institut Français d'Archéologie Orientale* 103: 439–457.

Servajean, F. 2004. Lune ou soleil d'or? Un épisode des *Aventures des d'Horus et de Seth* (P. Chester Beatty I R, 11, 1-13, 1). *Revue d'Egyptologie* 55: 125–148.

Sethe, K. 1922. Die Sprüche für das Kennen der Seelen der heiligen Orte (Totb. Kap. 107–109, 111–116). *Zeitschrift für ägyptische Sprache und Altertumskunde* 57: 1–50.

Sethe, K. and Firchow, O. 1957. *Thebanische Tempelinschriften aus griechisch-römischer Zeit*. Urkunden des ägyptischen Altertums 8/1. Berlin: Akademie-Verlag.
Shafer, B. E. 1997. Temples, Priests, and Rituals: An Overview, in B. E. Shafer (ed.), *Temples of Ancient Egypt*: 1–30. Ithaca: Cornell University Press.
Smith, M. 2002. *The Carlsberg Papyri 5: On the Primaeval Ocean*. Carsten Niebuhr Institute Publications 26. Copenhagen: Museum Tusculanum Press.
Smith, M. 2009a. *Traversing Eternity: Texts for the Afterlife from Ptolemaic and Roman Egypt*. Oxford: Oxford University Press.
Smith, M. 2009b. Democratization of the Afterlife, in J. Dieleman and W. Wendrich (eds), *UCLA Encyclopedia of Egyptology*. Los Angeles, http://digital2.library.ucla.edu/viewItem.do?ark=21198/zz001nf62b [29 March 2016].
Spalinger, A. 1996. *Private Feast Lists of Ancient Egypt*. Ägyptologische Abhandlungen 57. Wiesbaden: Harrassowitz Verlag.
Speleers, L. 1946. *Textes des cercueils du Moyen Empire égyptien*. Brussels.
Stadler, M. A. 2009. *Weiser und Wesir. Studien zu Vorkommen, Rolle und Wesen des Gottes Thot im ägyptischen Totenbuch*. Orientalische Religionen in der Antike 1. Tübingen: M. Siebeck.
Stadler, M. A. 2012. Thoth, in J. Dieleman and W. Wendrich (eds), *UCLA Encyclopedia of Egyptology*. Los Angeles, http://escholarship.org/uc/item/2xj8c3qg [30 July 2017].
Stählin, O. 1906. *Clemens Alexandrinus* II. Leipzig: Hinrichs.
Symons, S. 2014. Contexts and Elements of Decanal Star Lists in Ancient Egypt, in D. Bawanypeck and A. Imhausen (eds), *Traditions of Written Knowledge in Ancient Egypt and Mesopotamia: Proceedings of Two Workshops Held at Goethe-University, Frankfurt/Main in December 2011 and May 2012*: 91–122. Alter Orient und Altes Testament 403. Münster: Ugarit-Verlag.
Taylor, J. H. 2011a. Judgement, in J. H. Taylor (ed.), *Journey through the Afterlife: Ancient Egyptian Book of the Dead*: 204–237. London: British Museum Press.
Taylor, J. H. 2011b. The Perfect Afterlife, in J. H. Taylor (ed.), *Journey through the Afterlife: Ancient Egyptian Book of the Dead*: 238–261. London: British Museum Press.
Thausing, G. 1941. Zur Lesung eines Wortes in den Sprüchen vom «Kennen der Seelen von Hermopolis». *Bulletin de l'Institut Français d'Archéologie Orientale* 40: 51–52.
The Epigraphic Survey. 1934. *Medinet Habu III: The Calendar, the "Slaughterhouse" and Minor Records of Ramses III*. Oriental Institute Publications 23. Chicago: The University of Chicago Press.
The Epigraphic Survey. 1963. *Medinet Habu VI: The Temple Proper*. Oriental Institute Publications 84. Chicago: The University of Chicago Press
Thijs, A. 2010. The Lunar Eclipse of Takelot II and the Chronology of the Lybian Period. *Zeitschrift für ägyptische Sprache und Altertumskunde* 137: 171–190.
Tobin, V. A. 2001. Amun and Amun-Re, in D. B. Redford (ed.), *The Oxford Encyclopedia of Ancient Egypt* I: 82–85. Oxford: Oxford University Press.
Tooley, A. M. J. 1996. Osiris Bricks. *Journal of Egyptian Archaeology* 82: 167–179.
Tristant, Y. and Midant-Reynes, B. 2011. The Predynastic Cultures of the Nile Delta, in E. Teeter (ed.), *Before the Pyramids: The Origins of Egyptian Civilization*: 45–54. Oriental Institute Museum Publications 33. Chicago: The Oriental Institute.
Varga, E. 1998. Les hypocéphales. *Acta Archaeologica Academiae Sxientiarum Hungaricae* 50: 29–41.

Velde, H. te. 1967. *Seth, God of Confusion: A Study of His Role in Egyptian Mythology and Religion*. Probleme de Ägyptologie 6. Leiden: Brill.

Velde, H. te. 1992. Some Egyptian Deities and Their Piggishness, in U. Luft (ed.), *The Intellectual Heritage of Egypt: Studies Presented to László Kákosy by Friends and Colleagues on the Occasion of His 60th Birthday*: 571–578. Budapest: Eötvös Loránd University.

Velde, H. te. 2001. Seth, in D. B. Redford, (ed.), *The Oxford Encyclopedia of Ancient Egypt* III: 269–271. Oxford: Oxford University Press.

Verner, M. 2006. Contemporaneous Evidence for the Relative Chronology of Dyns. 4 and 5, in E. Hornung, R. Krauss and R. A. Warburton (eds), *Ancient Egyptian Chronology*: 124–143. Handbook der Orientalistik 83. Leiden: Brill.

Vernus, P. and Yoyotte, J. 2003. *The Book of the Pharaohs*. (transl. D. Lorton). Ithaca: Cornell University Press.

Vernus, P. and Yoyotte, J. 2005. *Bestiare des pharaons*. Paris: Perrin.

Vischak, D. 2001. Hathor, in D. B. Redford (ed.), *The Oxford Encyclopedia of Ancient Egypt* II: 82–85. Oxford: Oxford University Press.

Voss, M. H. van. 1980. Horuskinder, in W. Helck and E. Otto (eds), *Lexikon der Ägyptologie* III: 52–53. Wiesbaden: Harrassowitz.

Waerden, B. L. van der. 1953. History of the Zodiac. *Archiv für Orientforschung* 16: 216–230.

Wallin, P. 2002. *Celestial Cycles: Astronomical Concepts of Regeneration in the Ancient Egyptian Coffin Texts*. Uppsala Studies in Egyptology 1. Uppsala: Uppsala University.

Wb. = Erman, A. and Grapow, H. (eds). 1926–1931. *Wörterbuch der ägyptische Sprache* I–V. Berlin: Akademie-Verlag.

Wendrich, W. 2006. Entangled, Connected or Protected? The Power of Knots and Knotting in Ancient Egypt, in K. Szpakowska (ed.), *Through a Glass Darkly: Magic, Dreams & Prophecy in Ancient Egypt*: 243–269. Swansea: The Classical Press of Wales.

Westendorf, W. 1980. Horusauge, in W. Helck, E. Otto, and W. Westendorf (eds), *Lexikon der Ägyptologie* III: 48–51. Wiesbaden: Otto Harrassowitz.

Wilkinson, R. H. 1992. *Reading Egyiptian Art: A Hieroglyphic Guide to Ancient Egyptian Painting and Sculpture*. London: Thames and Hudson.

Wilkinson, R. H. 1994. *Symbol & Magic in Egyptian Art*. London: Thames and Hudson.

Wilkinson, R. H. 2003. *The Complete Gods and Goddesses of Ancient Egypt*. London: Thames & Hudson.

Wilkinson, T. A. H. 2000. *Royal Annals of Ancient Egypt: The Palermo Stone and Its Associated Fragments*. London: Kegan Paul International.

Willems, H. 1988. *Chests of Life: A Study of the Typology and Conceptual Development of Middle Kingdom, Standard Class Coffins*. Mededelingen en Verhandelingen Ex Oriente Lux 25. Leiden: Ex Oriente Lux.

Willems, H. 1996. *The Coffin of Heqata (Cairo JdE 36418): A Case Study of Egyptian Funerary Culture of the Early Middle Kingdom*. Orientalia Lovaniensia Analecta 70. Leuven: Peeters.

Willems, H. 2005. The Feather of the West. *Revue d'Égyptologie* 56: 208–213.

Willems, H. 2006. An Astronomer at Deir al-Barsha, in E. Czerny, I. Hein, H. Hunger, D. Melman, and A. Schwab (eds), *Timelines: Studies in Honour of Manfred Bietak* I: 437–445. Orientalia Lovaniensia Analecta 149. Leuven: Peeters.

Willems, H. 2007. *Dayr al-Barshā* I: *The Rock Tombs of Djehutinakht (No. 17K74/1), Khnumnakht (No. 17K74/2), and Iha (No. 17K74/3)*. Orientalia Lovaniensia Analecta 155. Leuven: Peeters.

Willems, H. 2008. *Les textes des sarcophages et la démocratie. Élements d'une histoire culturelle du Moyen Empre égyptien*. Paris: Cybele.

Willems , H. 2014. *Historical and Archaeological Aspects of Egyptian Funerary Culture: Religious Ideas and Ritual Practice in Middle Kingdom Elite Cemeteries*. Culture and History of the Ancient Near East 73. Leiden: Brill.

Wilson, P. 1997. *A Ptolemaic Lexicon: A Lexicographical Study of the Texts in the Temple of Edfu*. Orientalia Lovaniensia Analecta 78. Leuven: Peeters.

Winter, E. 1970. Nochmals zum *snwt*-Fest. *Zeitschrift für ägyptische Sprache und Altertumskunde* 96: 151–152.

Yoyotte, J. 1953. La ville de „Taremou" (Tell el-Muqdâm). *Bulletin de l'Institut Français d'Archéologie Orientale* 52: 179–192.

Zecchi, M. 2010. *Sobek of Shedet: The Crocodile God in the Fayyum in the Dynastic Period*. Studi sull'antico Egitto 2. Todi: Tau Editrice.

Zivie-Coche, C. 2008. Late Period Temples, in J. Dieleman and W. Wendrich (eds), *UCLA Encyclopedia of Egyptology*. Los Angeles, http://escholarship.org/uc/item/30k472vh [29 March 2016].

Žabkar, L. V. 1968. *A Study of the Ba Concept in Ancient Egyptian Texts*. Studies in Ancient Oriental Civilization 34. Chicago: Oriental Institute.

Index

Abydos, 11, 45, 46, 87, 110
Aelian, 106, 110
aetiological motif, 35, 190, 191, 192, 193, 208
Amarna, 15
Amun, 15
Anubis, 15, 44, 55, 58, 60, 61, 64, 66, 69, 70, 71, 217, 218
Apep, 164, 170, 171, 175, 226, 228, 232
archives, 189, 191, 193, 194, 199, 200, 203, 210
astronomical diagram, 11, 15, 148
Asyut, 4, 19, 20, 21, 24, 25, 26, 29, 39, 44, 48, 49, 50, 53, 62, 67, 75, 76, 77, 84, 87, 94, 95, 96, 97, 98, 113, 114, 125, 129, 132, 136, 138, 140, 143, 144, 148, 154, 161, 188, 189, 194, 202, 210
Atum, 12, 35, 86, 212, 213, 214, 215, 225, 226, 228
autumnal equinox, 104, 109, 119, 147, 148, 168, 231
ba, 12, 24, 43, 45, 59, 74, 89, 95, 96, 156, 161, 176, 191, 223, 224, 226, 228
Babi, 96
baboon, 96, 103, 104, 108, 168, 169
Bakhu, 162, 163, 164, 165, 175, 176, 186, 187, 205, 225, 226, 227, 228, 229
bald, 6, 31, 32, 37, 38, 172, 178
Banebdjedet, 96, 97
barley, 64, 65, 154, 155
bas, 3, 24, 25, 26, 30, 35, 39, 43, 44, 58, 65, 69, 70, 74, 75, 78, 87, 89, 93, 94, 95, 121, 125, 135, 139, 140, 142, 144, 145, 147, 153, 155, 156, 157, 161, 162, 163, 164, 175, 176, 179, 182, 184, 186, 189, 191, 193, 194, 199, 201, 203, 204, 205, 206, 207, 208, 209, 210, 211, 212, 213, 214, 215, 216, 217, 218, 219, 220, 221, 222, 223, 224, 225, 226, 227, 228, 229, 231, 232, 233
beer, 95, 98, 99, 138, 216, 217
blacked-out moon, 5, 7, 8, 10, 13, 16, 26, 27, 34, 38, 39, 75, 77, 79, 137, 148, 149, 205, 232, 233
Book of Gates, 108, 110, 184, 231
Book of Going Forth by Day, 9, 10, 11, 12, 21, 25, 46, 59, 64, 78, 81, 85, 86, 89, 98, 104, 105, 107, 108, 116, 119, 132, 139, 147, 149, 150, 151, 153, 156, 163, 171, 173, 174, 176, 177, 202, 203, 204, 205, 206, 209, 210, 211, 212, 213, 215, 216, 218, 221, 225, 229, 230, 231, 233
Book of the Fayum, 130, 185
Busiris, 44
Buto, 100
cannibal hymn, 6, 9
castrated bull, 68, 76, 181, 233
chronological seriation, 196
circumpolar stars, 4, 7
civil calendar, 13, 57, 106, 165, 178
Clement of Alexandria, 18, 83, 172
conjunction, 3, 8, 12, 15, 26, 27, 28, 29, 32, 34, 35, 36, 37, 38, 48, 54, 56, 57, 58, 62, 63, 64, 68, 103, 132, 134, 147, 149, 162, 166, 167, 177, 179, 186, 190, 193, 204
Contendings of Horus and Seth, 97, 101, 111, 128, 232
counting, 52, 53, 54, 65, 66, 70, 86, 88, 119, 120, 180, 213
cover basket, 131, 132, 133, 134, 185, 191, 219, 220, 221
Cusae, 203, 210, 211, 212, 213
dbḥ.w, 46, 48, 50, 51, 52, 56, 60, 70, 120, 192
decan, 109, 146, 147
decans, 16, 58, 109, 131, 146, 147, 202
Deir el-Bahari, 15, 60
Deir el-Bersha, 4, 9, 19, 20, 21, 24, 29, 43, 44, 49, 50, 51, 53, 58, 67, 74, 76, 80, 84, 87, 94, 95, 96, 98, 99, 113, 115, 118, 120, 129, 132, 136, 138, 143, 144, 154, 155, 161, 177, 188, 189, 193, 194, 195, 196, 197, 201, 202, 230
Deir el-Medina, 55
democratisation of the afterlife, 188
Dendera, 17, 18, 53, 68, 70, 94, 99, 104, 108, 109, 116, 117, 119, 146, 147, 151, 168, 231, 234
Dep, 100
divine power, 86, 207, 209, 211, 212, 213

Djedu, 43, 44, 45, 46
Djehutinakht, 24, 43, 45, 58, 74, 195, 196, 197, 198, 199, 202
Duamutef, 115, 116, 117, 118, 136, 137, 138, 139, 140, 169, 216, 218, 219, 220, 221
Edfu, 18, 28, 36, 75, 77, 83, 86, 103, 104, 106, 108, 111, 116, 117, 172, 183, 230, 231
el-Lisht, 4, 143, 144, 189, 193
emmer, 152, 154, 155, 186, 222, 223, 224
ennead, 29, 39, 108, 113, 156, 174
eye of Horus, 7, 8, 9, 10, 27, 34, 44, 48, 51, 59, 60, 64, 76, 77, 78, 80, 81, 85, 86, 97, 98, 100, 101, 104, 105, 113, 116, 117, 127, 128, 129, 133, 137, 139, 169, 182, 192, 201, 218, 231
eye of Tebi, 52, 53, 65, 66, 179
faience, 107, 163
feather, 7, 20, 75, 76, 78, 83, 85, 88, 127, 181, 199, 200, 211, 212, 213, 214, 231
ferryman, 6, 7, 10, 96, 116, 150, 230
Field of Reeds, 50, 143, 144, 152, 153, 154, 155, 156, 157, 185, 186, 193, 205, 221, 222, 223, 224, 233
Field of Rest, 8, 153, 154, 205
fiery bull, 53, 54, 68, 76, 86, 114, 233
fifteenth day, 6, 10, 12, 14, 30, 53, 64, 78, 80, 89, 94, 104, 134, 172, 182, 211, 214, 215, 231
filling of the eye, 10, 56, 127, 139
fingers, 59, 81, 86, 116, 127, 132, 139, 219, 220, 226
first-crescent day, 5, 6, 8, 99
fishing net, 9
flint, 33, 165, 166, 187, 225, 227, 229
fourth day, 8, 47, 82, 117, 180
full month, 35, 57, 180
full moon, 3, 6, 12, 14, 16, 20, 25, 26, 27, 30, 31, 32, 38, 44, 46, 47, 49, 50, 53, 54, 55, 56, 59, 64, 66, 68, 76, 78, 79, 80, 82, 84, 85, 88, 89, 90, 94, 95, 96, 99, 100, 102, 103, 104, 105, 106, 107, 108, 109, 111, 112, 113, 114, 118, 119, 120, 125, 127, 134, 135, 136, 139, 140, 148, 149, 168, 172, 178, 182, 183, 184, 192, 199, 203, 205, 212, 230, 231, 232
Fundamentals of the Course of the Stars, 11, 82, 110, 130, 180
geese, 144, 145, 146, 148, 164, 186, 222, 223, 224
golden disc, 112, 127
Great Eye, 68, 181
greatest of seers, 26, 28, 29, 30, 37, 38, 178, 207, 209
Gua, 74, 75, 80, 84, 195, 197, 198, 199, 201
half-month day, 8
hands of Horus, 112, 126, 127, 128, 129, 132, 133, 134, 135, 136, 139, 140, 184, 191, 219, 220, 221, 232
Hapi, 115, 116, 117, 118, 121, 136, 215, 216, 217, 218
Harakhty, 15, 155, 156, 170, 222, 224
harpoon, 34, 35, 113, 133, 170, 178, 207, 208, 209
Hathor, 95, 99, 100, 103, 113, 129, 151, 176, 205, 225, 226, 228
ḥbs tp, 47, 48, 110, 172, 225, 227, 228
Heliopolis, 24, 25, 26, 28, 29, 30, 31, 32, 35, 36, 37, 38, 39, 47, 135, 178, 189, 190, 191, 194, 205, 207, 208, 209, 214, 215, 230, 232
Hermopolis, 9, 17, 19, 21, 51, 52, 59, 67, 70, 74, 75, 77, 87, 89, 135, 177, 179, 182, 188, 189, 191, 192, 193, 194, 200, 201, 202, 205, 206, 210, 211, 212, 213, 214, 215, 230, 231, 232
Herodotus, 18, 106, 107
He-who-is-in-his-fire, 31, 32, 34, 35, 36, 165, 166, 167, 170, 171, 175, 178, 179, 187, 190, 193, 207, 209, 232
He-who-is-in-his-red-cloth, 35, 36, 37
He-who-is-in-the-broad-hall, 138, 139, 220
He-who-is-setting, 164
Hierakonpolis, 93
hollow month, 34, 35, 57
Horapollo, 104, 105, 183, 231
Horus, 7, 8, 9, 10, 27, 30, 31, 33, 34, 36, 39, 44, 47, 48, 51, 52, 57, 58, 59, 60, 61, 64, 76, 77, 78, 80, 81, 82, 85, 86, 95, 97, 98, 99, 100, 101, 102, 104, 105, 109, 110, 111, 112, 113, 114, 115, 116, 117, 118, 119, 121, 125, 126, 127, 128, 129, 130, 132, 133, 134, 135, 136, 137, 138, 139, 140, 147, 152, 156, 169, 170, 180, 182, 183, 184, 190, 191, 192, 201, 215, 216, 217, 218, 219, 220, 221, 231, 232, 234
Horus-eye fractions, 31, 52, 57, 58
Horus-on-his-papyrus-column, 116, 117, 118, 119, 216, 218, 234
House of Life, 200, 201, 202

Hyksos, 203, 210
hypocephalus, 12
imperishable (stars), 5, 39, 150
Imseti, 115, 116, 117, 118, 121, 136, 215, 216, 217, 218
injured eye, 25, 26, 27, 28, 53, 56, 85, 97, 100, 201
injury, 56, 63, 76, 85, 98, 100, 101, 105, 111, 113, 114, 128, 135, 169, 182, 183, 184, 216, 217, 218, 231
invisibility, 3, 5, 6, 9, 10, 15, 26, 27, 37, 38, 40, 43, 44, 45, 47, 48, 49, 50, 54, 55, 56, 58, 60, 63, 65, 68, 69, 70, 75, 76, 79, 82, 85, 99, 103, 115, 117, 131, 134, 143, 149, 150, 165, 166, 169, 179, 180, 181, 185, 187, 189, 192, 204, 205, 210, 232, 233
invisible moon, 8, 12, 29, 33, 34, 36, 37, 39, 75, 76, 77, 79, 93, 143, 148, 149, 150, 166, 171, 175, 179, 186, 224, 232, 233
Isden, 70
Isdes, 44, 69, 70, 71, 81
Isis, 11, 18, 36, 94, 99, 100, 111, 112, 113, 115, 116, 117, 126, 128, 129, 138, 151, 169, 171, 184, 185, 216, 218, 219, 220, 221, 228, 232
Jah, 15, 17, 18
Jahmes, 14, 17, 203
jꜥḥ, 5, 36, 39, 55, 59, 68, 77, 78, 114, 149
Karnak, 15, 17, 68, 83, 103, 114
Khemmis, 99, 100
Khepri, 130, 149, 207
Kheraha, 30, 35
Khoiak, 65
Khonsu, 6, 9, 10, 15, 17, 18, 68, 79, 83, 86, 103, 104, 106, 114, 120
Lake of Fire, 36
Lake of Knives, 167, 170, 187
last crescent, 3, 7, 26, 27, 32, 38, 44, 45, 49, 54, 55, 56, 63, 75, 143, 150, 166, 175, 185, 210
left eye, 12, 15, 28, 44, 61, 85, 86, 224
lunar calendar, 13
lunar crescent, 10, 13, 28, 54, 76, 131, 132, 147, 181, 184, 230, 232
lunar disc, 11, 15, 16, 20, 32, 45, 47, 48, 50, 55, 56, 60, 61, 63, 64, 70, 78, 80, 88, 100, 102, 104, 109, 115, 137, 148, 166, 170, 172, 182, 183, 184, 214, 232, 233
lunar eclipse, 16, 32, 101, 102, 104, 112, 129, 167, 169, 183, 216, 230, 231, 234
lunar month, 3, 5, 8, 10, 11, 13, 30, 31, 32, 35, 36, 44, 47, 48, 49, 50, 54, 55, 62, 75, 76, 78, 79, 80, 82, 89, 104, 107, 115, 116, 117, 119, 134, 163, 165, 172, 178, 179, 180, 182, 194, 210, 211, 214, 215, 219, 221, 230, 231
Maat, 213, 214
mansion of the moon, 8, 9, 10
Mansion of the Moon, 8, 70
Manu, 163
Mehetweret, 107
Meir, 4, 19, 188, 189
Mekhentiirti, 150
Mendes, 96, 97
mentjat-bowl, 78, 79, 80, 83, 84, 181, 211, 212, 213, 231, 232
Metternich stela, 100
Min, 12, 36, 79
monkey, 108, 110
Morning God, 5, 155, 156, 157, 223, 224
mummification, 12, 21, 58, 59, 60, 61, 64, 65, 70, 168
Mut, 15, 103
mythological papyrus, 47, 130, 170
Nakht, 20, 29, 115, 120, 161, 162, 171, 202
Neferi, 76, 84, 85, 195, 197, 198
Nehaher, 170
Neith, 213
Nekhen, 93, 94, 118, 125, 126, 135, 136, 137, 138, 139, 140, 169, 184, 190, 191, 205, 216, 218, 219, 220, 221
Nephthys, 36, 94, 151
Nile, 18, 93, 130, 136, 146, 162
Nut, 11, 36, 75, 76, 77, 80, 130, 151, 153, 182, 228
Orion, 77
oryx, 101, 102, 103, 104, 105, 109, 112, 113, 114, 129, 132, 133, 169, 182, 183, 190, 216, 231, 234
Osirieon, 11, 110
Osiris, 10, 11, 12, 16, 17, 18, 31, 43, 44, 45, 46, 48, 49, 53, 60, 63, 64, 65, 66, 69, 71, 74, 77, 94, 100, 101, 102, 106, 108, 109, 110, 111, 112, 117, 119, 126, 127, 137, 139, 152, 168, 169, 180, 181, 183, 192, 221, 231, 232
Osiris beds, 64, 65, 180

Pachons, 18, 79, 106, 109, 114
pBrooklyn, 32, 35, 56, 82, 106, 107, 110, 112
pCarlsberg, 57
Pe, 93, 94, 97, 98, 99, 100, 101, 118, 121, 125, 135, 136, 189, 191, 205, 216, 217, 218, 229, 231
Petubastis, 79, 231
pig, 14, 101, 105, 106, 107, 108, 109, 110, 111, 114, 168, 183, 184, 216, 217, 218, 231
pIufankh, 208, 212, 214, 217, 220, 221, 223, 226, 228
Plutarch, 18, 34, 49, 64, 65, 106, 110, 111, 119, 120, 169, 179, 183, 231
pNebseni, 105, 211, 213, 215, 218, 222, 225, 229
pNu, 206, 213
pork, 18, 106, 111, 114, 140, 183
pr.t-sm, 47, 82, 117, 180
psḏn.tjw, 3, 9, 10, 13, 15, 27, 36, 43, 44, 45, 47, 48, 54, 58, 67, 69, 75, 76, 77, 82, 89, 117, 143, 149, 179, 180, 181, 189, 204, 210, 232, 233
Punt, 9
Pyramid Texts, 4, 5, 6, 7, 8, 9, 10, 26, 31, 35, 36, 37, 39, 59, 61, 62, 69, 78, 83, 86, 88, 96, 98, 99, 101, 102, 111, 116, 138, 144, 145, 150, 152, 153, 155, 156, 157, 162, 188, 189, 191, 199, 209, 212, 230, 231
Qebehsenuf, 115, 116, 117, 118, 136, 137, 138, 139, 140, 169, 216, 218, 219, 220, 221
Ramesseum, 15, 16, 116, 117, 130, 148
Re, 6, 8, 10, 12, 15, 16, 18, 25, 28, 30, 31, 32, 33, 34, 35, 36, 37, 39, 83, 87, 95, 97, 98, 100, 101, 102, 105, 106, 107, 109, 110, 112, 114, 118, 120, 126, 128, 130, 133, 134, 135, 136, 137, 142, 143, 144, 145, 146, 148, 149, 150, 152, 153, 156, 157, 162, 163, 164, 166, 167, 169, 170, 171, 172, 173, 174, 175, 176, 178, 179, 182, 183, 185, 186, 187, 190, 191, 192, 193, 199, 205, 207, 208, 209, 211, 212, 213, 216, 217, 218, 219, 221, 222, 223, 224, 225, 226, 227, 228, 229
Red Crown, 78, 79, 80, 83, 84, 88, 118, 181, 182, 199, 211, 212, 213, 214, 231
Rhind Mathematical Papyrus, 51, 52
Saite recension, 205
sem-priest, 47, 82, 117, 180, 212, 213, 214, 215
Sen, 19, 20, 24, 27, 29, 43, 45, 48, 49, 50, 53, 56, 61, 62, 74, 85, 87, 94, 106, 113, 114, 115, 118, 120, 127, 129, 130, 135, 136, 137, 138, 140, 143, 154, 156, 161, 162, 166, 187, 194, 195, 197, 198, 199, 200, 201
Senenmut, 11, 116, 117
senut, 28, 29, 30, 31, 32, 34, 35, 38, 178, 208, 209, 232
Serqet, 164, 171
Seth, 7, 32, 47, 48, 76, 77, 82, 97, 101, 102, 105, 106, 111, 112, 113, 119, 126, 127, 128, 129, 130, 136, 137, 138, 139, 140, 167, 169, 170, 171, 172, 173, 174, 175, 182, 183, 184, 187, 216, 218, 219, 221, 226, 227, 228, 229, 231, 232
seventeenth day, 49, 119
seventh day, 5, 8, 30
She-who-lets-the-throat-breathe, 164, 171
Shu, 39, 144, 150, 151, 152, 153, 207, 208, 209, 212, 222, 224
Sia, 89, 170, 212, 213, 214, 215
sixth day, 5, 8, 30, 35, 38, 104, 178
sixth-day festival, 26
sjꜣ, 46, 48, 49, 50, 59, 82, 88, 89, 192, 211
small eye, 76, 80, 89, 182
snsn kA.wj, 68, 88
Sobek, 127, 129, 130, 131, 132, 133, 143, 162, 163, 165, 166, 176, 185, 187, 190, 191, 219, 220, 221, 225, 226, 227, 228, 229, 232
Sokar, 102
solar calf, 155, 156, 222, 223, 224, 233
solar disc, 6, 36, 104, 130, 143, 146, 150, 151, 152, 155, 156, 157, 165, 167, 170, 172, 175, 185, 186, 207
solar eclipse, 3, 34, 37, 108, 109, 134, 158, 162, 166, 167, 168, 169, 171, 172, 173, 174, 175, 176, 179, 186, 187, 193, 205, 226, 230, 232
sole eye, 26, 27, 29, 207, 208
Sole One, 8, 10
sons of Horus, 115, 116, 118, 125, 137
sound eye, 9, 12, 25, 85, 101, 113, 182, 190
stemma, 200
sun, 3, 4, 6, 7, 8, 10, 11, 12, 14, 15, 18, 20, 25, 26, 27, 28, 29, 32, 33, 34, 35, 36, 37, 38, 39, 53, 54, 65, 68, 78, 83, 85, 96, 97, 100, 103, 104, 105, 106, 107, 109, 112, 121, 127, 130, 131, 132, 133, 134, 135, 143, 145, 146, 147,

148, 149, 150, 151, 152, 153, 154, 155, 156, 157, 162, 163, 164, 165, 166, 167, 169, 170, 172, 174, 175, 176, 177, 178, 179, 180, 181, 182, 183, 184, 185, 186, 187, 190, 193, 204, 205, 207, 209, 226, 230, 232, 233
sunrise, 6, 7, 9, 27, 32, 36, 130, 131, 132, 143, 144, 145, 146, 151, 152, 153, 154, 156, 164, 179, 233
sycamore, 143, 144, 150, 151, 152, 222, 223, 224, 233
synodic month, 27, 31, 57, 178
Tanis, 146
Ta-remu, 136, 221
Tefnut, 39, 207, 208, 209
Ter-remu, 133, 134, 136, 219
Thebes, 1, 15, 203
Thoth, 6, 7, 8, 9, 10, 14, 15, 17, 18, 20, 24, 25, 33, 34, 44, 53, 59, 60, 61, 70, 75, 77, 78, 80, 81, 83, 86, 89, 97, 98, 100, 103, 107, 112, 116, 117, 120, 126, 127, 138, 139, 165, 166, 168, 179, 184, 188, 191, 192, 194, 202, 211, 212, 213, 214, 215, 224, 230, 232
turquoise, 144, 150, 152, 222, 224
Venus, 156, 157
vernal equinox, 147
Wadjet, 100
waning, 3, 5, 6, 7, 9, 26, 31, 32, 44, 47, 48, 49, 50, 56, 63, 64, 68, 75, 76, 79, 81, 85, 101, 102, 105, 106, 109, 110, 111, 114, 115, 118, 119, 120, 122, 126, 127, 128, 129, 131, 132, 133, 137, 140, 143, 166, 172, 178, 179, 180, 181, 183, 184, 185, 190, 193, 203, 205, 230, 231, 232, 233
waxing, 3, 5, 6, 7, 12, 20, 28, 31, 33, 37, 38, 47, 48, 50, 53, 54, 56, 63, 64, 65, 72, 76, 78, 79, 80, 81, 82, 84, 85, 86, 88, 89, 97, 107, 108, 114, 115, 116, 117, 118, 127, 128, 134, 136, 137, 139, 166, 178, 180, 181, 182, 192, 199, 201, 203, 205, 206, 230, 231, 233
wedjat-eye, 25, 28, 44, 51, 59, 70, 75, 79, 81, 86, 103, 104, 106, 108, 113, 116, 174, 183, 231, 232
wensheb, 104
White Crown, 78, 118, 120
Winding Waterway, 7, 98, 145, 153
wing, 20, 97, 98
winter solstice, 146, 147
wnšb, 103
zodiac, 17, 104, 108, 109, 145, 146, 147, 168, 231, 234